E. W. SWANTON

Also by E.W. SWANTON

A History of Cricket (with H.S. Altham)
Denis Compton: A Cricket Sketch
Elusive Victory
Cricket and the Clock
Best Cricket Stories
West Indian Adventure
Test Matches 1953
Victory in Australia 1954/5
Test Matches 1956
Report from South Africa
West Indies Revisited
The Ashes in Suspense 1962/3
World of Cricket 1966,
revised as Barclays World of Cricket, 1980,
3rd edn. 1986
Cricket from all Angles
Sort of a Cricket Person
Swanton in Australia
Follow On
As I Said at the Time: A Lifetime of Cricket
Gubby Allen: Man of Cricket
Kent Cricket: A Photographic History 1744–1984
(with C.H. Taylor)
The Anglican Church: A Layman's Sketch
Back Page Cricket
The Essential E.W. Swanton
Last Over

E. W. SWANTON

A Celebration of His Life and Work

E.W. SWANTON

With

DAVID RAYVERN ALLEN

RICHARD COHEN BOOKS
LONDON

British Library Cataloguing in Publication Data:
A catalogue record for this book is available from the British Library

First published in Great Britain by Richard Cohen Books, an imprint of
Metro Publishing, 19 Gerrard Street, London W1V 7LA in 2000

Last Over first published in Great Britain in 1996 by
Richard Cohen Books
7 Manchester Square
London W1M 5RE

Copyright © 1996, 2000 by E. W. Swanton and David Rayvern Allen

ISBN 1 86066 179 3

Design by Humphrey Stone

Typeset in 10¼/13pt Sabon
by Rowland Phototypesetting Ltd, Bury St Edmunds, Suffolk,
and MATS, Southend-on-Sea, Essex
Printed in Great Britain by CPD Group, Wales

Contents

PART FIVE 1956–1965

Introduction by David Rayvern Allen 132

PART SIX 1966–1975

Introduction by David Rayvern Allen 180

PART SEVEN 1975–1996

Introduction by David Rayvern Allen 216

viii

Foreword

I grew up with Jim Swanton. To me, he was one of the voices of cricket that filled my youth. At the end of a day's cricket I would listen to his fruity voice describing the play, and then the following morning I would read his commentary.

This book will bring alive memories of Jim for all those who knew him from near and far. I was lucky. I came to know him well and we spent many hours together watching and talking cricket at the the Oval or Lord's. Jim's memory was a treasure trove. I asked him once if he'd seen Bradman's great innings of 254 at Lord's in 1930. 'Oh yes,' he replied. 'Wonderful innings. The Don hit the first two balls for 4 - over there . . . 'the scene came alive as he pointed to an advertising hoarding ' . . . although'- a measure of distaste crept into his voice - 'there were no advertisements allowed then. I suppose it's progress.'

Once, Jim came to Chequers for lunch with his wife, Ann, who was an accomplished pianist. (Dickie Bird came too and arrived hours early: 'I didn't want to be late,' he explained.) Ann soon spotted the piano in the Great Hall and, after lunch, sat down to play. I asked her if she knew the ditty 'Our Don Bradman', but she didn't - Jim did, and the words too. Unfortunately, the piano was in need of tuning and our hope of musical entertainment came to naught.

Jim was a convinced traditionalist but not a crusty one. Over the D'Oliveira affair he led public opinion in his distaste for apartheid and did not advance the hoary argument that politics should not interfere with sport. Jim cared how the game was played, and racial prejudice was not cricket. He had no doubts and he was right.

When Jim died, despite his great age it was a shock. He seemed so fit and vigorous to the very end. He was mellow with years but his passion for cricket and cricketers was undimmed.

He had a long innings and he played the game to the end. It was written of Alfred Mynn - another great man of cricket from Kent - 'May the turf lie lightly upon you.' Jim loved that line - and once said to me that he wished he had written it. He didn't, but his writing was prodigious and his books have been on my shelves for decades greatly supplemented on my 50th birthday when Jim's good friend Jonathan Aitken presented me with volumes all personally inscribed. Jim sent me his last book only weeks before he died. I have, I think, a complete set of everything he ever published. I wish only that I had an archive of all he said to me about cricket as well.

There are so many memories of this Man of Cricket who became a national icon. May the turf lie lightly upon you, too, Jim.

The Right Hon. John Major, CH, MP
May 2000

Acknowledgements

(*Last Over*)

First, on a personal level, I must thank Jim for asking me to be a small part of what he foolishly expects to be his last work in hard covers. I, on the other hand, fully expect him to be producing well into the new Millennium. Only time will tell who is right.

Second, gratitude from us both to Richard Cohen who commissioned this book. And what is more, commissioned it with alacrity.

From that point, not so long ago, many others have helped considerably in the putting together thereof. Thanks are due to designer Humphrey Stone; and illustration researcher Gabrielle Allen; to Lindsay Allen for her herculean effort in transcribing a three-and-three-quarter-hour interview; to Gwyniver Jones at the BBC Written Archives Centre in Caversham for her help in tracing early broadcast scripts; to Patrick Eagar for so generously giving of his photographic brilliance when otherwise engaged; to Tina Langdon, who unearthed ancient family portraits; to Doreen Waite, Debra Skeen, Evelyn James and Janet Reeve for secretarial assistance; to Judith Cradock for her excursions to Colindale Newspaper Library; to Robert Brooke for unearthing potted and full scores; to Henry Hely-Hutchinson for proofreading; to Wendy Wimbush for indexing; to Margaret Body, Pat Chetwyn and Wendy Venis for work on the copy and covers; and to Valerie Hillier for making the tea.

We are also grateful to the *Daily* and *Sunday Telegraph*, *Sunday Express*, *The Evening Standard*, *The Field*, *The Spectator* and *The Cricketer* for permission to reproduce articles that first appeared on their pages.

Lastly, and most definitely in front of the equals that first were mentioned, a note of indebtedness to Ann Swanton not only and principally for her serenity and fortitude in actually putting up with the demands of the Old Man for far longer than anybody could reasonably expect, but also for her delightful renderings of 'evergreens' from the popular repertoire that, at those moments when most needed, kept the party going with a swing.

D.R.A.

Acknowledgements

(E. W. Swanton: A Celebration of His Life and Work)

As can be seen in the first paragraph of the Acknowledgements to *Last Over*, I was only partly right. One did not need to be prescient to know that as long as he lived Jim would never stop writing. As many will know, his book *Cricketers of My Time* followed *Last Over*, but he only just kept producing articles into this new Millennium.

For *E.W. Swanton, A Celebration*, I owe a great debt of gratitude to John Major for a wonderfully pithy foreword – nobody could have said so much so succinctly. My thanks also to Alan Brooke, Mary Remnant, Miriam Clift and Becke Parker at Metro Books for not only the idea and commission, but the good-humoured help in producing the book in such a short time. Helena Drakakis in working overtime with the editing, Wendy Wimbush with the indexing, and Penny Phillips should join them in taking a bow.

I would like to acknowledge as well the support of John Woodcock; of the Swanton Estate and the *Daily Telegraph*, in particular, Sports Editor, David Welch. And also that of Peter Perchard and his team at *The Cricketer*. I am in debt also to the *Daily Mail*, the *Guardian*, the *Independent*, *Scottish Herald* and *Scotsman* for permission to use extracts from their obituary columns.

Thank you too to Billy Carbutt and the Swanton family for their encouragement. And a special burst of applause to Valerie Hillier, Peter Knight and Doreen Waite for all their help at Delf House – it would have been impossible without them.

There now follows a long list of eminent contributors who each deserve a more fulsome commendation than it is possible to give. Many provided copy at short notice and with pressing deadlines. My heartfelt thanks.

First, much gratitude to Lord Runcie – who sadly has just passed away – and Lord Deedes for permission to use their moving addresses at the funeral and memorial services respectively. And to Jonathan Aitken for giving up much time to record personally his thought-provoking appreciation of Jim. First again – a double is, after all, a great commendation – with extended thanks to: Briony Allen, Peter Baxter, Daphne and Richie Benaud, Harold 'Dickie' Bird, MBE, Henry Blofeld, Richard Boyd, Paddy Briggs, Ben Brocklehurst, Billy Carbutt, Ted Corbett, Lord Cowdrey, CBE, Mike Denness, Ted Dexter, Hubert Doggart, OBE, Neil Durden-Smith, OBE, Patrick Eagar, Matthew Engel, David Faber, MP, Christine Field, Matthew Fleming, Charles Fry, John Paul Getty, KBE, David Gower, OBE, Stephen Green, Dr Gerald Howat, Robert Hudson, Richard Hutton, Colin Ingleby-Mackenzie, Roger Knight, Kay Knipe, Tony Lewis, F.G. Mann, CBE, MC, Christopher Martin-Jenkins, Sally Munton, Tony O'Reilly, Michael Parkinson, CBE, The Hon. George Plumptre, Sir Tim Rice, The Reverend Mark Roberts, Rector of Sandwich, Paul Sheahan, Sir Garfield Sobers, OCC, Sandy Strang, Fred Trueman, OBE, David Welch, Peter West, Mark Williams, John Woodcock, OBE, Ian Wooldridge, OBE.

D.R.A.

A Note on the Illustrations

The author and publisher wish to thank the following for permission to reproduce photographs: Frontispiece: Marylebone Cricket Club. Back Endpaper: Gary Prior. Plate Section One: Patrick Eagar, page 8 *below*; Hulton Getty Collection, pages 5 *above right*, 8 above right; Kent Messenger Group, page 4 *above right*; Popperfoto, page 8 *above left*. Plate Section Two: Hulton Getty Collection, page 4 *above left*; Kent Messenger Group, page 7 *above*; Popperfoto, page 5 *above right*; Gary Prior, page 8 *below*.

Except where indicated, all photographs are from the Swanton family's personal collection.

Editor's Note

I should explain straight away; this celebration is part ancient, part modern, or, if you prefer, in with the old, in with the new. It is *Last Over*, a book on which Jim Swanton and I collaborated in 1996 and it is also a compendium of much of Jim's writings from that year until his death at the beginning of this new Millennium, together with the remembrances of many friends, colleagues, foes? . . . who knew him well. Without actually counting, an estimate of the additional sections comprises around 50,000 words, so what readers have spread before them is, in effect, two books in one.

I began the note to *Last Over* with the thought that it may have appeared to some that Jim Swanton had outlived Methuselah and been part of cricket since the game began. He was then approaching his ninetieth birthday and had written twenty-two books and countless articles totalling well over eight million words. That calculation had, I think, been made blithely without too much fear of contradiction. After all, he had started as long ago as 1924 at Amalgamated Press before a transfer three years later to the *Evening Standard* where he wrote prolifically. Then, when he took his eventual place on the pantheon at the *Daily Telegraph* in 1946 – does it not now seem pre-ordained like an act of God? – he had already taken several excursions down branch lines to the *Sunday Express; Illustrated Sporting and Dramatic News* and *The Field* and was to later drop in on *The Spectator* and *Wisden Cricketers' Almanack*. His more or less uninterrupted residency at *The Cricketer* only added to the count.

Readers of Swanton knew they could expect balanced, reasoned accounts, sometimes augurous, but always constructive and founded on a sound basis. All that and something more for, as a former editor of the *Telegraph*, Lord Deedes, wrote on Jim's retirement: 'He put a stamp on his work – a majestic stamp which, I think, nobody else could quite equal.'

Well, how did the collaboration on *Last Over* begin? When asked whether the lyrics or music came first, songwriter Sammy Cahn always used to say: 'First, comes the phone call . . .' In this case, there were two phone calls.

I rang Jim and asked whether he was willing to subject himself to an interview for some BBC Radio 5 Live programmes to honour his ninetieth birthday. He then rang me and asked if I was willing to work with him on what was to become *Last Over*. We both of us said yes and so that is how it started.

At a very early stage I volunteered the thought that Jim's life fitted neatly into man's seven ages – albeit of a rather different kind from those handed down by that other well-known writer with almost the same initials – and so it was proposed that I provide introductions to each of these eras. It was also decided that *Last Over* should be more than just a compilation of Swanton's writings over the years and most of the articles included a new commentary specially written by him. And so, in that way the thread of autobiography and biography were combined.

Once embarked, there were frequent trips down the M2 to the Kentish coast where Ann and Jim were always kindly, generous and attentive hosts; there were car-boot loads of files and copy to ferry back and forth; there were meetings in London; much postage of material – especially for Jim – for comment and amendment (his suggestions mostly were written with a green felt pen. (His father too, had a penchant for green ink, a bent shared with Orson Welles.) There were lengthy conversations on the phone – my wife, holding an astronomical Telecom account in her hand, pointed out that I had spent over five hours on the blower to Sandwich in a period of just under two weeks; and deliveries of the typescript piecemeal to the publisher where, on one occasion, Richard Cohen memorably described Jim as 'the Claudia Schiffer of cricket'.

Since that time, Richard Cohen has embarked on new ventures in the USA and his book imprint has been subsumed by Metro Books under the wise guidance of Alan Brooke. Alan has yet to give a description of Jim Swanton, although he probably feels he does not need to having now commissioned this celebratory volume.

The formula used before has been repeated in a general sense in the new 'Part Eight: The End of the Innings' and 'Part Nine: Jim Swanton Remembered', although obviously without commentary from E.W.S., the concentration is biographical.

To collect recent copy has necessitated further trips to Sandwich, on these occasions with feelings of sadness at Ann and Jim's absence.

Given their advanced years both deaths were unexpected; they seemed immune to the frailties of age, because of their vitality and the fact that they always looked to the future.

Let us do the same, encouraged by a remark from former Australian Prime Minister Sir Robert Menzies: 'Swanton is a man whose maturity will be of value to those who read about cricket in a hundred years' time.'

Fortunately, we do not have to wait that long.

D.R.A.

Author's Preface

The perpetrator of an autobiography is self-evidently open to the charge of vanity: so what epithet can be expected by a man who connives at some sort of a sequel? I can remark, of course, that the personal content herein has been the work of another hand; also perhaps that *Sort of a Cricket Person*, my first innings, appeared almost a quarter of a century ago. In any case I have reached an age when so far as I am concerned people can more or less think and say what they like. It's family and friends now who really matter.

The first chapter of *Sort of a Cricket Person* I called 'The Universal Thread' because the thread that runs through all our lives, for better or worse, for richer, for poorer, would seem, whether or not it is guided by the hand of Providence, to be common or garden luck. A casual remark and an off-chance telegram diverted me at the outset of the Second World War from an ack-ack battery destined for Home defence to the 18th Division and surrender at Singapore. The day before that sickening disaster a Jap bullet hit me on the right arm an inch below the funny-bone. One inch higher and in the chaotic circumstances prevailing I would undoubtedly have lost an arm. My battery commander who took over from me was killed. Who cannot relate incidents but for which their lives would have taken a very different course? So far as my post-war activities are concerned my whole *Daily Telegraph* connection depended on a decision by Leonard Crawley in the winter of 1945/6. He was offered by the first Lord Camrose the choice of becoming either the cricket or the golf correspondent. He chose golf as being the one less disruptive of family life: if he had plumped for cricket – no Swanton.

Yes, for me fortune has been wonderfully kind. I have had an extremely happy life with cricket and the friendships it has brought at its centre, alongside a firm Christian faith. It has therefore been a pleasure to rekindle the memory and relive the high points in collaboration with my distinguished co-author, David Rayvern Allen.

E. W. Swanton
Sandwich, July 1996

PART ONE

1907–1924

1907–1924

E rnest William Swanton was born in south-east London or, depending on one's allegiance or preference, metropolitan Kent. The date was 11 February 1907 and at that time Forest Hill was a quiet, unpretentious suburb well endowed with medium-sized Victorian villas and surrounding parkland. To the north lay Nunhead and Brockley, to the west Dulwich, to the east Catford and Hither Green and, to the south, Sydenham.

At a very early age Ernest William became 'Jim', so-called by his mother after a favourite uncle. His mother was a kindly soul who espoused good causes in a practical way, for instance, as local secretary of the National Society for the Prevention of Cruelty to Children. Who knows? Perhaps she thought 'Jim' a preferable alternative to the abbreviations of Ernest that were likely to be inflicted on him, particularly by children. In time, the household was augmented by the arrival of two sisters for Jim: Ruth and Christine, shortened to Tina.

Both parents had been born within a few days of one another in January 1879. Jim's stockbroker father, William, was, for many years, treasurer of Forest Hill Cricket Club and an enthusiastic player, if somewhat limited, due to poor eyesight. He had a respectable baritone voice and rendered popular ballads such as 'Glorious Devon' at the alfresco smoking concerts which were part of the club's social calendar. For these occasions the pavilion was decked out with hundreds of coloured lights which sparkled, Jim recalls, 'ever more brightly as twilight closed in'.

Jim inherited his father's love of games. As a youngster at an early semi-detached residence at 19 Perry Hill in the district of Kirtley, he used to scramble through the fence at the end of the garden and practise his cricket on the adjoining Cuaco (Commercial Union) ground. That young love of cricket has remained constant throughout a long lifetime. He also used to look out of the window at the last of the horse-buses that passed by during the transition to motorised transport: 'I even remember the number,' declares Jim proudly. 'Number 75!'

Mostly, though, Jim is impatient of juvenile memories. An exhumation is not easy for those who wish to dig for more. It is not that he does not remember; his recall of detail from past years is outstandingly good, indeed positively elephantine. It is that he does not regard it as important to remember, thinking of his childhood as unremarkable and of no interest. But certain facts have emerged, more often than not vouchsafed with an apologetic smile.

Jim was told, although he does not actually remember, that he was present in his pram when the great W. G. Grace made 140 for London County against Forest Hill in 1907. On the other hand, he conjures up very clearly the memory of being hustled up to bed by his mother and hearing the big munitions explosion at Silvertown near Woolwich and also of seeing the glow over north London when the Zeppelin was brought down over Cuffley. There was, as well, the remembrance of indignation felt when Mr Wallace, the proprietor of a local ironmongers, inquired brusquely why his father was not away fighting in the war. Did the man not know that his beloved parent was a special constable, having been turned down for military service because of seriously deficient vision?

The terrible toll exacted by the First World War on foreign shores was reflected at home by considerable intolerance, not to say persecution, in some quarters of those who did not quite fit into the normal pattern of British life.

In Forest Hill there was a noticeable German community focused on a Lutheran church and they experienced, not unnaturally, some overt hostility: a neighbour of the Swantons was one such. His name was Streit and, to ward off potential problems, he quickly had it adapted to Street. Shortly before war was declared, Lillian Swanton, Jim's mother, was in the garden one evening, transfixed by a blood-red sunset. It seemed an omen. Turning to Mr Streit over the wall she said, 'This is a terrible foreboding, it must be war.'

Jim went to kindergarten school at the age of five and, having been ushered by his teacher Miss Watmough into morning assembly, stood next to a friend called Alec Edwards who eventually became a doctor. The first hymn was number four in *Ancient and Modern* – 'New every morning is the love.' Alec Edwards did not join in the singing because he was being brought up as a Roman Catholic. Jim has never forgotten this earliest evidence of the divide between Rome and Canterbury in 1912.

He then spent a few terms at St Dunstan's College, close to his home.

Coming out of class one day when about nine, he saw on the corner of Catford Hill a newspaper placard in purple type announcing the 'Death of Kitchener'. He can still see that placard today.

Preparatory schooling continued at Brightlands on the corner of Dulwich Common exactly opposite the football ground there and the College. Jim was a weekly boarder and remembers being released on a Saturday in May 1919, walking up the Common to the buses and trams which went to Kennington and arriving at the Oval just in time to see the Surrey side coming off the field, having been beaten by Hampshire inside two days. That briefest of brief encounters with the first-class game was not enough to dissuade him from returning to the Oval in August of the same year. Surrey were playing Yorkshire and the names of both sides are indelibly imprinted on his memory as if carved in tablets of stone. Two years later, Jim was elected a junior member of Surrey having been proposed by a friend of his father, N. A. Knox, the famous Surrey fast bowler. He soon found himself attending schoolboy nets under the supervision of Harry Baldwin, later renowned as an umpire, and young Jim was thrilled, not only to tread the famous turf, but to be in such close proximity to some of the great players of the time, notably Jack Hobbs.

Brightlands led to Cranleigh – eventually. First though, rather than seek entry to the nearby Dulwich College, and in order to help the family exchequer, Jim tried for an exhibition to Eastbourne College. This he just missed and so arrived by normal acceptance, although abnormally a year late, at Cranleigh in the summer term of 1921 when he was aged fourteen.

At Cranleigh, Jim says, he got by. 'I was not very good at anything. I had a very good Latin master called Antrobus and I always think that everybody ought to learn Latin as a basis for writing and talking English. I got the School Certificate from the fourth form, reasonably young, the London Matric. soon afterwards.'

The school had an enviable rugby tradition. 'I was never any good at rugger. Although I was fairly tall and slender, I was a little bit light. I wasn't a scrummaging forward and I wasn't really very fast.'

Jim was, however, good at cricket, although he never quite made the first eleven. At that time Cranleigh had a powerful side skippered by Maurice McCanlis, who went on to captain Oxford, and the last place was occupied by an Italian called Parlato. Young Swanton's sole appearance for the eleven was against the Masters in 1924 in which he scored 33. Four years later he made up lost ground by scoring his first hundred – 144 not out – for Old Cranleighans against Old Rossallians in a two-day match on the latter's southern tour.

During his first vacation at Cranleigh Jim had attended his first Test match – England v Australia at the Oval. In a drawn game Phil Mead shared a big stand with Lionel Tennyson, Mead remaining undefeated with 182 not out. The match remains in posterity for one incident. Warwick Armstrong became bored with proceedings and at the fall of one wicket lay down on the outfield reading the evening paper. When reproached later by Arthur Mailey, he retorted: 'I wanted to see who we were *plying*!'

Jim enjoyed his time at Cranleigh but the cost factor prohibited any thoughts of going on to University. Work beckoned. Every day his father travelled to London in the same railway carriage with a director of the Amalgamated Press. An approach was made. 'Does the boy write at all?' inquired Tod Anderson. 'Yes,' replied Mr Swanton, 'he writes a decentish sort of essay, I suppose.'

And so it was that the youthful Jim entered his first employment. Amalgamated Press was situated at Fleetway House in Farringdon Street in the City, from where was printed a variety of material ranging from Harmsworth's Encyclopaedias to *Comic Cuts*. Before long Jim was put to work on a paper aimed at those who liked their reading to be middle-brow and light, *All Sports Weekly*: more of that anon.

Meanwhile, let us leave him making the tea, teaching himself to type and doing the odd jobs around the office – at twenty-five bob a week . . .

D.R.A.

PART TWO

1924-1939

1924–1939

Amalgamated Press and, essentially, *All Sports Weekly* was an ideal training ground for Jim in the principles of journalism. The paper lived up to its name by being informative and chatty over a wide range of activity. For two-penn'orth every Thursday readers could usually find something in the twenty or more pages that interested them on their own favourite sport. For instance, cricket-lovers might learn of J. W. Hearne's thoughts on 'Modern Bowlers' or 'Surrey's Pressing Problem – can Peach fill the need?' or read Arthur Mailey on the googly, 'Cricket's Ugly Duckling'. In those pre-sexism days, there were also series for the lady of the house: 'The Dancing Girl, a Tale of Test Match Cricket, being the story of Rita the Girl who saved England. A Woman's influence on the Destiny of England in Test Match Cricket.' What have we missed?

Apart from keeping the tea-pot warm, Jim was soon inducted into the art of sub-editing and indeed within a few months was subbing none other than J. A. H. Catton, a familiar name in the sporting world of the 1920s, who, during the summer of 1925, ran profiles of 'Cricket Favourites', including the likes of Charlie Hallows of Lancashire and Fred Root of Worcestershire.

During his time with *All Sports Weekly*, Jim had the chance to do a couple of interviews. One was with Frank Woolley at Blackheath, the path to the great man having been cleared by a stockbroking friend of his father's, George Wood, the amateur who had in 1924 kept wicket in three Tests for England and was one of six Kent and England 'keepers. The result of that meeting is the first article in this section; the other interview was with Walter Hammond and took place in the Gloucestershire team's hotel during a visit to the metropolis.

By 1927 Jim was looking to better his lot or, at least, enlarge his pay packet. He had already contributed articles on club cricket under his own name to *The Evening Standard* and on schools' sport under the *nom-de-plume* 'Juventas'. So he wrote to the paper and said that 'as he was getting "x" pounds for these two articles they might care to have his full services for thirteen pounds a week.' The *Standard* replied saying they could not manage thirteen but would offer eleven – appreciably more than the 25/- he got a week at *All Sports*. And so in September 1927, Jim literally went up the road from Farringdon Street to 47 Shoe Lane to join *The Evening Standard*.

He was appointed onto the staff as rugger correspondent, thereby joining the famous England stand-off half W. J. A. Davies, with his weekly article, and Norman Hillson who had hitherto covered Internationals. In retrospect, Jim thinks his appointment ridiculous; there he was, not yet twenty-one, with only his Cranleigh background in rugby football, reporting on Internationals and England Trials and commenting critically on aspirants and veterans. Yet surely it was no more ridiculous than the case of Hillson, who was fundamentally a foreign correspondent, but happened to be an Old Rugbeian.

Catton – Jim could not get away from him – also spread his wings at *The Evening Standard*. He made up for his diminutive stature by writing voluminously; indeed, he gave the accurate impression of being paid by the word – he would never use one where three were viable. Jim recalls how, after sending off Catton's cheque, based on the number of words ordered and received, with youthful self-assurance, not to say arrogance, he proceeded to cut his copy to the bone.

When entering the press-box the young tyro was somewhat in awe of the company he was keeping: Stewart Caine, Hubert Preston, both, in turn, editors of *Wisden*; Harry Carson of the *Evening News*; 'Bertie' Henley of the *Daily Mail* who, as well as bringing a theatrical flavour and a lame leg to matches, persisted in calling Jim 'Jimmy'; Neville Cardus of the *Manchester Guardian*; Colonel Philip Trevor CBE – always CBE – of the *Telegraph*, mocked for his regular rider 'Good too, was so and so'; and Archie MacLaren, the old England captain, surrounded by pundits and who had an unbearably condescending manner when handing over his copy for young Swanton to pass on to the telephonist.

There were others too in the Press corps – though that was not a name used then – Sydney Southerton; William Pollock; the extraordinarily prolific C. B. Fry, accompanied by his butler called Brooks – Fry had *The Evening Standard* crying for mercy with the amount of copy he was producing; and the old Oxford blue and Gloucestershire player A. C. M. Croome writing for *The Times*, whose presence evoked memories for some of the time when Croome, on Grace's orders, was attempting to buy what was euphemistically termed an abdominal protector from an embarrassed young lady in a sports shop in Bristol.

He came away with an ill-fitting, cumbersome metal contraption which, when hit by George Hirst's left-arm in-swerver, produced a pitched-note pinging sound. Grace, batting at the other end, could not contain himself: 'I said a box, Arthur, not a musical box.'

Jim saw Croome, a distinguished schoolmaster journalist of his day, at the Old Trafford Test of 1930, but sadly missed the chance of his acquaintance, for Croome was dead within a week or two. Nonetheless Jim's memory of the press-box in the late 'twenties, and early 'thirties is a happy one. 'There was an innate feeling for the good of the game – and most of them were very kind and helpful to me.'

As far as his personal life was concerned, he had acquired his first car – an A.C. Tourer – and by 1928 was playing cricket and hockey for the Dulwich club. That year the West Indies, including in their side Challenor, Martindale, Constantine and Francis, began their tour with a game against Dulwich (R. K. Nunes, the West Indies captain, had schooled at the College) and Jim was 12th man.

Soon after that, having left home, Jim was to be found putting together his pieces in residence above a public house in Dorking and then in 1931 he began to share rooms with England leg-spinner Ian Peebles at 3 Grosvenor Cottages just off Sloane Square in London. Swanton's close friendship with Peebles had begun after a meeting at Aubrey Faulkner's Indoor Cricket School at Walham Green. In years to come Jim was to be godfather to Ian's son and Ian was best man at *his* wedding. Their stay at Grosvenor Cottages was not protracted. On a cold day the walls were streaming with damp and to their dismay they discovered the abode had been built over a plague pit.

8 King's Bench Walk in the Temple had no such problem and they were to remain there with intermissions until the outbreak of war in 1939. Their landlord was a retired barrister with mutton-chop side-boards called W. H. S. Truell. Truell was a Dickensian character whose florid handwriting was to be seen in idiosyncratic letters inquiring about his fifteen guineas a month. The letters always started: 'Dear Mr Swanton, In re the rental . . .' which became a pet phrase that always guaranteed a laugh between the two young lodgers. Their housekeeper, Mrs Smallbone, mothered them to perfection. Henry Longhurst, Jim's colleague on the *Standard* as golf correspondent, at first also lodged at King's Bench Walk, as later did John Mahaffy.

Whenever cash-flow became strained they would sub-let the rooms to rich Americans and move in with friends. During the 1930s Jim led a somewhat peripatetic existence. He rented for one winter No. 5

Holywell, Oxford, and then the next Palace Yard at Sonning-on-Thames in the Berkshire countryside. He moved into King Street, St James's, SW1 as paying guest to the editor of the *Illustrated Sporting and Dramatic News*, James Wentworth-Day. He frequented the Public Schools Club in Curzon Street in the heart of Mayfair. Here, obviously, was a young man on the go, ambitious and determined.

In 1931 he had been appointed cricket correspondent of *The Evening Standard* and as such reported on the England/New Zealand Tests of that year. But in 1932 came a setback. Shortly before reporting the only Test versus India he had covered the Essex match against Yorkshire at Leyton. It was the game in which Holmes and Sutcliffe amassed their famous record first-wicket partnership of 555, give the odd run. In those days there was but one public telephone to send copy. Jim was last in the queue. He missed the edition. His editor was not pleased – in fact, he was so put out as to change his mind about the reporting role for the forthcoming tour of Australia. Instead of Jim, he decided to send the Lawn Tennis correspondent S. Bruce Harris and with that end in view Harris was despatched at short notice to the Scarborough Festival to learn all he could about cricket! For young Swanton it was heartbreaking. Ever since he has wondered how he would have reacted to the volcanic events of 'Bodyline'. Certainly differently to Harris who, with the insecurity of a new boy, acted, in effect, as Jardine's mouthpiece.

In August 1933 Jim embarked – as a player – on a seven-week tour of Canada, the USA (Chicago and New York) and Bermuda with furniture magnate Sir Julien Cahn's side. In some cases they played teams with greater numbers; nevertheless they won sixteen of the twenty matches and drew the rest. Cahn's side contained four Test cricketers and one eventually to become so – Denijs Morkel of South Africa; Roger Blunt of New Zealand; Walter Robins, Ian Peebles and Paul Gibb, England. Jim scored fifties in Ottawa, Chicago and New York but had little chance to display his 'holy rollers' – which, in later years, is how his bowling was referred to, facetiously.

As a schoolboy at Brightlands, Jim had bowled lobs – incidentally in the side was Dilawarsinhji, cousin of Duleep – but now was busy developing leg-spin that kept a length and turned a little. As a batsman he liked to go in first as he was uneasy facing spinners. Perhaps that fact, and because he was in close company with a master leg-spinner Ian Peebles, persuaded him to try and unravel the mysteries of the art. There was no doubt in subsequent years that Jim had done so. To take one example just post-war: for Beckenham against Blackheath the local newspaper headline reads 'Swanton proved unplayable'. The narrative tells the tale: 'Swanton was in devastating form with the ball and took five of the later Blackheath wickets for seven runs. His last three came with five balls. He had previously opened the Beckenham innings with Collingwood and knocked up a useful 57.'

During the 1930s Jim managed somehow to find the time (as John Woodcock has pointed out in *The Cricketer* in April 1987) to 'play enough cricket himself to score 1,000 runs a season (except in 1933) and 2,000 in 1936, most of them for MCC, Wimbledon, Incogniti, the Romany, Eastbourne and the Cryptics.' He also played three matches for Middlesex in 1937 and '38 and, for the county second eleven against Kent at Folkestone, put on a hundred stand with a certain eighteen-year-old, Denis Compton.

The birth of his own wandering club, the Arabs, happened, in effect, because of an abortion. The success of Cahn's tour in 1933 led to an invitation to Jim to take a side to Bermuda in 1935. However the funding of the visit by the hosts fell through and so Jim was left with an expectant team but nowhere to go. He soon found somewhere – the Channel Islands – and so on Sunday 8 September 1935 our intrepid leader and his gallant men took off from Heston on their way to Jersey in what is believed to be the first air journey by a touring cricket side: it was certainly Jim's first flight.

Earlier in the same year Jim had played his first game at Lord's for MCC against Indian Gymkhana – Bill Edrich had got 60 and EWS was lbw b. Amar Singh for 7. He then scored 120 for Romany against the National Provincial Bank and 100 for MCC v Henley and, to recuperate from his exertions, took a river holiday from Wargrave with Henry Longhurst and two female companions. Jim made a lot of runs when playing qualifying matches for MCC. In 1934 he got 102 and 61 retired hurt in a two-day match against Eastbourne and two years later he was elected to membership of the club, having been proposed by the Hon. E. G. French and seconded by D. J. Knight.

But however much cricket he played, and he played a great deal, Jim's writing commitments predominated. As well as his regular output for the *Standard*, he was, by the early 'thirties, a contributor to the *Illustrated Sporting and Dramatic News*. Three series for that magazine in the next few years made considerable impact: 'Great Schools', 'Pavilion Parade', and 'County Cricket Club Histories'. The editor, J. Wentworth-Day, was kindly but quite specific in his requirements: 'My dear James, Forgive me if I seem a little exacting in my criticisms of copy but I have to watch the printer's bill for corrections pretty closely, so if you could see that all copy before being sent out is well and truly punctuated and that all the esquires, unless they merit it, are turned into Mr's and other small points, I would be glad. It really does make a difference of so many pence per line.'

Besides taking Swanton mildly to task, Wentworth-Day did enjoy fun at his expense too. Here is his editorial introduction to 'Pavilion Parade' in April, 1937:

That literary fay of the cricket and rugby fields, Mr E. W. Swanton, here gambols into print in a new and spring-like guise. During the course of an ill-spent youth, this pillar of the Old School Tie has contrived to build up not only an extensive and peculiar knowledge of the public schools of England, but a not inconsiderable reputation as an almost first-class cricketer. As a presumably paid agent wrote of him not long ago: 'He puts precept most charmingly into practice and shows an ease of footwork that belies his contour.' Mr. Swanton's notes and comments on the games of the week and the moving matters of public schools sport will, we trust, introduce a new, more personal, and hitherto lacking, feature into this newspaper. Readers who wish to earn immortality should address notes, comments, criticisms and contributions to him – or about him – at this office, 32, St. Bride Street, E.C.4.

In order perhaps not to be seen too obviously putting an excess of eggs into a couple of baskets, Jim invented a *nom-de-plume*. In 1935, reporting Tests for the *Sunday Express*, he wrote as Michael James, but for that year only. He also provided material for *The Field* and was to succeed Neville Cardus as their cricket correspondent. This transpired after Jim's job with *The Evening Standard* had been severed in 1938. For some time he had not seen eye to eye with the Sports Editor, a forthright Yorkshireman called Clucas who took exception to the amount of work Jim was doing elsewhere. Not that it mattered too much, because he continued to work for the paper on a freelance basis and at around the same time came an invitation from Harry Altham to assist in the updating of the definitive *A History of Cricket*.

But alongside all this literary activity was a burgeoning career in broadcasting. Jim had auditioned for producer Cecil Madden after proposing a topical talk on the Empire service on Cahn's North American tour in late '33. 'A good voice and a strong personality,' wrote Madden in his report. A year later Jim was giving 500-word summaries of the week's rugger. The story of his début in this series and the taxi-journey from a dinner at the Café Royal has been related in several of his books. Suffice to say that Madden's encouraging letter before the broadcast read, 'I hope this will be only the beginning and that you will do many more talks for us. Will you please remember to speak slowly and with plenty of emphasis, as rehearsed.'

Jim was his own harshest critic: 'Dear Mr Madden,' he responded, 'I enclose the script of my talk yesterday, as requested. Frankly, I was not altogether pleased with it, because, though it seemed to read well enough, when spoken it seemed somewhat stiff and disjointed. On another occasion this should be remedied quite easily.' Madden, however, thought it most effective.

An early voice test for the formidable Seymour de Lotbinière, Head of Outside Broadcasts, produced a more equivocal reaction: 'He struck me as having rather the Howard Marshall manner. I told him that we would bear his name in mind but that we were well satisfied with Howard Marshall.'

That sounds as if young Swanton was being rather too pushy. But it was not too long before Jim was involved in talking about sports other than rugby, such as cricket and golf, and there was even a proposal to have a try at commentating on tennis at Wimbledon, but that came to nothing because of the clash with the Lord's Test.

During the first years as a broadcaster Jim's performance attracted a lot of criticism, but probably not much more than anybody else coming to terms with the unforgiving microphone: 'tendency to slur your words'; 'slow down for overseas reception'; 'don't overrun your time'; 'I hear you had no notes of what you wanted to say, far less a script'; 'perturbation caused by your late arrival'; 'don't walk in during the reading of the News'; 'Swanton is a bit careless, I think'. And then an olive branch: 'These suggestions are made only in the friendliest spirit.' Jim occasionally offered a defence: 'I improvise a little for the sake of naturalness.' 'I would like to see any correspondence, as it may well be quite a guide to an as yet inexperienced broadcaster.'

Much of this makes surprising reading for those who know of Jim's predilection for organisation and method today. Could it be that with his many activities he was trying to do too much in too little time? The impression given is that of taking a few of life's responsibilities a touch lightly. But that, of course, is a young man's prerogative.

Eventually it all became acceptable and after a programme-saving performance on 31 August 1938 at the Oval, when Percy Fender at Hove handed over commentary to a lubricated (Henry Longhurst's wedding) but articulate Swanton, the path ahead was not so strewn with boulders. A Surrey last-wicket partnership was not a promising precursor to filling a half hour but when it ended with many minutes yet to fill, Jim still managed and, moreover, managed well. Back in Broadcasting House 'Lobby' was pleased. Jim was now definitely on the boat to South Africa. For the five Tests (ten minutes of commentary each day, twenty-five on Saturdays, followed by five-minute summaries) – *the first English commentary from abroad* – he was to receive 120 guineas, 24 per match, with the added bonus of work for the South African Broadcasting Corporation and articles for local papers, as well as *The Field*. Cricket broadcasting was new in South Africa; the SABC initially ordered twenty broadcasts but ended up taking two hundred so obviously they were pleased with what they heard.

Tom Goddard's hat-trick on Boxing Day; the 'Timeless' Test and much else lay ahead.

D.R.A.

TWENTY YEARS A KENTISHMAN

Not being much addicted to quoting verse, it amuses me that my very first venture into print in July 1926 opens as it does. Further, it is about the only time I wrote under my Christian name. I suppose for a nineteen-year-old it is just passable. All Sports, on which I was a sub-editor, had quite a following up to the war. I missed the point that that first hundred, against Hampshire, was made at Woolley's home town and, says Wisden, in 'about an hour and a half'. Much worse was a fact unchecked. It was at Headingley in the Third Test not the Second that Tennyson batted one-handed. He made 5 and 74 not out at Lord's.

BY ERNEST SWANTON

It's good to be born
At Tonbridge in May.
You'll say, I'll be sworn,
It's good to be born,
For Life's at the morn,
And the umpire calls 'Play!'
It's good to be born
At Tonbridge in May!

And Frank Woolley was! In the very heart of Kent, the county which produced the great Alfred Mynn and his heroes who did battle against the great Hambledon Club and against All England, too, in the days when cricket was first! In so far he was lucky. His whole environment suggested cricket, as anyone who knows Tonbridge in the summer will testify. And from the first Woolley suggested the cricketer.

If you win his confidence – which in itself is not easy, because he is inclined to be shy and retiring with strangers, and talks about anything or anybody rather than himself – you may learn something about his cricket before the day on which he first played for Kent.

Cricket was always for him the 'grande passion.' Many hours he spent as a boy, he has told me, with his brother Claude by the side of the New Wharf Bridge. A tennis-ball, an old broomstick, and a post were their impedimenta, and the close of play only came with darkness or an extra hefty smack that landed the ball in the river.

That was all when Frank was very young. At fifteen he was introduced into the Kent nursery. In the hands of Captain McCanlis he developed so quickly that four years later, and just twenty years ago, he was chosen to play for Kent. At Old Trafford, against Lancashire – stern test for a youngster – was the spot-light of cricket first concentrated upon him. It blinded him then no more than it does to-day, as a score of 64 will testify. That innings, played when Kent had their backs to the wall, for 'Johnny' Tyldesley had hit his record score of 295 not out the day before, proclaimed him as a man of great possibilities – possibilities which have since been realised a hundredfold.

Against Surrey in the same year he made his first appearance in London. He won the game for Kent. When the rest of the side failed he had a splendid innings to his credit in the first venture, and in the second, when Fielder went in No. 11, and twenty odd runs were required, he took command of the situation and knocked off the runs himself!

A century against Hampshire followed immediately, and from such a fine beginning Woolley has never looked back. To-day, at thirty-nine, he is almost at the zenith of his powers – as a batsman, at any rate. There should be plenty of cricket ahead of him yet. In a record which scintillates with a myriad brilliant feats, it is difficult to pick out any one and say it was his best.

He has to his name 305 not out against Tasmania, he shares with Fielder the last-wicket record of 235 against Worcestershire, he has no less than seventy centuries to his credit, yet I hesitate to think that he has ever done anything finer than his two innings against Australia at Lord's in 1921.

In this match when no other Englishman except Lionel Tennyson, who played his historic 'one-handed' innings, scored over 40 in either innings, Woolley stood head and shoulders above anyone else on either side. His two superb efforts of 95 and 93 were from an English point of view like twin stars in a black and gloomy sky. If ever a man deserved a century in both those innings, he did. He batted easily and without restraint against McDonald and Gregory; the others, literally, 'couldn't look at them.'

Most attractive of batsmen, it is small wonder that he is popular with the crowd; he is accorded almost as fine a reception in the North as on the cricket grounds of Kent. Only one exception have I met to this: it took the form of a disgruntled Ovalite who, on an occasion when Woolley was treating the Surrey attack with scant respect, referred to him as 'that elongated hop-pole!' Lucky for that Ovalite he wasn't at Tonbridge or Canterbury!

He always gets runs at the Oval. I remember a wonderful piece of hitting in which he took part there two years ago when playing for the Rest of England against Yorkshire. Before lunch on the second day, he was joined at the wicket by A. P. F. Chapman. The amateur took ten minutes or so to get going, but when he did the two left-handers set about the bowling in amazing fashion. At one period they actually scored 49 runs in seven minutes, including 6, 3, 6, 6, off Rhodes from successive balls!

Reminiscent of the great Colin Blythe, his contemporary in the Kent eleven before the War, on whom he has obviously modelled himself, he bowls slow left-arm with a high, easy action. Has eight times taken 100 wickets in a season, the last being in 1923. Since then he seems to have lost some of his old spin and has been very wisely rested and nursed for his batting, but he is still deadly on sticky wicket.

In the slips his height and long reach make him one of the best fielders in this position in the country. Truly a wonderful cricketer!

ENTER 'JUVENTAS'

I was still employed by the Amalgamated Press when I began contributing regularly to The Evening Standard *on public school sport and club cricket. This is the first half of a column under the pseudonym 'Juventas', a Latin word with youthful – or possibly juvenile – connotations which I somehow lit upon. Note that (aged twenty) I refrained from echoing the dashing advice propounded for the improvement of school cricket. The rest of the article dealt with the prospects of Eton and Harrow, followed by current news of St Paul's and Charterhouse.* The Evening Standard, *May 1927.*

BY 'JUVENTAS'

I have received correspondence in connection with my remarks last week on the subject of cricket coaching at the Public Schools.

One who in the course of the season plays against several of the leading schools is most emphatic in his denunciation of the instruction given to young batsmen. They are taught, he says, to play gently forward to half-volley after half-volley, to play carefully back to a long-hop, instead of going for such balls with might and main. My correspondent would have a notice in every school pavilion thus:–

PLAY HARD.

Where any ball gives the player the chance of swinging the body, he should play it with his whole strength, and not be content to play it back to the bowler or letting it pass altogether. His whole concern should be in hitting it hard and keeping it low.

My experience does not prompt me to make such a wholesale condemnation of coaching methods as this. Batting is encouraged on the right lines at most schools, but there is no doubt that there are some where batsmen are over-coached.

Too often their style is moulded for them, instead of being just guided, with the result that many boys become possessed of a 'robotish' style instead of a natural one. However, this is an evil that is passing, and coaches are, I think, beginning to realise that a boy's individuality must be given play.

More serious is the almost total lack of coaching that prejudices young bowlers. The well-worn dictum that bowlers are 'born, not made,' is but a half-truth. A successful bowler must have some natural inclinations, but to say that he cannot be taught anything is absurd. However good a boy's action, however fast he may be off the pitch, he will never make the most of his talent until he finds the value of length, and the variation of it, and the intricacies of spin and swing.

Harrow have not beaten Eton at Lord's since 1908. Since, Eton have won on eight occasions, and six times the match has been drawn. From this it would seem that there is a great disparity between the cricket at the two schools, but actually, though both have better years and worse, the standard is much the same.

Last summer the match produced the fifth successive draw, but Harrow, as in the last three years, had the better of the play, and would probably have won if there had been a third day. Though it is admittedly early in the season to judge, I think that Harrow will again be the stronger side this year.

EPIC AT LORD'S

I can see the great 1930 Lord's Test against Australia in clearer detail than any since. It was my first as a reporter for early editions of The Evening Standard. *Hence this piece out of chronological order from a Daily Telegraph book,* I was There, *published in 1966.*

There were so many memorable things about the Lord's Test Match of 1930 that the picture of it, in all its splendour and excitement, remains fresh in the mind's eye to this day. It contained some wonderful batsmanship by some of the greatest players in the game's history, and for all four days the sun poured down on what was then the largest crowd (115,000) ever to see a cricket match in England.

There were four hundreds, by K. S. Duleepsinhji, Woodfull, Bradman, and Chapman. 'Duleep's' 173 came in his first Test against Australia and Bradman's 254 was at the moment of its making the highest score ever made by an Australian in a Test. Yet England, whose two innings totalled exactly 800, were brought, on the fourth and last day, from the brink of defeat to a real prospect of a draw, and when finally the ending of their second innings at half past three meant that a definite result was certain it seemed for a palpitating half-hour that they might even defy all possibility and snatch a victory.

That did not happen, but when young McCabe made the winning hit in the evening sunshine to give Australia their first win in England in nine Test Matches there was such an aura of content at a battle bravely fought, such a sense of honour being satisfied all round, as characterises only the great sporting occasions.

This, however, was not only in itself a tremendous contest that put the emotions under the severest strain from first to last; it was also one that marked, and was seen to mark by all who were at Lord's on Saturday the 28th and Monday the 30th of June, the arrival of a cricketer of unique gifts whose play would henceforth dominate the game as it had not been dominated since the era of W. G. Don Bradman had come to England two months before, a young man of 21 who, after being dropped for one match during the Australian series of 1928–29, had scored a hundred in the Fifth Test. Here he had opened the season in a burst of glory at Worcester, reached a thousand runs by the last day of May, and followed this with a hundred of rare skill and maturity that came near to denying England victory in the First

Test at Trent Bridge. 'Plum' Warner was already announcing the arrival of a new star of extraordinary brightness. But it was this Lord's innings that clinched the matter.

When in Australia nearly seventeen years later, with almost every batting record then to his name, and his fame supreme, I asked Don what was the best innings he had ever played, he said at once 'My 254 at Lord's,' going on, characteristically, to give as his reasons 'because I never hit the ball anywhere but in the middle of the bat, and I never lifted one off the ground until the stroke from which I was out.' Bradman's innings turned the match and made the foundation from which Australia were to regain the Ashes. But before passing on to the story of the game let us make a brief survey of the company.

The England XI, led by Percy Chapman, contained Jack Hobbs, greatest of all professional batsmen, at the age of 47 playing in his *tenth* and final series against Australia. It contained in Maurice Tate probably the finest bowler of his type ever seen. It contained two of the greatest all-round cricketers of any country or generation, Frank Woolley and Walter Hammond. It contained 'Duleep', whose illness at the height of his powers was soon to deprive the game of a genius. It contained two of cricket's immortal characters, 'Patsy' Hendren and George Duckworth. Not least it contained as many as five past, present or future captains of England – Percy Chapman, Jack White, 'Gubby' Allen, Walter Robins and Walter Hammond.

Allow for the enthusiasm of youth, and the enchantment that time lends to the distant view, and it still seems an incomparable collection of talent and personality. Note, by the way, that Herbert Sutcliffe and Harold Larwood were missing, both because of injury. The latter, contrary to general belief, was as a rule expensive on the English Test wickets of his day, but Sutcliffe, of course, was and had been since 1924 the inseparable complement to Hobbs. How he might have relished England's long rearguard in the second innings!

If some of the Australian names by comparison suffer a little in lustre and tend to be dwarfed by Bradman, they likewise include a rich assortment of the great. When has Australia had a better opening pair than Woodfull and Ponsford, a finer wicket-keeper than Oldfield, a leg-spin bowler superior to Grimmett, batsmen more gracious in style than McCabe and Kippax?

In Sutcliffe's absence Woolley went in first with Hobbs. Wall, from the Pavilion end, began the game with a maiden to Hobbs. Fairfax bowled at the other, and Woolley simply leaned on his first ball and sent it flashing up the hill, to rattle among the seats under the Grand Stand balcony behind cover point. (I know because I was sitting there in the Press Box annexe.) The next three-quarters of an hour were pure heaven. Even the dismissal of Hobbs, soon caught behind off Wall, seemed a relatively minor incident as one watched the Australian attack plundered with a succession of strokes that held the crowd in wonder and fascination.

Forty minutes after he had received his first ball, his score now 41, Woolley faced Fairfax, who had taken over from Wall at the Pavilion end. Fairfax dropped one a little short and Woolley came down on the ball and cut it left-handed just behind square with the speed of light. No gully could conceivably have arrested the stroke, but Wall had retreated until he was almost a pitch's length from the bat. Instinctively he grabbed at something red hurtling straight at his boots, and incredibly the catch stuck. So ended one of the little masterpieces of batting, and the hundred before lunch – before one o'clock, I dare say – that never was.

Hammond batted hesitantly. At this stage of his career he was in Tests at home only a shadow of his great self, probably because he was trying to repeat the very cautious methods he had employed to make his huge scores on the flawless Australian wickets of 1928–29 when time was no object. When he was drawn forward by Grimmett and bowled off his pads England were 105 for three. But Woolley had lit the torch, and it was the batting from now on that held the stage throughout the game.

So far as the two England innings went this was despite the excellence of Grimmett. The wicket was particularly comfortable in pace but the little man kept pegging away from the Nursery end, using all his resources of spin and flight, bowling a little 'flatter' and faster to the quicker-footed, tossing the ball a little higher to the rest, and giving it an accordingly sharper tweak. He was the foundation of the Australian attack of 1930, and it was the punishment he took after lunch at the hands of Duleep and Hendren that put England, temporarily at least, on top. No one was more nimble at coming to meet slow bowling than little Patsy, while the lithe Duleep, with his oriental speed of eye, though he moved much more deliberately, achieved the same results.

These two made 104 together in an hour and a half. However, the new ball accounted not only for Hendren but also for Chapman and Allen, the latter playing in his first Test Match. For a second time the innings was set on its feet, thanks now to Tate. Many a great bowler fancies himself as a batsman but few of his kind have been as effective as Maurice, who in his youth used to open the Sussex innings and over his Test career had the more than useful average for a number eight bat of 25. No stylist, he played straight in defence and gave the half-volley a hearty thump. In a boyish way Maurice had a keen sense of theatre. The scene and the situation were just up his street. The seventh wicket added 98 in seventy minutes, and, when Tate left, Duleep embarked on an all-out assault.

There is some uncertainty over the tactical plan late in the day which at this distance cannot be exactly determined. This was only the second four-day Test to be contested in England, and the critics all had different ideas as to how it should be planned. At six o'clock, so legend has it, Archie MacLaren, the arch-pundit, was brandishing his umbrella in the Long Room and declaiming that 'Percy must be mad'. A declaration was the obvious policy, thought he, with the aim a couple of wickets before close of play.

Did Duleep receive a hurry-up signal from the dressing-room balcony? Evidence is conflicting, but when at quarter past six he was caught at long-off by Bradman off Grimmett, his uncle, 'Ranji', though expressing the greatest pride in his nephew's achievement, is said also to have exclaimed, 'the boy was always careless'. Well, the careless boy had made 173 in five hours, and, far from declaring, Chapman let the innings run its course next morning.

By close of play that hot, eventful Saturday everyone, including presumably MacLaren, was a little wiser about the waging of a four-day match, at any rate when Bradman was around. Who does not remember the Saturday of his first Lord's Test? With me the picture of this one stands clear: the crowd in baking heat, spilling out on to the grass, watching quietly while Woodfull and Ponsford laid their careful foundations, equally at home against all the English bowling except for an occasional tester from Tate; the inspection of troops by the King in mid-afternoon, the small, slight, bearded figure of King George with grey bowler hat, button-hole, and rather high walking-stick, moving up and down the lines of the teams while the crowd stood, thankfully taking the chance to stretch their legs; the fall of Ponsford to the first ball afterwards, caught Hammond, bowled White – the origin, this, of the tradition that the monarch's visit is generally worth a wicket to England; and finally the brilliant, relentless taking to pieces of the England bowling by Bradman.

Over his career Bradman was rarely a spectacular starter. His innings tended to come gradually to full glory from quiet, methodical beginnings. But now he almost leapt down the pitch at White's first ball, reached it on the full-pitch and smacked it crisply to the outfield under the Nursery clock-tower. This was his first sight in England of 'Farmer' White, whose length and wonderful control had pegged down the Australians so completely on their own wickets the previous year. Bradman literally jumped at the chance of showing his mastery, and White was known afterwards to say that such was Don's speed of eye and foot he believed he need never have let him bounce unless he had wanted to. But Bradman was equally at home with everyone, and while Woodfull, almost unnoticed, pursued his worthy way the runs accrued at a remarkable rate at the other end.

In the last two hours forty minutes of play Australia went from 162 for one to 404 for two: 242 runs, of which Bradman's share was 155. In fact he caught up Woodfull who, having had three hours start, was stumped off Robins for 155 just before the close. The implications of Bradman's assault were quickly realised. My predecessor, Colonel Philip Trevor, remarked on Monday's *Daily Telegraph* that no one before had seen a side get more than 400 in a Test in England, 'and at the end of the second day's play have to ask themselves if they are going to be beaten'.

In fact Australia made 325 more and declared at the tea interval, with all sorts of records lying strewn in their wake: notably, Bradman's 254, the highest Test score in England and the second highest in England–Australia matches, while 729 for six was the largest of all totals by either side in either country. And there was the somewhat grim comedy of the delay in finding the figure seven for the hundreds column on the Tavern score-board. Kippax, batting with the utmost polish, scored almost run for run with Bradman in their long partnership for the third wicket, whereafter all the Australians who got to the crease made runs and made them fast. This was despite a high standard of English fielding, wherein Chapman was the brightest ornament. It was a superb one-handed catch by the captain, wide to his right, at silly-mid-off that at last disposed of Bradman. The Australian run-rate over their innings was just over 70 an hour, probably the most rapid in the history of Anglo-Australian Tests – and be it noted that England in those less sophisticated days bowled their overs at only a fraction under 23 an hour. Twenty-three! The attack, well-assorted in method if expensive in result, comprised Allen, Tate, White, Robins, Hammond, and Woolley. Your modern cynic may remark that had the captain and his bowlers connived in 'going slow', and delivered, say, at the average rate of the recent series in Australia, the protraction of the Australian innings would have resulted in England easily saving the match. But let me not philosophise painfully about that!

As it was, England's task was in the highest degree formidable, and at nightfall it was still more so with Hobbs bowled round his legs sweeping at a ball that pitched in the follow-through marks and Woolley out hit wicket, having brushed the stumps with his leg as he forced Grimmett to the mid-wicket boundary. Hammond and Duleep lasted out and next morning took the score to 129, but with both of them, and Hendren also, out with 147 on the board England were apparently sliding fast to an innings defeat.

Now came the last of the batting episodes that lifts this game high among the classics. Allen, with a hitherto unsuccessful First Test behind him, joined Chapman around 12 o'clock, their side still 157 runs in arrear. The stand began inauspiciously, for Chapman, misreading Grimmett's googly, so his partner maintains, at once spooned the ball up into the covers where Richardson and Ponsford each left the catch to the other. Thus reprieved, Chapman turned his particular attention to Grimmett while Allen batted in an orthodox and attractive way.

At lunch both had reached 50, and only 42 were needed to make Australian bat again. We had seen some intelligent, aggressive cricket, with Allen mostly at the Nursery end taking the faster bowling while Grimmett was attacked by the left-hander. But here is another tactical curiosity. 'Gubby' Allen was under the impression all the morning that so far as possible this was the plan that was being followed, but when on going out again in the afternoon he asked whether they should carry on as before, Percy surprised him by saying, 'Oh, you can't do that in a Test Match.' Chapman had great personal qualities as a captain – indeed, in my time I doubt that England has had another as good when all virtues are weighed in the scales – but his make-up was an unusual mixture of the shrewd and the naïve.

As it happened, Allen was soon out, but Chapman went from strength to strength, hitting four sixes and twelve fours in an innings of 121 that lasted just over two hours and a half. There could be no clearer example of the old axiom about attack being so often the best mode of defence.

Chapman's play, sketchy at first and growing in power and certainty the longer he batted, was of course just the medicine the crowd were praying for. In particular they enjoyed his onslaught on Grimmett, who was in almost permanent occupation of the Nursery End, and whose spin down the Lords 'hill' the right-handers found so difficult to confront. Here Chapman was at an advantage, for to him the ball turned in, towards the bat, not away, threatening its outer edge for a catch at slip or behind the wicket.

After lunch he discarded the Cambridge Quidnunc cap of blue with the vertical yellow stripes which was his normal wear, and the change in appearance was symbolic. Bare-headed, literally, he went for the Australian bowling, hitting Grimmett not only into the boundary fence but over it into the crowd. Did not one such blow whistle through the narrow aperture between the score-board and the Tavern and land in St John's Wood Road? Such details are not easy to confirm getting on for forty years later, but I fancy so. At all events the bombardment in that quarter was pretty severe, and it was fine disciplined hitting calling for a nice coordination of cool head and eye attuned. This undoubtedly was Chapman's finest hour. When at last Chapman was caught behind the wicket there was now a real chance of saving the game, but Robins, with the impetuosity of youth, called White for a hard hit to Bradman lying deep at mid-off, and 'the Farmer', in his fortieth year, was easily beaten by a fast return. This incident, followed as it was by an ill-judged rebuke in the dressing-room between innings from 'Shrimp' Leveson-Gower, the chairman of selectors, and a characteristically blunt rejoinder by Robins, caused the latter's dropping for the subsequent Tests of the series – but he still had a dramatic part to play in this one.

Australia went in half an hour before tea, needing only 72 to win, but the wicket after all the traffic of the four days and having been baked by unusual heat was now definitely dusty. Robins was brought on for the fifth over and at once should have had Woodfull caught at mid-on. But with the next ball Robins bowled Ponsford, while at the other end Bradman was marvellously caught in the gully by Chapman off a genuine late cut. Robins' wrist-spin for several overs continued to look infinitely dangerous, and the crowd was on the tip-toe of excitement. Duckworth caught Kippax off him (23 for three) and if the 'keeper could have taken a second chance offered by Woodfull, Australia would probably have been struggling for their lives. But the magic moment passed, Robins' length grew uncertain, and the placid Woodfull was sensibly supported by McCabe.

So Australia coasted home, and, though there was some grumbling afterwards about the poor state of English bowling, no one grudged the winners their success: certainly not Chapman, who after winning six successive Tests against Australia now found himself on the losing end for the one and only time. 'It has been a great match,' he said, 'and I think that the people who came each day to see it must have been well rewarded by the fine struggle they saw. Australia fully deserved their victory, for they played splendid cricket at every point.' Woodfull's comment was equally congratulatory and generous. Those were courteous days.

England v Australia, at Lord's, June 27–1 July 1930

ENGLAND

J. B. Hobbs c Oldfield b Fairfax	1	b Grimmett.....................	19
F. E. Woolley c Wall b Fairfax	41	hit wkt b Grimmett	28
W. R. Hammond b Grimmett	38	c Fairfax b Grimmett.............	32
K. S. Duleepsinhji c Bradman b Grimmett...................	173	c Oldfield b Hornibrook	48
E. H. Hendren c McCabe b Fairfax .	48	c Richardson b Grimmett..........	9
A. P. F. Chapman c Oldfield b Wall .	11	c Oldfield b Fairfax	121
G. O. B. Allen b Fairfax	3	lbw b Grimmett	57
M. W. Tate c McCabe b Wall......	54	c Ponsford b Grimmett...........	10
R. W. V. Robins c Oldfield b Hornibrook	5	not out	11
J. C. White not out	23	run out	10
G. Duckworth c Oldfield b Wall....	18	c Oldfield b Wall	18
Extras b 2, lb 7,n-b 1	10	b 16, l-b 13, w 1	30
Total	425		375

FOW: 1–13 2–53 3–105 4–209 5–236 6–239 7–337 8–363 9–387 10–425;
1–45 2–58 3–129 4–141 5–147 6–272 7–329 8–354 9–372 10–375.

Bowling: *1st inns:* Wall 29.4–2–118–3; Fairfax 31–6–101–4; Grimmett 33–4–105–2; Hornibrook 26–6–62–1; McCabe 9–1–29–0; *2nd inns:* Wall 25–2–80–0; Fairfax 12.4–2–37–2; Grimmett 53–13–167–6; Hornibrook 22–6–49–1; McCabe 3–1–11–0; Bradman 1–0–1–0.

AUSTRALIA

W. M. Woodfull st Duckworth b Robins.........................	155	not out	26
W. H. Pondsford c Hammond b White	81	b Robins.......................	14
D. G. Bradman c Chapman b White	254	c Chapman b Tate	1
A. F. Kippax b White.............	83	c Duckworth b Robins...........	3
S. J. McCabe c Woolley b Hammond	44	not out	25
V. Y. Richardson c Hobbs b Tate...	30		
W. A S. Oldfield not out	43		
A. G. Fairfax not out.............	20		
C. V. Grimmett, P. M. Hornibrook, T. W. Wall did not bat			
Extras b 6, l-b 8, w 5	19	b 1, l-b 2	3
Total (6 wkts. dec.)	729	(3 wkts)	72

FOW: 1–162 2–393 3–585 4–588 5–643 6–672: (2) 1–16 2–17 3–22

Bowling: *1st inns;* Allen 34–7–115–0; Tate 64–16–148–1; White 51–7–158–3; Robins 42–1–172–1; Hammond 35–8–82–1; Woolley 6–0–35–0; *2nd inns:* Tate 13–6–21–1; Whte 2–0–8–0; Robins 9–1–34–2; Hammond 4.2–6–0

Umpires: F. Chester and T. Oates
Australia won by 7 wickets.

A BRILLIANT HAMMOND

I cannot recall just when I heard that Sam (later S. Bruce) Harris and not I was to accompany MCC to Australia, but I continued all the 1932 summer to report the leading fixtures and, although I sez it, considering one was writing in an evening paper to produce for the telephonist a running narrative in small doses, I don't think these reports read too badly. My clearest recollection of this 'G and P' is of the great Duleep/Pataudi stand on the second day. The Evening Standard, *14 July 1932.*

The Players won the toss and batted first at Lord's, and the play before lunch went rather in favour of the Gentlemen, who got rid of four such illustrious batsmen as Hobbs, Sutcliffe, Woolley and Hendren for 108 runs. The wicket was moist enough from dew and the effects of the storm to necessitate the use of sawdust, but there was a certain life about it that made the bowling of Allen and Allom at the start look most dangerous.

Hobbs soon showed that despite a recent period of scant success he is in very good form; but Sutcliffe played in his most passive manner and encouraged the bowlers to pitch the ball right up to him without fear of being hit. Hobbs played a ball from Allen beautifully for four off his legs in the first over, and scored another by a perfectly executed forward stroke against Allen in his second.

The best Sutcliffe did to entertain anybody was to call for one or two of those short runs that could not be runs at all to any other pair. Allom swung the ball very late, and against a lesser player than Hobbs the slips would have had catches to take; but his eye is so good that he may leave alone at the last moment balls that others have to play at.

Allen, too, bowled splendidly and kept up his pace for an hour. Hobbs was out at 29, somewhat unluckily playing a ball very hard with his bat, whence it spun on to the wicket.

Woolley paid Allen the compliment of a maiden over, but then straight-drove Brown for 4 and made other strokes that showed he was seeing the ball well. Brown bowled a maiden or two to Sutcliffe, not in itself a great achievement on this occasion, but did not look much like getting a wicket, and eventually gave way to Wyatt, who bowled several half-volleys and fielded them with agility.

Sutcliffe ended a strangely unhappy innings by applying an off-drive with his left foot many inches from the line of the ball, and 'holed out' quite gently into cover-point's hands.

Wyatt, having accomplished his mission, was taken off forthwith and Allom and Peebles bowled several most interesting overs to Woolley and Hammond. Woolley was out, as he has been several times lately, from a full pitch. He tried to make a big hit wide of mid-on, caught the ball approximately on the oil hole at the very bottom of the blade, and was very well taken low down by Hazlerigg who made the catch running in.

It should be added that hereabouts the light was very bad.

Hendren, fresh from his triumph at Southampton, began as if the Gentlemen's success was going to end here, but he found a ball from Allom that would have been too good for most men, and there were four out for 98.

Paynter had an uncomfortable quarter of an hour to face, but he stuck it out while Hammond played superbly to the end of a most enjoyable and distinguished morning's cricket.

After lunch came the stand that was almost certain to take place sooner or later in such a batting side as that of the Players.

Paynter was not wholly comfortable, once at least snicking a ball from Allen through the slips and again playing out at the pitch and not getting a catch. However, he did not get out, which was the main thing.

At the other end Hammond played in inspired mood. He immediately drove Brown over mid off's head for two 4's, and when Brown was promptly taken off treated Allom in the same way with two most powerful clumps that rebounded yards off the fence.

Hammond's 50 took him only an hour, and he then proceeded to score even more quickly. Allen, who had another long spell from the Pavilion end, was the only bowler able to check him.

Peebles occasionally was able to make Hammond hit the ball to a different place than he intended, but it always fell safely. He hit one terrific off-drive for six into the litter basket in the players' enclosure – a contemptuous gesture that well expressed his treatment of the bowling.

Hammond was out at last to Allen, caught at short square leg after as admirable an innings as he can ever have played. He had hit twelve 4's and a 6, and had been in only two hours for 110.

Larwood was caught at the wicket, second ball, and when Tate left 13 runs later, the advantage had passed once again to the Gentlemen.

Gentlemen v Players, July 1932. Players 301 (Hammond 110, G.O. Allen 5 for 71) and 320 (Hobbs 161 not out); Gentlemen 430 for 8 wts. (Nawab of Pataudi 165, KS Duleepsinhji 132, D.R. Jardine 64, Larwood 4 for 54). Match Drawn.

LBW AND THE CLUB UMPIRE

By 1933 I was now writing regularly for the Illustrated Sporting and Dramatic News, *edited by James Wentworth-Day.*
10 June 1933.

Of all the controversial topics associated with cricket I suppose alteration of the leg-before-wicket law is the one upon which the venerable old gentlemen whose playing experience ended with, or was cut short by, the Boer War most frequently seize upon.

There may be a case for revision as it affects first-class cricket, but if you ask a hundred club players their opinion, ninety-nine will say that so far as their class of cricket is concerned the present law is all right.

In club cricket the balance of power as between batsman and bowler is well enough adjusted. To be sure there are, in fine weather, too many tamely-drawn matches, but the reasons for these are to be found in unintelligent, even stark bad, captaincy, as regards bowling changes, disposition of the field and an over-timid use of the declaration, rather than any advantage possessed by one side in the duel between the bat and the ball. But if the law, so far as it concerns the club player, is well and good as it stands, there is much room for improvement in its interpretation.

It is probably more true than most generalisations are, to say that, whereas in first-class cricket more wrong decisions concerning leg-before-wicket are given in favour of the batsman than the bowler; in club cricket the reverse is the case. Stung by what I, in my unbalanced state, considered was an infamous decision against me, I conducted, one evening last summer in an Eastbourne garden, certain lbw. experiments. Stumps were pitched in the regulation manner, and string was tied taut from stump to stump so that three parallel lines were formed the length of the wicket. I bowled right arm over the wicket, my assistant left-arm round.

The first thing that was made abundantly clear was the difficulty that a right-arm over-the-wicket bowler has in obtaining a legitimate lbw. Everything depends upon the point from which the bowler delivers the ball. The average right-arm bowler bowls from a point about mid-way between the stumps and the end of the crease. From here the good length ball which goes straight through must pitch in line with a spot between the middle and off stumps to hit the leg stump. The good length straight ball on the middle stump will either shave the leg stump or miss it altogether.

As soon as a right-arm bowler over the wicket brings to work his natural break, which is the off-break, his chance of getting a legitimate lbw. virtually disappears. On the other hand, if he bowls the leg-break he has the angle in his favour, and he may turn the ball a good deal and still be justified in appealing. Yet how often is an lbw. explained by the bowler thus: 'Yes, I know it broke back; but it pitched on the off-stump and would have hit the leg.' Actually, unless he delivered the ball from right over the stumps, it must have missed the wicket by the best part of a foot.

If anyone is unwilling to take these observations on trust, let him experiment for himself, and the results will quickly be confirmed. Their importance in any case lies not so much in themselves as in the lesson that most of us know a good deal less about cricket than we think we do. Umpiring is a very much more difficult business than one who has had no experience of it would allow.

I recently umpired in a club match and the fact was forcibly and very rapidly brought home to me. To begin with, there is considerable physical discomfort in standing stock still for any length of time in an attitude of concentration. Then there is so much to watch for. You must decide *whether* the ball pitched on the wicket *and* would have hit it. I found it a help to say to myself 'yes' or 'no' simultaneously as the ball pitched, one's mind thus being cleared of one doubt in the next vital second.

But if an occasional experience of umpiring has the effect of making the batsman more sympathetic towards his traditional enemy, it also emphasises the need of getting some physically and mentally reliable and withal conscientious person to do the job.

The club umpire is commonly portrayed as a somewhat decrepit individual, weary of eye and limb; and too often the portrait is more or less true to life. When one considers to how great an extent the general enjoyment of a day's cricket depends on the efficiency, not to say probity, of the umpire, one realises the importance of finding the right man and the expediency of paying well for his services. Still more easily evident is the advisability, at least in so far as club cricket is concerned, of leaving the lbw law alone. As it is, its interpretation is difficult enough. The results of a change, apart from any intrinsic merit it might possess, would be chaotic.

GREAT SCHOOLS – REPTON

In 1934 I began a series in the Illustrated Sporting and Dramatic *called 'Great Schools in Sport'. It ran for three years and included nearly a hundred well illustrated articles covering seventy-odd schools. I visited many, but not by any means all of them, finding Headmasters and their sporting assistant-masters extremely co-operative. I give here only one severely edited piece, chiefly confined to cricket. In the light of experience I would have modified the adjective 'great', for less illustrious schools were the most keen to be included. 20 July 1934.*

Though Repton dates from 1557, its history, so far as games are concerned, is comparatively modern. A word must suffice about the place itself. A Benedictine monastery was founded at Repton, then the important city of Hrepandune, in the seventh century. In 874 the Norsemen stole up the Trent, and wreaked their customarily thorough devastation, but at least from Norman times the monastery continued to be the religious and social centre of the community. With the Dissolution in 1536 came a general need for schools to replace the teaching of the monks, and twenty-one years later, a certain Sir John Port founded a free grammar-school, known as Repton Priory School.

The fortunes of Repton varied greatly during the next three hundred years, but at its most prosperous it was never a big school, and the wave of athleticism which had affected such places as Eton, Harrow, Westminster, and Rugby by the second quarter of the nineteenth century, left Repton untouched.

No doubt the Reptonians of those days bird's-nested, fished, poached, and over-ran the countryside generally like young barbarians, as indeed the Rugby boys were still doing in the time of Tom Hughes, but the only form of semi-organised amusement seems to have been the old Repton game of football that took place in the school yard. A rough-and-tumble affair was this, whose rules probably varied with the years; played by as many as cared to risk their shins, not to say their heads, against the Priory wall.

Repton's crisis occurred in the 'fifties. In 1854 the celebrated Dr. Pears came from Harrow to find a miserable establishment inhabited by some forty-eight pupils. Upon this precarious foundation Dr. Pears built what had become, by the time of his retirement in 1879, the great public-school that Repton is to-day. In the list of great headmasters, Dr. Pears must take a very high place. Dr. Pears encouraged games. Five years after his arrival there is a record of the first colours being decided upon – a white coat, trimmed with magenta, with cap to match, and a magenta scarf. In those days this was considered the last word in style, for magenta, one of the first three aniline dyes, had only just 'come in.'

By 1865 Dr. Pears' energies had resulted in the arrangement, after much correspondence, of a match against Uppingham, and that was the start of the famous series which still produces one of the outstanding school matches of the season.

The saga of the famous Ford family dates from 1870, when W.J., the eldest of the seven brothers, opened the innings against Uppingham, and was put out for 1 in the first innings and a duck in the second. Little did Uppingham realise then what terror the name was to strike.

The Fords so monopolised Repton cricket of the period that their name is missing from only two sides out of seventeen consecutive ones. All seven of them came from the Priory house, and they may be said to have initiated the sporting tradition which the Priory preserves strongly to this day.

The eighties found Repton cricket at its very greatest. There have been splendid sides afterwards in isolated seasons, and the standard, it does not need recording, has always been exceptionally high. But for sustained excellence there can be no beating this decade, in which twenty-two consecutive school matches contained only one defeat, and that, incidentally, by a matter of nine runs.

Lionel Ford, Headmaster of Repton, then of Harrow, and Dean of York until his death two years ago, a great hitter; Alfred Cochrane, a left-arm bowler who subsequently played for the Gentlemen as well as for Oxford; Francis Ford, the most illustrious of all the family, most polished and graceful of left-handers, and one of five Reptonians who have played for England against Australia; the brothers Palairet, classic models of right-handed batsmanship; P. R. Farrant, a great schoolboy bowler; and, lastly, C. B. Fry, whose later deeds outshone them all; the 'eighties saw the rise of every one of them.

Small wonder that poor Uppingham and Malvern measured their success by the margin of defeat. Francis Ford, as a schoolboy, was in this galaxy the undisputed star.

Fry's, of course, was the genius that consisted in taking infinite pains. He was far from being the natural cricketer that the others were, although his ultimate success transcended theirs. His record as a schoolboy suffered by comparison with his remarkable predecessors.

In 1902 there appeared on the horizon one who, by mathematical account and almost universal testimony was the greatest schoolboy cricketer of any generation. The genius of J. N. Crawford in four years revived Repton to its old eminence. 'A medium-paced bowler of beautiful action,' says Mr. H. S. Altham, 'great accuracy, and every possible device, a batsman of extraordinary power but classic method, and a magnificent field in any position, he dominated, during his last two years, every school match in which he took part, and appeared what indeed he was, a first-class cricketer playing in a class below him.'

In his four years Crawford made more than two thousand runs for Repton, a figure only R. A. Young begins to approach, and took more than two hundred wickets, where no one else has ever taken a hundred and fifty. As a schoolboy he took nearly a hundred wickets for Surrey; the year after leaving he 'did the double' and played for the Gentlemen at Lord's.

Contemporary with Crawford were Young, who afterwards played for England in Australia as a batsman and wicket-keeper, E. A. Greswell, and the brothers Turner, so Repton's triumphs were hardly surprising. In 1905 Repton went through the year unbeaten, winning eight and drawing one, both school opponents being mercilessly crushed by hundreds in each match and a huge haul of wickets by the captain, Crawford. This, indeed, must have been almost, if not quite, as good as the 1908 side, although it is the latter that has earned fame as the best school eleven of all time. Such were its deeds that four members, Altham (Surrey), W. T. Greswell (Somerset), R. Sale (Derbyshire), and A. T. Sharp (Leicestershire) played for their counties in the following August and, rumour had it, three more were invited but could not accept. At any rate, in the end five of the side got Blues, and two more played for the Gentlemen. Immediately before the war there were two more remarkable boy cricketers at Repton, named Howell. Miles since has earned renown with Oxford and Surrey, but all seem agreed that he was second to John. Just as the Palairets owed much to the home teaching of Dick Attewell, so did the Howells benefit from the instruction of Tom Hayward. John, in particular, had much of the watchfulness and sound defence of that great player, and he surely was destined to play one day for England. But in 1915 John Howell fell in France, and the school pavilion contains a room to his memory, presented by his mother.

Within recent years there has been no lack of Repton cricketers worthy to be mentioned with the great ones. R. L. Holdsworth was, no doubt, the best of the war-time players, and in this year of grace, B. H. Valentine and J. H. Human are household names. A modern Gentlemen's eleven is not complete without either, and when he is in practice there is no better amateur wicket-keeper than P. C. Oldfield.

PAVILION PARADE

This was the third of the three regular features which I contributed to the Illustrated Sporting and Dramatic News *in the 1930s before the war put a sudden end to such (for me) agreeable scribbling. One returned to England at the war's end to find the magazine transformed in character, entitled* Town and Country, *the sporting tradition discarded. The item on Donald Knight must have given me much pleasure to write. He had seconded me for MCC and in the 'thirties we often played club cricket together on Sundays, for the Romany and a splendid Sunday wandering club called the Musketeers. He played a dozen matches for Surrey in 1937, batting in much the manner of my first sight of him when in the first county match I ever saw, against Yorkshire at the Oval (2 days only in 1919), he made a hundred in each innings. In 1937 he averaged 25, but at forty-three by the end of June found the effort of continuous cricket a bit beyond him.* Illustrated Sporting and Dramatic News, *23 April 1937.*

'Rugby is not a spectacular game – and pray heaven it never will be!' An old sentiment this, but it is well we should be reminded of it by Rugby Union Presidents. Thus, Mr. J. E. Greenwood at the inaugural luncheon of the twelfth Middlesex Seven-a-Side Tournament.

*

Mr. Greenwood's two years of office are almost over. He has spoken too controversially for some – though he tells me he has not always been accurately construed. But he has been a great success – zealous, friendly, delightfully unpompous.

*

Sir Alfred Webb-Johnson, the eminent surgeon, welcomed us on behalf of Middlesex Hospital, in aid of whose Cancer Research Fund 'Sevens' take place. Praising the luncheon Sir Alfred remarked he could say, with Luther after the Diet of Worms, 'I could have taken no other course.'

*

The medical profession seems to tell stories against itself better than any other. Sir Alfred introduced us to the bibulous doctor who, called in unexpectedly to a sudden illness, swayed uncertainly over the lady patient, murmured 'Drunk, by God!' and hurriedly departed. Next morning came a cheque for twenty guineas and a fervid request to say nothing about it.

*

Fleet Street, as might be expected, has not taken kindly to the criticisms of the rowing press expressed in a joint letter to *The Times* by the Presidents of the University Boat Clubs. They condemn, perhaps with good reason, the 'highly impertinent' behaviour of 'The Isis' who, in a strident leader, called for changes in the bows of the Oxford boat a few days before they were made.

*

Yet I wish Messrs. Lewes and Lonnon had held their peace. To the non-expert the Boat Race seemed on the whole to be reported very adequately. And if the oarsman is really so thin-skinned, he can always adopt the strong-minded attitude of W. W. Wakefield and other University sportsmen who, in their undergraduate years, never read the sporting pages.

*

So after ten years we are to see Donald Knight once more in the Surrey XI. He is good enough to play cricket for me sometimes, and I am sufficiently vain and selfish to put myself in first with him.

*

An innings in such company is a revelation of the art of batting. Like Woolley, like Hammond, like the great stylists of the former days, Knight is pre-eminently orthodox. It is merely some exceptional facility of eye and movement that transforms the prosaic into the beautiful.

*

Knight has been away a long time. He is forty-three – and a county match lasts three days. For the sake of the young, and those to whom cricket still means more than dirt-track riding, greyhound racing and baseball, may his experiment succeed!

HENDREN'S LAST MATCH

The Evening Standard [30 August 1937] went to press too early for me to record the hundred which Pat Hendren went on to score in his last match. Next day he followed with a duck. It was his 170th hundred, and it brought his aggregate to 57,611, a total exceeded only by Hobbs and Woolley. I had the privilege of playing with this genial little man earlier in the summer for Middlesex against Cambridge at Fenner's. He allowed himself to be bowled out by an aspiring leg-spinner, Rab Bruce-Lockhart, the Scottish rugger International. Pat's was the only first-class wicket he ever got.

LORD'S, Monday

Surrey showed no mercy to-day, Holmes deciding there were too many runs in the pitch to justify a declaration, and that Parker and Brooks might well be capable of a substantial addition. In fact, 61 more runs were made in 50 minutes, and the innings ended for 509.

If anyone had suggested, a week ago, that Surrey were likely to make such a score in this match, he would have been regarded by his friends as slightly queer in the head.

Yet such is the reaction Middlesex are feeling after their efforts, and such the excellence of this Lord's pitch.

Surrey had the heavy roller on it early, no doubt to bring out a heavy dew, and so did Middlesex when at last it came to Robins' turn to decide. Allen led Middlesex for some time until Robins arrived on the field, and apparently had lost count of new balls. He put on Gray and Owen-Smith, and Robins' first move was to call for the third new ball and introduce Smith.

But the batsmen were not noticeably more liable to error than before. Parker played normally, and like a most extraordinarily good No. 8, while Brooks' self assurance was quite appalling. Even when he executed the Surrey cut, between legs and wicket, which was quite frequent against the fast bowlers, he managed to convey the impression that it was wholly intentional. Perhaps it was only a ridiculously sentimental handful of Middlesex followers who would have been spared the scene.

When Robins came on himself, Brooks's chief weapon was a niblick stroke over mid-on, which was fed in vain. He reached 50 by hooking a long hop for four, and decided that that was enough. In the next over Parker was out to a nicely-judged catch in the deep field.

In the absence of an alternative No. 1, Price came out to bat with Hart, despite his injured hand, and faced the first fury of Gover. It is still, of course, very much a question of Gover first, the others far behind, and when Hart played at his first three balls and missed them all, one was almost prepared for the opening sacrifice.

In fact both Price and Hart were out with four runs on the board, and Hendren came in to bat in his last match in just such a situation as he has faced and dealt with many hundreds of times since he first played for Middlesex as a boy of 18 thirty summers ago.

There were, perhaps, 10,000 of us to applaud his journey to the wicket, and to see the Surrey eleven cheer him in unison. Hendren's composure was not noticeably affected by these tokens. In fact, he began to bat with the greatest possible assurance, and Gover at once looked a yard slower.

Hendren pushed Watts off his legs for four, late cut Gover and drove him to the boundary past cover's left hand.

Edrich stuck there without attempting to do more, and Hendren treated the arrival of Parker and Squires with affable unconcern.

He placed Squires's first ball for four past mid-on, and then decided to leave further stroke-making until after luncheon. *He had made 32 out of the 53 which Middlesex had scored, and a better or more characteristic piece of batting could not have been wished for.*

Middlesex continued with a rush, and now Edrich played his part. He late cut Gover for four, hooked him for four, and glided him for four more. Gover, who had seemed so terrible, was almost docile, and in a longish spell Squires did not threaten to beat the bat. Hendren reached 50 in a few minutes over the hour, and no one on the ground would have given very long odds against him getting 50 more.

Middlesex v Surrey, at Lord's, 28–31 August 1937. Surrey 509 (Fishlock 127, Barling 114, Holmes 82, Brooks 52) and 204 for 6 dec. (Barling 71 not out, Holmes 58); Middlesex 419 (Hendren 103, Edrich 96, Owen-Smith 55, Allen 53, Gover 5 for 130) and 202 for 7 (Compton 64, Watts 5 for 62). Match Drawn.

PROBABLES V POSSIBLES

This is the sort of eye-witness contribution I regularly made in national, regional and Empire service programmes in the 1930s. Empire service broadcast, December 1937.

I spent a pleasant afternoon yesterday watching the second Rugby Union Trial at Ipswich. It was the first time there had ever been a Trial in East Anglia and they used the Ipswich Town soccer ground because there was no rugger ground capable of taking the crowd. Well, we had a soccer pitch (it seemed very broad; though I wouldn't say it was beyond the maximum width) and for the most part a soccer crowd; and the ingenuous willing-to-be-entertained sort of atmosphere helped to make it a very enjoyable occasion. The Probables won in the end by 18-11; but there was a time in the second half when they were being led, and in danger of losing quite convincingly enough to cause the selectors considerable embarrassment.

I have my programme in front of me and I think probably the best thing I can do is to go through the names and give you an idea of the various personalities as they struck me:

[There followed comments off the cuff, unfortunately not scripted. It was scarcely a vintage period for England. Scotland won the Triple Crown, England's only win being a wholesale one in which they scored seven tries in Dublin. Peter Cranmer was captain.]

The RU was luckier than their rivals the Scotch whose Trial at Melrose had to be postponed because of the frost. This was only one of many football matches which were held up. In London we were pretty fortunate, except that Blackheath v Richmond could not take place. But in Scotland, the North and the West the conditions were pretty bad.

Among the RU results just one or two call for particular comment – firstly the [London] Scottish's victory over Birkenhead. The Scottish are having a run just now, and when this happens they seem to go on getting better in geometrical progression. To beat Birkenhead (perhaps the best side on the North-West coast) by 19-3, even at Richmond, is a bit above what one expects from either of the two clubs renting Richmond Athletic Ground. Then we find Bedford beating Leicester 3-0, their second victory over Leicester this season. That is not an astonishing result to us at home, but it may emphasise to some of you who have been away some time that the balance of power in Midland football has changed somewhat. Nowadays Coventry and Bedford are the best sides in the Midlands, and Leicester and Northampton come next in that order. The Harlequins contributed six men to the Trial and, that being so, their performance in running Cardiff to a score of 13-9 was a particularly good one, for Cliff Jones was against them, even if W. Wooller was not. The 'Quins are unquestionably the best side in London and it was a great pity they could not have met Cardiff with a full side.

HANDSOME OFFER

This letter from H. S. Altham represented an accolade to a young journalist. I accepted his proposal without delay and undertook the writing of the post-war history. Allen and Unwin had the second edition of A History of Cricket *on sale in June 1938. I had taken a brief summer holiday in the early 1930s playing two-day cricket for Eastbourne and first met Harry Altham, luckily for me, when he brought down the Harlequins to that lovely Saffrons ground.*

Chernocke House
Winchester
Hants

14th February, 1938

My dear Jim,

I don't know what you will say to the following proposal, but at least it can do no harm to make it.

Allen and Unwin, who published my 'History' have been at me for a year past to bring it up to date. The old edition is completely sold out, and it is, I believe, almost impossible to obtain a copy second-hand. They seem pretty confident that a new edition at a lower price should enjoy a steady sale for some years to come.

Now I simply do not see how I am going to effect this revision myself, or rather the writing of the new chapters necessary to bring the book up to date, for of actual revision work there would, I think, be little necessary. I cannot possibly do it in term time, and I cannot in justice to my family bury myself for a fortnight or so in the holidays.

In my last letter to the publishers I asked them whether they would consider me offering you the work involved. They wrote to-day welcoming the suggestion, and asking me to get in touch with you. The whole question of payment involved would, of course, have to be discussed between us, but there is first the question as to whether you find the idea palatable at all. You know the book yourself, and my idea would be to bring it up to date on the lines that I have followed throughout, i.e. by dealing separately with (1) International cricket; (2) County cricket; (3) Gentleman players from the Varsity; (4) Public Schools. I don't think that we could work on the same scale as I did for 1900–14. There has been so much cricket, especially international, that the edition would be unwieldy.

I should like to have the last say in any general verdict on major issues, e.g. body line, and the policy of the MCC, but I don't think that we should often be at variance.

If you would entertain this proposal, would you come down and spend a night with me, and we can go into details together. The publishers are anxious to produce the book by the early summer, as they seem confident that there would be a considerable sale for it straight away.

All good wishes
Yrs ever
Harry Altham

LORD'S CLASSIC

My earliest BBC radio cricket work was scripted eye-witness pieces in the 1930s such as this [13 July 1938] on the 1938 Gents. and Players. Hugh Bartlett played a glorious innings. After he had taken out his bat for 175 not out and the Gentlemen's innings ended for 411,

*Kenneth Farnes bowled one over of ferocious speed before the close,
Bill Edrich and Fred Price going for ducks. Ken had been omitted from
the England team for the Third Test at Old Trafford (in which not a
ball was bowled) and had a point to make. He took eight Players'
wickets for 43 with some of the fastest bowling I ever saw at Lord's.
The only men whose technique sustained them against him were Len
Hutton and Frank Woolley who, aged fifty-one and in his retirement
season, was given the honour of leading the Players and made a felici-
tious 41.*

The Gentlemen made a great score at Lord's today against the
Players, and some ten thousand of us sat in the sunshine and
watched them do it. I hope you won't think I am moralising when I
say I consider it an important event that the best eleven amateurs
should achieve a score like this against the best professional bowling.
First-class cricket needs the special qualities of both amateur and professional, and the game has always been at its most prosperous and
most attractive when the balance was even between them: when Mac-
Laren and Jackson and Ranji and Fry scourged the Players' bowling:
earlier than that, when 'W.G.' himself was their particular enemy.

In these less spacious times, of course, the strain of good amateur
talent sometimes runs somewhat thin, and days like today are therefore
doubly welcome.

The sad fiasco at Manchester, which has led to so many astonishing
and impractical suggestions for the future of Test Matches in England,
has had its compensations, for there is a life and character in this
Gentlemen versus Players match which there could hardly have been
had it come after four days of hard warfare between England and
Australia.

The best, if not the most spectacular, innings today was played by
the Cambridge Captain, Norman Yardley. The Gentlemen began none
too well, Gibb, Wyatt, and B. O. Allen of Gloucester all being out
before forty runs were on the board. At this critical moment Yardley
joined his captain, Hammond, and together they put on 120 runs. Of
these Yardley made 75 and Hammond 43, and that fact is the most
eloquent tribute to Yardley that could be made. There is indeed a
distinct resemblance to the great Hammond in Yardley's batsmanship.
The impression of bat and leg forming an impassable barrier, the
remarkable composure of both at the wicket, the strength of wrist and
forearm that puts such great power into quite gentle strokes. By the

time Hammond had hit Pollard right off the drive of the bat into Compton's middle, and this remarkable young man, standing about six yards away, had somehow caught it, the Players' bowling had been, as it were, half-tamed.

Yardley made 88 before he was caught behind the wicket from his first inaccurate stroke, and I should be prepared to prophecy that if his invitation to go to South Africa for the MCC tour this winter was ever in doubt, this innings has clinched it.

Bartlett of Sussex, the large lad whom you will remember as captain of Cambridge two years ago, began by alternately playing at the ball, missing it, and hitting it really hard. Gradually he grew more certain, and at tea he had made 59 and the Gentlemen's score stood at 263 for 6. Afterwards Bartlett hit quite magnificently. The last man was out at ten past six, and by that time he had made 175 not out, the last hundred in an hour and a half. He hit four sixes, one from the Pavilion end to mid-wicket that landed half way up the Mound, a most enormous carry, another that pitched on the Grand Stand roof and rolled into the gutter so that Nichols had to dry the ball before he could bowl with it.

> Gentlemen v Players, at Lord's, 13–15 July 1938. Gentlemen 411 (Bartlett 175 not out. Yardley 88) and 172 for 8 wts. dec. (Smith (T. P. B.) 5 for 68); Players 218 (Hutton 52, Farnes 8 for 43) and 232 (Edrich 78). Gentlemen won by 133 runs.

THAT OVAL PITCH

This was my first sizeable contribution to The Cricketer. *To me the tone of it has a somewhat over-confident ring: crossing swords mildly even with Plum Warner! 3 September 1938.*

I imagine that a large number of past and present practising crickteters, either in spite of or because of what they have read concerning the fifth Test Match, must be feeling extremely perplexed as to what truly occurred during those four momentous days at the Oval. Remembering how cheaply England was twice bowled out by the chosen Australian bowlers at Leeds only a month before, they may well be finding it hard to believe that our runs were made (as has been said) against the weakest Test attack in history. And yet there stands that bloated mountain of runs – 903 for 7, scored by England over a weary span of fifteen hours and a quarter. How to account for so thorough and merciless a butchery?

I would not attempt by a single word to belittle that astonishing exhibition of physical effort and mental control that went to make Hutton's record innings – or, for that matter, the dour contribution of Leyland. A batsman can only utilise the conditions in which he finds himself to the limit of his ability; the conditions in which England batted were such that the mere act of staying in meant an inevitable, if slow, accumulation of runs.

The whole protracted course of the England innings, the batting tactics, the bowling tactics, and the field placing, were dictated by the state of the wicket. Now the wicket (for those of you who were not present) was nothing like the kind of wicket on which time-limitless matches are decided in Australia; nor did it closely resemble the ordinarily good wicket we get in England. It was infinitely easier because there was so little pace left in it. However spotless and true a pitch may be (and no one, of course, seriously wants to see a Test played on other than a plumb wicket), the great bowler (like O'Reilly) can worry the great batsman so long as the ball can be made to zip reasonably quickly off the turf. But by ceaseless watering, and rolling when the turf is saturated, you get a surface that acts like a thick hearth-rug, or a huge piece of felt. I do not say that on all wickets this procedure need be forestalled by the use of liquid chemical dressings, though these undoubtedly are applied generously on many grounds in spite of official abjuration against them. On the Oval wicket, the bowler was helpless, and the batsman knew that *patience*, almost alone, bought him a long lease of it.

To make O'Reilly bowl on that wicket, said Howard Marshall, was like asking Kreisler to play on a one-string fiddle. Such surfaces (and I have seen them on all the Test grounds at one time or another) bring the great artist down to the common level. So don't belittle Australia by thinking she was a lamentably weak bowling side – though I must allow myself to say, by the way, that on his previous Test form, McCormick, their fast bowler, would have strengthened them, for his speed might well have banged some trace of life out of the pitch after the showers, and it would in any case have provided variety. Nevertheless, had Australia won the toss, I think that England might have had to field out to just as vast a score. The difference would probably have been that the Australians would have exploited their normal strokes, and thus made their runs a good deal more quickly. The unkindest comments which England's innings brought forth were those to the effect that the Australians were being played 'at their own game.' Truly the legend of Collins and Kelleway lingers on a long while! For every Woodfull and every Brown that Australia sends over here she produces several stroke-players of the temper of Ponsford, McCabe, Kippax and Hassett, to say nothing of Bradman. There have indeed been moments this summer when one has blushed for the Cyclopian sense of chivalry of which this astounding *volte-face* provides only the most glaring of a number of examples.

Finally, what of the Oval Test in so far as it may have affected the future playing of the last match of an English series to a finish? The Editor of *The Cricketer* emphasises two main points in his advocacy of Test reform. He condemns the over-prepared wicket as 'the bane of cricket,' and he wants to see five days allotted to every Test Match, including the last. Of these points, the first seems to me to be infinitely the more important. Five days would probably not have yielded a finish on the Oval wicket if the Australians could have played for a draw. Four days would almost certainly have been sufficient at Lord's but for the rain.

If I may be allowed to dissent from the Editor in his own pages, I would say that the fifth Test of a series had best be allowed to take its course to the end, either to insure a result to the 'rubber' if the teams are equal in wins, or to prevent the team in the lead playing for a draw. It is, however, my contention that a time-limitless match need call for a technique very little different from any other match – so long as the surface gives the bowler a chance to attack. And if the bowler attacks, the batsman must attack him back. That is cricket as it must be, whether at Kennington or on the village green: a fight between bat and ball.

TIMELESS DRAW

The culminating irony of the ten-day Test at Durban in March 1939 was that, after all the weary hours of defensive, attritional cricket, it had to be left drawn. Neither side had the bowling to offset the utter docility of a pitch which, after two dawn rollings following over-night rain (a regulation applying only to this series), emerged, if possible, easier than ever. Soon after lunch on the tenth afternoon, with England cruising along at 600-odd for 4 in pursuit of the 696 they needed to win, I had a message in the broadcast-box telling us it was raining down the coast at Isipingo. This I passed on to Jack Holmes, the MCC manager, who sent out a message to the captain. Walter Hammond stepped up the pace, but was stumped for 140, and at 654 for 5 the rain duly arrived. I think both sides equally welcomed the release.

This last message betrays my deficient news-sense. The match could have been concluded next day had MCC not prohibited air travel as involving an unacceptable risk: hence the drudgery of the long train trip. What I failed to reveal was that soon after I had written this last dispatch our aircraft, following the coast-line, was obliged to make a forced landing short of the Cape at Mossel Bay. We got off again, but the emergency amply justified MCC's caution.

Fond farewells to a team which had greatly magnified cricket interest in South Africa looked forward to Alan Melville bringing the team to England in 1940. He duly did so – but in 1947. Illustrated Sporting and Dramatic News, *April 1939.*

The interminable Test is at last behind us, and I am flying from it, quite literally, as fast as I can. To be precise, we are at this moment several thousand feet above the Indian Ocean following the verdant coastline that curves gently down from Durban to Table Bay. (Just now the pilot dipped low to show us the wrecks of two cargo ships lying with their noses on the rocks, their sterns beaten away by the fierce Mozambique current that drove them to their unhappy destination). The Cape in all its glory lies ahead – and the *Athlone Castle*, and England.

For the team things are neither so swift nor so convenient. Two hours after the 'emergency committee' had decided that time, after all, must be up, they were beginning a trip by train involving the last three nights and two days of their tour. It must be proving an irksome end to a tour in which there has been singularly little hardship of such a kind.

The most hopeful news item from home concerning the last Test, among many which have read so queerly to us on the spot, has been that announcing the determination of Yorkshire to propose legislation to deal with the preparation of wickets. If this monstrous affair at Durban does lead to a positive step of such a kind, it will not have been played or watched in vain.

Below Cheerful first exposure

My mother, Lillian Emily Swanton

Little Lord Fauntleroy with sister Ruth

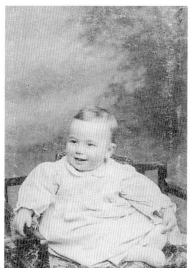

With sisters Tina (*left*) and Ruth

With my father, William

My parents at Ruth's wedding, 1939

Earliest heroes: Jack Hobbs and
Frank Woolley open their innings
against Australia at Lords in
1930.

With Hugh Bartlett: the Arab flag
flies at our opening match on the
Victoria College ground, Jersey,
September 1935.

In February 1941 Service dress was still the off-duty uniform of 148 Field Regiment, R.A. Note the Bedfordshire Yeomanry lapel badges. The 18th (East Anglian) Division sailed for the Far East in October 1941.

This 1939 Wisden accompanied me throughout the war. It survived many jungle POW camps, and was re-bound in gas-cape material. At one point borrowers had to return it within 12 hours.

"B" Troop, 419 Battery, 148 Field Regiment, R.A. at Poona en route to Singapore, December 1941. Sitting from left Sgt. E.L. Samuel, Sgt L. Webster, B.S.M. J.W. Gardner, Lt. D.C. Powell, E.W.S., Lt P.L. Marriott, Sgt. A.K. Brantom, Sgt A.W. Cavalier.

Window display in the *Daily Telegraph*'s Fleet Street building. England's first post-war Test win against Australia in the last Test of 1950/51 gave the title for the book and film.

A debonair Denis Compton, at the peak of his fame in 1949, dances with Anna Neagle.

On the mat. The Cricket Writers' Club played many matches in Australia during the early post-war MCC tours.

Off parade, England's post-war best. A relaxed Peter May, Captain of MCC in Australia, 1958/9.

Charity Match for victims of the North Devon flood disaster, September 1952. In front from the left, Denis Compton, Maurice Tremlett, EWS and John Warr.

T.E. Bailey, c. McWatt b. Sobers 23. West Indies v. England, Sabina Park, Jamaica, March 1954. The first of Gary Sobers's 235 Test wickets.

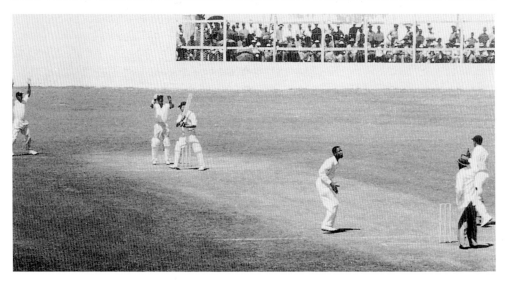

With an over-large but very comfortable Austin Sheerline.

The rose between... Katharine, daughter of Sir William Worsley, whose XI, including Len Hutton (not quite yet Sir Leonard), at Hovingham in 1955 entertained the Arabs on their Northern Tour. Scorer in the match, some years later she became HRH the Duchess of Kent.

Ian Peebles (*Sunday Times*), EWS, John Woodcock (*The Times*) and Denis Compton. In 1954/5 three of us toured the Eastern States of Australia in this Rover car.

Champions. W.G. (1848–1915) The initials suffice – who found the game a country pastime and left it a national institution.

The Don (1908–) A contrast in physique but likewise massive in achievement.

Gary, soon to become Sir Garfield Sobers, in 1973 on his fifth and last tour of England. He signed off with 150 not out at Lord's: his 26th and last Test hundred. The final tally in Tests of the greatest of all all-rounders was 8,032 runs (average 57), 235 wickets (34 runs each), 109 catches.

The last Test resolved itself into an affair of stamina and concentration – great virtues themselves, and splendidly exemplified by all twenty-two players involved. But purely attritional batsmanship opposed by negative bowling tactics do not spell cricket.

From the widest viewpoint, the most pleasing feature at Durban was the proof, renewed after the very favourable draw at Johannesburg had helped to soften the somewhat alarming happenings of the Third Test, that South Africa could stand up to England toe to toe. England was the better side in this series, but there was no discrepancy of class, and we should look forward to the English season of 1940, when the South Africans will be with us, as providing a Test preparation for our cricketers due the following winter in Australia.

South Africa v England, at Durban, 3–14 March 1939. South Africa 530 (van der Bijl 125, Nourse 103, Melville 78, Grieveson 75, Dalton 57, Perks 5 for 100) and 481 (Melville 103, van der Bijl 97, Mitchell 89, Viljoen 74); England 316 (Ames 84, Paynter 62) and 654 for 5 (Edrich 219, Hammond 140, Gibb 120, Paynter 75, Hutton 55). Match Drawn.

TOUR TO REMEMBER

An off-the-field, euphoric impression of my first MCC tour, broadcast on the Empire service on my return [11 April 1939]. Note the absence of any reference to blacks or coloureds, except that a mixed bag bowled in the nets to Len Hutton. We were socially unaware in 1938/39 and even on the next tour ten years later. The atmosphere was very different when the Nationalists were in power in 1956/57.

When I joined the MCC at Johannesburg they played six first-class matches, against most of the South African provinces, and they were waiting for the First Test, which began at Johannesburg on Christmas Eve. Just about a third of the tour was over, but of course the most momentous part lay ahead of us.

Those first days of mine were really very hectic. Over Christmas we had the First Test. Then the morning after it was over both teams got into the train and swirled away in the dust down to the Cape. And the Second Test, (over the New Year) began the day after we arrived.

The night that was finished off we went again, this time to Port Elizabeth. I was under firm instruction when at Port Elizabeth from the
designer of the links there, Colonel Hotchkin of Woodhall Spa, to
report to him on its condition. He had fashioned it out of bush five
or six foot high, plunging about on horseback armed with a bell with
which he used to tell his assistants where he was. Humewood reminds
you of Sandwich or Deal – and it has what I rather think is a very
unusual distinction: you can see the sea from every single hole. In my
opinion it's one of the world's courses, and I personally spent every
minute I could on it.

At Port Elizabeth, as elsewhere, we had a mayoral lunch, and a lot
of Scotch jokes from the Scotch mayor. It was one of the things I
noticed – that if a man had been born in Scotland, no matter if he had
been fifty years in South Africa, he spoke with a Scotch accent – in
fact some of them must have become broader and broader as they
went on. Talking of mayors, by the way, there was one who put up
a very good turn. He very kindly gave a big cocktail party in honour
of the team. In due course he got on to his hind legs and said how happy
he was to welcome the MCC team and particularly their distinguished
Captain Mr . . . ('What was your name again?') . . . Mr Hammond!

All round the coast you get the most excellent surf-bathing, and Port
Elizabeth was just as good as anywhere else. When we'd finished bath-
ing my particular host asked me whether I'd like to have a look at the
cricket ground. Of course I said yes, and when we got there some time
after tea we found Len Hutton having some net practice, and he had
bowling to him the oddest collection I have ever seen on a cricket field.
Old men in braces, young boys in shorts, Indians and some Malays,
including one rather elderly one with what I took to be a very doubtful
action who (after they had been going well over an hour) claimed the
shilling that Len had put on his stumps. Somehow or other he had
managed to play on. Genius is said to consist of an infinite capacity
for taking pains – I remembered that the great W. G. Grace always
used to begin strenuous practice around the middle of March. Len
Hutton made 200 the following day.

It was not a terribly strenuous tour. There was always just the one
match every weekend, and according to how far off the next match
was one had leisure for the sort of warm hospitality which we enjoyed
everywhere. The heat wasn't really tiresome either. The hottest day I
remember was at Victoria Falls, where it was ninety-nine in the shade,
but we were not up there for cricket. There was one real scorcher at

Pietermaritzburg, but at Durban (where it can be stifling) we were lucky and there was always a bit of wind in the Final Test to make our vigil easier.

The average South African, of course, is keener about Rugby football than about cricket: almost anyone you meet will talk about the technique of rugger as eagerly as he'll discuss politics. Cricket is not his national game. Yet I'm sure that as a result of this tour cricket has gained a lot of ground. Take my own case. I went out to do twenty broadcasts for the South African Broadcasting Corporation. By the end I'd done over two hundred – so that some of my rather ruder friends out there said they couldn't switch on their wirelesses during the Tests without hearing how Verity had bowled another maiden to Bruce Mitchell – or that Paul Gibb had let another one from Gordon go by!

I was very struck by the exceptional fairness of the crowds. When in the last Test England was scoring even more slowly than South Africa had done there wasn't a sign of barracking. I remember one incident which convinced me of the South African essential good sportsmanship. Hutton and Gibb came in in England's second innings at 5.55 p.m. in a poorish light. After one ball Hutton appealed against the light and from the crowd beneath my box there was a general cry of 'Uphold it – Uphold it' which the umpire proceeded to do.

The grounds themselves are most attractive. Johannesburg has a magnificent cricket ground with probably the best playing surface in the world and Newlands, with the Table Mountain in the background, is simply lovely. Durban is pretty too, with a charm about it which carried us through ten days as well as can be expected. If the last Test Match had been played in some settings I can think of we should all have turned a little bit mental before the end of it.

There are days on this tour I shall never forget.

There was a night at the Durban Country Club (talking of Country Clubs) when Lord Nuffield announced his gift of ten thousand pounds to South African cricket – and incidentally I remember showed himself a very nimble performer of the Lambeth Walk.

Then there was the trip to the Falls – a quite unforgettable experience – and an afternoon when we went up the Zambesi in a launch to a place called Kandahar Island, and saw on the way great crocodiles slipping into the water as they heard us approach, and when we got to the island the monkeys were so tame that they came and ate out of our hands. Personally I found that a rather more pleasing experience than when the baboons came just as close to us, no doubt with the most amiable intentions, in the Rain Forest back at the Falls themselves.

Lastly you cannot forget the Cape with its glorious flowers, and those fine Dutch farmhouses, with the great mountain as a backcloth. It was a great trip. And as to the kindness which we met everywhere I have tried to convey an impression of it – but you must go to South Africa yourself really to know its charm. They say that if you want to return to South Africa you must throw a tickey (that's a South African threepenny bit) into Table Bay as you leave. I threw my tickey in all right.

PART THREE

1939–1945

1939-1945

Jim had plenty of warning of the imminence of war. On the boat back from South Africa in March 1939 a colonel in the Bedfordshire Yeomanry, S. W. Harris, who had played rugby for Blackheath and England, had told him; 'The harvest will be gathered in at the end of the summer and then it will all start. Mark my words. Why don't you come and join my regiment when it does?'

It was not really a question, more an offer and Jim *did* mark his words. After all, Stanley Harris was a man of many parts and knew what he was about; apart from his rugby distinctions, he had boxed in the Olympics and played Davis Cup tennis for South Africa. And so a few months later the erstwhile cricket and rugger correspondent of the *Evening Standard*, together with his friend, the Middlesex captain, Ian Peebles, found themselves in a dingy recruiting office in Victoria. The formalities of signing-on were supervised by a somewhat seedy Army major. Having put their names on the dotted line there was, for both of them, a sense of relief. 'It was rather like joining a club,' recalls Jim. 'You didn't want to miss the boat and you were not sure whether you would be accepted or if lists would be closed.' It had been a splendid if somewhat shortened summer after an initial setback. While in South Africa Jim had written to the Editor-in-Chief of the *Daily Telegraph*, Seymour Berry, in the hope of landing the job of cricket correspondent which had become available. On his return, Berry offered Jim first refusal if Douglas Jardine declined. He didn't!

Never mind, George Headley's hundred for the West Indies in each innings of the Lord's Test; Learie Constantine's electrifying all-round performance at the Oval, including a whirlwind 79, the majority in boundaries; and the happy thought of a winter ahead giving broadcast eye-witness accounts, in conjunction with Teddy Wakelam, of the Wallabies' rugby tour helped to dispel any lingering disappointment.

The latter, of course, was not to be, nor indeed, was it possible to consummate an engagement offered by the editor of *The Field*. Brian Vesey-Fitzgerald had written on 18th August, 1939:

Dear Mr Swanton,

I should be very glad if you would do our cricket for us next year commencing at the beginning of May at a fee of 5 guineas per week. We should require about 1,200 words each week and certainly not more than 1,500. This matter will have to be in our office by first post each Monday morning. We should also require from time to time during the winter, but at no specified times, further articles on cricket particularly during those winters when there are Test Matches abroad. In these circumstances we write to you for an article and we expect – and hitherto have always received – an article in return. I very much hope that you will accept this offer and let me know fairly soon.

Jim did accept fairly soon but by 1940 matters were, of course, out of his hands. Commendably, the post was kept for him, awaiting his return from the Far East in 1945.

After a short induction at Woolwich and Dunstable, Jim became Second-Lieutenant Swanton in the 148 Field Regiment, Royal Artillery (Bedfordshire Yeomanry) which was part of the 18th Division. The 18th was an East Anglian division and very soon he was supervising a convoy of impressed vehicles – lorries pulling the guns, trucks, civilian cars – on a journey to the wind-swept wastes of Norfolk and north Suffolk. Lowestoft, Great Yarmouth, and particularly North Walsham were unexciting places for those geared for action. The Regiment was supposed to be guarding the coast and so was placed a mile or two inland in order to facilitate fire on any invasion force.

It was a time of manning promenades, taking part in training exercises and waiting for something to happen. Boredom and frustration were relieved, for Jim at least, by the occasional game of cricket once summer had returned, and inquiries to the BBC regarding further broadcasting. A missive from the Red Lion Hotel in Colchester in May, 1940, informed that he was free to play for the Corporation in a match against the Ministry of Information. Or as Swanton preferred to refer to it, 'the noisy service versus the silent one'.

There was a game, too, on the August bank holiday of that same year in which the Battery took on Ingham Cricket Club or, in effect, a side full of Edriches.

The following new year – that of 1941 – saw the Regiment posted to Hawick where they received their G1098's, or in layman's language, the full equipment for battle. But even now, not yet unto the breach! For after a snowy winter in Border country, they were all sent down to Lancashire where Jim found himself comfortably ensconced in Lord Derby's house, Knowsley Hall. He was so encouraged that he scored a hundred in an Army match.

But such an event becomes nugatory when set alongside the tragic air raids on Liverpool to which he was witness. On the first Saturday of May, Swanton, by now a captain, was named in the Liverpool side against Bootle in the Liverpool and District Competition for a match on the Aigburth ground. A major air raid on the city had taken place the night before. When he turned up for the game, he found the field full of shrapnel from the ack-ack shells. A small hole in front of the pavilion was a numbing reminder of a rogue shell that had killed an ARP warden in the unlikeliest of horrible accidents.

Later that year, and from the same ground, Jim commentated for the BBC on a match between the Army and the RAF. BBC Archives reveal a letter that arrived soon afterwards, from the Training Ship *Mercury* anchored at Hamble, Southampton:

> Dear Swanton,
> You may be amazed to hear that your broadcast on Saturday from Old Trafford or somewhere [*ed: geographically not too far distant*] – with no particular objective material to put across – was the best I've ever heard on cricket.
>
> All the best,
> Yours truly,
> C. B. Fry

The Regiment's final billet on British soil was at Monmouth, where they paraded before the King in the courtyard of the castle. Nothing was said, but everyone realised the significance of the event. And so it proved. At last they were off. Trains back to Liverpool and 148 Field embarked on the lavishly appointed cruise ship, *Andes*, to cross the Atlantic. A vast amount of alcohol also embarked but did not survive the voyage. Halfway across, the American Navy took over and escorted the convoy to a docking at Halifax, Nova Scotia.

At this stage, October 1941, the USA was supposedly uninvolved or rather non-belligerent; Pearl Harbor was a few weeks away. Therefore the transfer to an American cabin-class cruiser was a surprise to say the least. The *Wakefield* was cramped, uncomfortable and dry – in direct comparison with the *Andes*. The Regiment now proceeded south, hugging the coastline with zig-zags past the West Indies before leaving the security of the South American shore and risking interception from enemy submarines with a crossing of the South Atlantic towards the Cape.

As always with Jim, even in the most alien of circumstances, cricket was never far from his thoughts. A couple of days short of the Cape, he sent a cable to 'Sport' Pienaar, a famous figure in the cricket and rugby world of South Africa, and one of those amiable entrepreneurs who knew everybody and could arrange anything. The cable ran: '54 Brigade challenge Western Province to a Match.' A positive reply was soon forthcoming and the game was played at Newlands where the home side were duly defeated. The Province borrowed a couple of sailors from the aircraft-carrier *Hermes* to make up their team – distressingly, it sank shortly afterwards with total loss of life.

Onwards once more, up the east coast of Africa while their ultimate destination was being decided in exchanges between Churchill and the Australian Prime Minister, Curtin. Was it to be the Middle East or Malaya? In the event one Brigade went to Malaya and the other two were sent to Singapore, but not before a stiff training interlude at Poona. During the three weeks spent on the sub-continent Jim again donned his flannels and in 'marvellous dry heat' bowled all afternoon from lunch to tea against gritty opposition provided by league cricketers from the York and Lancaster Regiment and King's Own Yorkshire Light Infantry.

All too soon it was back to reality and incarceration in the dreaded *Wakefield*. The journey south-east went round Ceylon and then headed through the Sunda Strait to a final berthing in Singapore where a large Japanese bomber force greeted the new arrivals in head-on diamond formation. Fortunately, their target was not the ship, but if with some there had been any illusions about the tallage of war, that unwelcome reception left them in no doubt.

After over two years preparing to get to grips with the enemy, it was the enemy who were about to get to grips with them. The 18th British Division were now to be sacrificed on the high altar of expediency, left exposed, defenceless and in hostile hands. For the newly appointed *Major* Swanton and his proud men the capitulation to the Japs, after so brief a fight, was deeply wounding. Far more so than any physical injury, such as the bullet wound from a sniper which put Jim in Singapore General Hospital on the day before the surrender.

The next three and a half years contained much deprivation and degradation. Yet the shared plight produced a human bonding which so many times surmounted the dreadful circumstances. A spirit, a quality which perhaps only truly manifests itself in extremity. Looking back to those days now, Jim says he would not have missed them.

D.R.A.

LIFE UNDER THE JAPS

This is a shortened version of a talk I wrote on 6 October 1945
on board the SS Corfu *which brought me home from Rangoon.*

I have set myself the task, as we return home by ship, of trying to put before you, in a very brief form, what life as a prisoner with the Japanese was like. But I must make it quite clear that this is nothing more than a personal account. I was one of the lucky ones, and most people had a more arduous time than I. My reactions are quite individual, and others would paint a different picture, for it is one of the features of the whole business that men's experiences varied so much. Some happened to be kept at the base, or happened to follow the less unpleasant or evil of the Jap camp commanders. Others just went from bad to worse, and most of these, of course, are among the 20,000 who now lie in the overgrown cemeteries – or communal graves – that stretch from Bangkok at one end of the railway to Moulmein at the other.

By the end of April, that is less than three months after the capitulation, we were in a camp in Singapore called River-Valley Road. There the other ranks had their first experience of working for the Japs. They were amazingly quick at weighing them up, and at once set to work to make capital out of their stupidity. For the guards mostly were very stupid little men, and they laboured under the disadvantage of being unable to 'lose face' by asking about what they didn't understand – not, of course, that they would have got very helpful answers if they had. Just one story to illustrate this: some Australians were put in charge of a steam-roller, the common-or-garden kind that one sees repairing the roads. They at once asked for petrol from the Japanese *gunso* (that means sergeant) in charge. The *gunso* looked puzzled, but the Aussies stood firm: 'No petrol, roller no go.' So the *gunso* produced petrol, which was duly hidden away. Every day from then onwards, the Aussies drew forty gallons of petrol – 'Roller very thirsty' – which proved extremely useful to the Chinese outside, who couldn't get any, while the dollars they paid were made good use of by the Aussies. At another camp on Singapore where there was a lot of petrol, there was so much trade between the inhabitants and the prisoners that the prisoners laid a pipe line outside the camp one night. Thereafter trade was even brisker! From the start our fellows got morally 'on top' of the Japs – and in most places, except when they were starving and shockingly sick, they remained on top.

In the middle of October we were moved up by cattle-truck to Banpong in Thailand. In our truck – it was a closed iron affair – we only had twenty-two officers, so that most of us throughout the three-day journey were able to lie on the floor, sardine-fashion, at the same time. Most trucks had more than thirty, and that meant, of course, one could only squat.

From Banpong where we got out, to the jungle camp of Tarsao was eighty miles, and we did the march in five days. This march was a very stiff affair, the last part of it over the slippery raised ridges of paddy-fields and through jungle tracks in which, more often than not, the guards lost their way. It would probably have been all right if there had been food at the other end, but we found only a diet of rice and marrow – very, very poor broken rice, and a particularly watery marrow. For weeks this was all there was, and by the time the traders started coming up the river about the middle of January several hundreds had died of dysentery, or malaria, or beri-beri, or more probably, a combination of all three.

As soon as we began to get some eggs and a little sugar the Japs put pressure on the job of making the railway. I leave this part of the show to your imagination – the clearing of the jungle; the eternal digging of the red clay soil, and the carrying of it in baskets to build up the embankment; the blasting and drilling of rock; and the whole rigmarole – all in great heat, and accompanied by much shouting by excitable guards, hitting with bamboo, and so on. At Wampo, where we were, the officers never worked on the railway. We did the administrative jobs, and some of the camp chores, and did all we could in the way of arranging some sort of entertainment in the evenings. Nearly every evening there was something on, a talk, a quiz, a Brains Trust. One found all the way up the line that this sort of thing kept up the morale almost more than anything else.

There was a tremendous rush to get our part of the line finished, and the men got on with it because the Japs promised us a holiday at the end of it. We didn't yet know them well enough. As soon as one job was over, everyone was marched further up the line to help in the next stage.

The following four months or so were for us, and for everyone on the railway, the very worst time. We arrived at Tonchan to find a camp in very low spirits – much sickness, little food and hardly any work done. Everything now went wrong. The rains made the camp a glutinous mess, and the tents, with no linings, leaked persistently. The Japs had given the best tents to the Tamils in the adjoining camp. In the middle of all this came cholera. The Tamils, who were upstream of us, went down in hundreds, and the officers were put to burying them. Then, of course, our own water was infected and the scourge ran through the camp. Sometimes a man died in a few hours, sometimes he lasted several days. A number, nearly fifty per cent, thanks to the British doctors, pulled through.

Now, of course, the railway was behind schedule, and the Japs sent out men whose weakness only just enabled them to reach the railway. Up the line it was even worse – at Kanyu and Kinsayok men died literally at their work. By the time the railway was through the casualty lists were enormous, and men evacuated down river were still dying from the effects of this period nine months later. At Kinsayok cattle began to come through, and the feeding for a short time was almost reasonable. The men picked up, though still hard at it maintaining the line. It was bad food much more than the work which was doing the damage.

I came down in November to the Number 4 Group Headquarters Camp at Tarsao, and found a hospital of two thousand, the doctors doing their best with a handful of drugs, and a general atmosphere of squalor. Here it was possible to get the talks and such-like diversions going. The convalescents would come out and listen to talks on every topic under the sun. Personally I found that anything about cricket was certain to find an audience, and some of my pleasantest memories are of evenings with a mixed crowd of British and Australians shooting questions from all angles, and barracking sometimes in a friendly way from 'the Hill'.

At last, in April 1944, we were moved south, after eighteen months in the jungle, and the sight of a flat plain again, and to be able to watch sunrise and sunset, put new life into one. Soon I found myself in the Base Hospital camp at Nakom Patom and I stayed there until January this year [1945] when they put all Allied officers in Thailand into an officers' camp at Kanburi. It was there that I heard the news of the Jap surrender.

What, you may ask, was the Japanese attitude towards us? In the early part, when they thought they were going to win the war, I believe that our survival was only of interest to them in so far as we were a source of labour. In late 1943, when I suppose the Jap Navy had taken some rough knocks and the tide was turning in Europe, there seemed to be some change in the official policy but, as always, the local commander was a complete autocrat, and by this time his sadistic instincts in most cases had long got the better of him.

Overriding the whole Japanese attitude was the idea that a prisoner, by letting himself be captured, lost his honour. Their feelings towards us seemed to be torn between this theory on the one hand and a pronounced inferiority complex on the other. In different Japs one or the other influence was the stronger, but in either case the result was apt to be the same.

I only met one Englishman who really understood them, and he had spent many years in Japan. For most of us, to read their minds was like trying to decode a cipher with the wrong key. Again, their characters were so unstable that it was impossible to predict how they were going to behave. Frequently I have known a Jap who was a reasonable sort of individual in one camp become a cruel tyrant in another, and vice versa. By nature they were tremendously jealous of their dignity. They loved to build themselves impressive houses. Once a major or a colonel took over a headquarters from a Japanese captain. His senior officer, on seeing the former commandant's magnificent bamboo and attap house, called him over and gave him a good beating up for his extravagance in front of everyone before moving in himself.

Officers lying on bamboo staging in two rows, with about two feet three inches headroom each, is a strain on anyone's nerves. But one let off steam, as it were, against the common enemy rather than one's neighbours. The other ranks came through the show with colours flying. Just at the start in Thailand, when the unexpectedness of the conditions and the fact that working battalions had been formed haphazardly into a mixed bag of all sorts of units, discipline faltered. But as soon as everyone realised they were all in the same boat, and that the officers were doing their best for them, the British troop settled down to make the best of it. I think the fraternisation between British and Australians was good for both of us. The Australians certainly taught our lads a lesson in self-reliance and improvisation, while perhaps the Aussies drew something from the Britishers' irrepressible sense of humour. There were clashes of temperament, of course, both with the Australians and the Dutch; but individually there were many firm friendships, and all pulled together pretty well.

One thing is quite certain: when life is reduced to a primitive struggle for existence everyone is seen for what they really are – in our case literally stripped almost naked! None got away with what we call 'a line of bull'.

A great many men made things much more tolerable for themselves by finding some interest that carried their minds away from the surrounding scene. Nearly everyone humped at least one book on the march up, and it was really astonishing how they lasted, rebound time and again, with gas-cape covers. At the officers' camp at Kanburi we had a staff of amateur and professional bookbinders, twenty strong. In six months they rebound 1,500 books. I treasure myself a *Wisden Cricketers' Almanack* which must have been thumbed by thousands in twelve different camps. One found quite unexpected people anxious to discuss the problems of the times – politics, religion, sociology, science, and so on. It was a wonderful time for sorting out one's ideas and getting down to the fundamental things. One seemed to see the world so clearly in an oddly detached way – as you might say through a telescope.

The religious side of life varied greatly, according to the presence or otherwise, and also the quality, of the padres. The Japs almost invariably made things as difficult as they could, partly I suppose because they considered services were good for morale and partly because they suspected their being used for plots and propaganda. In that sense the padres had a difficult time; on the other hand, many men were receptive who, in the ordinary run of things, the padres would not have reached.

One of the older Roman Catholic priests was talking one day to a Eurasian lad, who began to dream about the great day when he would be free. 'Yes, my son, for you it will indeed be wonderful,' the old Father replied. 'But for me, you see, it is not the same. Wherever I am is my parish – and I shall never have a more wonderful parish than this.'

Examples of courage, both physical and moral, are stored plentifully in one's mind. Perhaps the bravest were those who kept us in touch with the world by the use of secret wireless sets. After the news came up-river of officers at Kanburi being beaten to death for being found with a set, everyone knew there was little hope for anyone who was caught. But they continued to work, with sets in water-bottles, and sets in four-gallon containers fitted with false bottoms. Scores of times, in the searches that took place every month or so, only the stupidity of the Koreans saved them.

Once, two of our fellows were taking a wireless set to pieces when a Korean came in unexpectedly. Even a Korean knew a wireless set when he saw one, and he began to look menacing. But one of the two with great presence of mind explained that he was a very fine radio engineer at home – 'Him no good, so I teach, we no listen Churchill'. With that the Korean, astonishing to relate, was apparently satisfied, but I dare say that to divert his attention someone finally produced a few photographs of a wife or sweetheart. This trick always worked, so that anyone who had anything to hide always stuck some photos, or some other thing that the Korean might want to purchase, on top of his kit. 'She wife?' 'Yes, she wife.' 'How many children?' was the next enquiry. It was best to say five or six.

The stories of these searches are legion. For instance, a Korean found an oil-compass, which would have been about the next most dangerous thing to a wireless set. The owner not unnaturally was highly apprehensive. But the Korean put the compass to his ear, shook it, and gave it back saying, 'No good, watchee no go.' The great thing was to get wind of the searches in good time. Often a friendly Korean would give the tip – they grew more and more anti-Jap as time went on. But a bugler of the Norfolk Regiment at Tarsao had the best idea. When the first guard appeared with his bag, the bugler promptly blew a few bars of 'A hunting we will go' and thus everyone was warned!

The Japanese efforts to lower our morale provided a certain humour, for they naively passed on items put over by their own propaganda system. For instance, an officer once summoned a big parade to announce the total annihilation of London.

London, he said, was finished. 'Boom-boom come, no rice, all men go jungle.' To him food meant rice, and any place that wasn't a town was jungle. He was quite mystified by the merriment this caused, and went on to complete the desolate picture by saying London could not be rebuilt because there was no bamboo!

The whole show was a tremendous test of the virtues – of self-discipline, bravery, charity. In a sense, indeed, it was an experience of great value. You might say it was like a dose of castor oil. It was very good for those of us who survived – but we didn't much like the taste.

. . . AND CRICKET

This is an account of a little proper cricket played in the early days of our captivity and of a highly improper match towards the end of it. It is reproduced courtesy of the Editor of Wisden *who published it in the 1946 edition.*

It is strange, perhaps, but true, how many of us agreed on this: that we were never so thankful for having been cricketers as we were when we were guests of the Japanese. There were periods when we could play 'cricket', if our antics do not desecrate the word. There were occasions when we could lecture, and be lectured, about it. It was a subject that filled countless hours in pitch-dark huts between sundown and the moment that continued to be euphemistically known as lights-out. And it inspired many a day-dream, contrived often in the most gruesome setting, whereby one combated the present by living either in the future or the past.

In the days that followed shortly on the fall of Singapore, before work for prisoners had become widely organized, there was a certain amount of play on the padangs of Changi camp that really deserved the name of cricket. It is true that one never seemed able to hit the ball very far, a fact probably attributable about equally to the sudden change to a particularly sparse diet of rice, and the conscientious labours of generations of corporals in charge of sports gear, for whom a daily oiling of the bats had clearly been a solemn, unvarying rite. These Changi bats must have reached saturation point in the early thirties, and I never found one that came up lighter than W. H. Ponsford's three pounder. However, the pitches were true – matting over concrete – and there were even such refinements as pads and gloves. After most of us had been moved to Singapore City on the first stage of the journey up to Thailand, Lieut.-Colonel A. A. Johnson, of the Suffolk Regiment, promoted some excellent matches with the Australians, whose captain was none other than B. A. Barnett; I cannot write of these from first-hand knowledge, but this was, so to speak, Cricket de Luxe, and our jungle cricket bore little outward relation to it.

That sort of cricket played with a tennis-ball soaked in water and a narrow bat produced by the carpenters reached its climax at Nakom Patom on New Year's Day, 1945, when a fresh, and certainly hitherto unrecorded, page was written in the saga of England v. Australia. The scene is not easy to put before you, but I must try. The playing area is small, perhaps sixty yards by thirty, and the batsman's crease is right up against the spectators, with the pitch longways on. There are no runs behind the wicket, where many men squat in the shade of tall trees. The sides are flanked by long huts, with parallel ditches – one into the ditch, two over the hut. In fact all runs by boundaries, 1, 2, 4 or 6. An additional hazard is washing hung on bamboo 'lines.' Over the bowler's head are more trees, squaring the thing off, and in the distance a thick, high, mud wall – the camp bund – on which stands a bored and sulky Korean sentry. (Over the bund no runs and out, for balls are precious.) In effect, the spectators are the boundaries, many hundreds of them taking every inch of room. The dress is fairly uniform, wooden clogs, and a scanty triangular piece of loin-cloth known (why?) as a 'Jap-Happy.' Only the swells wear patched and tattered shorts. The mound at long-on is an Australian preserve, their 'Hill.' The sun beats down, as tropical suns do, on the flat beaten earth which is the wicket. At the bowler's end is a single bamboo stump, at the other five – yes, five – high ones. There is the hum of anticipation that you get on the first morning at Old Trafford or Trent Bridge, though there are no score cards, and no 'Three penn'orth of comfort' to be bought from our old friend 'Cushions.'

The story of the match is very much the story of that fantastic occasion at the Oval in August 1938. Flt-Lieut. John Cocks, well known to the cricketers of Ashtead, is our Hutton; Lieut. Norman Smith, from Halifax, an even squarer, even squatter Leyland. With the regulation bat – it is two and a half inches wide and a foot shorter than normal – they play beautifully down the line of the ball, forcing the length ball past cover, squeezing the leg one square off their toes. There seems little room on the field with the eight Australian fielders poised there, but a tennis ball goes quickly off wood, the gaps are found, and there are delays while it is rescued from the swill basket, or fished out from under the hut. As the runs mount up the barracking gains in volume, and in wit at the expense of the fielders. When at last the English captain declares, the score is acknowledged to be a Thailand record.

With the Australian innings comes sensation. Captain 'Fizzer' Pearson, of Sedbergh and Lincolnshire, the English fast bowler, is wearing BOOTS! No other cricketer has anything on his feet at all, the hot earth, the occasional flint being accepted as part of the game. The moral effect of these boots is tremendous. Captain Pearson bowls with shattering speed and ferocity, and as each fresh lamb arrives for the slaughter the stumps seem more vast, the bat even punier. One last defiant cheer from 'the Hill' when their captain, Lieut.-Colonel E. E. Dunlop, comes in, another and bigger one from the English when his stumps go flying.

While these exciting things proceed one of the fielders anxiously asks himself whether they will brew trouble. 'Should fast bowlers wear

boots? Pearson's ruse condemned – where did he get those boots? . . .
boots bought from camp funds: Official denial . . . Board of Control's
strong note . . .' headlines seem to grow in size. Then he remembers
gratefully that here is no Press box full of slick columnists and Test
captains, no microphones for the players to run to – in fact, no papers
and no broadcasting. The field clears at last. As he hurries off to
roll-call he thinks of a New Year's Day six years before when the bund
was Table Mountain, the field was the green of Newlands, and he
decided that even the South Africans who jostled their way cheerfully
back into Cape Town that evening had not enjoyed their outing more
than the spectators of this grotesque 'Cricket Match.'

Eight months later and a few days after the Japanese surrender our
camp at Kanburi began to assemble frequently for news bulletins.
Emissaries, we heard, were flying hither and thither, instructions and
encouragement were being relayed from Governments to POW's; the
air was heavy with the most momentous happenings. Moreover, many
of those present had had no news of the outside world for months, or
longer; yet, no item commanded so much attention as the Test match
at Manchester.

I had, by then, already taken my first walk for three and a half years
as a free man. We found ourselves in a Thai village on the edge of
the jungle. In the little café our hosts politely turned on the English
programme. Yes, we were at Old Trafford, and a gentleman called
Cristofani was getting a hundred . . .

LONG LOOK BACK

*This article, in which I tried to see our situation in the general context
of the War in early 1942, in addition to picturing life as a POW as I
saw and experienced it, was published in* The Spectator *of 15 February
1992, marking the fiftieth anniversary of the fall of Singapore.*

This weekend sees a sombre jubilee. I suppose that the picture of
the last days of the Battle of Singapore will stand out equally
clearly in the recollection of most of my fellow survivors. We had
ample time to relive the chaotic scene in the three and a half years

from the Allied surrender on 15 February 1942 to that of the Japanese in Tokyo Bay on 15 August 1945.

On Thursday 29 January, 17 days before the largest capitulation in the history of British arms, we slid into Singapore harbour, the only significant reinforcements to have arrived there since the Japanese invasion of Malaya seven weeks before. As the American troop-ship SS *Wakefield*, carrying 54 Brigade of the 18th Division, was being berthed, the decks thick with men in full order, a flight of 27 Jap bombers flew straight at us. If ever there was a sitting duck we were it. Almost overhead they came, then veered off and dropped their bombs on the pre-selected prey, a gasworks perhaps. The leader ignored the target of his dreams, for in the Jap code obedience came before initiative. It was my first glimpse of his mentality.

The Australian truck drivers who took us to a staging camp in a rubber plantation told us we had arrived too late. By contrast, an official communication from Army HQ at Fort Canning suggested things were normal enough. A letter from the Deputy Provost Marshal requested a photograph in duplicate for the issue of an identity card – this when by the weekend or thereabouts the advancing Japs would have arrived at the Johore Strait dividing the island from the Malayan mainland, a fortnight, as it turned out, before surrender. It was incidental in my case that the signatory of the letter, Lt Colonel Brian K. Castor, the pre-war secretary of Essex County Cricket Club, would have had no difficulty in recognising his cricket partner in a pre-war opening stand or two.

The shape of Singapore Island is much like a full-blown rose, twice as wide as it is deep, with the city on its southern coast. The naval base and the causeway connecting with the mainland lie centrally, with the military area of Changi to the north-east.

This was the area assigned to our 18th Division, which was composed of Territorials from the eastern counties. With what remained of the Indian 11th Division, we took up positions on the 31st, the battle-weary Australians and the other Indian and British troops who had been fighting a gallant, hopeless retreat on the mainland being deployed on the left flank. Churchill, in Book IV of *The Second World War*, notes that there were no permanent fortifications on the landward side and, what was 'even more astounding', no field defences had been attempted after the war in the East had begun. This is the exact truth. Not a coil of wire did we find, and when we sent to the RAOC depot on the afternoon of Saturday the 31st to get some, we found they had closed down for the weekend.

We made what defensive provisions we could in that first week of February, and provided some custom to an Officers' Club bar with well-laundered staff down by the shore. I signed my last chits there (thinking a bottle or two of whisky would come in handy) on 8 February, the very night that the Japs (after a strong bombardment, in small craft and with blood-curdling cries) penetrated the north-west coast.

The 18th Division, wrote the Prime Minister to General Wavell, the Supreme Commander, on 10 February, 'has a chance to make its name in history'. Vain hope! After two years of hard home training, commanded by General 'Becky' Beckwith-Smith, in whom we had confidence and who held the affection of all, we were denied any such glory. Leaving us unscathed, apart from spasmodic bombardment from the air and artillery on the mainland, the Japs made such inroads in the north-west that by 11 February (my 35th birthday) all troops east of the causeway were withdrawn to a circular perimeter in defence of the city. Units were thrown in piecemeal to plug the gaps. Beckwith-Smith saw his beloved division dismembered bit by bit.

Once the Jap had gained a foothold on the island, surrender was inevitable. In 17 days I never saw a single Allied aircraft, only Japs either bombing from high altitude or, in the final days, spotting disdainfully for their guns almost at tree-top height. They even had balloons doing the same job. Denied any vestige of air support, even the finest fighting troops would have been pressed to maintain morale.

On 12 and 13 February, the 25-pounder guns of 148 Field Regiment supported the centre-right of the perimeter defence of the city facing the MacRitchie, the southernmost of the three island reservoirs, with the Bukit Timah golf course just west of it. From a convenient observation post, I had the satisfaction of directing heavy concentrations of fire from the 12 guns of 419 Battery at and in the area of the clubhouse and down the Sime Road.

The left of the line came under the heaviest enemy pressure, and on 14 February we received orders to conform to a further withdrawal. It was in establishing a new OP that I came to grief. Wireless communication between OPs and guns was extremely unreliable, making archaic telephone lines essential. While my OP Ack was away directing the signallers laying the wire, I saw up an adjacent tree a pair of spectacles glinting in the sun. Using my Ack's rifle I aimed a few shots into the foliage, but was rewarded by no falling body. A while later, rather forgetting the fellow, I got up to investigate the wire-laying situation. In a burst from, I suppose, his sub-machine-gun I was hit by a single bullet at the right elbow. I was taken to an advanced dressing-station, being succeeded at the OP by my battery commander, Major Bill Merry. During the night of the 14th/15th the situation on our front rapidly deteriorated and in the early morning of the day of surrender poor Merry, in the act of rallying some straggling infantry, was killed.

I, by contrast, had been wonderfully lucky. The bullet had passed through my arm an inch below the funny bone. Sent back to Singapore General Hospital, I passed through corridors lined with civilian stretcher cases, and was directed to the last but one vacant bed.

I found on returning to my Battery a medley of emotions: frustration ('We were thrown away,' says a staunch bombadier, recalling the moment), indignation in some, indifference in a few, and in many – for those at the guns' end had had no direct contact with the enemy – sheer surprise. For our losses were negligible, four killed out of 202, one of them our battery commander.

In his summary of the immediate reasons behind the surrender, General Percival mentioned dwindled food reserves, shortages of ammunition, petrol and water. I can vouch for the water shortage, for in 24 hours at the General Hospital I received one cup, which was the ration. (It was ten days before the water supply was restored to this teeming hospital.) Once the Japs took the MacRitchie reservoir, the struggle was over. Could the General have exposed the civilian population of nearly a million to the threat of death by thirst? His only alternative to surrender on the morning of 15 February was a counter-attack to regain possession of the reservoirs and the food depots. His commanders ruled out this option as impracticable. They doubted – with ample reason – whether their forces could resist another determined attack which would have meant Jap troops running loose in the city.

So the white flag was hoisted and, shortly after dusk in the Ford factory at Bukit Timah, General Percival acceded to the demand of unconditional surrender made by his opposite number, Lieutenant General Yamashita. The Jap army had shown all the military virtues, as well as a capacity to inflict acts of unbridled savagery that boded ill for their captives. After the action at Muar, non-walking wounded were massacred in cold blood. At the Alexandra Military Hospital at Singapore two days before the surrender, 150 patients and staff, having been confined all night to a space allowing standing-room only, were executed the next morning.

The feeling that we were implicated, however helplessly, in the humiliation of Singapore, coupled with the sudden change from normal food to a diet exclusively of rice and jungle vegetables, did nothing for morale in the early days of captivity. I recall a dark moment in March or April when a string of heavy Jap cruisers – we counted 11 in line ahead – steamed past Changi to the naval base. Our release at that moment seemed a very long way off. There was no means of knowing that the spring of 1942 marked the limit of Jap expansion, that in early June the Americans shifted the balance of naval strength by destroying four of their carrier fleet in 10 minutes in the Battle of Midway. This astonishing victory, John Keegan has written, 'turned the tide of the war at a stroke'.

For most of us, I think, depression lifted when there was work to be done. In River Valley Road camp in Singapore city, as the so-called camp Welfare Officer, I formed a library of several thousand books brought back by working parties employed by the Japs to clean up the European quarter. They were the sort to be expected on the shelves of expatriate Englishmen: Priestley, Waugh, Galsworthy, Bryant, H. V. Morton, Gunther. When we were sent away to make the Burma-Siam railway, two books a man were doled out. The result was that in the next three years modest libraries were set up all along the railway, once the line had been laid and work pressure eased. The tattered contents were kept in reasonable shape by book-binders using paste and remnants of gas-cape for cover. At one point my 1939 *Wisden* was in such demand that it could be lent out only for periods of six hours.

In September 1942, I found myself transported up through Malaya by rail. There were, luckily, only 22 to our officers' cattle-truck and not the usual 40, so that, over the several days of a journey punctuated by station stops to consume pails of rice and water, we were just able to lie sardine-fashion head to tail. From the rail-head at Banpong, we marched 25 miles (with all the belongings we possessed or could carry on a tarmac road in much heat) past amiably curious Siamese to Kanburi, and thence by jungle track to the headquarters camp at Tarsao. This was the route travelled by all the Allied POWs engaged on building the railway: there were 66,000 of us, of whom 16,000 failed to return. These were military casualties exclusive of Tamils, Malays, Chinese and other sources of impressed labour who died like flies.

I owe it to the memory of Colonel Sir Philip Toosey and to my

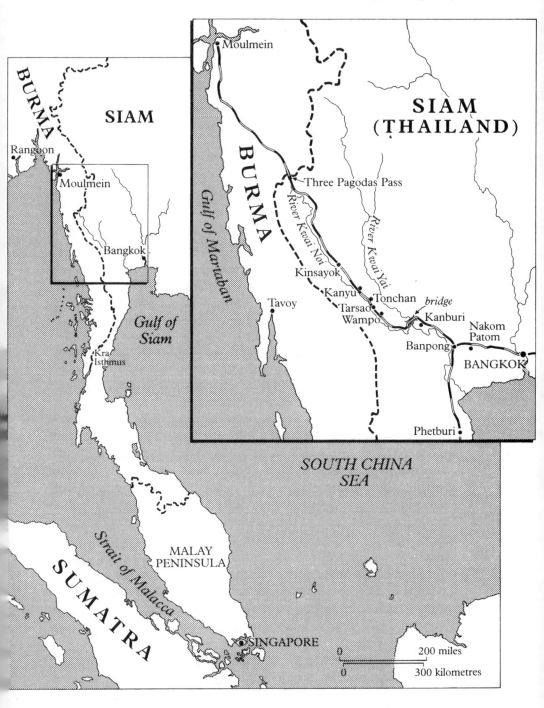

fellow Far Eastern POWs to object to the portrayal by Alec Guinness of the British colonel in the film *Bridge Over the River Kwai*, which, though purporting to be a version of the fictional book of that name by Pierre Boulle, was assumed by the public to be fact.

The building of the bridge at the junction between the Kwai Yai and Kwai Noi was the essential first step in the construction of the railway that was to follow the line of the Kwai Noi up to the Burmese border at the Three Pagodas pass. As the senior British officer in a group of prisoners that swelled ultimately to 2,600, including many Dutch, Toosey was ordered to command the camp at the site and provide all fit men for the work, which was supervised by the Jap railway regiment.

He protested without avail that under the Hague and Geneva Conventions prisoners must not be used for tasks helpful to the war effort as, of course, did other senior POW officers elsewhere, but equally to no avail. He therefore pursued a policy of limited co-operation, which he considered the best way of ensuring that as many of his men as possible should survive captivity. By insisting on strict discipline – no beards, by the way, for fear of lice – keeping constant pressure on the Nips to improve food and conditions, and protesting against every instance of brutality, he succeeded marvellously. In many ways the film gave a graphic, realistic picture of the scene apart from the character of the Jap-happy, half-crazed 'Colonel Nicholson'.

Sir Alec Guinness won an Oscar for a virtuoso performance that was nevertheless seen by Toosey's fellow-prisoners as a gross calumny against one of the heroes both of the war in Malaya and of the captivity.

If circumstances thrust Philip Toosey most prominently into the spotlight, other senior officers of the 18th Division shouldered with outstanding success throughout our captivity the utterly wearing, frustrating, dangerous duty of representing their fellow-POWs in negotiations with the Nips. They lived with the knowledge of secret wireless-sets, illicit traffic in money and medicines, and other matters which, if the Nips had known of them, would have resulted in torture, if not death. Two lieutenant-colonels, H. H. Lilly of the 1/5 Sherwood Foresters and A. E. Knights of the 4th Norfolk Regiment, known as 'Knocker', small men both but tough as old boots, were respected up and down the river.

I eventually got down to the 'hospital' camp beside the golden temple at Nakom Patom. The 'hospital', by the way, was so only in name. We still slept all together on bamboo platforms, though perhaps there was a little more head-room, say 30 inches each, rather than the uniform 18 inches.

The railway layers passed us at Kinsayok on 30 July 1943, after which the work pressure eased and the camp death-rate decreased, perhaps from five or six a day to one or two – or even none. In a clearing we made a sort of open-air chapel, with a wooden altar and cross in case a padre came our way. A Harvest Festival was planned, and one of the Korean guards, who was a Christian, contributed to our meagre display a hand of bananas. This was noticed. The guard was beaten up and I, the Welfare Officer, apparently a subversive influence, was slapped a time or two and sent down to headquarters at Tarsao.

The journey down river in a pom-pom would have been agreeable but for the prospect of being handed over to the tender care of the Kempi-Tai, the secret police. Luckily, the camp commandant dismissed the frivolous charge and I was passed on down to the new hospital at Nakom Patom. At Tonchan I recall the climax of a much more serious case. At a transit point on the march up through the jungle, Major I. J. Mackinlay of the Scotch whisky firm was so provoked by the Nip NCO in charge that, with a blow to the jaw, he knocked him senseless. The Nip was dragged off by other guards, feet first. Astonishingly, next morning Mackinlay and his party, under another Nip, were moved on with no word said or action taken. Now, weeks later, the boss of the Tonchan camp, Sergeant-Major Hiramatsu, known as the Tiger, called for Mackinlay Chosa and confronted him with the NCO he had KO'd. Mackinlay for a while protested he had never seen the fellow before, but finally gave in. Thereupon there was laughter and back-slapping and the three sat down to sake and food.

The normal penalty for striking a guard was death. There was a jovial side to the Tiger, but he did not come by his sinister nickname for nothing. At the War Crimes Trials at Singapore in 1946, he was sentenced to be hanged, as were others of our tormentors such as Noguchi, commander of the Kanburi camp for officers, set up in January 1945 when the Nips, anticipating an Allied invasion, separated officers from other ranks.

The trials, which took place under the authority of the Judge Advocate-General, imposed the death sentence on many; others were committed to various terms of imprisonment; a few more acquitted. Notorious sadists like Donald Duck, the Frog and the Undertaker – the worst of them all had their labels – were strung up on evidence given by senior Allied officers.

These included some of those who administered 300 lashes and worse tortures to Leonard Wilson, Bishop of Singapore (accused of spying), as told so dreadfully by his chaplain, John Hayter, in his book *Priest in Prison*.

To the natural comment 'you must have had a terrible time', when the subject of our POW life has since come up, my answer is equivocal. On the face of it, conditions were appalling. Yet the body can be extraordinarily adjustable to conditions, however horrific, while the spirit takes courage from friendship, the feeling of burden shared, and the sense of humour it nourishes, macabre though it often was. The American wife of an RAMC officer incarcerated in Changi Prison put it this way: 'It wasn't unrelieved gloom. I wouldn't have missed it in terms of human experience. It made me grow up. I became a little less self-concerned.' I would go along with that.

Many have found it difficult to live with the stigma that attached to the Malayan campaign and capitulation. Yet the odds facing the Australian, Indian and British forces were enormous. The aerodromes, foolishly sited pre-war in northern Malaya and manned mostly by obsolete or obsolescent aircraft, were overrun within the first few days. The truth was that British Far Eastern strategy was based from pre-war days wholly on sea power: hence Singapore's big guns and static defences all faced seawards, on the assumption that it would be necessary only to protect the fortress from an attack by sea until the Allied navies arrived within a matter of days. From the moment that the *Prince of Wales* and *Repulse* failed to survive their first encounter, our fate was sealed.

We had ample time in the next three-and-a-half years both to reflect on the malignancy of fate and, at the same time, to wonder at the deep resources of the human spirit which the extremities of captivity revealed in many. I had lost something physically which was soon put right. But I had gained much that would always remain.

BOON PONG'S POM-POMS

In this follow-up letter to The Spectator *(21st March 1992) I was able to draw attention to the scale of the little-known, clandestine resistance movement directed by Colonel Smiley; and of the invaluable information regarding Jap plans provided courtesy of the Regent of Thai-*

land to the British Brigadier holed up in his attic. I was grateful also
for the chance to salute the brave, life-saving work of Boon Pong.

S ir: My article 'A cricketer under the Japs' (15 February) has elicited
from readers much hitherto unknown to me which I hope you will
feel is worth a postscript. Thanks to Colonel David Smiley of the Royal
Horse Guards (The Blues), who was parachuted into Thailand early
in 1945 with other SOE officers to organise Thai resistance, I have
seen Colonel Sir Philip Toosey's report on the six POW camps he
commanded during three and a half years of our captivity and also a
remarkably detailed medical report by Major E. A. Smyth, RAMC. It
was Toosey's wonderfully comprehensive report running into 15,000
words and completed, despite his other duties, within a month of the
Jap surrender which, I expect, helped to win him an immediate DSO.

Whereas one Allied POW in four perished in the building of the
Burma-Siam railway on the Siamese or Thai side of the border, the
ratio would have been much higher but for the brave devotion of a
handful of people prepared to risk discovery and torture by the dreaded
Kempe-Tai (secret police). The chief underground source of money
and medical supplies were Messrs Heath and Gairdner of the Civil
Internees Camp in Bangkok. Major R. S. Sykes, RASC (sadly, later
one of 100 victims of Allied bombing) was thus able to bring back
among the rations bags of tapioca in which were hidden thousands of
Thai ticals.

Boon Pong was a Thai trader known throughout the camps, who
brought canteen goods up the river on barges drawn by pom-poms
(onomatopoeic). This little man was our life-line, regularly smuggling
in medicines under the noses of the Nips, saving hundreds of lives with
emetine, the specific cure for amoebic dysentery. At Tonchan, with the
monsoon at its height and our spirits at their lowest, laden elephants
arrived at the camp headed by a smiling Boon Pong aloft.

After the war he was awarded the George Medal and British officers
combined to set him up in business. When my Commonwealth team
toured the Far East in 1961 he proudly showed me over the garage of
the Boon Pong Bus Company.

We knew little of the degree of Thai resistance as now told me by
Colonel Smiley. He commanded 12 Thai camps of 1,000 men each,
secreted in the jungle and eager to turn on their allies-under-duress
when Mountbatten's forces were due to invade. This was a bare few
weeks after the atom bombs forced their surrender. The Thai Regent

secreted a British brigadier, Hector Jacques, in his palace. After the Japanese Commander-in-Chief gave the Regent his daily briefing, the gist was duly passed on via the Brigadier's transmitter to Mountbatten's headquarters.

Whether or not in the event of the invasion the Thai guerillas could have reached the POW camps before we were gunned down is nevertheless a point verging on the moot.

E. W. SWANTON
Sandwich, Kent

PORTRAIT OF 'WEARY'

A review for the Daily Telegraph *[4 June 1994] of* Weary:
the Life of Sir Edward Dunlop *by Sue Ebury,*
published by Viking.

Weary Dunlop at Tarsao POW camp on the Menam-Kwai-Noi river beside the Thai-Burma railway, accused of having a secret wireless set, after being heavily beaten, was stood against a tree. His arms were manacled behind his back, encircling the trunk. Four soldiers with fixed bayonets worked themselves up with yells and grunts. He was given 30 seconds to confess. Having uttered a contemptuous last message, with ten seconds to go he was released. Next day he suffered similarly and was similarly reprieved.

Another time at a so-called hospital camp at Nakom Patom after hours of torture he announced to his captors that if they would excuse him he would amputate a Dutchman's arm, and with tremulous hands proceeded to do so.

I saw him at Kinsayok camp, having been stood for hours at attention in the sun, being assailed by a Korean guard with a length of bamboo from a pile nearby. Weary caught it and threw it away as he did others that followed. Luckily fellow-guards enjoyed the man's humiliation, and Weary was released. Life was like that, the austerities alongside the bizarre, even the comical.

This tall, supremely tough, utterly determined, tireless, soft-spoken Australian surgeon saved many hundreds of lives on the railway. He and his medical staffs of British and Australians did all possible, with few drugs and improvised instruments to put a brake on the death-rate among men emaciated by over-work on a diet of rice, and racked with dysentery, malaria, and beri-beri. The Japanese camp commanders, recognizing his skills as an aid to their labour-force, were angered by Weary's unending demands for supplies and protection of the sick. Clashes of will were inevitable. So they likewise were with another hero of the captivity, Major Cyril Wild. A staff officer in the Malayan campaign, a fluent Japanese linguist who had been official interpreter at both surrender ceremonies and had spent the captivity endlessly and often with dramatic effect arguing prisoners' cases with the Nips, Wild was killed in an air crash when working as War Crimes Liaison Officer.

Lady Ebury, a New Zealander and by profession a publisher, edited Sir Edward Dunlop's War Diaries which were secreted on odd scraps of paper and miraculously undiscovered by the enemy. In 1984 they were a best-seller and form the basis of this book. But there is vastly more.

Weary, a Victorian country-boy whose Scots grandfather had emigrated from Dumfries, came to England for his F.R.C.S. with a First in Medicine at Melbourne University and an Australian Rugby Union cap in 1938. He was a star forward for St Mary's Hospital and became a Barbarian before being commissioned in London into the R.A.A.M.C. He served in the Middle East, Greece and Crete before being shipped in early 1942 to Java.

Weary, now a lieutenant-colonel, commanding No. 1 Allied General hospital in Bandoeng, prevented Aircraftsman Griffiths from being bayonetted by standing in front of him. Blinded and with face shattered by a mine his execution had been ordered by a Jap officer. Bill Griffiths has lived to write his saviour's obituary. Colonel (now Sir) Laurens van der Post, British Army fellow-prisoner, fortified Weary's responsibility for mixed Allied camps in Java prior to their transportation to Thailand.

Weary Dunlop's post-war career comprised more than 40 years of ceaseless, selfless service within and outside the world of medicine. Invitations to lecture and preside at POW reunions, professional seminars, congresses, took him to every continent. He visited Japan and entertained Japanese students in his Melbourne home. He never forgot Boon Pong, the prime figure in the Thai Resistance whose supply of hundreds of thousands of duck eggs brought by barges up-river (along with secreted drugs) were literally a lifeline. Honours abounded. He was appointed OBE and CMG before being knighted in 1969. In 1977 he became Australian of the Year. Eight medical fellowships and two doctorates came his way. He was made a Companion of the Order of Australia.

In his 80s, after losing his beloved wife Helen, and in increasing weakness and ill-health, he fulfilled demands both overseas and at home until the end came within 10 days of his 86th birthday. Wrote his biographer: 'He gave his country a vision of sacrifice, compassion and service. Race and creed had been no barrier to his understanding.' This book is a worthy testament to the most heroic figure I ever knew.

YOUNG HEROES

First printed in the Saint Clement's Church, Sandwich,
parish paper,
The Signal, *August 1995.*

Resistance in our POW existence varied astonishingly, so that the phrase turning one's face to the wall was being illustrated literally all the time. Two men might be more or less identically ill and weak. To A you would give no chance while B, you felt, might have the will to pull himself through. Of all the sad cases that come to mind I will select that of Francis Millward, a young signaller of my own troop, a Derbyshire lad who at some stage of our training had been drafted to us as a recruit. He was a practising Christian, and we had no nicer man or more reliable soldier. He went down at the worst time in Tonchan South, one of the worst camps where to the usual scourges cholera was added, the infection coming from a Tamil camp a little way up-river. One tried to keep in touch with men of one's own Battery as far as possible, though gradually they became scattered far and wide, and the story of Millward's amazing cheerfulness and prolonged fight for life came to us at the main Tonchan camp.

Though there were several deaths each day, and everyone was working from dawn to dusk, Millward's refusal to give up long after complete debility had set in became something of an epic. On 7 July 1943, I got Jap permission to walk the few miles between camps to see him. As it happened I was an hour too late, but was in time for the funeral.

They were such regular occurrences as to attract little notice. At times all that could be done was a mass burial, with no accompanying words from the Prayer Book. But for this one every man in camp seemed to have turned out, and to have saved a clean if tattered shirt for the occasion. It was as though we were all expressing our gratitude for a shining example of quiet courage which had put heart into the whole community.

I recall, too, the case of a man who had volunteered for the most dangerous of all jobs, orderly in the hut containing the worst of the dysentery cases. He invested this most gruesome of occupations with much zeal and humour until his own condition was so bad that he had himself to take to the bamboo slats which formed one's bed. The specific for amoebic dysentery was Atabrine, and though the doctors had none there were sometimes a few tablets to be had on the black market. I caused inquiries to be made, and was brought some which, I was told, had come from some Australians who admired his guts and would take no money.

When I gave him the news the relief was a joy to see. It was literally a reprieve from death – in ninety-nine cases out of a hundred. The injections were duly given, but this was the hundredth case of the man who was impervious to the drug. So hope went out almost as swiftly as it had been engendered. Why I specially remember this case is because this fellow, who held a key rôle in the battery, was one of the only ones who during his brief experience of battle had reacted badly under fire. Maybe, given time, he would have faced the music as well as the next. As it was, everyone knew it. I believe the work among the dysentery cases which cost him his life was a deliberate act of self-redemption.

I found one could never begin to gauge in advance individual reaction to danger. During the sea passage through Sunda Strait I happened to observe at an air-raid alert that a timid young signaller was plainly petrified, and made a mental note. The first thing I heard on rejoining the battery after being slightly wounded was how this same man had shown the greatest courage manning his post hour after hour while his truck was under constant shell-fire. Conquest of fear is surely the height of bravery.

Every survivor had his own memories of an unforgettable experience. One saw human nature in the raw, and it made for a common bond of fellowship which helped to sustain us until the glad moment came. For many of us it had a deeper significance. If our minds were not led towards the spiritual in such circumstances they surely never could have been.

THE RAILWAY MAN

The end of my review of The Railway Man *by Eric Lomax (Jonathan Cape) in* The Sunday Telegraph *(13th August, 1995) makes, it may be thought, an uplifting epilogue to our sombre story.*

O f all the actions by prisoners-of-war of the Japs which carried, if detected, the certainty of extreme torture and the probability of death, the most dangerous – just as it was of the greatest value to the POW communities – was the setting-up and use of radio sets.

To men in the ultimate stages of weakness and malnutrition, any scrap of news suggesting that there might be light at the end of the tunnel nourished hope. Those who with infinite ingenuity and stealth contrived from improvised materials to put sets together were, need it be said, the bravest of the brave. In the nature of things, the operators were likely to be members of the Royal Corps of Signals.

Eric Lomax, a Scot born in Edinburgh and educated at the Royal High School, joined the Supplementary Reserve of that Corps in the spring of 1939. He was a lonely 20-year-old with a passion for train-spotting. Hence the brutally ironic title of the book, in which he tells the horrifying story of his detection and sufferings at the hands of the Japanese secret police, the dreaded Kempei-tai, at Kanchanaburi, a headquarters camp on the Siam-Burma railway.

Lomax's story, which describes in relentless detail both the author's physical and psychological torture, makes almost unbearable reading. It is no book for the faint-hearted. In the literature of the Far East POW-dom, even the sufferings of the Bishop of Singapore as related by his chaplain, John Hayter (*Priest in Prison*), are almost mild in comparison. Lomax's story certainly makes more comprehensible the feelings of those POWs who still think with utter contempt of their former enemies, 'the Nips'.

Yet there is a redeeming moral to the book. It is the cleansing virtue of forgiveness. Lomax after all but half a century, during which he was perpetually racked by nightmares and ever haunted by the memories, arranges to meet his chief tormentor, the interpreter Nagase Takashi.

They meet – the Christian and the Buddhist – where river and railway run side-by-side downstream of the bridge over the River Kwai. Nagase had spent the intervening years assisting the Allied War Graves Commission in their grim exploration of the jungle camps up into Burma. Presumably their need of an interpreter saved him from arrest. He worked also for Japanese-Allied reconciliation in Japan and Thailand. At Chungkai, he had built a Buddhist shrine in memory of the fallen.

They reminisce endlessly. Lomax finds himself consoling Nagase, whose relief was palpable. He said, 'I think I can die safely now.' The final chapter sees them with their wives visiting the museum at Hiroshima where a relative of Nagase was a victim.

PART FOUR

1946–1955

1946–1955

The immediate reaction at Kanchanaburi to the Jap surrender was decidedly anti-climactic. Overwhelming relief, of course, that the hideous privations were soon to end, but feelings ran far too deep and bodies were too much drained for any expression of wild elation. The Nippon guards had been ordered to remain in place until they could be relieved, so freedom arrived by degrees. Union jacks unfolded from secretion in bamboo canes; national songs sung without fear of reprisals; stores, medicine and mail released from confiscation; and visits to local cafés – these were the initial signs of change.

At a café owned by the remarkable Thai trader Boon Pong, Jim experienced his first post-war shock. From the large radiogram in the corner came the unmistakable sounds of cricket. Commentating in the fifth 'Victory' Test between England and Australia from Old Trafford was none other than Rex Alston and the BBC Overseas service, as it was then, was relaying his words as New South Wales all-rounder Bob Cristofani was approaching his hundred. What were Major Swanton's thoughts at that moment? 'Oh, delight that cricket was being played again, but also a twinge of anxiety that my place behind the microphone had been taken.'

Jim's thoughts might well have dwelt on his own recent cricketing enterprises. Just over eight months previously, on New Year's Day 1945, he had organised an English and Australian POW 'Test match' between the huts at Nakom Patom in the shadow of a giant pagoda. Before that at Tarsao, a base camp in the jungle by the river Kwai Noi, he had produced a 'Radio Newsreel' every Tuesday night in which, more often than not, the main subject was cricket.

For the Newsreel the camp entertainment committee had created a simple open-air theatre on a flat area at the foot of a steep concave hill. A large stage-prop wireless made of bamboo and matting was placed centre stage with the performers screened behind and the audience out front sitting on the slopes of the hill.

A memorable 'broadcast' was 'The Life of Bradman' which Jim narrated with statistics provided by his much-read 1939 *Wisden*, the cherished copy preserved with remnants of gas-cape and rice paste. In this documentary there was even simulated running commentary with sound effects, but it was the Swanton delivery that captured the crowd: 'Donald George Bradman was born at Cootamundra in New South Wales on 27 August 1908. He was the youngest of five children and in 1911, the family moved to Bowral, about eighty-five miles south-west of Sydney...' At the end of the evening the audience was on its feet applauding enthusiastically. Such escapism had been infinitely precious to each and every one of them.

Back at Kanchanaburi in the aftermath of the cease-fire Jim was brought quickly in tune with reality. He was shortly to be sent as commander of Phetburi camp down towards the Kra Isthmus where several thousand troops – British, American, Netherlanders, Australians, East Indians – had been deployed. It was not easy without a sanction of any kind to keep discipline among so many nationalities whose sole thought was when could they return home. But before long an American Air Force plane took all the POW's to Rangoon for a spell of recuperation in hospital and a morale-boosting visit from Lady Mountbatten. The Allied staff at the hospital were genuinely surprised to see Service personnel as they knew of Hirohito's orders to wipe them out if Japanese territory was invaded. The atomic bombing of Nagasaki and Hiroshima could not have come soon enough for thousands of Allied troops.

The boat trip back to Blighty on the *Corfu* was restful and the train journey from Southampton to Waterloo bewildering: so much had happened, so much time had passed. What had once been familiar now seemed strange. On the platform at Waterloo Jim's father walked straight past him. His son now weighed five stone less than he had four years previously. At ten and a half stone it was a slim-line Swanton. At the sight of him, his mother burst into tears. When Singapore had fallen on 15 February 1942, it had been ten months before news of his safety had reached home; although home itself, for his parents, had changed several times during the war. They had been bombed out of two houses and at the time of their son's return were living in rather makeshift fashion in a hotel at Chislehurst in Kent. Soon they were to move into the bottom floor of a large Victorian house in Beckenham where Jim kept a room. He spent weekends with them and took the opportunity to play for the local cricket club.

But it was whether or not he would be allowed to commentate on cricket that was his main concern when re-adjusting to civilian life.

The knowledge that Rex Alston and others had been occupying the 'box' chairs during the Victory Tests of 1945 did not help his peace of mind. He therefore decided to register the fact that he was now back in circulation with the BBC's Head of Outside Broadcasts, Seymour J. de Lotbinière, who at six foot seven was every bit as lanky as his name was long. A meeting duly took place a few weeks after his return from captivity in October 1945. 'Lobby' was normally nothing if not decisive. On this occasion, however, he was noticeably non-committal, although he did promise an early chance behind the microphone the following season.

Gloucestershire versus Lancashire at Gloucester in May and a Wally Hammond century provided plenty of action for a good audition and very soon Jim was contracted for the Test Matches. Later 'Lobby' confided in Jim that he had been taken aback by the latter's debilitated appearance and that his hesitancy was the result of wondering whether Swanton's faculties would be sharp enough for broadcasting.

By now, Jim had mapped out his summer – or thought he had: broadcasting, writing a piece for *The Field* every week, and as much cricket as he could fit in with any club that offered a game. Unexpectedly, however, the job of cricket reporter on the *Daily Telegraph* became vacant and so Jim filled in, initially as Special Correspondent on a monthly basis and then from July onwards under his own name. Little did he know, he was to make the seat his own for the next thirty years.

During that first year after the war Jim occupied two rooms at Pusey House in Oxford. Pusey House, so called after Edward Pusey, a leading figure of the Oxford Movement, is a centre for the Catholic Revival within the Church of England. It is a truism to say that nobody came through the war unchanged and in Jim's case the change was of a religious nature. In the 'thirties he had been a nominal Anglican, an occasional church-goer who could have aptly fitted the label 'conventional C of E'. As a prisoner of the Japanese he came into contact with a number of fellow-captives who were Anglo-Catholics. In discussions with them and after reading several books on the subject Jim came round to adopting what he determined was the full Faith based on the Apostolic Succession and there was a period during 1943–44 when he seriously considered a life in holy orders. This, of course, was at a time when he was often called on to conduct funeral services for those unfortunate men who had succumbed to the inhuman regime imposed by the Japanese. By the end of the war he was a committed Anglo-

Catholic and ever since has been a devoted church-goer, who has played an active role in ecclesiastical affairs.

One of the POWs with whom Jim talked about religious matters had been Lawrence Turner, later to be the MP for Oxford. Turner gave Swanton an introduction to the Principal of Pusey House, Canon Frederic Hood, and Hood it was who offered the rooms. Jim was to base himself at Pusey House for six years, until 1952, in what was to prove a very happy and fulfilling time.

The principal reason for leaving Oxford and buying a house near to Lord's at 17 Loudoun Road, St John's Wood was the declining health of his mother. In the past few years she had suffered more than one stroke and was reduced to moving around in a wheelchair, so Jim decided to take both parents under his wing and into his new home. The house, incidentally, was next door to that of the renowned concert pianist, Solomon, who was most concerned that his practice did not disturb his new neighbours. A married couple were employed to help keep the Swanton household ticking over – Jim was, of course, frequently away on the cricket circuit – and the plan was eventually to install Mrs Swanton in the St John and St Elizabeth Hospital nearby. Sadly, before that could take place, at the beginning of January 1953, she had a final stroke and died.

This post-war decade up to the mid-'fifties was a regenerative time for cricket, particularly cricket in England. Foremost in most people's minds was the need to construct a worthy Test side both before and after the nadir of defeat by the rampaging Aussies of '48. When such a side did materialise and triumphantly reclaim the Ashes in 1953, it was as if the whole of Britain had at last thrown off the cloak of post-war gloom and austerity. Today, the names of that team seem little short of legendary.

But much else took place to relieve England's insularity: transitory times in South Africa; the New Zealanders holding their own; the effervescent West Indians of 1950; and the sudden emergence of Pakistan in 1954. A County Championship, too, that was being dominated by Surrey – arguably, for several years, the best county side of all time. And, as always, the concerns of cricket were just as hotly contested off the field as well.

At the centre of all this was Jim, whether writing in the *Daily Telegraph* or in *The Field* or sitting in the commentary box with Alston and Arlott – he was there, in pole position, enjoying himself immensely, ready to relate whatever was happening.

D.R.A.

BACK TO PRE-WAR CRICKET

Spring is in the air and every prospect pleases.
The Field, *27 April 1946.*

No deep psychological exercise is needed to predict that, for all the grave issues overhanging us, cricket is going to be in the fore-front of attention this summer. All over the country clubs have used the winter in preparation – from the great Yorkshire club, with its many thousand adherents and its fat bank balance, down to the most modest village. The fighting ended at a convenient time of year, for there has been much for faithful hands to do. To those who say, 'Cricket is not what it used to be,' the stock answer suffices, 'It never has been.' But though we may have no fears for the spirit behind it all, it will be astonishing if the general technical level does not reflect the gap of six summers that separates us from the last season of peace.

So far as the counties are concerned they have no alternative but to recruit their teams very largely from among those who were the 'stars' of seven years ago; no alternative because the generation that has grown up in the interval, or rather the surviving part of it, has had no chance of developing its powers, and the great bulk still remains in the Services, for the most part abroad. A British crowd generally surveys its 'old 'uns' with a warm, nostalgic eye, and it will be splendid to see once more the heroes of the 'twenties and 'thirties.

But even the greatest of them cannot cheat nature indefinitely, and as some of the names have been announced in the Prospects Columns I have thought of the remark made, and accompanied by an indulgent smile, when Mead was batting in his later years, 'He plays from memory now!' There will be more than a few of them 'playing from memory' in 1946, and I dare say they may play uncommonly well. The fear one has is that, in the absence of young bowlers, and with fielding inevitably on the slow side, age may take root and persuade us into a false scale of values. For it is axiomatic that batsmen 'last' longer than bowlers.

I see that in his latest book (*English Cricket*: Collins) Neville Cardus stresses how eloquent is cricket at any time of the English mood and temper. In the tired and disillusioned 'twenties, 'beautiful and brave stroke-play gave way to a sort of trench warfare, conducted behind the sandbag of broad pads. . . . A shrewd professionalism decided on a compromise; enough of pace, pitched just short of a length, and a suggestion of spin and more of swerve, the attack directed on the leg stump – the main idea being to obtain a reasonably good bowling analysis every season at the expenditure of a minimum of risk and physical endurance.'

On Mr. Cardus' analogy our immediate cricket future would seem somewhat depressing, for a certain weariness there is in the air, and must be. But if the cricket of the 'twenties reflected the trench battles of Flanders, maybe that of 1946 will be conditioned by the spirit of the commandos and the paratroopers. And if Mr. Cardus is right, as I think he certainly is, in putting much of the blame upon a new genus of post-Great War county captains who, like the Duke of Plaza Toro, 'led their regiments from behind,' we may certainly take heart from the present. For there has probably never been a better collection than those who have been appointed for this year: better in the sense of having a truer notion of the essentials of a cricket match, of whatever kind.

There will be a lively note of conflict engendered right enough. To sustain it there must be bowling of quality – and a fair wicket. To a large degree the former depends upon the latter. The captains indeed can do much, but not everything, to set first-class cricket (from which all other in some degree takes its tone) going on the right lines.

AN UNEXPECTED ENCORE

The King came to this celebration (delayed by a year) of Surrey's Centenary. The sun shone, 15,000 came, and I had the honour of manning the public address system, a post-war novelty which swiftly spread. Woolley (aged fifty-nine) and Hendren (fifty-seven) batted felicitously. The Field, May 1946.

There has never been an occasion quite like the Oval Centenary Match between the old England cricketers and Surrey, and the only regret one has is that it is so clearly unrepeatable. Such a success was it that to risk an almost inevitable anti-climax next year would be to jeopardise the pleasantest of memories.

Was it a *match*, as distinct from an event? Did Surrey 'hold their punches'? Or did 12 players averaging 50½ years prove themselves the equals of one of the major county teams?

The truth is that, so far as the Surrey innings went, both Gregory and Squires batted, after they had each made 50, with a light-heartedness which pointed to an only brief survival. Surrey made their runs very comfortably at 100 an hour on a very docile wicket, and set their opponents to get 249, or 75 an hour.

It is no disparagement of anyone to say that the Surrey bowlers were as anxious as anyone on the ground to see the great ones 'off the mark.' They did not bowl as though attacking Notts on a bank holiday, and only one lbw was asked for – and given. After Sutcliffe and Sandham had fallen to the new ball the attack sensibly eased. The fact detracts little from the efforts of Hendren, Woolley, and D. R. Jardine, each of whom, in his own style, demonstrated how a sound technique ground in by the years can remain almost unaffected by age and lack of practice. Whether these three and those to follow would have withstood a Surrey team anxious to catch an early evening train to the provinces cannot be said, for they were not faced with such a proposition. What they succeeded in doing was a test not only of their surviving skill but of their sportsmanship in facing the arc-lights once again.

WHAT FORTUNE IN AUSTRALIA?

This article (reduced here) was preceded by an announcement on page one that I was to sail with the team to cover the MCC tour. All was anticipation and high hopes, doomed to founder. Daily Telegraph, *September 1946.*

When the 17 cricketers selected by the MCC board their steamer tomorrow, they will be following in the wake of nearly all (though not quite all) of the foremost English cricketers of every generation over little short of 100 years.

The historically-minded perhaps may contrast the palaver of to-morrow's departure, with the array of journalists and all the impedimenta of modern publicity, with the pioneer journey of 1861.

In that remote year, even before Bismarck had begun to alarm the chancelleries of Europe, 12 bewhiskered heroes stepped aboard a paddle-boat at Liverpool on their precarious journey.

They arrived in Melbourne on Christmas Eve, and it is interesting to observe that then, as now, the enthusiasm and glamour of cricket was set in a higher key in Australia than over here.

It was W. G. Grace who aroused the national consciousness of England for cricket, and in 1861 the triumphs of that great man were still confined to the apple orchard at Downend, with the dogs and his mother and Uncle Pocock scouting out.

Yet at Melbourne the obscure company from Liverpool were met by 10,000, and, as Mr. H. S. Altham tells us, were driven off for their first practice to a secret destination in the bush in order that they might have some peace from their admirers.

Twelve years were to pass after the first Englishmen had landed in Australia to play cricket until W. G. himself appeared there. He found in his antagonists a tough combativeness exceeding even his own and that of his brother 'E. M.' It may perhaps be said that he set a standard in that direction of which Australians have rarely fallen short.

From W. G.'s visit to our own day the series of battles has gone on, and the heroes of 'the Golden Age,' MacLaren, Jackson, Fry and Jessop on the one side, Noble, Hill, Gregory and the immortal Trumper on the other, are still household names.

The question which exercises the followers of cricket at present is the measure of skill of the team which Hammond leads from home to-morrow. There are some factors which are better set down now than when the battle is joined.

The most important is that this tour, undertaken relatively so soon after the close of six years of war, takes place specifically because the interest of millions of Australians and Englishmen seemed to the authorities to demand it.

There is no need to disguise the fact that many would have liked to see our cricketers tuned up for the business by the full dress series of the Test matches due to be played over here against the South Africans next summer. The gap of six seasons has prevented a whole generation from showing its mettle, and the older players from keeping their skill from going to rust.

The English golfers, one may note, have declared a two-year truce before continuing engagements with their enemies from America. But cricket's spotlight has a brighter and more powerful beam. It must be added that Australia, too, have had their losses and their interruptions. Further (what we often overlook) their source of supply is a small fraction of ours. The population of Australia can still be contained within that of Greater London.

Where the selectors of the present side have been particularly handicapped is in the generally low standard of our cricket this summer. It is an inevitable thing, but none the less tiresome, that long scores made against many of the counties in 1946 have been valueless from the point of view of appraising the likelihood of a batsman's success against Australian bowling on Australia's wickets. Equally, it is little criterion that a bowler may have taken eight for 45 against Blankshire, or even captured 100 wickets and be sixth in the averages.

As for the fielding, there are several fine natural athletes in the party and few real weaknesses. But they will have a tremendous standard to live up to. A. P. F. Chapman's team did not miss a catch in Australia until the rubber was won. I believe that D. R. Jardine's missed only one. In two series Ames missed only one chance behind the wicket. Here, in his Kentish successor, Evans, I think we are still well provided.

It is generally agreed, I think, that the selectors were a little hasty in announcing 12 names in the first batch. My personal opinion is that there are two specially lucky choices, perhaps three. But no side has ever left these shores approved by one and all. It is enough to say that the team as a whole will carry the confidence of English followers, from the captain down to the youngest member.

A BALANCE OF HOPES

A fifty-fifty chance in the rubber? Not, retrospectively, a very clever prognosis. I was not to know that England would be drowned by the weather at Brisbane, or that Australia's young unknowns, under Bradman's leadership, would transform so swiftly and formidably. Daily Telegraph, 28 November 1946.

BRISBANE, Wednesday

The first Anglo-Australian Test match since Hutton made his fame at the Oval eight years ago begins here on Friday in an atmosphere of the greatest excitement. Everyone is busy picking his own England team. Indeed, the official selectors are in session as these words are being written.

This committee of three – Hammond, Yardley and Edrich – has been augmented to-night, as has happened on previous occasions during the tour, by the co-option of Hutton and Washbrook.

What are England's chances? Or what are the prospects of either side winning outright?

Well, hopes have been expressed here more than once that the Brisbane pitch would at some stage or other of the match help the wretched bowler.

It can be taken for granted that the Test wicket will be every bit as good as this last one, if not better, so that all the bowlers can hope for is rain at the appropriate time. At present the barometer is set fair, but it will apparently be unusual if the next week passes without a storm.

The importance of the toss thus needs no elaboration. In the absence of rain it will be a perfect batting wicket, calculated to have tested the giants of the past.

I wish I could be truthfully optimistic of our chances of winning a match – if such a one has ever been played – in which the luck breaks even. But to say we have a fifty-fifty chance is to take inadequate account of the advantage that Australia seems to enjoy in the important respect of getting the enemy out.

Their bowling, if it may not compare with that which Warwick Armstrong had at his disposal after the last war, looks to have a thrust and also a balance more dangerous than our own. In the field the Australians have greater speed and throwing power and fewer men to tuck away into corners while linking bowlers and fielders, and a wicket-keeper of the highest class in Tallon.

Lindwall is perhaps the man one fears most, at any rate when the pitch shows an atom of response, which may or may not be at Brisbane. Tribe also is a potential danger if he can drop that left-arm googly.

The Australian side, like our own, is largely unfledged in affairs of this nature, and the first blow will be proportionately more valuable than with some hard-bitten teams of the past.

The MCC touring party stands at present very much at the crossroads. There is a deal of natural ability contained in it with the respective genius of Hammond, Compton and Hutton in the van.

The MCC have not had a particularly lucky break so far. If things go well this next week they can certainly win this match and so ensure what we all fervently hope for, a rubber that goes the full distance – that is until the fifth Test at Sydney in March.

COMPTON, EDRICH – AND MELVILLE

Much rich batting against limited attacks. Alan Melville
was out next day for 117, England winning the first of their
three victories. Daily Telegraph, *24 June 1947.*

LORD'S, Monday

Once again South Africa, thanks to her captain, has emerged from the day's play in the Test match with an equal share of the honours and upon the third morning's play probably rests the issue of whether England can win victory or must be happy with a draw.

Compton and Edrich inscribed their names deep in cricket history in the early part of the day only to be answered in the evening by Melville, who needs four runs more to complete four hundreds in a row in Tests against England.

This would appeal to most as an obvious if not an unapproachable record, but that admirable batsman and critic, J. H. Fingleton, made four successive Test hundreds against South Africa and England in the middle thirties.

However, a wonderful performance Melville's certainly was and is, and his duel with Wright as soon as that bowler, around whom controversy is never silent, took the ball about four o'clock, lifted the cricket to a higher plane than anything I have seen since Compton's innings against Amarnath and Mankad on a bad wicket at Manchester last July.

Indeed, one makes bold to say with due respect to Nourse, who is also still there, that if Melville had got out at any time before six o'clock the South Africans would have been hard put to save four of their wickets till the morning, so dangerously did Wright bowl to a close attacking field.

England's innings was monopolised by Compton and Edrich as no two men have monopolised the crease since those partnerships of almost wearisome perfection – to English eyes – between Bradman and Ponsford.

The 370 these Middlesex players added in 5½ hours has been exceeded only once, when Yorkshire, in the persons of Hutton and Leyland, made 382 together at the Oval nine years ago.

Again the South Africans kept them at full stretch so that only 55 came in the first hour, though four 4's from successive balls by Edrich at Smith's expense stepped up the second hour's total to 76. The batsmanship was enterprising, polished, expressing eloquently the cricket character of each.

One flaw there was only, the running between wickets, which was an almost perfect example of how not to do it. Generally the wrong man called and when the right man did he was as often as not sent back.

When Edrich left at last Barnett transformed the whole tempo by running properly and inducing Compton to do the same. Compton caught the idea and the 25 minutes in which these two put on 49 was the most delightful phase of the match.

Barnett drove in a way to warm the cockles of the most ardent Victorian in the pavilion. The rest of the innings served only to emphasise the stamina and zeal of Tuckett and the difficulties involved in batsmen hitting accurate bowling before they are set.

Melville and Mitchell dealt with the quicker bowlers set against them with the very minimum of trouble when South Africa went in just after 3.30, so that one has rarely seen the bat hit in the middle with greater consistency.

Mitchell was in his more fluent vein but just when some may have been thinking the early arrival of Compton at the bowling crease was a gloomy augury, he enticed Mitchell forward and Evans made a beautiful stumping during the split second when the toe was raised.

Wright had missed a low, difficult catch and bowl offered by Melville just previously, but he swiftly sent back Viljoen with his very quick one that just hit the leg stump behind the batsman's pads.

Yardley rested Wright directly on Nourse's arrival, which, from the ring, seemed a questionable decision. I feel that in similar circumstances O'Reilly would not have been easily deprived of the ball.

The last stages were notable for much easeful stroke play by Melville, and some excellent overs by Compton, who may yet make for himself a reputation as a bowler that he might easily have had years ago.

England v South Africa, at Lords, 21–25 June 1947. England 554 for 8 dec. (Compton 208, Edrich 189, Washbrook 65, Tuckett 5 for 115) and 26 for 0; South Africa 327 (Melville 117, Nourse 61, Wright 5 for 95) and 252 (Mitchell 80, Nourse 58, Wright 5 for 80). England won by 10 wickets.

A DONNELLY CLASSIC

Daily Telegraph, 18 July 1947.

There were 17,000 at Lord's yesterday for Gentlemen and Players, a fact that is a sufficient answer in itself to any foolish and perverse suggestions that the match has outlived its fame. And the day was made for ever memorable for them by Donnelly, who played one of the classic innings of modern cricket history.

From lunch until the innings ended he batted, scoring 162 out of 240 in 175 minutes, and at the end the members in the pavilion seats all rose to give the innings its final hall-mark. This has not happened at Lord's since Hammond made 240 against Australia nine years ago.

It is remarkable how in so short a time Donnelly has been accepted quite universally by cricketers as comparable to the best left-handers who ever played, that is, of course, to Woolley and Clem Hill.

To-day he showed all the strokes, except, possibly, the leg glide, so that even Ames's ingenuity in setting a field went for very little. His special delight was the ball just barely short of a length on the middle and leg.

Wright was the only bowler to whom Donnelly accorded anything approaching respect. The rest he deposited hither and thither in the most arbitrary way and none more nonchalantly than Walsh, whose left-arm googlies were apt to puzzle everyone else.

Butler was the better of the opening Players' bowlers, and both opening batsmen should have fallen to him, but Willatt was missed at leg slip. Willatt stayed long enough to justify his place in this distinguished company, and would be a better batsman if he could reassemble his stance, which at present precludes his swinging the bat straight to the on-side ball.

Edrich's confidence set the Gentlemen's innings on a profitable course on a good wicket, and 37 of the score of 64 for two at lunch were his.

Afterwards Donnelly pulverised Walsh and the quicker bowlers until Wright settled down to a long and admirably steady bowl, during which no doubt he thinned the ranks of his detractors. Edrich, who seemed the master of everyone else, was anything but confident against him, and justice was served when he was lbw for 79.

The rest of the Gentlemen's innings, apart from Donnelly, contained much rather paltry cricket with a strange disregard for the text-book. But Simpson stayed long enough to show a pleasing similarity to Hardstaff's better method, and Cranston played some good strokes.

The Players batted in a poor light. Bailey bowled fairly quickly but rather short, and Mallett perhaps looked just the more dangerous. Robertson showed many a cultivated stroke, and when he left it was a pity that Ames, coming in to save a younger player, should not have had his proper reward.

> Gentlemen v Players, at Lord's, 16–18 July 1947. Gentlemen 302 (Donnelly 162 not out, Edrich 79) and 209; Players 334 for 8 dec. (Washbrook 101, Fletcher 77) and 3 for 0. Match Drawn.

COMPTON'S GOLDEN SUMMER

Daily Telegraph, September 1947.

At Middlesex v. The Rest the other day, as we sat watching the Champion County indicating so firmly to all cricketers their right to the honour they have won, my neighbour remarked: 'This season will always seem to us, looking back, the most brilliant we have known.'

I did not contradict him, for no doubt we shall instinctively remember the glamorous things: the triumphs of Compton, with W. J. Edrich pursuing him so closely and making a firm niche for himself in the hall of fame; the entirely delightful tour of the South Africans; the hard and exciting fight for the Championship; above all, and over-spreading all, the glorious sunshine in which vastly bigger numbers have watched cricket than ever before.

There are, after a World War, sociological causes for the boom in cricket, as in other games, that are more powerful than the attraction exercised by any one individual; yet undeniably the crowds have been swelled this summer by Denis Compton as by no one since Don Bradman came into his kingdom.

This is Compton's year, just as 1930 belonged to Bradman, 1925 to Jack Hobbs, 1902 to Victor Trumper, and 1895, to the immortal W. G. In each case statistical milestones have needed to be passed, or freakish figures set up, for a universal acceptance of genius.

FINE BOWLING BY LAKER

This was an early portent of greatness to come.
Daily Telegraph, *20 January 1948.*

BRIDGETOWN, Monday

There was an ending of tense interest this evening to the MCC's return match with Barbados, who lost five wickets for 29 runs in a few overs from Laker and Howorth.

At tea Barbados wanted only these 29 to save an innings defeat and had three men out. Twenty minutes later they were in dire danger from which they just struggled clear, thanks to some brave hitting by E. A. V. Williams and an uncharacteristic defensive innings by Walcott, who kept Laker's bowling to himself when his side had shown symptoms of being demoralised.

When Barbados went in 115 behind with three hours to play, Laker again started straight away pitching his offbreaks to a length, and Wardle bowled much better than in the first innings and was unlucky not to have had Taylor stumped.

The MCC maintained their skill in the field, the Barbados batsmen showing marked reluctance to run until the ball was through the inside ring.

There were three explanations of the purple patch after tea. At Laker's end the pitch showed a tendency to crumble, and the suddenness of the crisis found the Barbados batsmen temporarily unbalanced.

But the primary cause was some very fine bowling by Laker. Not often has a young cricketer made a happier introduction to the best class, and for the heartening prelude to the Test he has been chiefly to thank.

Barbados v. MCC, at Bridgetown, 15–19 January 1948. Barbados 243 for 6 dec. (Carew 81, Lucas 56) and 182 for 8 (Laker 5 for 76); MCC 358 (Brookes 108, Hardstaff 105). Match Drawn.

This was one of the better performances by the weak MCC side which toured the West Indies under G. O. Allen in 1947–8.

AUSSIES AHOY!

*After ten years expectation was at its height. The Don had so matured meantime that his speech at the Cricket Writers' dinner, which caused the BBC to delay the nine o'clock News, touched every cord of kinship. This was Prince Philip's introduction to a major cricket occasion, and an early masterpiece by the prince of after-dinner speakers, Mr Justice, later Lord, Birkett.*Daily Telegraph, 23 April 1948.

Nothing shakes this country in the sporting sense like the visit of an Australian team and to-day, before they have played a single match, there can hardly be a hermit in the Shetland Islands who does not know that Don Bradman and his players are among us again.

The prospect of seeing Bradman bat once more is one which has been lightening the days for many thousand folk since it was first evident, some months ago, that he would pay his fourth visit to England. The prospect is the more intriguing since, a few years ago, it must have seemed so fantastic a thought that he would again lead an Australian eleven on to that gracious field which lies beneath the Cathedral tower of Worcester.

*

It will be found, I think, at any rate if no young fast bowler steps out of obscurity into the headlines, that the greatest of all modern batsmen is almost, if not quite, as effective as in the days of his youth.

Perhaps he is just a shade less nimble (though there is precious little falling off in that respect), but still he exemplifies beyond compare so many of the virtues of batsmanship and, not least, that quality of concentration which he himself places as the most important of all. There is surely no one in whom the instinct of self-preservation is so strong!

Australia's captain is so easy and interesting a subject for the writer that one needs to guard strongly against letting one's pen run too far, for he has brought with him a band of cricketers each of whom deserves close attention. There will be plenty of opportunity to do them all justice, however, from the time the Worcestershire match begins next Wednesday.

For the moment one notes especially the presence of Keith Miller, undoubtedly an even finer cricketer now than when he was giving so much pleasure to English spectators in the Victory Matches three years ago; a great deal of sound batsmanship as represented by such men as Hassett, Barnes, Morris and Brown; and a wonderfully 'complete' attack, of which the main strength is likely to be the opening overs of Lindwall and Miller.

It is the one real regret, so far as English cricket is concerned, that we apparently have no authentic fast bowler to match against these two. Would that some Nottingham coalpit, or a country place where the larders are relatively well-filled, would produce a Larwood, a Kenneth Farnes or a G. O. Allen!

The Australians will find, of course, that our cricket stock, is still impoverished by the war, and indeed the fear I have for this tour is that so few of the counties may prove able to give them a reasonable game of cricket.

I was surprised to see, in the interesting correspondence of the *Daily Telegraph* at the end of last season, that so many of the writers seemed quite oblivious of the drop in our standard of play. I fancy the Australian tour may bring the extent of this rather cruelly home.

It is inevitable, and I firmly believe it need only be temporary; but it seems equally evident that nothing less than a co-ordinated effort to provide more and more true matting or concrete wickets on fields where money and conditions do not admit of good turf ones, allied with some centralised scheme of coaching, can make good the old standard.

We must face and offset the fact that the number of amateurs with the luck to have been brought up in a cricket atmosphere, and with the leisure to play, is declining all the time.

It is one thing to submit this critical judgment of English first-class cricket, and quite another to proceed, as so many are doing, to a deduction that England has little chance in the Test matches.

This does not seem to me in the least to follow, for there happens to be, integral to the England eleven, a nucleus of very gifted players who have already proved themselves in the fire of Test cricket.

Denis Compton, of course, comes first to mind, and this for him must be the season in which to prove the claim of his admirers that he is the best English batsman since Hobbs. Wright, Hutton, W. J. Edrich, Washbrook, N. W. D. Yardley, Bedser, Evans, all these are fine cricketers who, in an expressive phase, 'have what it takes'.

Perhaps the most sanguine follower would hardly expect England to win a Test series fought without rain. But in an English season it does rain and if it should do so at the right time, as it did last year in the Tests against South Africa at Leeds and Old Trafford, I hardly think we should need any incidental luck to show ourselves the better-equipped side.

AUSTRALIA TRIUMPHANT

The Field, *21 August 1948.*

When the wireless commentators were each saying their valedictory pieces after the stumps had been pulled up at the end of the Fifth Test Match, Mr. Arthur Gilligan observed that we had lost not only the Ashes but our sackcloth as well. That, perhaps, was a fair way of expressing the utterness and completeness of Australia's victory in the series. No team before has won four Tests in an English summer, and if that in itself is not extraordinarily significant because this is the first time they have stretched over five days, the figures are conclusive indeed.

How good are they? Better than Warwick Armstrong's side of '21, or Joe Darling's of 1902? The inevitable question can demand only one answer. A game that is perpetually in development and change no more allows comparisons of this sort to be made than does a study of warfare the relative merits of armies. This time, too, there is the important and conclusive factor that we can hardly know the Australians' strength because they have not been properly tested. 1902 was a vintage year for England, as well as Australia; even in 1921 our team had been pulled together fairly successfully by Lord Tennyson by the time of the last Test. This year, the first day at the Oval was the sorriest of all, with the fight virtually all over when England's last wicket rattled down for 52.

Taken by itself the performance that followed, of bowling out Australia for 389 on a pitch which never gave the bowlers very much, was a perfectly good one. But the heart was really out of the match, and though Hutton and Edrich and Compton, especially Hutton, batted thoroughly well in the second innings we never seemed likely to have the pleasure of watching Bradman bat again in a Test.

The Australian heroes were Lindwall and Johnston in the bowling, and Morris, once more, in the batting. Lindwall has, from first to last, been the main danger, and it was on the last day but one of the series that he brought his total of wickets level with the twenty-seven which McDonald took against England in '21. Three English wickets remained on the fourth morning, and Lindwall thus might have gone one better than Grimmett's twenty-nine in '30. But it was Johnston who, by taking all three, brought his own number equal with Lindwall, a fact which, in the general wind-up, escaped much notice.

I mention it because Johnston himself has rather been obscured by the more spectacular efforts of Lindwall and, when he has bowled, of Miller. Johnston, as the stock bowler, equally happy bowling fast-medium over the wicket, or medium-pace round it, swinging the new ball or cutting the old one across from leg, and always keeping it straight and well up, has been the success and surprise of the tour. Outside these three, Toshack and Johnson have had a good deal of bowling to do, mostly in a more or less defensive rôle, and have illustrated the virtues of control of length and direction that one looks for in all Australian bowlers, without often threatening great danger.

Incidentally, what Australian bowler has not been notably accurate above all things? I can recall only Arthur Mailey, that erratic genius, and the left-arm googly bowler, Fleetwood-Smith, whose style of attack has never been adopted economically by anyone since it was first practised by G. C. B. Llewellyn, of Hampshire and Natal.

The fielding in support of this formidable band was scarcely ever anything but adequate, and often it was extremely brilliant. Tallon, behind the wicket, generally was magnificent, and some of his catches, such as the one from a full-pitch off the inside edge, standing up to Toshack, which sent back Washbrook at Lord's, and the low one, diving left-handed at Hutton's snick off Lindwall at the Oval, will be pictured in many memories. There was no great first slip, of the quality of Gregory or Chipperfield, but Miller at second slip or gully, in this respect if no other, was showing his genius all the time.

On the subject of Miller it would need much space to sift out the reasons for his not bulking larger in this series, but perhaps the main point is that he seems to need the spur of danger and responsibility. His influence was greater than his figure would suggest, but, however you look at it, his batting was the one Australian disappointment. Other fielders who must be mentioned are Harvey, probably the finest of long fielders, Loxton, Lindwall and, of course, Barnes close up on the leg-side.

The Australian batting was only slightly less devastating than in some recent years by the measure of Bradman's more modest achievements.

Morris, Barnes, Bradman, Hassett, Miller, Harvey, Loxton was an order which, against contemporary English bowling, could hardly go wrong, and the proof of its strength is that Brown, averaging sixty and playing almost as well as ever, could be safely excluded. Add to all this virtue the calculated skill of Bradman's captaincy, and the result is a most formidable side – formidable, and singularly attractive.

CAPTAINCY CANDIDATES

Norman Yardley declared himself unavailable for South Africa, as George Mann for Australia was to do two years later. Meanwhile Freddie Brown had come into the picture. The exclusion of D. R. Jardine may be noted. The Field, 1948.

I suppose that the matter of the England captaincy commands more interest among cricketers and followers than almost any other, for there is to be considered the problem of the future as to whether the modern practice of confining the responsibility to amateurs can be maintained. There are certainly few candidates with good qualifications for the England captaincy just at the moment.

At the beginning of the season it was hoped that F. R. Brown could be considered, and his intention was to play regularly enough to keep in form and practice, but a series of accidents ruled him out, and so what he would have made of the chance, if it had been given him, we shall never know. R. W. V. Robins was the only other feasible alternative to N. W. D. Yardley, when the series against Australia started. His reluctance on the score of age was well known as also was the wide degree of support for him among those who recognised that he had no rival, from the point of view of either tactics or experience.

It is now just a matter of abstract interest what course the Test series might have taken if Yardley had been bowled for nought in the Middlesex–Yorkshire match at the beginning of June. If he had been, Robins would certainly have led England in the match following, against Australia at Nottingham. I believe Yardley considers the ball hit his wicket: at any rate it did not miss by more than a coat of varnish – and he went on to make 90. Such is the luck of cricket, with the momentous consequences it so often involves!

Whatever happens at the Oval, we are to have a new captain in

South Africa, and it is good to know that F. G. Mann has accepted the position. An even more exacting set of qualities is needed by an MCC captain abroad than an England captain at home, and I confess it is difficult to see who else, of the right age, would fill the place satisfactorily, if Mann had not been able to. It would certainly have been necessary to retrogress, to the extent of choosing someone in the region of forty and, though the immediate object could perhaps have been served well enough, nothing would have been done towards finding a captain for Australia in two winters' time.

One cannot be sure, of course, that Mann would either be quite a good enough batsman, or quite a shrewd enough captain for the Australian tour, but at least the winter in South Africa will give him the chance of making up what is necessary in both departments. It can only be a help to him that F. T. Mann, his father, was one of the most popular and excellent of all MCC touring captains, in South Africa twenty-six years ago.

Looking back across the gulf that separates the cricket of to-day from that the 'twenties and 'thirties one cannot help sighing for an A. P. F. Chapman, whose cheerful and infectious enthusiasm was coupled with such outstanding natural gifts as a cricketer. I suppose that a reckoning of the best English captains of the period between the wars would include P. F. Warner, P. G. H. Fender, R. W. V. Robins, and A. B. Sellers, all excellent leaders of counties – though 'Plum' Warner, of course, was a great touring captain as well. But as a Test captain, Chapman at his best was, perhaps, second to none.

An England captain must essentially have the breadth and buoyancy of a leader, and if the ranks of the professionals could supply such a man, any lurking prejudice would soon be disarmed by performance.

ZEST IN THE FIELD

Daily Telegraph, 22 *January 1949.*

DURBAN

Denis Compton was walking back to the pavilion at Cape Town the other day having been bowled out for 1. A cheerfully precocious small boy rushed out on to the field with the inevitable autograph book, choosing, I suppose, the most inauspicious of all possible moments for his request. The English champion ruffled the boy's hair in the friendliest manner and promised to sign after the day's play.

This, no doubt, is a remarkably trivial incident with which to introduce a short survey of the MCC's tour of South Africa, but it symbolises, I think, that aspect of it with which people at home cannot be so familiar as they are with happenings in the middle.

What is the object of these tours abroad? It can be covered surely in the phrase: 'To play good cricket and to make and renew friendships.' The more cynically minded might be disposed to add 'to make money,' but that would be inaccurate so far as the MCC are concerned, for they have never taken a penny from a tour in any Dominion or Colony except Australia.

In the last few weeks I have seen enough of F. G. Mann's team to gauge pretty well just how generally successful is this latest campaign of the MCC. That it is a trebly welcome thing in view of the West Indies tour last winter and the tour of Australia immediately before that needs little emphasis.

Probably the most important combined factor in the success of these intricate enterprises is the work of the captain and the manager. The one is the complement of the other, and if the partnership fits happily many of those troubles which can occur so easily and are often provoked so unknowingly just do not happen.

Every follower of cricket of reasonable insight will have credited George Mann with considerable powers of leadership. They are, of course, quite right, and they should know, too, that Brig. M. A. Green is playing his own rather less colourful rôle with equal sureness of touch.

Before the first ball was bowled captain and manager set down some pretty stern and quelling restrictions on social affairs during matches, and especially during Tests. In the spirit, if not perhaps exactly to the letter, these have been honoured right through, and their reflection can be seen well enough in the cricket.

VISIT TO WALES

The Field, 21 May 1949.

There are seventeen counties in the championship, but only one at a time are the champions, and it seemed right and fitting, therefore, that one of one's first pilgrimages of the summer should be to Glamorgan to see the team which Wilfred Wooller led to victory last summer play in front of their own folk.

Last Saturday was a memorable day for those who came down to Swansea from the valleys to watch Glamorgan play their first county match as champions on the St. Helen's Field. They will recall it for the excellent score their team put up – 388 for five it was when Wooller declared against Warwickshire at half-past six. And they will be reminded of it, especially those from his own Llanelly, by Emrys Davies' grand score of 158: some no doubt, after a few years, will be confusing this innings of Emrys with another, as big to within a few runs, that he played against Nottinghamshire on the same ground in the summer before the war. That, incidentally, is engraved on my own mind, because then, as now, I happened to be broadcasting, and had the always pleasant feeling of bringing good news to so many.

The Welsh feel deeply for their heroes; for their cricketers now, it seems, almost as intensely as for their footballers. In regard to that, a friend was describing the deep fervour of the crowd at Cardiff on that day, at the end of last season, when Glamorgan rattled out Surrey and so put themselves strongly in line for the championship. They did not take their pleasures silently; apparently one could have imagined oneself at Cardiff Arms Park next door, with Wales narrowly leading and time drawing near.

Alas! that I did not see this vanquishing of Surrey. (But I did see the most dramatic of all finishes, when Wales beat the All Blacks of 1935, and that memory, in which, incidentally, the present Glamorgan cricket captain was the central figure, will live for ever.) Watching a great sporting event in Wales is an unforgettable experience, and as for the chivalry of the spectators, it was one of that beaten Surrey team who afterwards described the Cardiff crowd as the best in the country, the most appreciative and the most fair-minded.

SOUTH AFRICA BY FLYING BOAT

The Field, *21 January 1950.*

From the dark mists of Twickenham to the dry, exhilarating heat of Johannesburg; it has been my happy chance for a second year to leave England and Rugby football for a few brief weeks of cricket in South Africa, this time, too, by the novel and utterly fascinating means of the flying-boat. Southampton – Augusta – Alexandria – Luxor – Khartoum – Kampala – Cape Maclear on Lake Nyasa; those were our ports of call, and one finally touched water at the B.O.A.C. base on the Vaaldam above Johannesburg with what the guide-books call a kaleidoscope of impressions, of the treasures of ancient civilisations and of new ones, of Sicilian olive-groves, the great temples of Thebes under the moon, the Nile threading endlessly through sand and forest and, at last, the engineering triumph of the dam on the Vaal river which was the journey's end.

As these notes are being read, another Test series will be beginning, one which can be followed in England without the agonised hopes and fears, which are inseparable from the doings of an MCC side abroad. All the indications are, of course, that the South Africans will find the Australians rather too strong for them, and it needs a lot of faith, or perhaps powers of self-delusion for anyone out here to suppose that Australia's colours will be lowered. As a matter of fact, it is the disinclination on the part of South Africans to consider their side as being in the same class as Australia and England which is one of the bars against their success. There is plenty of ability within the Union which needs only some inspiration to reach a full blossoming in Test Matches. With the utmost respect to A. D. Nourse, what is wanted is a Sherwell or a Deane to make the side believe in itself.

PRESIDENT PLUM

The Field, 8 May 1950.

Since my last notes were written Sir Pelham Warner has become President of MCC, and Mr. H. S. Altham has been appointed Treasurer. In these days of change and of inherent difficulties the two most distinguished and important positions in the Club carry a particularly heavy responsibility, and it may be as well to turn attention to their new occupants. For if I can perhaps add little that is new to their own contemporaries it is easy to fall into the erroneous supposition that what are household names to one generation may be very much more than dim legendary figures to the next.

The MCC system whereby the President is alone responsible for the nomination of his successor is one which some have recently considered might be changed. There may well be those who feel that the matter is one in which it is preferable for the view of the majority of the Committee to be discovered. Yet even if they might not be disposed to agree with what I fancy is the opinion of the majority, and retain the present custom on the good practical ground that 'it works,' few indeed would cavil at the Duke of Edinburgh's choice this year. More probably among the members of MCC would be found those who based an objection to the arrangement on the fact that one who has given such long and faithful service to cricket in so many spheres has had to wait so long for his acknowledgment.

Sir Pelham Warner must be gratefully remembered by cricketers in all of three different capacities for a succession of achievements which are sufficiently notable when considered separately. He was a very fine player and, by all credible witness a great captain; he has had a career of vast utility as an administrator, legislator and selector; and he has enriched the literature of the game with many worthy books and a period of notable daily journalistic work. It will be the work of some future biographer to set all these activities in their due perspective, for his labours are still proceeding, and the year of his Presidency, the 77th of his age, is only beginning.

There is, I suppose, no doubt as to what was the turning point of his cricket career; no doubt either of his able and successful grasp of the opportunity. In 1903 P. F. Warner, the Middlesex captain, was apparently a pretty good and clearly improving county batsman. He had had a blue in his third year at Oxford in '95, and gone in first at Lord's that year and the next without achieving anything particularly notable. And he had played, I think, once at Lord's for the Gentlemen in that vintage time when the names of Jackson, Fry, Ranjitsinhji and MacLaren were automatically to be found high in the batting order. For Middlesex he was certainly a growing force as a batsman, particularly at Lord's, and especially on awkward wickets. Both at Rugby and at Oxford he had been slight and far from strong, and one assumes that physically he 'developed late.'

In that summer MCC undertook for the first time to sponsor a tour to Australia. Hitherto, of course, these had been theoretically private enterprises, unofficially arranged; and it no doubt weighed in the decision that the last two sides, captained by Stoddart and Maclaren, had been heavily defeated and, in fact, despite all the riches of English cricket at that time, that the last four rubbers, two home and two away, had been lost. It must have needed much courage to choose the young man of 29 in face of cricketers so much senior, and of so much greater repute. It is a wistful thought at this moment that England under Warner were able to win the 1903/4 Tests in Australia without the services of any of the four great amateurs whose names I have mentioned. And, incidentally, the fact of MCC sending so young a side on their first expedition and being so handsomely justified in the result, is not without its implications at this time when the context of events has so many parallels with forty-seven years ago.

Warner went again, of course, to Australia in 1911–12, and although taken severely ill and unable to play in any of the Test Matches, his leadership in the broader sense was not the least factor in the Ashes being rescued and brought home again. Since then he has had one supreme moment on an English cricket field, when Middlesex in his last season of captaincy, and by dint of winning the last match at Lord's against Surrey, won the Championship. The administrative work and the writing overlapped the latter part of his playing time, and have gone on in full flood until now. All in all, as was recently written of him, 'it may well be argued that he has exerted a wider influence on the game than anyone since the Champion himself.'

A STAR IS BORN

David Sheppard, Bishop of Liverpool, was one of a quintet of contemporary Cambridge and England batsmen, Peter May, Hubert Doggart, John Dewes and Doug Insole being the others, who blossomed on the Fenner's pitches. My first view of him, in 1950, had just preceded the astonishing match wherein the University had declared at 507 for 4, to which West Indies replied with 730 for 3. The Field, May 1950.

L et us take the new boys first, giving D. S. Sheppard, of Sherborne, pride of place in token of his 227 against the West Indies. He is largely built, especially long in the arms and legs, and, in his batting, he develops all the advantages of an unusual reach. Against Lancashire, when the University were anxious to hurry the game along, he scored 76 in something just under two hours against very steady .bowling without giving any reckless signs of hustle. As one might expect, he leans on the ball easefully in the off-side strokes, and persuades it away powerfully in all the segment between point and the bowler. He has an aggressive back stroke with which he plays the ball square-ish, and there were the indications that he could cut, though mostly the ball kept too low. Against the slower bowlers he was always looking for the chance to go down the wicket, and when he did he was usually admirably balanced for the stroke in mind. A wise old professor (of cricket) said: 'He looks a bit "clodhopperish," yet when he goes out he seems to get there so easy.' And he went on, of course, to conclude that the young man must get an enviably early sight of the ball. I will not fall to the temptation of making prophecies, but only recall that in rather less than six playing weeks, beginning in the middle of last August and ending at the moment of writing, he has collected over a thousand runs with an average away up round the eighties.

CLIFF-HANGER AT BRAMALL LANE

M ay 1950. Lancashire beat Yorkshire here this afternoon at Bramall Lane, Sheffield, by 14 runs after a day of agonizing excitement which, many a year from now, will set tingling the blood of all those

– and there were some 16,000 of us – who were lucky enough to have been present.

After the Yorkshire innings this afternoon had gone through many palpitating changes of fortune Wardle, at No. 9, came in to join his captain, Yardley, with only 125 on the board of the 182 needed, and, with respect to Brennan, no substantial batting to follow. The wicket was spasmodically spiteful still, though scarcely the venomous, treacherous thing on which Lancashire had been bowled out for 117 in the morning.

The odds seemed long, but Yardley was playing most admirably, and whatever impious critics may say of certain technical limitations on faster wickets, he is, as he has always been, an excellent batsman when the turf is taking the spin. No one who saw his partnership with Hammond on that evil day at Brisbane in the First Test of 1946 could doubt that.

The mood of the whole day's cricket had been to 'get at him before he gets at you'. Only Hutton, with his superb method, had been above and beyond the necessity of chancing his arm. Wardle was the last man to close up at such a moment, and in hardly more than a quarter of an hour 27 more came for the eighth wicket, mostly runs truly made against bowling that remained steady and fielding that took inspiration from the occasion. This was a moment, almost the only one in the match, when Yorkshire seemed really on top. And then when another four or two would have counted beyond price, Wardle drove Berry hard off the meat of the bat straight back. Berry clung safely to the ball, and in that there was poetic justice since the game from its beginning had developed largely into a duel between these two left-arm bowlers and the Lancastrian had proved a clear and worthy winner.

With 30 needed Brennan took Wardle's place and began with a fine snick for four past the wicket-keeper to a roar that must have been heard far away in the heart of the city. Yardley now monopolized the situation, drawing everything off his stumps with an easy dexterity that made it all look almost safe. His 50 arrived to a crescendo of cheering, and then Brennan swung at an off-break and Wharton held a good, hard hit chest-high at short mid-wicket.

Now it was simply Yardley or no one. He declined single runs from each of the first three balls of Berry's next over, tried for the last time to flick the fourth off his wicket round the corner and so get the next over, and the ball, lifting, lobbed gently in the air to within reach of any of three men round the bat.

Thus it ended and Lancashire had beaten their ancient enemies for the first time since on this same ground Iddon's fine bowling had won the day 13 years before. Since the Second World War all the eight matches before this had been drawn, but in the late 1930s Yorkshire had usually won with conclusive emphasis, and in recent times Lancashire has a long leeway to make up.

This has not been a happy match for young Close, but he had his brief moments of glory, pulling his first ball, from outside the off stump, for a thrilling six to square-leg, sending Berry whistling over extra cover to the boundary, and giving his captain cause to hope that the improbable might after all be brought to pass. The manner of his end was a tragedy for Yorkshire. Yardley declined a youthfully optimistic call for a second run. Close turned and could no doubt have made his ground, but slipped up badly (was he properly studded?) and a quick pick up by Berry, followed by the slickest of returns, ran him out.

In a match of this kind there are always many 'might-have-beens', and it seems hard after such a struggle that either side should have to lose, but tolerably composed afterthoughts emphasize that justice was certainly done in the result.

On Saturday Yardley gave Lancashire a more vicious wicket to bat on than Yorkshire themselves found yesterday; and when he declared after three overs this morning 64 behind with two wickets left including his own, he obliged them to bat on the unpleasantest one of all.

I wrote last evening that a further judicious fall of rain might make for a battle, and so indeed it proved. Lancashire had a desperately sticky time of it this morning, and how few they might have been skittled for but for Grieves no one can say. The first three wickets had gone for 35 when he came to the crease, and he made 52 out of the next 76 in well under the hour. As with Yardley, it was a case of a fine eye and quickness of judgment overcoming the attack against all the odds. As ever, when an Australian is assaulted, he hits back good and hard.

Wardle at any rate, though still inclined to drop short on the leg stump, bowled a fuller length than in the first innings, yet Grieves found a variety of strokes with which to belabour him and to put heart into a succession of young partners at the other end.

Grieves batted grandly, and it was not the least thing about this happy day for Lancashire that nearly everyone in the team contributed something notable to the success. For this critical enthusiast it was the best day, and the most exciting finish, since England won off the last ball at Durban 18 months ago.

> Yorkshire v Lancashire, at Sheffield, 27–30 May 1950. Lancashire 257 (Wharton 93, Edrich 70) and 117 (Grieves 52, Wardle 6 for 44); Yorkshire 193 for 8 dec. and 167 (Yardley 51, Tattersall 5 for 60). Lancashire won by 14 runs.

WEST INDIES MAKE HISTORY

This tour of 1950 established West Indies in the front rank of Test countries. This match followed their wholesale victory at Lord's, and was in turn followed by one of equal emphasis at the Oval. In making 283 together for the fourth wicket Worrell and Weekes showed batting of the highest class. Daily Telegraph, *25 July 1950.*

TRENT BRIDGE, Tuesday

West Indies won the Third Test by 10 wickets here at 4 o'clock this afternoon, the game having veered towards them without a check since the moment when the sixth-wicket stand of 58 between Evans and Dewes was ended at half-past twelve.

That first hour had seen a lively prolongation of the long defensive action begun by England's batsmen just before lunch on Saturday. Evans played yet another audaciously skilful innings for England, his third incidentally in successive Tests at Trent Bridge.

As long as he was there the fight was very much alive, although the wicket was taking rather more spin than it had done previously. But soon after Dewes was lbw Stollmeyer caught Evans brilliantly just behind square-leg, right-handed high above his head and leaping to his right and the vain hopes of setting West Indies a score that needed thinking about disappeared.

The victors, of course, were full value for this second success in a Test which makes them dormy in the rubber of four. As at Lord's, their better batsmanship touched a class that left the England players groping well behind; and once more Ramadhin and Valentine stuck to their work and bowled with unwearied persistence and ever-growing appreciation of their craft.

This is an astonishing partnership to have sprung suddenly from obscurity into fame from the rough playing fields of Trinidad and Jamaica. They were chosen, these two, with no figures to support them by good judges of cricket bold enough to back their opinions – a pertinent and encouraging reflection, it may well be considered, on the eve of the selection of MCC's team for Australia.

During the long innings Valentine bowled 92 overs, the greatest number sent down by any player during one innings of a Test match. Ramadhin bowled 81. The previous highest were by the Australians W. J. O'Reilly and L. O'B. Fleetwood-Smith against England in the Fifth Test at The Oval in 1938. Fleetwood-Smith bowled 87 overs and O'Reilly 85, when England made a record Test score of 903 for seven declared.

Although Valentine has established this record, his total number of balls bowled, 552, falls well short of the 648 delivered in 81 eight-ball overs by George Geary, Leicestershire, for England against Australia in the Fifth Test at Melbourne in 1929.

Evans's play to-day was a tonic and his duel with the spinners must have compensated those who risked the journey. He hit the ball as crisply as ever off the back foot and made a lot of runs with the sweep before it was his downfall. He got a few off the edges in various directions, including four for a missed catch between first and second slip off Valentine, and the unintended strokes added to the general air of excitement and hope.

Dewes's part was to resist more quietly. He batted with more poise than yesterday and did particularly well to circumvent the efforts of Valentine bowling over the wicket and using the turf worn by the bowler's follow-through to turn the ball into him from the off. He snicked once to Walcott – who missed the chance – and seemed to have an accurate and profitable knowledge of where his legs were in relation to the stumps.

I suspect that Goddard was almost in the act of taking the new ball that had been due some time and thus surrendering a tactical point when Dewes suddenly shocked everyone by hooking across a shortish ball that did not deserve the name of long hop and which, but for his legs, would probably have hit about the middle and off.

This was a sad disappointment and Shackleton's return soon afterwards further put the lid on things. He was caught at slip from a ball that straightened, whereupon Jenkins obstructed while Evans continued to try to keep the opposition at bay by counter-attack.

When he fell to Stollmeyer's catch the last two wickets subsided quickly, and West Indies had all the afternoon to make the 102 they needed.

England v West Indies, at Trent Bridge, 20–25 July 1950. England 223 and 436 (Washbrook 102, Simpson 94, Parkhouse 69, Dewes 67, Evans 63, Ramadhin 5 for 135); West Indies 558 (Worrell 261, Weekes 129, Rae 68, Bedser 5 for 127) and 103 for 0 (Stollmeyer 52 not out). West Indies won by 10 wickets.

AMES'S MILESTONE

Four great counties, two spirited finishes and I on the air for both. Alas! that cricket at Bramall Lane surrendered to the football. I always enjoyed broadcasting there at a table in the groundsman's preserve within sound of the members. Hearing the lunch score, the Sheffield faithful doubled the gate, much to the surprise and pleasure of John Nash, the Yorkshire secretary. Les Ames's hundred proved his last for Kent. At Gravesend in May, 1951 his back seized up and he could play no more. Kent had decided to offer him the captaincy for 1952. Daily Telegraph, August 1950.

The story here is of a match well won and gallantly lost on the St Lawrence ground at Canterbury and of a notable feat by a great English cricketer.

Kent, after they had been set by Middlesex to score 237 in two hours and a half, reached their target with three effective wickets and seven minutes to spare and Ames, whose innings was the inspiration of the whole effort, became the 12th batsman in the game's history to score 100 hundreds. It was Clark's declaration as soon as the Middlesex score was passed on Thursday afternoon that invigorated the game to the degree of ensuring a combative last day. Edrich, who has led his side with a sure and easy touch in this match, was not the man to decline a challenge. Yesterday morning he himself batted in his best vein. To come into the ground soon after eleven o'clock and hear the sound of bat on ball a couple of times was all the assurance one needed on the matter. In 70 minutes Edrich added 54 to his score. With Brown also pushing along well runs came so quickly that Edrich could declare soon after noon, leaving Kent to make their runs at a rate of 95 an hour to win.

Fagg left at once and Clark very quickly, Warr, after much empty grasping at the ball, picking it up eventually and running him out at the bowler's end with a second run uncompleted. Before lunch Ames had to do all the scoring himself and so Kent did not progress at anything like the required speed, Edrich finding it expedient to feed them an over of donkey-drops to increase their ardour. The arrival of Pawson coincided with a spate of fours by Ames, now in punishing form.

It was a delight to see him cracking away in very much the old style. No one seems to play with a better bat than Ames when he is in full cry. His hundred was rapturously greeted, after which he flung away all care and bombarded the president's tent and that of the Band of Brothers, just to the on-side of the sight screen, with a series of the grandest on-drives. Pawson, too, flung his bat at anything and everything, and in the 35 minutes he and Ames were together the score leapt by 85. Mallett helped Pawson when Ames went at last, and so Kent coasted to a victory which had seemed almost a forlorn hope an hour earlier. Thus Ames joins a glorious band.

Since at the age of 21 he played first for Kent in only two matches in 1926, he has reached his milestone after 18 English seasons. In all he has scored 36,371 runs, which gives him an average in the neighbourhood of 44. From his batting yesterday one would imagine, as all Kent will hope, that these figures are due to be considerably augmented before he puts his pads on for the last time.

> Kent v Middlesex, at Canterbury, 9–11 August 1950. Middlesex 249 (Sharp 62, Dewes 60, Wright 5 for 61) and 241 for 3 dec. (Edrich 77 not out, Robertson 54, Brown 51 not out); Kent 254 for 6 dec. (Pawson 103 not out, Fagg 88) and 239 for 6 (Ames 131, Pawson 57). Kent won by 4 wickets.

ELUSIVE VICTORY

On the day following the events related below, at the fifteenth time of asking post-war, came the Elusive Victory which gave me the title for both a book on the tour and the first of a series of cricket films, photographed for the BBC by my assistant, John Woodcock. Daily Telegraph, 28 February 1951.

MELBOURNE, Tuesday

The Fifth Test match rose to a fine pitch of gripping interest on this fourth day, and when the cricket ended England had snatched back every bit of the advantage that had been lost by the inadequate batting of the preceding evening.

On his 31st birthday the honours went first and foremost to Simpson for one of the finest innings played by an English batsman since the war. By means of it, with most commendable assistance from the No. 11, Tattersall, England's lead did after all at least reach three figures, and when Australia batted again with a deficit of 103 Bedser once more filled the bill as a penetrative open bowler.

Four wickets were down before Australia's runs began to count against England's second innings, and although Hassett and Hole have so far added 40 for the fifth wicket, the position remains advantageous to England. The difference now is 26 and the Australian middle and tail have much to do to set England a testing task.

The weather is fine as I write. Let it be hoped that rain does not come now to befriend either side at the end of the fight.

I cannot praise Simpson more highly than to say that no batsman on either side, not even Hutton in his second innings at Brisbane, has looked more thoroughly in command of both himself and of the situation than Simpson to-day. He has hovered on the brink of great things for a long time.

You might say that he has been the victim either of natural caution or of an inborn modesty. At any rate, he will surely not be able to look back on this Melbourne innings in which, first with Hutton and latterly quite alone, he supported the whole English performance over a spell of more than five hours and a half, without recharging himself with whatever degree of confidence the situation may demand.

Simpson took some while to change gear. In the first 50 minutes of the day he went only from 80 to 92 while the wickets of Bedser, Bailey and Wright were being captured.

Bedser was bowled in the third over playing back to a ball not very far short of a half-volley, and though Bailey promised better he immediately began to grope at Iverson, who promptly had him caught at short fine-leg.

Lindwall and Miller were both off by now, which presaged a better chance to Wright, on whose arrival Simpson began to manage the game. But Wright was less convincing than usual batting at the dizzy height of No. 10 and was lbw, not offering a stroke.

Tattersall played out the remainder of Iverson's over in a scarifying way, but soon discovered that his best counter to all types of bowling was a forward defensive prod.

Simpson, in going for the bowling off the last ball of an over, had given an unaccepted slip catch when 89. But the effort of manipulating nearly all the bowling and adding to his score by a stream of free and attractive strokes, did not find him wanting.

First, he reached his 100 by means of that fine persuading hit off his legs which he makes so easily. The Blue Riband gained, with all the elevation that must accompany that supreme moment, he really let himself go.

He was timing so well that he hit several fours early in the over, despite four or five men on the boundary, and he was using such a wide repertoire that he usually found a hole through which to place a single when the field closed in for the last two or three balls. Once, Lindwall, at deep mid-wicket, let a hard, flat hit go through his hands to the boundary off Iverson – a nasty chance.

When lunch arrived the morning's tally had risen to 85, of which Simpson's share was 63. The whole game had been lifted up and England could not be accounted to have less than a sporting chance. Not least important was the moral value of this unexpected last-wicket stand.

It seemed too much to hope that it would be able to re-establish itself after the interval, but Simpson, beginning with a grand square cut for four off Miller, proceeded as before. At last Tattersall's resistance was broken, and broken properly, by a fast ball from Miller that knocked the stumps all ways.

The 10th wicket in five minutes over the hour had made a priceless 74 – as someone observed with some bitterness, it was only one run fewer than had been contributed by the seven preceding wickets, from the third to the ninth inclusive. Simpson had earned, and was given, a great ovation.

Australia went in 103 to the bad, and within 10 minutes Morris and Burke were back. Morris was out, not for the first time on this tour, playing the half-hook, half-sweep peculiar to himself to a ball that pitched on the wicket. It made the seventh time on the tour that Morris has fallen to Bedser.

Bedser was bowling to three short-legs, all perching very close – Compton, Bailey and Sheppard – and his normal movement with the new ball is legward. It was therefore no great blame to Burke when he was well caught at first slip off a ball that pitched somewhere around the middle stump and turned away off the wicket.

I had fears of Harvey as soon as he arrived, but Hassett was not at first comfortable, and from a similar ball to Burke's he gave an easier unaccepted chance to Hutton. Small blame to Hutton, for he is an improvised slip who has made a succession of wonderfully good catches in what is essentially an expert's post. But 25 for three, with Hassett out of the way, would have been an acceptable beginning.

The Victorian third-wicket partnership existed until tea, Hassett playing the goose game and Harvey batting with all the ease and polish that come so naturally to him when he is in his stride.

After tea, when Harvey tried to hit Wright on the leg-side he was beaten by pace off the ground, and the ball keeping low, and was lbw.

Brown had just relieved Bedser at the other end on Miller's arrival, which was palpably a critical moment. Wright bowled him a taxing maiden, whereupon Miller, who always strains until he is off the mark, once more pushed out at Brown strongly but too soon. This time the ball was returned low and wide to his right, and the captain made a first-rate catch. It is marvellous how often Brown has accomplished the needful, prayed for, thing on this tour.

> Australia v England, at Melbourne, 23–28 February 1951. Australia 217 (Hassett 92, Morris 50, Bedser 5 for 46, Brown 5 for 49) and 197 (Hole 63, Harvey 52, Bedser 5 for 59); England 329 (Simpson 156 not out, Hutton 79) and 95 for 2 (Hutton 60 not out). England won by 8 wickets.

PETER MAY'S AUSPICIOUS START

Daily Telegraph, 30 July 1951.

HEADINGLEY, Tuesday

The big happening on this third day of the Fourth Test against South Africa was the arrival of another young batsman, England in quality as well as in name. May, like Lowson, was lucky in having so favourable a setting for his first Test Match, and in the encouraging presence of Hutton at the other end.

But it is one thing to be given the chance and another to seize it. Both these young cricketers batted with a poise and style most refreshing to see, and if they have faults of technique which might become apparent on a less friendly wicket, Saturday's play gave little hint of them.

To May, of course, must go the palm, and when in the evening he reached his hundred with a handsome straight drive to the boundary off Rowan, the crowd stood and applauded with a warm, prolonged intensity which was an acknowledgment of the virtues which Yorkshiremen especially appreciate in a cricketer.

His batting, over nearly five hours of a tense and grilling day, had a steadfast calmness and concentration of purpose remarkable in a young man of 21. He not only gave no chance, but his false strokes can be recalled on the fingers of one hand.

If the opportunities came he made a swift succession of telling hits, the best being his drives to all points of the arc between extra cover and mid-wicket. Tall and slim, he is built to hit the ball off the forward foot.

If the bowling pegged him down, as happened for a quarter of an hour with his score at 49, he accepted the fact with cool detachment. The basis of his play was the forward defensive push, with which he safely countered Rowan's off-breaks for over after over. But his range included most of the orthodox strokes except the cut.

May's success brought fresh laurels to Cambridge cricket. The last English batsman to make a hundred in his first Test was a Cambridge Blue, S. C. Griffith, and so was the one before that, P. A. Gibb. And from Cambridge came the only other man ever to score a hundred for England while an undergraduate, F. S. Jackson, who made 103 against Australia at the Oval in 1893.

England v South Africa, at Headingley, 26–30 July 1951. South Africa 538 (Rowan (E. A. B.) 236, Mansell 90, van Ryneveld 83, McLean 67) and 87 for 0 (Rowan (E. A. B.) 60 not out); England 505 (May 138, Hutton 100, Bailey 95, Lowson 58, Rowan (A. M. B.) 5 for 174). Match Drawn.

TRUEMAN TAKES EIGHT

Led by Len Hutton, the first modern professional England captain, this third successive victory clinched the series at Old Trafford. Daily Telegraph, *21 July 1952.*

Engley won the Third Test and the rubber, to be precise, at 20 minutes past five on Saturday, but India's defeat was as certain as anything could be the moment the Manchester weather changed for the worse the night before the match.

The 1902 Test at Old Trafford, which Australia won by three runs, was not only the last Test that England lost on this ground, it was the last Test England lost anywhere on a wicket wet from the first ball to the last. The handicap is too great for visiting sides from sunny countries, whether Indians or South Africans, New Zealanders, West Indians – yes, or Australians.

These thoughts bring one to a consideration of the true merit of England's performance. To what extent was it flattered by unworthy play? Would other Test sides have been likely to do substantially better?

I would say, taking the wicket, the bowling, and the fielding into consideration, that while 347 would nearly always be a winning score, a reputable Test batting side should have been capable of a much longer and more productive resistance in the first innings.

The irresistible pressure of events submerged the Indians so swiftly that they were bowled out a second time in the day, an indignity that has not happened to a Test side since the 'nineties.

That was only one of a fistful of facts and figures that zealous mathematical experts unearthed while the slaughter was going on.

The scope of international conflict at all games is so greatly enlarged that most modern 'records' become entirely irrelevant. The mention of them is agreeable chiefly because it revives memories of the giants of old.

Thus, no England bowler has taken eight wickets in an innings, as Trueman did, since Verity bowled out Australia at Lord's on a sticky-dog. And though everyone remembered how Tom Richardson, heroically unavailing in one of the classic pieces of fast bowling, took all seven Australia wickets that fell in the Old Trafford Test of '96 no one could quote a case of an English fast bowler getting eight.

If it came to the point, nor could anyone remember such suicidal batting in a Test match from accredited batsmen, as that of Umrigar and Phadkar. So bowling comparisons, on the strength of figures, if not odious, are at any rate valueless.

Nevertheless, make whatever reservations you like and Trueman still performed an impressive and highly encouraging feat. He bowled down a strong wind, blowing from about mid-off, and he had the stimulus of the occasional ball that kicked.

It was certainly not a thoroughly spiteful wicket: nothing like that, for instance, on which Hutton and Ikin stood and took a battering from McCarthy this time a year ago. However, it had enough life to raise apprehension and worse in several of the batsmen, and such a state of mind causes only one sort of reaction in the fast bowler.

Trueman bowled faster than at Headingley, when the wind also blew stiffly behind him, and he bowled straighter. Furthermore, thanks to the combination of a native shrewdness and the quiet advice of his captain, he bowled very sensibly.

All comparisons with famous fast bowlers may be discounted at the moment. For all his 24 wickets in this series the real testing is yet to come.

The remaining factor in the day's sensations, and in some respects it was the most satisfying as well as the most spectacular of all, was England's close fielding, which was the best I remember seeing in a Test match.

Not only was every one of 14 chances taken but there were a great many thrilling stops, wide, one-handed by the slips, by gullies, and short-legs that encircled the bat. The ball adhered in the most uncanny way, as though each man was trying to outshine his neighbour.

England v India, at Old Trafford, 17–19 July 1952. England 347 for 9 dec.) Hutton 104, Evans 71, May 69); India 58 (Trueman 8 for 31) and 82 (Bedser 5 for 27). England won by an innings and 207 runs.

RETURN OF THE ASHES

Daily Telegraph, *August 1953.*

The Fifth Test at the Oval, which had seemed to turn so sharply England's way when Australia were battling against the spin bowlers yesterday, duly ended in victory here shortly before three o'clock this afternoon: that elusive victory which has been awaited ever since D. R. Jardine's side won the Ashes 20 years ago.

The margin of eight wickets was conclusive enough, but the result was not gained without a fight to the last ball as between Edrich, May and Compton on the one hand, and Johnston, Lindwall and Miller, supported magnificently as ever in the field, on the other. Johnston bowled today without respite until Hassett came on, as at Melbourne on a similar occasion in 1951, to bowl a final comedy over at his end. Lindwall, likewise, from the pavilion end kept up a ceaseless, fast and accurate attack, apart from five overs from Miller, until he gave the ball finally to Morris off whom Compton hit the last four needed.

It took 2 hours and 40 minutes of resolute batsmanship to make the final 94 runs. May's wicket being the Australians' only reward. All this was as it should be, a hard struggle to the finish, and the final scenes were equally fitting. At the end some 15,000 clamoured in front of the pavilion. Hutton and Hassett obliged with speeches, and the players were cheered on their respective balconies.

It all took one back 27 years to the August evening when for the first time since the First World War Australia's colours were lowered in a Test rubber, and the crowd let themselves go as though a reproach had been wiped away. Then, as now, England's side was a blend of the ages, from the youthful Chapman and Larwood to the grizzled Rhodes, and Strudwick playing, too, in his last match against Australia. It cannot be said that any of Hutton's present team are anywhere near the end of their tethers but certainly several are, or should be, at the beginnings of fine achievements. One thinks of the four in this team who were not born when Hobbs and Sutcliffe were fashioning that former victory on an Oval sticky-dog: Graveney, May, Trueman and Lock. The performance of the latter three over these last few days was rich in promise.

In 1926 it was universally said that the change in the tide would be all for the good of cricket in Australia. They had won three rubbers with consummate ease, and the keen edge of competition was worn blunt. Exactly the same situation exists, so our Australian friends assure us, in their country today. Three rubbers have been won against England, and now, after the warning jolt of the drawn series against Cheetham's admirable young South Africans in the last Australian summer, it is established that the supremacy has passed to other hands. It will prove to be the spur that has been needed in Melbourne, Sydney and Adelaide, and one can almost savour the unholy relish with which the next MCC side will be received at Perth in October next year.

Of the England side Bedser must take the palm, but the honours of the series have not been monopolized by the captain and his foremost bowler. Everyone of today's XI has played a part at one time or another along with several not called upon in this match: Watson, Wardle, Tattersall, Statham, Simpson and, not least, Brown. Bailey's unique contribution will not quickly be forgotten, while in support of all the bowling Evans, apart from a few off-moments at Old Trafford, has been, as usual, quite admirable. On Hutton has been the greatest strain. Anyone who has seen all five Tests, and who has realized how he has upheld the batting and appreciated the difficulties he has encountered in the field, three times with only four bowlers, almost always irked by the presence of a left-handed batsman and with several fieldsmen of limited mobility, will give him a high degree of praise for his efforts.

Edrich and May played with excellent poise and judgment when the last phase of the game began this morning. Australia, of course, desperately needed a quick break-through and though Compton and Graveney were waiting with their pads on, steeled no doubt to put right their contributions of Monday, no Englishman on the ground can have relished the thought of watching them doing so at the start of the day.

The crowd was hushed and still, bursting into a loud and fevered sort of applause whenever there was a specially good stroke. These, it may be added, very frequently produced no runs, for Harvey in the cover country was in the most scintillating order even by his own standards, and Davidson, as usual, was leaping about like a cat. He is not only a magnificent fieldsman close in but is extraordinarily quick on the chase and turn. So, again is Archer, while the older brigade, Hassett, Miller and, despite his long bowl, Lindwall, more than once cut off hits that seemed certain to go through.

Considering how often Lock and Laker were hitting the edge of the bat and passing it yesterday it was extraordinary how few streaky strokes there were this morning. Once May snicked four between the wicket-keeper and first slip off Johnston, who had changed to bowling over the wicket, and next over Edrich from a sharply spinning ball gave a very difficult low fast catch at second slip to Hole. This was the one and only catch missed by Hole in this series, and he has caught seven, including some wonderfully good ones.

May was out just after one o'clock. He had just hit the stroke of the innings, a thrilling cover drive off Miller. Then he glanced to leg firmly off the middle of the bat and Davidson, close though he was standing at leg slip, made the catch look simple.

Compton this time caused no qualms while Edrich was impervious to error and temptation, batting slowly, resolutely on. When luncheon came with the score at 101 for 2 only 31 runs short of the goal, everyone knew the game was won. Still Johnston and Lindwall had a final fling and Edrich and Compton had to watch with all their eyes and wits. The crowd relaxed now, cheered Edrich's 50, laughed as Hassett made great play breaking down the ridges of Johnston's bowling hole before delivering his over, and finally swarmed the field happy and exultant.

England v Australia, at The Oval, 15–19 August 1953

AUSTRALIA

A. L. Hassett c Evans b Bedser	53	lbw b Laker	10
A. R. Morris lbw b Bedser	16	lbw b Lock	26
K. R. Miller lbw b Bailey	1	(5) c Trueman b Laker	0
R. N. Harvey c Hutton b Trueman	36	b Lock	1
G. B. Hole c Evans b Trueman	37	(3) lbw b Laker	17
J. H. de Courcy c Evans b Trueman	5	run out	4
R. G. Archer c and b Bedser	10	c Edrich b Lock	49
A. K. Davidson c Edrich b Laker	22	b Lock	21
R. R. Lindwall c Evans b Trueman	62	c Compton b Laker	12
G. R. A. Langley c Edrich b Lock	18	c Trueman b Lock	2
W. A. Johnston not out	9	not out	6
Extras b 4, nb 2	6	b 11, lb 3	14
Total	275		162

FOW: 1–38 2–41 3–107 4–107 5–118 6–160 7–160 8–207 9–245 10–275;
1–23 2–59 3–60 4–61 5–61 6–85 7–135 8–140 9–144 10–162.

Bowling: *1st inns*: Bedser 29–3–88–3; Trueman 24.3–3–86–4; Bailey 14–3–42–1; Lock 9–2–19–1; Laker 5–0–34–1; *2nd inns*: Bedser 11–2–24–0; Trueman 2–1–4–0; Lock 21–9–45–5; Laker 16.5–2–75–4

ENGLAND

L. Hutton b Johnston	82	run out	17
W. J. Edrich lbw b Lindwall	21	not out	55
P. B. H. May c Archer b Johnston	39	c Davidson b Miller	37
D. C. S. Compton c Langley b Lindwall	16	not out	22
T. W. Graveney c Miller b Lindwall	4		
T. E. Bailey b Archer	64		
T. G. Evans run out	28		
J. C. Laker c Langley b Miller	1		
G. A. R. Lock c Davidson b Lindwall	4		
F. S. Trueman b Johnston	10		
A. V. Bedser not out	22		
Extras b 9, lb 5, w 1	15	lb 1	1
Total	306	(2 wkts)	132

FOW: 1–37 2–137 3–154 4–167 5–170 6–210 7–225 8–237 9–262 10–306;
1–24 2–88

Bowling: *1st inns*: Lindwall 32–7–70–4; Miller 34–12–65–1; Johnston 45–16–94–3; Davidson 10–1–26–0; Archer 10.3–2–25–1; Hole 11–6–11–0; *2nd inns*: Lindwall 21–5–46–0; Miller 11–3–24–1; Johnston 29–14–52–0; Archer 1–1–0–0; Hassett 1–0–4–0; Morris 0.5–0–5–0

Umpires: D. Davies and F. S. Lee
England won by 8 wickets.

ECHOES OF ENGLAND, THEIR ENGLAND

Daily Telegraph, *8 July 1953.*

LORD'S, Tuesday

Cambridge won the University match here this evening by two wickets at 27 minutes past six, a statement that may picture to those who have ever watched the matches between Oxford and Cambridge, something of the tenseness and excitements of the scene. The way the result was achieved, however, was something that defied imagination, for in cold truth it defeated all logical analysis.

The facts were these: Cambridge went in at 10 minutes past 12 to score 238 runs to win in 5 hrs. 20 mins, a rate of 45 an hour. Despite a fair start, which by luncheon had produced 57 in an hour and 20 minutes for the loss of Bushby's wicket, they scarcely kept pace even with this sluggish tempo, although until after tea wickets fell at irregular intervals.

At tea Cambridge had six wickets in hand and needed to make 93. An hour later they still needed 66 with only three wickets left, including certainly that of Silk, who had been batting from the beginning.

Silk, as he had from the start, was going with the utmost sedateness, while Crookes his partner, who batted 35 minutes for five, was making no apparent effort to push the score along. In the first innings while making 25 in three-quarters of an hour Crookes had revealed himself as a somewhat cross-bat hitter.

The only inference was that Cambridge by then were not prepared to embark on what had become a pretty sizeable order, and that the limit of their ambition was a draw. The next 23 minutes produced 14 runs in an air of sorry anti-climax.

These thoughts, with all their depressing implications so far as cricket generally is concerned, persisted until suddenly Crookes left his ground to hit Allan and was stumped. By now only some 37 minutes remained, and the last two Cambridge wickets needed to make 52.

Marlar's dilatory stroll to the crease, which was received with some ironic hand clapping, seemed only to underline the Cambridge tactics.

He walked to the far end to speak to Silk. And one recalled the captain's advice in A. G. MacDonell's immortal cricket match: 'Play carefully, Bobby. Keep your end up. Runs don't matter.'

'Very well, Bill,' replied Mr. Southcott sedately, and proceeded to deliver such an assault on the bowling as the village of Fordenden had not seen in many a long year.

Silk did not take the bull by the horns quite in the manner of Mr. Southcott, but he began to hit the ball in a way that everyone, I verily believe of whatever persuasion, had been hoping and praying to see for hours past.

At Marlar's arrival Silk's score, after more than four and three-quarter hours' batting, stood at 77. A quarter of an hour later we were applauding his 100.

Once more the batsmen conferred, and again the scene of MacDonell came to mind. 'You needn't play safe any more, Bob. Play your own game.' A maiden played by Marlar from Allan between 6.20 and 6.22, the score then being 232, roused visions of a further crescendo of drama if anything happened to either batsman.

But at 6.25 Silk late-cut Allan for four down to the Clock Tower boxes (which were by no means the calmest places on the ground), and the scores were level. Off the fourth ball of the over he had to make a last-second dive into his crease when the winning run was pro-jected and turned down, off the fifth the single came and all was over.

Thus ended the closest finish to the University match since 1908 when at the climax C. E. Hatfield was the hero for Oxford and the margin was the same as this.

> Oxford v Cambridge, at Lord's, 4–7 July 1953. Oxford 312 (Cowdrey 116, Marlar 5 for 94) and 116 (Marlar 7 for 49); Cambridge 191 and 238 for 8 (Silk 116 not out). Cambridge won by 2 wickets.

TO WEST INDIES WITH HUTTON

Daily Telegraph, 14 December 1953.

Cricket history will move on a step this morning when the MCC team fly away from London Airport to Bermuda on the first stage of the West Indies tour. It is the first time an MCC team have been sent abroad under a professional captain; it is the first time they will have made the outward journey by air; and it is the first time the West Indies will have been visited by a side ostensibly representing England's best.

Hitherto only Australia and, in 1938 and 1948, South Africa have received England's full strength on a full-scale tour. The addition of a major West Indies tour, on the indisputable evidence of their visit here three years ago, means a further load on the hard programme that stretches ahead of our leading cricketers.

They are still in the early stages of a programme that involves, in a month or two more than two years, 12 Test matches abroad and 14 at home; all of five or six days each.

Hutton's side are to play five Tests, five first-class colony matches, and six lesser matches in a tour lasting four months. The tour takes in, in addition to the four traditional centres, Bridgetown, Port-of-Spain, Georgetown, and Kingston, several places where MCC's flag has never flown before.

The games will all be played on grass wickets, except at Trinidad (where I am glad to hear they are to experiment with a turf wicket to succeed the lifeless jute mat), at Bermuda, and in the Windward Isles.

You cannot travel far in West Indies without becoming aware of the West Indian's passion for cricket. He loves it, and, what is more, he has a natural aptitude for it, and, of course, it is the game he specially identifies with England.

In the minds of humble folk there are two links between their country and this: the Crown and cricket. Such is the measure of the responsibility borne by Hutton and his team.

MASTERLY INNINGS

Having lost the first two Tests heavily, England won the Third and drew the Fourth. Trevor Bailey's inspired 7 for 34 on the first day of the Fifth Test was followed by Hutton's masterly marathon and the win that halved the series. Off the field (and sometimes on it) the team did not endear themselves. Hutton asked in vain for S. C. (Billy) Griffith as manager. Instead MCC appointed C. H. Palmer player-manager, a division of duties unfair to him and all concerned. Daily Telegraph, 2 April 1954.

KINGSTON, Jamaica, Thursday

England in the indomitable person of Hutton thrust home the advantage they had gained on the first two days of the Fifth Test. West Indies went in again at five o'clock this evening 275 runs to the bad and it would seem that only some exceptional batting over these next two days can save the game for them.

One has been watching Hutton now for the best part of 20 years and in that time he has built a record of achievement second only to Sir Donald Bradman's. Whatever he does, he has almost lost the capacity to surprise us. Yet from the viewpoint of physical stamina and mental concentration this latest innings is a thing apart, at any rate so far as the post-war years are concerned.

In his youth he once stayed in 13 hours 20 minutes against Australia, but it was in English summer weather after his captain had won the toss and there was a Sunday break intervening. In this match he batted a few minutes short of nine hours in tropical heat. When he was finally got out after the tea interval he had been on the field continuously for the best part of three days. This, moreover, was the hottest of the three.

As to the technical side of the job, need more be said than that he gave only one extremely difficult chance (immediately after reaching his 100) and that one could count on the fingers of the hands the number of times he was beaten.

By this afternoon he had forced his opponents to their knees and one will long retain the picture of the West Indies trailing wearily into their tea preceded by a figure pale and with a slight stoop of the shoulders, but walking briskly as though anxious to get the interval done with so that he could continue to chase them.

As it happened, he made no more, but if Hutton's innings has not won the match, the West Indies will either have to bat superlatively well or England will have to bowl and field indifferently ill.

West Indies v England, at Kingston, 30–31 March, 1–3 April 1954. West Indies 139 (Walcott 50, Bailey 7 for 34) and 346 (Walcott 116, Stollmeyer 64); England 414 (Hutton 205, Wardle 66) and 72 for 1. England won by 9 wickets.

A GREAT YORKSHIREMAN

In 1906 Hirst made 2385 runs and took 208 wickets,
an unparalleled all-round achievement.
A Daily Telegraph *obituary, 11 May 1954.*

George Hirst, the former Yorkshire and England cricketer, who has died, aged 82, was one of the greatest all-rounders in the history of the game. He was born at Kirkheaton, near Huddersfield, and was playing for Yorkshire by the time he was 18. He continued to play for them until 1929, when he was 58.

Cricketers of several generations, back to the very small band of his near-contemporaries that survive him, will be saddened by the news of George Hirst's death. He was a magnificent player, one of the best, on the evidence of indisputable figures, who ever lived.

But he was also in the estimation of all who knew him, a great and good man. It was George Hirst and the likes of that generation from whom derived that most over-worn and over-done of all sporting phrases: 'It isn't cricket.'

There was a gentle steadfastness, and yet at times clear outspokenness, about Hirst that proclaimed his honesty and integrity. There was surrounding him a naturalness that made him equally beloved at Eton, where he taught the game for 18 seasons, retiring in 1938, and with such good effect; and among the young men from mine and mill who came, spring after spring, to the Yorkshire nets to try their skill for the county of their birth.

Hirst was in at the first real flowering of Yorkshire cricket. In the early 90s Surrey were supreme. The Yorkshire elevens, for all their native talent, were not much better than a crowd of ill-disciplined roisterers.

Lord Hawke's assumption of the captaincy coincided with the arrival of Hirst, Brown and Tunnicliffe. In the 10 years from 1893 Yorkshire won the championship six times, and it is true to say that from that moment Yorkshire cricket has never looked back.

AUSTRALIA BEATEN BY SPEED

Daily Telegraph, *3 February 1955.*

ADELAIDE, Wednesday

Nine weeks ago this evening Australia inflicted upon Len Hutton's England team one of the more conclusive defeats of Test history by an innings and 154 runs. If anyone on that depressing day at Brisbane had expressed the belief that England would have won the series by the end of the Adelaide Test he would have been supposed an insane optimist.

Yet there it is. The thing has happened, and no Australian doubts that the English victory by five wickets here to-day is thoroughly deserved.

This fifth and last day's play was full of excitements, of disappointments, of surging hopes, and long suspense. The bowling out of Australia for 111 appeared to foreshadow a task achieved without any prolonged difficulty.

There came a great piece of cricket by a great cricketer, Keith Miller, and when May walked out this afternoon close on the tea interval, having made 26 out of England's score of 49 for four, there were those who harboured unworthy fears of a continuation of the collapse, and of England's failing to make the 94 needed to win.

In fact there followed a partnership between Compton and Bailey which practically signed and sealed the contract, and by twenty minutes past five the crowd were applauding the first victory by an English side in an Australian series since 1933.

Last November the English side at Brisbane looked very poor, even by the standards of Hammond's and Brown's teams, neither of which were strong. Their improvement has coincided with an Australian decline which will always be one of the curiosities of Test history, so that by the climax of the rubber to-day there was no doubt which was the more confident, the better organised, indeed the more determined side.

The turning point of the series, of course, was the fine bowling of Tyson and Statham on the last day of the second Test at Sydney. These two snatched the match from Australia when overnight they had made 72 of the 223 they needed with only two wickets down.

As one of the England cricketers remarked to-day: 'When we drove to the ground at Sydney that morning we felt we had "had it." ' It was Tyson and Statham who tilted the scale then and it has been these two, with significant help on occasion from Appleyard and Bailey, who have completed the job.

Of the 66 Australian wickets credited to the bowlers in the four Tests, Tyson and Statham have taken 43 between them. No more need be said.

The English batting owes most, as the averages show, to Cowdrey and May; but in this fourth Test most of the side contributed usefully and Hutton himself played much more like the man who has supported the England batting, often singlehanded, for so long.

England needed 94. That did not seem very much when Hutton and Edrich came out to bat, but it looked a little larger when Edrich was straightway yorked by Miller. It seemed quite a target when Hutton, in Miller's second over, was magnificently caught low and left-handed by Davidson at second slip: and the most fearsome possibilities were apparent when the injured Cowdrey, after off-driving Miller once for four, was caught at first slip: 18 for three.

Both Hutton and Cowdrey were out to balls that went viciously from leg to off after pitching. We were watching a spell by Miller of the order of that first morning at Melbourne.

No praise now could be too high for May who met the Australian challenge with a series of fine forceful strokes and yet never verged upon rashness. He and Compton withstood Miller, and at the other end Archer who had relieved Davidson, then Benaud, then Johnston.

May and Compton, with the utmost skill and discretion, had steered the game into calmer waters when May launched an off-drive at Johnston and saw Miller catch a stinging hit at extra-cover, throwing himself to his left and rolling over as he made the brilliant catch.

After tea it needed an hour to finish the game. Happily for England, Compton was in his very best form while Bailey met the situation as usual with the straightest defensive bat in cricket.

Compton has had much ill luck to fight against these last few years. It was good indeed to see him playing so masterfully in the crisis and taking out his bat at the finish as he had done at the Oval on Aug. 19, 1953.

Australia v England, at Adelaide, 28 January–2 February 1955. Australia 323 (Maddocks 69) and 111; England 341 (Hutton 80, Cowdrey 79) and 97 for 5. England won by 5 wickets.

PART FIVE

1956–1965

1956–1965

As the 'fifties approached the 'sixties cricket got increasingly out of step with the spirit of the times. In any activity whenever such separation occurs change is imminent. First comes a general feeling of dissatisfaction, then the clarion calls of distemper from those in a position to make them, leading to a moment where, when the masses are sufficiently vocal, either tentative steps or positive leaps are taken.

A new youth culture was abroad in Britain with a developing sense of adventure. Cricket was very much at odds with that. The first-class game around the shires had become staid, almost moribund, trapped in a straitjacket, seemingly unable to get out. In essence, it was unhappy with itself. Bowling directed predominantly at the leg-stump, slow over rates, batsmen concerned with defence rather than attack, captains unwilling to take risks and, crucially, absent crowds making the hearts of county committees grow noticeably less fond. Virtually in unison, the press bemoaned tepid, predictable cricket; Jim's voice along with the rest. So what was to be done? There was no shortage of suggestions, though resolutions were fewer in number. Nor was there a lack of issue and controversy: amateur status; the state of pitches; overseas qualification; players' writing about games in which they had just taken part; the Wardle case; the no-balling of Griffin and so on. As cricket suffered from the aches and pains of transition, it seemed to take an age before it would become comfortable with the new one-day fling.

At the beginning of this period Jim took an active role in pouring proverbial oil on troubled seas. During the MCC visit to the West Indies in 1953/54 under Len Hutton there had been considerable unhappiness in the Caribbean over aspects of the tourists' behaviour; markedly when displaying dissension at umpires' decisions. And so the following year Jim was asked to take an 'unofficial' side to Barbados, Trinidad and Bermuda in order to, in his own words, 'heal the damage'. The team was captained by Colin Cowdrey and consisted of high-class players including Gamini Goonesena, Tom Graveney, Frank Tyson, Robin Marlar, Hubert Doggart and Mickey Stewart. The first three named were the most successful members of the party – indeed,

Graveney scored hundreds in successive innings – although only one of the four first-class matches in an itinerary of seven games was won. Not unnaturally the players found some difficulty in adapting to Caribbean conditions in such a short time-span. Nevertheless they created a favourable impression both on and off the field.

Jim also managed an international side to the West Indies in 1961 – *international* being the operative word as Everton Weekes, the Nawab of Pataudi, A. A. Baig and Ray Lindwall were among the team. In a month's tour nine matches were played and the only defeat was against British Guiana. In the other three first-class matches the Windward Islands and Trinidad were beaten and the game against Berbice was drawn. Overall five matches were won. The Lancashire captain Bob Barber epitomised the attractive cricket that was played by topping the batting averages in the first-class games and notching nineteen wickets with his leg-breaks. Incidentally, the match against St Kitts was the first in the island involving a touring team for over sixty years.

It should not be thought that this era in English cricket was all despair and repair. There was much to be lauded and enjoyed. Not least the national side's success during the first half of this decade and individual performances as well: Laker's destruction of the Australians at Old Trafford in 1956, and of course, Dexter's magisterial riposte to Hall and Griffith at Lord's in 1963. There were excitements too in Jim's own life.

Surprising many people, including perhaps even himself, he had, in 1958, entered the state of holy matrimony. It had all started at a Golf Foundation Ball at Grosvenor House in Park Lane. Ann Carbutt, a highly attractive widow in her mid-forties, was attending the Ball in a party of ten as a guest of Brigadier-General A. C. Critchley. Critchley was not only a very good golfer but also the initiator of greyhound racing at White City in London. Ann, too, was a very good golfer, playing at Championship level with a four-handicap and having inherited her skill, no doubt, from her father, a celebrated golfer and cricketer of pre-war days, R. H. de Montmorency. She was, and still is, a fine musician and a sensitive exponent of the keyboard – thankfully, musicians are not expected to play with handicaps! As if that were not enough, she has a list of compositions to her credit including a *Rhapsody for Piano and Orchestra*; specially commissioned music to the Diana Wynyard/Godfrey Tearle 1948 production of *Othello* at Stratford for the Royal Shakespeare Company; and published popular songs such as 'Sometimes I Think of Spring' which was featured in broadcasts by Geraldo and his orchestra.

Of all this, of course, Jim was totally unaware. His own musical tastes are largely underdeveloped and confined to Gilbert and Sullivan and the *English Hymnal*. Anyway, as the Ball drew to a close Ann helped Critchley, who was blind, into the foyer of the hotel and towards the door in search of a cab. She too was intending to leave as she had not totally recovered from a recent bout of 'flu. Suddenly Jim materialised, seemingly from nowhere – he had, in fact, been in the bar area with golfing correspondent Henry Longhurst with whom he had spent the entire evening – and led the way to Critch's taxi. At the same time he ordered Ann not to go and get her coat. When, naturally, she demurred, he told her to 'go straight back to the table'. Obviously Jim's required bedside reading had not included Dale Carnegie's famous treatise. Ann herself laughingly says: 'He'd ignored me for the whole evening and I said to myself "Shall I? Shan't I? Shall I? Shan't I?" And obviously if I'd stood my ground, gone and got my coat, I should never have seen him again, but I didn't and that's how it all began.'

The Golf Ball took place on 11 December 1956. One month later, on 11 January, Ann and Jim became engaged and then a month after that, on 11 February, they married. After short spells in St. John's Wood and Ann's cottage in Bowling Street, Sandwich, they became established at Delf House in Sandwich, where Ann used her skill in interior design in helping to renovate what had been a rather run-down lodging house for homeless men. The property dates back to at least 1700 and is an integral part of the historic Cinque Port. Along the front of the house runs a moat, in fact, a section of the Delf Stream, which functioned as the town's main water supply and sewerage for nearly seven hundred years up until the end of the last century. Another distinction that Ann Swanton retains is to be the only person to have played piano duets with both Don Bradman and Noël Coward, but that is another story.

Cupid was obviously lingering around the Swanton clan in the later 'fifties because shortly before Jim and Ann's marriage at All Saints, Margaret Street, his widowed father had also taken the same vows with his physiotherapist, Helen Baker, who came from a well-known family of West Country doctors. Jim's father continued to work at the Stock Exchange until he was in his early eighties, before finally moving with his wife from their Kensington home to Upper Welland near Malvern in Worcestershire. He died from emphysema at the age of eighty-seven in 1966.

Meanwhile, Jim continued to write for the *Daily Telegraph*, broadcast for the BBC and also, from 1960, take on the role of editor of *The Cricketer*. He was of course, by now, a respected and influential figure in the cricket world, not least because of his growing participation in MCC affairs.

In the English spring of 1964, he organised a tour of the Far East which was sponsored by a group of businessmen with interests in the newly created Federation of Malaysia. A representative side of Commonwealth cricketers led by the Hampshire captain A. C. D. Ingleby-Mackenzie visited Penang, Singapore, Kuala Lumpur, Hong Kong, Bangkok and Calcutta. They played a dozen matches, won eleven, drew the other and whetted the appetites of the local people wherever they went. The victory in Calcutta was notable for being against what was virtually an Indian Test side – Pataudi was playing for the Commonwealth team – and, in fact, it was the only first-class game involving an English side not drawn during that season in India.

The tour was not just limited to success *on* the field. Unqualified praise came from all quarters – including Prime Minister Tunku Abdul Rahman Putra – regarding the ambassadorial spirit of the team and their generosity and friendliness which engendered so much goodwill. Jim's well deserved OBE, awarded the following year, was surely a direct consequence.

The demands of cricket in the summer and now winter led Jim to relinquish the job of rugby correspondent to the *Telegraph* in the year of that tour, 1964. Even he, with an extraordinary penchant for organisation, could not manage everything. He was also falling a little out of love with the way the game was often being played. After an encounter between Ireland and Wales at Dublin, which former international Cliff Jones described as 'the roughest game of rugger I ever saw', Jim was threatened with libel by a member of the Welsh fifteen, whose performance he had criticised. Subsequent inquiry revealed a 'biter's Club', with evidence of teeth-marks as victims' qualification for membership. The *Telegraph* were prepared to justify Swanton's comments in court; however, the plaintiff hastily withdrew.

But Jim had not fallen out of love with cricket and his writing on that carried on undiminished.

D.R.A.

COCONUTS AND CENTURIES

This was the first of the three first-class teams I took overseas. It consisted of M. C. Cowdrey (captain), G. H. G. Doggart (vice-captain), D. E. Blake, G. Goonesena, T. W. Graveney, A. C. D. Ingleby-Mackenzie, R. C. M. Kimpton, R. G. Marlar, A. S. M. Oakman, M. J. Stewart, Swaranjit Singh, F. H. Tyson, J. J. Warr. Daily Telegraph, *3 March 1956.*

One cannot travel for long in a West Indian island without meeting the signs of cricket. It is the common bond of interest with Englishmen to an intense degree not to be found elsewhere in the Commonwealth.

To the average Barbadian and Trinidadian, I suppose, England tends to mean the place where the Queen lives and the place where the cricketers come from. English teams of one sort or another have been arriving at irregular intervals for 60 years.

The first amateur parties contained such distinguished names as Warner, Stoddart, Woods, Leveson-Gower, and 'the Odysseus of cricket,' Lord Hawke. At the time of these early visits, in the 'nineties, coloured men first found their way into representative colony teams, hitherto exclusively white.

The roots of cricket in the West Indies go back at least twice as far as this. When one sees a group of barefooted boys playing on a rough plot with a coconut husk for a ball and a stump of palm branch to hit with, they are imitating the grandees, the Weekes, the Walcotts and the Worrells, just as boys were aping the garrison players and the planters who first sowed the seed soon after Trafalgar had made the islands safe under British rule.

The West Indian is a natural cricketer if ever there was one. I remember on my first visit to the Kensington ground at Bridgetown, Barbados, where G. O. Allen's MCC team were preparing for their tour, shaking hands with young Everton Weekes. John Goddard explained how Weekes, having joined the West Indian Regiment as a boy, was spotted as a likely cricketer, and when the war ended was given a job under the groundsman which would afford a chance of practice on good wickets. 'We hope he's going to make some runs against you.'

How many has he got! And what great pleasure have 'the three Ws' given to crowds all over the world these last eight years.

Weekes, Walcott and Worrell, all are Barbadians born and bred, though Frank Worrell has since migrated to Jamaica and Clyde Walcott now coaches in British Guiana. It is remarkable, to say the least, that these three heroes should have sprung, in the same vintage, from an island just about as large as the Isle of Wight.

Unlike the other islands, Barbados since its colonisation in 1627 has always been British, and its inhabitants naturally perhaps took most thoroughly, in the early days, to the English game introduced by the Army and Navy. Since the Challenors and Austins first laid the basis of the West Indies' cricket reputation Barbados has occupied a position corresponding in some way to that of Yorkshire, in the cricket world, in relation to England.

When Hutton and Compton, late in their careers, played for the first time in Barbados each, as he came in to bat, was applauded and cheered all the way to the wicket, just as an artist of world reputation would be received on a first visit to Covent Garden. The crowds are noisy but fair-minded, and they like to see batsmen taking advantage of their beautiful wickets by hitting the ball.

In Trinidad, which contrasts in almost every way with Barbados, cricket needed longer to take root. The island is ten times as big, hilly and largely covered with luxuriant tropical vegetation. Where Barbados is almost aggressively British, Trinidad with its mingling of the blood of former conquerors, Spanish, French and Portuguese, with its East Indians, Chinese, and those of African descent, is utterly cosmopolitan.

Thus in Trinidad sides are to be found names like Stollmeyer and Gomez, Asgarali and Ganteaume, Tang Choon and Achong. Yet the Constantines, father and son, and Pascall, uncle of the great Learie, had helped, before these men came to notice, to found a cricket tradition at least comparable to that of Barbados and British Guiana, and stronger than that of Jamaica some thousand miles to the north-westward. (Caribbean distances are not always appreciated: people sometimes speak of the British West Indies as though they were clustered like the Channel Islands.)

To-day at the week-end you may see 30 matches at a time in progress on the Queen's Park Savannah in Port-of-Spain, while at colony and Test matches there may be crowds of 25,000. Though he has long retired, the magic name in Trinidad is still that of Constantine, and as one rides to the golf course the driver will point with awe to the little field at Maraval where, according to legend, father and son practised together.

The team which I have the honour to be taking on a short tour to the West Indies next week is treading where famous men have trod in the main centres at Bridgetown and Port-of-Spain.

We are also, in three minor matches, breaking fresher ground. At Pointe-a-Pierre there is a match against South Trinidad, where we will be in the hospitable hands of Trinidad Leaseholds. There is also to be a brief visit to the reputedly enchanting island of Tobago, a dependency of Trinidad, and the legendary scene of the adventures of Robinson Crusoe.

And as we fly home, we stop for a day to play in Bermuda, where one understands the American influence has not weakened the islanders' zest for cricket.

CARDUS IN SPATE

Neville Cardus spent his last years in London and much of his summers at Lord's. He was the only man I ever saw – and felt – emphasise his talk by grasping the lapel of his hearer's coat. Daily Telegraph, 21 *May 1956.*

It was agreeable to discover at Lord's recently that Neville Cardus retains his form as a commentator of the cricket scene. (I use that phrase advisedly, rather than 'conversationalist.' Cardus orates. The best conversationalist, in many estimations, would be Ian Peebles.)

A young cricketer on being told by Mr. Cardus that he had recently been in Vienna took the liberty of asking him what the cricket was like there. 'Exactly as it is here,' came the bland answer with a wave of the hand that embraced St. John's Wood, Kennington, and all the countryside beyond, 'NON-EXISTENT.'

Mr. Cardus is unashamedly 'laudator temporis acti,' romanticising the style and opulence of MacLaren, Spooner, and J. T. Tyldesley, and finding little that is admirable in the utilitarian cricket of the 'fifties. Yet his standards can occasionally be approached, and I was not surprised that the Sussex batting on Saturday sent him home purring contentedly.

Compton, of course, exactly fulfils his notion of a cricketer. 'To think it was Denis's knee-cap they had to take away!' A chortle and another expansive wave. 'You could remove both legs from most of them, and they'd bat just the same with wooden ones.'

All of which, and much else besides, made one glad to hear that his third, and avowedly final autobiographical book, 'Close of Play,' published by Collins, is shortly due. What a refreshing thing to look forward to amid all the phoney books, ostensibly written by cricketers, but mostly thrown together by 'ghosts,' and frequently of such little merit, in point of either taste or truth – to say nothing of style.

NINETEEN TO LAKER

The contrast between the relative effectiveness of Jim Laker and Tony Lock seems no more credible today than it did at the time.

Old Trafford, Fourth Test, last day

July 1956. For many nervous hours since last Friday evening it has seemed that England would be robbed of victory in the Fourth Test match. But Manchester expiated its sins of weather this afternoon, and it was in bright sunshine tempering the wind that the game ended in an innings win, which meant the safe-keeping of the Ashes until MCC next sail in their defence two years from now. The only proper formal announcement of the result is that J. C. Laker defeated Australia by an innings and 170 runs. Unprecedented things are always happening in cricket because it is so charmingly unpredictable a pastime. But now and then occurs something of which one feels certain there can be no repetition or bettering. Laker followed his capture of nine first innings wickets with all 10 in the second. What is left in the vocabulary to describe and applaud such a *tour de force*? It is quite fabulous.

Laker's first innings performance was phenomenal enough, but its merit was perhaps clouded by the deficiencies of the Australian batting, as also by the palaver over the condition of the wicket. There was no room whatever for argument regarding his bowling today. He bowled 36 overs, practically non-stop except for the taking of the new ball, all the time attacking the stumps and compelling the batsman to play, never wilting or falling short in terms either of length or direction. Nor was he mechanical. Each ball presented the batsman with a separate problem. Laker never let up and neither for an instant could his adversary.

It is, of course, scarcely less remarkable that while Laker was building up new heights of fame at one end Lock was toiling just as zealously, albeit fruitlessly, at the other. On a wicket on which one famous cricketer captured 19 wickets the other, scarcely less successful and dangerous, taking one day with another, in 69 overs had 1 for 106. Still, the comparison between the figures is in one sense unarguable evidence of Laker's great performance. If the wicket had been such a natural graveyard for batsmen it is inconceivable that Lock, even below his peak, even with the other arm tied to his side, would not have taken more than one wicket.

So long as McDonald was in the odds were still fairly balanced. When he was beaten at last directly after tea the latter-end batsmen carried on in the same spirit, and there was a bare hour to go when Maddocks, the No. 11, played back and slightly across to Laker, fell leg-before and advanced up the wicket to shake the hero by the hand. One of the Australian party summed up the day, as the crowd that massed round the pavilion dispersed and Laker, glass in hand, had turned from the balcony to the dressing-room by saying: 'Well, it was a good scrap after all.' There was relief in his voice, just as there was jubilation in the surrounding English faces.

The captains having formally disagreed, there was a delay of 10 minutes before play was continued this morning. The wicket was just about as sluggish as yesterday. McDonald and Craig, by high-class defensive play, withstood the session of an hour and 50 minutes without many moments of difficulty. Just before lunch Evans and Lock, those tireless propagandists, when the latter was bowling, tried their hardest by expression and gesture to suggest that the dormant pitch was stirring. But McDonald and Craig came in calm and unscathed, having incidentally added 28 runs.

There were early signs after lunch that the batsmanship might be more severely tested. Craig was twice beaten by lifting balls from Lock, who naturally enough was sharing the bowling with Laker. After a quarter of an hour Craig went back to the latter and was lbw to an off-break. Thus he retired full of honour after an innings of 4 hours and 20 minutes, in which his stature had grown surely and steadily. The breaking of the stand was the signal for the second Australian collapse of the game. Within half an hour Mackay, Miller and Archer had all followed Craig, all to Laker, and all for ducks. Granted the ball was doing a little more during this phase in answer to bursts of sun, these batting failures underlined the worth and value of the third-wicket partnership. Where before the judgment of length and direction had been good enough to ensure a smooth, well-considered defensive stroke, now the new batsmen were floundering about and either using their pads or offering a last-minute jab. Mackay was surrounded by slips, silly mid-off, and short-legs, six in all within a five-yard radius. One could hardly see how he could survive, for in going forward he plays so far in front of the front leg. This had been evident against the slow bowlers even while he was putting up his celebrated resistance at Lord's. Now Mackay probed out, and edged a short sharp catch to Oakman, the middle of the slips. I have never seen a batsman whose value rose and fell so abruptly according to the state of the wicket. On a good one he wants blasting out. When the ball is doing anything it is hard to see how he can last five minutes. As it was, Mackay today, like Harvey on Friday, bagged a pair.

McDonald was seemingly impervious, immovable, and he and Benaud came in to tea, having stayed together an hour and 20 minutes. Australia were still breathing. But McDonald did not take root afterwards and it was the inevitable Laker who got the most valuable wicket of all. This was a sharp off-break which for once went too quickly for McDonald, who edged it to the sure hands of Oakman in the middle position just behind square. So ended a valiant effort lasting without a chance for more than five hours and a half.

Lindwall made a steady partner for Benaud and at five o'clock these two looked ominously settled and determined: there was still Johnson and Maddocks to come. It was not yet 'in the bag'. But Benaud now went back where he might have gone forward and was bowled middle-and-off stumps or thereabouts. Twenty minutes later Lindwall, like so many before him, fell in the leg-trap. Then, with Johnson looking on, Maddocks made his entry and speedy, gracious exit. So the game ended. The post-mortems no doubt will linger on. But whatever is added one thing cannot be gainsaid: Laker was magnificent.

England v Australia, at Old Trafford, 26–31 July 1956. England 459 (Sheppard 113, Richardson 104, Cowdrey 80); Australia 84 (Laker 9 for 37) and 205 (McDonald 89, Laker 10 for 53). England won by an innings and 170 runs.

THE INIMITABLE ROCKLEY

The bon mots were legendary. He didn't much care for our Australian cousins. They were reputedly formidable scroungers. Scene in Middle East mess: 'Where are your troops, brigadier?' 'I left them by the Sea of Galilee.' E.R. in stage whisper, 'I bet the shepherds watch their flocks tonight.' Daily Telegraph, *July 1957.*

At the Leeds Test match this week-end the familiar figure of E. R. Wilson, who has died at the age of 78, will be greatly missed. He was never absent from a big match at Lord's or a Test at Leeds, where he loved to sit and talk with Wilfred Rhodes and the other great Yorkshire players of his time.

Rockley Wilson's life was centred on Winchester, where he taught for 40 years and where, after his retirement, he lived and died. In one sense he was as 'complete' a cricketer as could be imagined.

A good enough batsman to score a 100 for Cambridge in the University match of 1901 he is chiefly remembered as a slow medium bowler of remarkable accuracy, possibly the best length bowler since Alfred Shaw. He reached his prime after the first war when, over 40, he was selected to tour Australia with MCC in 1920–21, and, bowling only for Yorkshire in August, he once headed the English averages with 51 wickets in the month.

Playing only in the school holidays on coming down from Cambridge he took nearly 500 wickets in first-class cricket and made more than 3,500 runs. He toured abroad with English teams in the United States, West Indies, and Argentina, as well as Australia.

He was a most successful school coach, through whose hands passed more than a score of Blues, including such distinguished players as D. R. Jardine, A. J. Evans, J. L. Guise, and the three Ashton brothers.

He was an extraordinary repository of cricket knowledge of the most diverse kind, historical, practical, technical, topical. He wrote all too little about the game, though the bound volumes of The Cricketer contain a number of excellent essays and articles. He was the most difficult of all men to 'stump' on any cricket matters.

If, as is often said, the number of anecdotes surrounding a man are a measure of affection, there have been few more popular cricketers, for no one had a bigger fund of stories, and of none were more and better stories told. He was a master of the cricket idiom.

'My boy,' he once said to a complete duffer in the nets: 'You must hit *one* ball in the middle of the bat before you meet your Maker.'

EVIL GHOSTING

I was surprised that Bill Edrich lent himself to this form of journalism, and suppose he later regretted doing so – as Jim Laker did openly in a more notorious case, the result being that membership privileges which had been taken away were restored to him. Letter to the Editor of the Daily Telegraph, *July 1958.*

Sir – Some of your readers, though not perhaps very many will have seen the latest cricket 'shockers,' the series of articles published during the last month under the name of W. J. Edrich.

Beginning with the fashionable decrying of Sir Leonard Hutton (who was saved apparently from throwing away a Test series against Australia by the astuteness of Mr. Edrich) we have been led behind the scenes and introduced to numerous petty feuds, in which many of the most distinguished figures in cricket are alleged to have been involved.

One such feud, it seems, concerned the author and a very famous cricketer and England captain, Mr. R. E. S Wyatt.

The broad story here seems to be that, when chairman of the Test selectors, Mr. Wyatt, having a grudge against Mr. Edrich, seized the chance of a 'harmless' party during a Test match to have the culprit 'court-martialled' by MCC, as a result of which he was kept out of Test cricket for three years. I have no doubt that Mr. Wyatt could establish a very different set of facts if he had recourse to law, or if MCC, on their own account and in justice to Mr. Wyatt's reputation, were to institute an inquiry into this public defamation of one of their members by another.

MCC have, of course, the machinery to take extreme action against a member. Equally such a course would be thoroughly repugnant to them, as no doubt in this instance would legal action be to Mr. Wyatt.

But, Sir, where is this sort of journalism going next? There is an ever-increasing traffic in 'reminiscences', peddled by agents, which give an entirely false picture of the first-class cricket scene.

It may not be appreciated by those who go to more respectable sources for their cricket reading that to a very wide public the modern player is being portrayed as just about everything that a sportsman is not.

Yours faithfully,
E. W. SWANTON
London, N.W.8.

THE END FOR WARDLE

Yorkshire's decision not to re-engage Johnny Wardle would not itself have affected his travelling to Australia with MCC, had he not subsequently in the Daily Mail *abused the Club and his captain, J. R. Burnet. This led to the Club withdrawing their invitation, and so considerably weakening the team. Wardle was a distinctly better bowler than Tony Lock on overseas pitches, and I never heard of him putting a foot wrong on tour.* Daily Telegraph, *July 1958.*

Yorkshire yesterday decided to terminate forthwith the engagement of J. H. Wardle.

It was open to Yorkshire to reply specifically to the version of his recent experiences with the county as written by Wardle. But they have preferred the more dignified course of allowing the articles to speak for themselves, and I suppose that most people will approve their decision not to pursue the business of washing dirty linen in public. It will have been appreciated by any sensible follower of cricket that Yorkshire would not have disposed of their most experienced and distinguished cricketer without good and proper reason.

It was perhaps somewhat ingenuous of them to imagine that the euphemistic phrase in their original announcement of the news that they were concentrating on building a new young team would be accepted as it stood, especially in the light of comments subsequently made to newspapers by members of their committee.

However, if Wardle had set about obtaining other employment without demur his reputation need not have suffered as it has done, nor would any question have arisen as to his going to Australia. As it is MCC may, or may not, confirm their invitation, made before the trouble blew up. Their decision was a great disappointment to the

Captain, Peter May, who remembered how very effective Wardle's wrist-spin had been in South Africa two years previously.

NETT NOTHING

From the Peterborough column, Daily Telegraph, *August 1958.*

Mr Ronnie Aird, secretary of MCC, did the eighth hole at Royal St George's in one yesterday morning. He was partnering Mr E. W. Swanton against Mr G. O. Allen and Marshal of the RAF Sir William Dickson, Allen's brother-in-law.

As they had started at the 10th this was the 17th of the match. Dickson and Allen were one hole down. Allen himself, fighting to get square before the last hole, had hit a challenging tee shot. But Aird received a stroke – so his and Swanton's score was nett nothing. That settled the match.

ODDS ON AUSTRALIA

My estimate differed sharply from most media opinion. As the tour unfolded and the scale of England's defeat grew elements of the press without the slightest justification blamed the presence of the captain's fiancée, Miss Virginia Gilligan, as an unsettling factor, a slur which, of course, Peter May bitterly resented. The presence of several Australian fast bowlers with dubious actions was an important factor in the result. Daily Telegraph, *September 1958.*

For the fourth time since the war ended an MCC team is leaving for Australia. On the day before sailing it might be as well to stress what an exacting job is likely to lie before May and his team in the Test series. People have come very much to expect England to win Test matches nowadays, and it is true that *at home* we have lost only two Test rubbers since the war.

This is an excellent team in several respects. But Anglo-Australian form in this country is only a very hazy guide to what may be expected overseas. It is a stark fact that on the last three tours abroad, to

West Indies, Australia and South Africa, England have won seven Test matches, lost five and drawn four.

There is no conclusive story of superiority in hard-wicket conditions to be drawn from these figures, and one's feeling is that if they bring home the Ashes once more, May's team will probably have done extremely well.

A great part of English hopes must rest on Bailey as the one all-rounder. If he can come off again in both departments the tail will not start too early. Otherwise, in what is sure to be a much higher-scoring series than last time, Australia will have an important advantage in the presence of Benaud, Davidson, and possibly Archer, in the lower part of the order.

If pressed for a view I would say that the proper odds at this stage may be just a shade in Australia's favour. But the position could obviously have shifted a good deal by the time of the first Test on Dec. 5.

Let us hope that MCC have shown cricket of real quality by then, and that whatever the result, Australian interest is stimulated by a memorable tour and series.

ENGLAND CRUSHED

Daily Telegraph, 20 February 1959.

MELBOURNE, Wednesday

The last chapter of one of the most surprising of all Anglo-Australian rubbers was written this morning when Australia made short work of scoring the 69 runs needed to win.

Trueman and Tyson bowled fast and often pretty short to a close attacking field and McDonald steered the ball so deftly through the gaps that he managed to add a further 50 to his two recent hundreds before making the winning hit.

Australia lost Burke to an lbw decision when only three runs were needed. So they followed previous victories by eight, eight again, and ten wickets with a fourth by nine.

I describe the outcome as surprising only because of the extent of Australia's success. England were always likely to be extremely hard pressed.

What is extraordinary is that not after even a single day's play in the series have we been able to say that England were in the stronger position. The good phases, the better days, have only cancelled an Australian advantage which Benaud's team have been quick to snatch back.

It is this which has made the series so disappointing to watch and describe from the English viewpoint – and no doubt also to read about.

The satisfactory aspects of the tour boil down more or less to two. In the first place the admirable performances of Benaud and of his team have helped a great deal to restore interest in and respect for the game in Australia, which, of course, is an important matter in itself, both to English and Australian cricket.

Also, thanks to the higher gate charges rather than an overall increase in attendances the tour has made a record profit both for MCC and the State Associations. It seems as though MCC will hand over something just short of £30,000 for distribution among the counties, Major and Minor, and the two Universities.

Australia v England, at Melbourne, 13–18 February 1959. England 205 (Richardson 68) and 214 (Graveney 54); Australia 351 (McDonald 133, Grout 74, Benaud 64) and 69 for 1 (McDonald 51 not out). Australia won by 9 wickets.

YORKSHIRE RACE TO VICTORY

After thirteen years, much the longest gap between titles in their history.
Daily Telegraph, *2 September 1959.*

HOVE, Tuesday

Yorkshire won the Championship here this afternoon thanks to two innings of exemplary hitting, each in its way a model, by Stott and Padgett. In 61 minutes they scored 141 together, starting at 40 for two and taking their side to the brink of victory.

Needing 215 in a shade under 1¾ hours Yorkshire got them for five wickets with seven minutes to spare. Thus they put themselves beyond the reach of Surrey, Gloucestershire and Warwickshire, and the prize is theirs at last, for the first time, apart from one tie, since 1946.

A more detailed analysis can wait for a calmer moment when the last games are finished on Saturday. For now it is enough to congratulate Yorkshire with all possible warmth, and in particular their captain Burnet. When the unhappy domestic events of last summer are brought to mind to-day's victory will seem all the sweeter to him. From 11th to the top is a transition indeed!There was every possible ingredient of a perfect day's cricket when play began at 11 except one which seemed definitely scarce: time. When Dexter and Parks continued the Sussex innings at 143 for three the difference between the two sides was 46. The number of minutes left, deducting ten minutes between innings, was 280.

In all human possibility Marlar would not be able to think in terms of a declaration. So one's thoughts ran before the start. Yorkshire, if they wanted the Championship, would have to bowl Sussex out.

That no doubt was how Yorkshire approached the matter, and Trueman, downhill and downwind, fired the first salvoes with authentic fire and speed. But he was worthily opposed. Dexter generally plays Trueman well, but Parks's certainty against speed is perhaps more open to question.

To-day his batting could scarcely have been improved upon – until perhaps he grew a shade over-venturesome against the spinners, notably Wilson.

It was this tall young successor to Wardle, with the steady length and steep flight, who was to bother Sussex more than anyone. Yesterday he had accounted for Lenham and Suttle. This morning after 40 minutes he had Dexter, driving, well taken at extra-cover. The catcher was Birkenshaw, and it was the first of four held by him at varying distances, none of them completely easy.

Doggart, not the steadiest of beginners, soon had a lot of attention round the bat, including Close at the end of the popping crease. Having tried to disperse them with a 6 to mid-wicket off Illingworth. Doggart was caught at deep square-leg sweeping.

Parks's dismissal for 85, and the entry of the Nawab of Pataudi, persuaded Burnet to take the new ball which had been due for some time. Trueman summoned his best speed, but was extremely well played by Smith and also by Pataudi, whose class and promise have been amply illustrated in this game.

Smith was caught at third man off Taylor trying to play what to him was an outswinger on the leg side. But at lunch Sussex were 280 for seven, 183 runs on.

Pataudi continued to play well and freely afterwards until he seemed to think his part had been played. Thomson followed him, then finally Marlar, caught first ball at deep square-leg.

There was a strange notion current during the interval between innings that Yorkshire had only the slimmest chance. They would try, of course, because they had nothing to lose. But 215 in 1¾ hours – well!

In fact, of course, a much higher rate has been gone for and achieved hundreds of times. And what better circumstances could be imagined than a combination of the Sussex bowling and a brick-hard field?

This having been said, all possible praise to Stott and Padgett for the way they played. The batting was brilliant and it was well matched by the Sussex ground fielding and throwing which, despite the hottest pressure, never faltered. There was scarcely a run lost by misfielding, and only one chance went to hand, a scorching low hit which Doggart clung to, then lost as he fell at short mid-off. Dexter was the bowler and Stott was 39, the total 77.

One other incident might possibly have affected the result. When Stott was 77 he made a big hit to long-on which Pataudi jumped for and caught, landing, after making the catch, a foot or so over the rope.

Is the ball 'under control' when the fielder is in mid air? Was it a fair catch? It was a nice point which the fielder decided instantaneously by signalling 'six.' That was in the spirit of the occasion. The only criticism indeed that might have been levelled against Sussex was that they were almost too generous in that they bowled all the time at the stumps.

Taylor showed Yorkshire's mettle in the first over by scoring 14, he and Stott running up and down the pitch like scalded cats.

But Taylor was lbw in Dexter's first over, and although Close made some thrilling strokes, including a 6 out of the ground over square-leg, he was caught behind the wicket at 40, made in 13 minutes.

The stroke-play of Stott and Padgett that followed was unforgettable. It was not in any sense blind hitting. They made ground to almost everything, so dictating the length, and in turn they showed every stroke.

Their driving especially was magnificent and the number of false strokes remarkably small. They ran very fast between wickets, and though with five men as a rule on the boundary there were not many 4's, the number of 2's was unusually large.

One wondered how much harder the batsmen's job would have been made if Sussex had attacked outside the off-stump with a strong off-field. As it was, they split invariably five-four, and there were holes galore.

By the time Padgett was caught at deep mid-wicket Yorkshire had only to coast comfortably and keep their heads. Only 34 more were needed and there was all but half an hour.

Marlar, who had induced more mistakes than anyone, got Trueman stumped and Stott caught at long-on. But time was not now a problem, and the difficulty Illingworth and Bolus had in squeezing the last runs only emphasised the excellence of the batting that had gone before.

Sussex v Yorkshire, at Hove, 29 August–1 September 1959. Sussex 210 (Nawab of Pataudi 52) and 311 (Parks 85, Lenham 66); Yorkshire 307 (Illingworth 122, Wilson 55) and 218 for 5 (Stott 96, Padgett 79). Yorkshire won by 5 wickets.

SUCCESS IN THE CARIBBEAN

Daily Telegraph, *31 March 1960.*

PORT OF SPAIN, TRINIDAD, Thursday

England won the rubber here this morning when by batting on until lunch and beyond they deprived the West Indies of the slightest prospect of winning the Fifth Test match. Nature merely took its course.

It was not an heroic way to achieve history – for, as all now must surely know, England have not hitherto won a series over here. England, however, like the West Indies, were the victims of circumstances. The latter can be commiserated with in being deprived of three hours' play in this game following two hours in the last. Apart from the loss of five successive tosses one's impression is that providence has not smiled on their efforts, taking the five matches as a whole.

Yet no one who has watched from first to last should be inclined to deny England full credit for their success. Considering the limitations of their bowling it is one of the most remarkable and praiseworthy victories of the recent past. It is, of course, all the more notable following the wholesale defeat in Australia a year ago. The fruits of picking a largely fresh side have been amply gathered.

May and Cowdrey have instilled an emphasis on unselfish team effort and keenness. The results of this have been seen especially in the fielding which overall has been the best I remember by an English side since the tour of F. G. Mann's team to South Africa in 1948–9. If there is one aspect more than another that has contributed to the result it has been the English rate of scoring which at something over 42 runs per hundred balls has been substantially ahead of the West Indian. Dexter's arrival has been the chief individual factor in this new approach and everyone will fervently hope that similar tactics will be applied in the forthcoming series in England against South Africa and Australia.

The fact of four Tests out of five having been drawn is not of course satisfactory. On the other hand the draw at Kingston was more exciting than most finished games and the result was in the balance almost to the very last.

In the two draws since then the weather has played a part and so have the West Indian methods which have been strangely lacking in thrust. Their cricket has been unorganised and unco-ordinated in several respects as compared with England's.

There is only one really disquieting item in the cricket from the English viewpoint, and that is that where the rate of bowling the overs has been the slowest in all recorded history, England should have been the worse offenders.

The MCC manager was surely not overstating things when he said this afternoon that of all the problems confronting the legislators to-day this was the most pressing.

It can always be said by those who are not special admirers of the game of cricket that it is often spoiled by its endings. This is a charge that can scarcely be denied, and all the lover of the game can do is to point to the great moments and say that they much more than compensate for the dull. That has been the case here in this Test. The situation these last two days in mid-afternoon has been thrilling, on Tuesday when Trueman and Moss were making a hole in the West Indies middle batting and yesterday when the reverse process was happening.

Just after three o'clock, at 148 for six, England were likely to lose the game unless Smith and Parks had stayed. In terms of dramatic perfection, of course, they did their job infinitely too well.

When the game was continued this morning England were 293 runs on with four wickets in hand. The pitch was almost as good as new. A draw was enough to give England the rubber. Having striven for 29 days England could scarcely be expected to risk depriving themselves of the result of their efforts by a quixotic declaration. They did not do so. They batted on until some while after the result was utterly and completely safe, latterly no doubt to give Parks and Smith the chance of making their hundreds.

Parks got his, Smith was caught behind the wicket four runs short, and the loss of one arithmetical item in this case was the making of another, for Alexander's catch brought the number of his victims to 23: now he tops the roll of Test wicketkeepers in this respect of wickets in a series, being bracketed with Waite of South Africa.

With nothing more positive to do than to mark time and try and make things agreeable for the spectators, the West Indies batsmen had a thankless job when they went in with all but three hours of the match to go.

They promptly lost McMorris, and although Hunte and Kanhai played pleasantly in a partnership of 71 both of these and Walcott got out to the spinners. With an hour to go we had the familiar sight at the wicket once more of Sobers, whose batting has dominated the series.

Sobers and Worrell. These are at once the most effective and the most polished of modern West Indian batsmen, and it was some salve to wounded pride that the crowd – admitted free from the tea interval onwards – should have seen them this evening in such handsome form.

The front page of the Trinidad *Guardian* this morning carries a tribute to Mr. Robins, the manager, of a warmth which must strain his modesty to the uttermost, and the team altogether have departed in an aura of good will.

West Indies v England, at Port-of-Spain, 25–31 March 1960. England 393 (Cowdrey 119, Dexter 76, Barrington 69) and 350 for 7 dec. (Parks 101 not out, Smith 96, Pullar 54); West Indies 338 for 8 dec. (Sobers 92, Hunte 72, Walcott 53) and 209 for 5 (Worrell 61). Match Drawn.

BBC SAVE £2.10.0

They were only safeguarding the public purse, after all.

The British Broadcasting Corporation
Broadcasting House
Piccadilly
Manchester, 1

15 June 1960

Dear Mr Swanton,

As you will be aware, the cricket match between Yorkshire and Lancashire at Headingley scheduled for June the 4th, 6th and 7th was finished in two days. The cheque covering this match has already been sent you and I am afraid a mistake has occurred in that you have been sent one overnight allowance too many.

In order to rectify this position I propose with your permission to offset the overpayment amounting to £2.10s.0d. against another match, and I am asking our Talks Booking Manager to make the necessary arrangements accordingly.

Yours sincerely,

M. S. Taylor, Programme Executive, North Region.

THE GRIFFIN DRAMA

The frequent no-balling of Griffin, which reached a climax in the Lord's Test, took the heart out of the tour.
Daily Telegraph, *25 June 1960.*

LORD'S, Friday

England made a substantial score here to-day and Smith, for the third time in Test cricket inside 12 months, got out after a fine innings in the late 90's – this time at 99.

Yet the position of the game, and the successes of the English batsmen, seemed almost subordinated this evening to the astonishing fact that Griffin, who had been no-balled for throwing six times during the day, came back in his last spell and achieved the hat-trick. Poor Smith, who when 97, had just had a seemingly certain 4 brilliantly saved at short-leg by Wesley, flashed twice outside the off-stump and the second time was picked up by Waite behind the wicket.

That was the last ball of an over, and from the first ball of the next Walker, his head in the clouds maybe after the intoxicating moment wherein with two successive 6s in the intervening over from Goddard, he had reached his 50, was bowled playing back. Trueman came in, the light bad, and England plainly interested more in a few more quick 4s than anything else. (I assume a declaration first thing). The ingredients for a hat-trick were richly mixed, and sure enough Trueman swung across the next ball and was bowled.

So Griffin in one extraordinary moment became the first man ever to achieve a hat-trick in a Test at Lord's, and the first of his countrymen to do so in a Test match anywhere. On the reverse of the ledger, stands a tally of 11 no-balls for throwing in this match to date, 28 in all so far this summer. To be frank, one does not relish the prospect of the series being fought to the finish on the present note.

England v South Africa, at Lord's, 23–27 June 1960. England 362 for 8 dec. (Smith 99, Subba Row 90, Dexter 56, Walker 52); South Africa 152 (Statham 6 for 63) and 137 (Statham 5 for 34). England won by an innings and 73 runs.

REFLECTIONS ON AN EPIC

Daily Telegraph, 15 December 1960.

As our correspondent remarks in his cable from Brisbane, yesterday was a wonderful day for cricket: not only for Test cricket, and not only for the teams led apparently so bravely and so well by Benaud and Worrell. If ever the game needed some revivifying event to remind the world of its unique dramatic possibility and of its capacity, *when played in the right spirit*, to sustain an enthralling appeal over the full length of a match, this indeed was the moment.

The fact of this First Test ending in a tie of course inscribes its fame in history with a capital letter. A tie, need one say, is a glorious fluke, having some analogy with a hole in one, or a dead heat in a Boat Race.

To imagine the odds against it one need only reflect that in around 500 Test Matches played since Tests began this is the first tie. (Among the many thousand games of first-class cricket played since the 1914–18 war only 19 have ended in ties.)

But, if one weighs the matter as properly as is possible, looking on enviously from afar, it would seem – as Benaud afterwards remarked – that in a tie poetic justice was perfectly served. The course of the game was certainly such that either side could have counted itself desperately unlucky to lose.

Australia especially must have felt so when late on the fifth and last afternoon their captain along with that magnificent cricketer, Davidson, were pulling the game round so gallantly after Hall's great burst of fast bowling. Yet Benaud, despite the obvious fallibility of those due to follow, kept his sights fixed on victory. Thus he maintained at the last the challenging spirit set by the West Indian batsmen on the first day.

Bearing in mind the West Indies' caution against the England bowling last winter one naturally wondered whether the attacking approach of their early games would extend to the Tests. Sobers' tremendous 100 – in two hours! – on the first day did a good deal to provide the answer.

Inevitably odious comparisons are being made between this West Indies tour and the last to Australia by MCC. It was in Brisbane just two years ago that England were ingloriously beaten in just about the worst game ever played, and Bailey made 68 in seven and a half hours of the most misguided effort ever perpetrated in the name of cricket.

The contrast is astonishing: 665 in the one game, 1,474 in seemingly very similar conditions and a few hours less in the other; frustration and recriminations in the first place, to-day a joyful echo of courage and excitement that penetrates to us at home through the cold murk of winter.

But this is a good moment to remind ourselves that the recent MCC tour of West Indies gave evidence of a welcome change of heart on the part of a rejuvenated England team. Brilliant though much of the batting was at Brisbane, it cannot have been much better than that of Cowdrey at Kingston, or of Dexter at Bridgetown and Port-of-Spain.

All eyes and ears now will be trained on the next Test that begins at Melbourne on Dec. 30. But whatever occurs it will not dim the recollection of a game fit to rank with Manchester and the Oval, 1902, or Melbourne, 1908, or Durban, 1948 (when England won by two wickets from the last ball of the last over), and other tight-run classics of the past.

The nearest parallel probably was that Melbourne game wherein Barnes and Fielder put on 39 together to win for England by one wicket. With the scores level they embarked on an apparently suicidal run, but scrambled home as Hazlitt threw a wide return. When the scene was re-enacted yesterday, more than half a century later, the West Indian concerned kept his head a good deal better: at the climax his side owed all to the judgment of Solomon!

DIARY FOR 'THE SUNDAY'

Robert Menzies' aphorism gave me the first paragraph of the sporting diary in the opening issue of the Sunday Telegraph *on 5 February 1961. After writing the first six diaries I flew off (with the blessing of Michael Berry, our Editor-in-Chief) to manage my second touring side to the West Indies. When I returned I found that the diary was to be permanently in other hands, while I began a feature called 'In the Pavilion'. I shared a room with Kenneth Rose, whose Albany column, wonderful to relate, is still in his distinguished hands thirty-five years later. I quite enjoyed dabbling in other fields, but could never have permanently combined the cricket job and diary-writing. Besides, Donald McLachlan, my Editor, wanted the paragraphs short and pithy. I doubt if I could have been pithy enough.*

Herewith a few entries over the period: I never knew Jack White but John Morrison, Ernest Tyldesley, George Duckworth and Donald Steel were friends. Morrison's partner in trousers a while later became my wife. I never went to Upton Park but have always had a soft spot for West Ham.

'A sporting diary should combine wit with accuracy, and humanity with judgment.' Pondering this new assignment I sought light, among others, from one of the great modern patrons of sport, the Prime Minister of Australia, who was kind enough to wire these launching words.

Mr. Menzies describes the job as daunting, but is good enough to hold out hope for my success. Respecting his sentiments absolutely I can only endeavour to live up to them.

The date of the Prime Ministers' Conference next month will not please Mr. Menzies, for he must be home in early April while the Australian team are still on their way. His political wicket, it seems, is at last taking a little spin.

As to the wonderful Australia–West Indies series I dare not comment for fear of spilling over to the detriment of all else. But here is an agreeable news item. When Benaud's team – it will be his, of course – come first to London they will experience the novel compliment of being entertained to lunch at Lord's by the Lord's Taverners in the Long Room under the Chairmanship of their President, the Duke of Edinburgh.

Only one meal has ever previously been served, to my knowledge, in the Long Room, the dinner to mark Sir Pelham Warner's 80th birthday. MCC's gesture is a tribute to our visitors, to their own Royal ex-President, and to a club which has served the National Playing Fields with singular imagination and profit.

*

J. S. F. Morrison's death will recall many memories to the fraternities of soccer, golf and cricket, for he was a most clubable, genial man.

As it happens the anniversary falls this week of the first and not the least of the Corinthian victories in the F.A. Cup, against Blackburn at Crystal Palace in 1924. John Morrison was captain and played the game of his life. I watched as a young man, and was duly thrilled.

*

Today is J. C. White's 70th birthday. Though he bowled beautifully for Somerset summer after summer his real fame is based on his exploits in Australia with A. P. F. Chapman's team. It is a romantic story.

'Farmer' White was 37 before, in 1928, he played one Test against the West Indians. His subsequent choice to tour Australia was a tremendous surprise, owing itself, I believe, to Sir Jack Hobbs, who had been co-opted by the selectors.

As a foil to Larwood, Tate and Geary, he easily outdid all three, taking 25 wickets in the Tests and 65 altogether. These are the best figures of any visiting slow bowler in Australia since the 1914–18 war.

The secret of his slow left-arm bowling (delivered round the wicket) was such control and subtlety of flight that he never needed more than two men on the leg-side. Brilliant fielding, notably by the captain at silly mid-off, helped him to taunt his prey to their doom.

*

Of the memories evoked by my note on John Morrison I like best the picture of him with Ann de Montmorency (as she then was) winning the Central England Mixed Foursomes.

A deer-stalker on his head, he wore a vast mackintosh skirt of his own design. His partner – one of the first women to do so – wore waterproof trousers. (Years later this intrepid lady became Mrs E. W. S.)

*

My note on J. C. White prompts another member of the great 1928 MCC side, George Duckworth, to send news of a third, his old Lancashire friend Ernest Tyldesley.

'I am pleased to say,' he writes, 'that Tyldesley (E.) can now see to read.' He has had a cataract removed, having been blind for a year, and is so riddled with arthritis that he has had his neck in a plaster cast.

Despite these tribulations Tyldesley 'is in great heart, and very much on the Lancashire cricket ball.' This most respected of Old Trafford figures was the first pro elected to the County Committee. Now he is a vice-president.

*

By the time next season starts West Ham will have put to good use the £29,500 they received from Manchester United in exchange for their Eire full-back Cantwell. Covered accommodation for more than 10,000 on the north bank takes £18,000 of it, new floodlights 60ft. higher than the present ones the remainder, plus a further £5,000 to be raised from the bank.

LINDWALL DELIGHTS

The second of the tours under my name and the captaincy of Colin Ingleby-Mackenzie to the West Indies in 1961 was more ambitious than the first, taking in Grenada, Guiana, and St Kitts, in addition to Barbados, Trinidad and Tobago. As in 1956, the invitation came from the West Indies Board of Control. I was luckily able to recruit an ideal side, capable equally of distinguishing itself on the field and enjoying itself afterwards. Our captain and his deputy, the inimitable Everton Weekes, complemented one another perfectly. Eight of our side were or became Test cricketers, the leading performer being Bob Barber, then Lancashire captain, whom I rate among post-war English all-rounders second in natural ability only to Ian Botham. Ian McLachlan of South Australia, as I write, has recently been appointed Minister of Defence in the Australian Government. My side was: A. C. D. Ingleby-Mackenzie (captain), E. de C. Weekes (vice-captain), A. A. Baig, R. W. Barber, R. A. Gale, R. R. Lindwall, I. M. McLachlan, Nawab of Pataudi, H. J. Rhodes, A. C. Smith, P. M. Walker, B. D. Wells, O. S. Wheatley. Treasurer J. S. O. Haslewood. Daily Telegraph, *April 1961.*

ST KITTS, Saturday

There is an end to the best of parties and we begin to-morrow the ninth and last game of this short tour, the first visitors from overseas to play at St. Kitts in the memory of all but the oldest. The field has been levelled and re-sown for the occasion.

This week has brought two wins at different levels. Against Trinidad an even game swung strongly against us so that at one point we were only 45 runs on with half the side out in the second innings. But though the top batting has failed the tail never has and four innings of diverse style and character from Walker, Ingleby-Mackenzie, Smith and Lindwall put us in a position to declare, setting Trinidad to make 252 in 225 minutes.

Young Davis played so well that his side were ahead of the clock at half way with only two men out before Barber once again (with 5-44) showed the infinite value of a good class leg spinner. It was leg-spin again, this time purveyed by McLachlan, that flummoxed the enthusiastic cricketers of Tobago after they had bowled us out for 192, the lowest total of the tour.

Here, as at Port of Spain, Lindwall delighted all with a robust half-century, hooking the local fast bowler almost into the blue Caribbean. This great cricketer approaches his last games of consequence with the zest of a schoolboy: a moral here, of course, which is not lost on crowd or fellow players.

MENS SANA . . .

I knew and admired so many sporting schoolmasters who combined the qualities of scholar and gamester and who were dedicated to teaching, alike in classroom and on playing field. Charles Blackshaw was one such. A letter to the Editor of The Times, *30 May 1961.*

E. W. S. writes:

May I beg a few lines to express what many of your readers must have felt on hearing of the very sudden death at Cranleigh School of Charles Blackshaw?

It was there, over a span of all but 37 years, that his work lay, for most of that time as housemaster of East House and latterly as Master of the Junior School. From Rossall and Oriel he was appointed straight to Cranleigh, which from the end of his undergraduate days to the very eve of his retirement he served with singular ability, devotion, and cheerfulness. It would be hard to name a more admirable example of the 'all-round' schoolmaster, identifying himself with every facet of a boy's activities from the chapel and the class room to the playing field.

He coached many generations of cricketers, Rugby footballers, and hockey and Eton Fives players. But though Cranleigh was his life it was not his whole life. In the world of cricket his range of acquaintance was unusually wide, for he worked for the game in addition to playing it, on many club committees, and as manager of a host of sides, MCC, the Cryptics, Grasshoppers, Incogniti, Oxford Authentics, *et al.*

His special pride was the Cryptics, and it was he as president who largely directed the ambitious and wonderfully happy Jubilee Reunion at St. Edward's, Oxford, last September – perhaps the most comprehensive gathering of its kind ever assembled. It is safe to say that of the several hundred cricketers present there was scarcely a handful who did not know him as a warmhearted friend: few who had not sampled the hospitality that always flowed so generously.

PATAUDI'S ACCIDENT

The Oxford captain, the Nawab of Pataudi, was injured in a car crash at Hove last Saturday evening in company with R. H. C. Waters.

I gather from the Sussex secretary, Col. Grimston, that the doctors cannot yet commit themselves regarding the eye on which they operated. There is certainly a chance of its being saved.

There is, I gather, no possibility of his being able to play in the University Match on Saturday week. What a bitter blow for his side, which he was leading so well and for which he was batting so brilliantly!

C. D. Drybrough, the secretary, who automatically takes over the captaincy, is a highly promising all-round cricketer. But nothing can make up for the Nawab's batting and fielding. He has made 1,216 runs with an average of 55, and held 25 catches. Nothing, by the way, seemed more likely with three matches to go and only 90 more to get, than that he would outdo his father, who just 30 years ago made the most runs, 1,307, ever scored by an undergraduate in an Oxford season.

In the event he remained almost blind in the right eye, but played nevertheless for India against England six months later. Gubby Allen saw him during the Calcutta Test, saying in admiration, 'Tell me, Tiger, when did you think you might be able to make runs with only one eye?' Tiger smiled wickedly and said, 'When I saw the English bowling.' His overflowing talent, I believe, would have carried him to the very top of the tree but for the accident. Daily Telegraph, *June 1961.*

HAMPSHIRE'S TITLE

Daily Telegraph, *2 September 1961.*

The Championship to Hampshire! Leaving aside the natural disappointment of Yorkshiremen in general at seeing their side come so near to a hat-trick of victories everyone, I am sure, will be glad for Hampshire, and will salute them as worthy winners in what has been once more quite an open field.

Yorkshire patently could have won again, and so might Middlesex. But for both these giants of the Championship it would have been just another year on the roll of honour. Hampshire, like eight other of the counties, have never finished at the top since the competition was widely expanded in 1895.

It is appropriate, indeed, that a club which has given such cricketers as Philip Mead, Lionel Tennyson, George Brown, and Alec Kennedy, to name merely a few, should join the elect. The more historically-minded may delve back further, and recall that Broad-Halfpenny Down is the very cradle of cricket. We can imagine William Beldham chanting a Te Deum somewhere aloft, John Small striking triumphant chords on the violin.

The virtues that have won the day are patent to see, the consistent excellence of Shackleton, the strength and stamina of White, on the one hand, and on the other the brilliance of Marshall, supported less spectacularly by Horton, Gray, Sainsbury, and Livingstone, with frequent flourishes by Ingleby-Mackenzie.

Perhaps the outstanding characteristic of Hampshire has been their form on the third day in any sort of tight situation. Whether batting or bowling they have produced the goods, and this is where morale and leadership have come in.

This win is to a considerable extent a triumph for Ingleby-Mackenzie, and it will give particular delight to those who see in his approach the antithesis to the drab formality of much present-day cricket. Those who regard Ingleby-Mackenzie as a tactical cavalier are not wholly on the mark. In the field, at least, this is scarcely so. Equally it is a slight exaggeration to imagine the Hampshire dressing room is a focus for trainers and tipsters, with private wires to Newmarket and Burlington Street.

At the same time Ingleby-Mackenzie rules with a light touch and plays cricket with a smile that is reflected in his team. This is not the worst reason why Hampshire will be hailed as the welcome and popular Champions of 1961.

ENTER ONE-DAY CRICKET

Daily Telegraph, *December 1961.*

It was announced from Lord's after the MCC Inquiry Committee had met there yesterday that they are recommending to the counties the addition of a one-day knockout competition in the 1963 season.

To accommodate this all the first-class counties would play 28 three-day matches, and the Championship would be decided on points instead of the present percentage system, which is made necessary by the fact that eight counties now play 32 matches (i.e. all others twice) whereas nine prefer to play 28.

There is to be an Advisory County Committee meeting at Lord's on Dec. 20, by which time the various county committees will have met and decided on their support or otherwise.

It is to be hoped that they will be more sympathetic than was the case four years ago when the Altham Special Committee recommended a knock-out cup, and the counties duly rejected it.

VINCENT'S EMBLEM

To my vast surprise and pleasure I was notified not many years
ago that I had been elected an honorary member.
Daily Telegraph, *8 July 1962.*

There is, I suppose, no institution which personifies the ideal of 'Mens sana in corpore sano' – *a healthy mind in a healthy body* – to such effect as Vincent's Club, Oxford.

The Greeks had a word for it long before the Romans, but it was in Victorian England that the philosophy for which Vincent's stands found its most vigorous expression. The 1860s was a decade unparalleled for the founding of schools and the formation of games organisations of every sort and kind. Hence the great rush of centenary celebrations which have either taken place or are in prospect, that of Vincent's included.

Why, by the way, 'Vincent's'? Who was he? The facts have that element of chance upon which so much history depends. The original spirits were still debating the proposal of the founder, an oarsman from Brasenose called W. B. Woodgate, to call their club 'The Century' when the clock of the University Church began to strike midnight and all had to repair rapidly to their colleges. Someone said 'Vincent's, pro tem,' and thus it still is 99 years later.

Vincent was the publisher and stationer in the High Street who hired out the rooms above his shop, so the club got its name much as did Lord's, which was simply the field rented out to the Marylebone Cricket Club by Thomas of that ilk.

In this case surely there is much in a name. The idea of the founders, in which they succeeded from the first, was to gather an all-round elite of a hundred, but one wonders if they would have succeeded nearly as well if they had settled on the self-conscious 'Century' rather than the informal Vincent's.

To a regular and ever-grateful guest it would seem that the amiable atmosphere of Vincent's – the ethos, if you like – has changed little over at least the last quarter or third of its span. Part of the reason probably lies in the fact that though the emphasis has always been on games-minded people there has never been a sporting qualification for membership.

Though most of those who represent the University are members it does not at all follow that membership accompanies a Blue. A few precocious young gentlemen have had to wait a long time – or even for ever. Nor are most of the members Blues. Vincent's in fact is not a Bluetocracy.

As to colours, the old Vincent's was unusual – unique even – in having none. When after the first war the club decided on a tie they broke unfamiliar ground. The dark blue tie with silver crowns – perhaps, along with that of The Hawks of Cambridge, the most famous of all sporting ties – is a prototype of all the myriad others following that feature crests and emblems.

It cannot be necessary to emphasise the influence of Vincent's on Oxford games, but the club's *raison d'être* has been reflected in a far wider field. Cecil Rhodes was a member, and the qualifications for the Rhodes Scholarships that bring men to Oxford from over half the world are, as expressed in his will, very similar to those of Woodgate, the founder, who ordained that members should be 'selected for all-round qualities: social, physical, and intellectual.'

The reigning president, J. J. McPartlin, captain of the Rugby club and a Scottish international, is the 104th, and the latest of a roll that includes such present, or relatively modern, heroes as Sir George Abell, Alan Melville, the late Jack Lovelock, J. O. Newton-Thompson, Roger Bannister, D. B. Carr, M. J. K. Smith and Lord Home.

DUKE TO MANAGE

Among sporting surprises this appointment ranks very high. The Duke, with Alec Bedser alongside, ran a happy tour with a light but firm touch. As was commonly said, the real peer was the captain, 'Lord Ted' Dexter. Daily Telegraph, *25 July 1962.*

MCC created a surprise of the first order at Lord's last evening by announcing that the Duke of Norfolk would manage the team to tour Australia and New Zealand. His assistant manager will be A. V. Bedser.

It has been a point of criticism that several touring parties have been what might be described as 'underweight' on the management side, and the showing of MCC teams abroad has suffered severely in consequence.

No one can use this phrase, either metaphorically, literally, or in any other way, as regards the MCC tour of 1962–3.

The Duke will bring to his appointment not only a zeal for the game that is second to none, but also a shrewd knowledge of its practical politics, going as president of Sussex and past president of MCC. He is now serving his second term as a member of the MCC committee.

The necessary counterpart to a figure of such eminence at the head of affairs is clearly a man close to the players in age and one with the prestige that comes from great experience as a Test cricketer. Who therefore could fill the bill more admirably than Mr. Bedser?

DEXTER IN EXCELSIS

An exhilarating day altogether. I never remember an English side abroad scoring 458 in a day.
Daily Telegraph, *10 November 1962.*

MELBOURNE, Friday

It is just 100 years since a team of English cricketers first stepped on to this Melbourne field and it is safe to say that rarely if ever in the intervening century have their descendants given bowling a worse hammering than in this match against an Australian XI.

Dexter showed the way with the innings of a lifetime and this was the opening act of a drama that reached a climax in the last hour, wherein Knight punished the tired bowling for 57 out of an unbroken partnership with Barrington of 92.

It was all invigorating to a degree and the lift that has been given to the tour by the events of to-day is prodigious. There were 15,000 present – a good gate for a Friday – and it is now to be expected that everyone will want to see MCC bat, especially, of course, Dexter.

After a good many years of watching, relatively few innings stand out sharply in the mind above hundreds of others that become distinct again when one refers to them in books or in conversation.

Before to-day one has connected four pieces of English batsmanship with this vast and somewhat awesome arena. There were the hundreds by Compton and Hutton on the first appearance here of MCC since the war. There was Simpson's 156 not out that brought England's first post-war Test victory and there was Cowdrey's first Test hundred against Australia made a few days after his 22nd birthday.

Dexter's innings to-day brings the number as far as I am concerned to five. It was in every sense a *tour de force* that had the crowd humming with excitement and the Englishmen basking happily in reflected glory.

Dexter came in when MCC after three-quarters of an hour had reached a rather uncomfortable 26 for one. The authority and power he immediately brought to the scene were remarkable.

He began so audaciously in fact that one felt it was all rather too good to last. But last it did and that with the very minimum of false hits. He sliced a four over slips in the 20's and went slightly off the boil as it were in the 90's when Simpson bowled a couple of very good overs of leg-spin to him and both he and Veivers appealed vehemently for lbw.

These small items apart, his stroke-play was not only extraordinarily powerful but practically devoid of mistake. He hit 13 fours and two sixes and reached his hundred in 106 minutes.

It was one of the fastest seen in recent years in Australia and it was assuredly the hardest hit. Walcott is the name that one thinks of in terms of muzzle velocity, but I never remember seeing the ball travel faster even when there was a pile of runs on the board, let alone at the start of a game with the bowlers theoretically fresh.

Dexter having taken the Australian attack apart, the following MCC batting on a wicket now mild after its fretful first period took full toll. Everyone made runs and made them attractively, though, of course, the innings that mattered most was Cowdrey's.

He had at first the ideal role for a batsman out of luck – that of playing second fiddle to one in full command. By the time Dexter left Cowdrey was playing easily and well and in that vein he continued drawing the short ball at the angles he wanted on the leg-side and thrusting the fuller-pitched ones through the covers with that final persuasion of the wrists that those at home know so well. He had left his bad form behind him long before he got out, having incidentally batted only two hours 10 minutes for his 88.

After Cowdrey and Barrington had added 89 Barrington and Titmus put on a brisk 94. Harvey took another lovely catch down on his boots at deep mid-off to dispose of Titmus but this only let in Knight, who, while Barrington pursued his normal way, swung the bat and treated the bowling almost as though this were a charity match. At times one half-supposed it must be.

> Australian XI v MCC, at Melbourne, 9–13 November 1962. MCC 633 for 7 dec. (Barrington 219 not out, Knight 108, Dexter 102, Cowdrey 88) and 68 for 5 dec.; Australian XI 451 (Simpson 130, Shepherd 114, McLachlan 55, Harvey 51) and 201 for 4 (Shepherd 91 not out, McLachlan 68). Match Drawn.

THE ASHES IN SUSPENSE

Daily Telegraph, *22 February 1963*.

SYDNEY, Thursday

No Test tour is complete without its post mortems. The song is over but the melody lingers on. What sort of a melody? How happy are one's recollections?

Well, the Ashes are left in Australia or, as I prefer to put it, they remain in suspense. In a sense this is unsatisfactory and for some the sterile ending leaves a taste of ashes in the mouth.

But now is the time surely to try and see a tour in perspective and if one can adjust the focus at such a short distance the good, it would seem, more than counterbalances the bad.

Upwards of a million people have watched MCC since they landed at Fremantle four and a half months ago – in days of falling attendances in all sports that is a bare quarter of a million fewer than the highest ever figure of a quarter of a century ago – and the memories of most of them will I expect be satisfying ones.

Glamorous individual things are, of course, too numerous to count. But certain items stand out at random; Dexter's hundred, for instance, against the Australian XI at Melbourne, one of the finest pieces of forcing batsmanship I have ever seen; the prolonged felicity of Cowdrey's 307 at Adelaide; the composite effort by Sheppard, Dexter and Cowdrey that won the Second Test.

Most of England's batting in the Brisbane Test was effective and satisfying. Graveney had his moments of quality and the prolific Barrington, cast in a more sombre role, was by no means always quiet and restrained. The English out-cricket, certainly, was generally less satisfying.

Trueman's fire in the second innings at Melbourne was one conclusive performance, while Titmus, surely the find of the tour, had several. Allen, except for one bad day in the State match at Sydney when some odd notion or other was being put to the test, usually showed the arts of slow bowling at their best, while if many, too many, catches were missed some beauties were taken by Cowdrey, Graveney, Titmus, Barrington, Smith and others.

This last Sydney Test has been analysed enough already. It was unfinished because of England's tactical misappreciation on the first day, thought the most unsatisfactory episode of the tour, because of the sluggishness of the wicket and, indeed, the whole field which surely needs the urgent attention of Australian cricket officialdom, and not least because the fact of their holding the Ashes persuaded Benaud's team to wage defensive war from the beginning of the England second innings.

From the broad English viewpoint, granted certain reservations, the picture is not unsatisfactory. Few people expected Dexter's side to escape with a halved series. They have done so against more mature opponents for whom with the retirement from touring of Benaud, Harvey, Davidson and Mackay this marks the end of an era.

England must find replacements in certain places before Australia come next year especially in the way of opening batsmen and bowlers. Otherwise the framework of the present side should serve well for a while. Titmus has found himself as a Test all-rounder, and here let me say how pleasant it is to applaud his success. There are good tourers, moderate tourers and, alas, sometimes downright bad tourers, and when an exemplary one takes the palm all who know what these expeditions involve for captains and managements are doubly delighted.

Again there is no keener or fitter cricketer than Barrington and he has his reward in a batting record in Australia second only to Walter Hammond's back in 1928–29.

What now of the captain? He is an arresting figure of course and my belief is that both as leader and batsman the best of him lies immediately ahead. He has made a lot of mistakes of a tactical kind but he has the intelligence to learn from them. A certain combination of impulsiveness and a wayward concentration has prevented his making quite such an impact as a batsman as he promised in the first two Tests. Yet he ranks with Sobers as one of the two most exciting batsmen in world cricket to-day.

It is characteristic of the modern hypercritical attitude to those at the top that his supposed limitations are stressed and his virtues taken for granted.

Dexter, it seems to me, has the constitution and the temperament to withstand the strong tensions surrounding the leadership of the England XI at home and abroad. Not least he can combine toughness on the field with amiability towards the enemy off it. It may seem trivial to mention but it will not be so to those who have had close connection with touring teams that on the eve of the final Test the two captains and their wives should have been seen together happily enjoying the performance of Nat King Cole. So far as the off-field impressions of his team is concerned Dexter could hardly have been luckier than to be surrounded as he was.

Not many cricket visitors to Australia will have left behind more friends than the Duke of Norfolk, Alec Bedser, Colin Cowdrey and David Sheppard.

INNINGS UNFORGETTABLE

Within a few months Dexter played two innings only
to be described as superlative.
Daily Telegraph, 22 *June 1963.*

Great things were afoot to-day and Lord's, alternately silent in anticipation and a-jabber with excitement, has not for years seen better cricket or a tougher fight. Dexter played, I think, his finest innings for England, Old Trafford and Edgbaston in '61, Brisbane in '62, and earlier deeds at Bridgetown and elsewhere not forgotten. Barrington gave him most doughty support, and yet, despite an injury to Hall's foot that prevented his bowling more than nine overs, the position of the game to-night favours the West Indies.

Dexter's innings would have been remarkable whatever the circumstances had happened to be. In the context of the game it had an epic quality that one had to be here to appreciate. It was certainly recognised for what it was by the crowd who stood all round the ground and applauded Dexter back to the pavilion.

It was one of those occasions when men bask in the reflected virtue of great deeds. We will talk of this batting for weeks, and many years on cricketers will say to one another: 'But did you see Dexter that day at Lord's?'

The England innings began on that taut note which always accompanies great speed. Worrell caused some surprise by setting Hall at the Nursery end into the breeze, probably supposing that Griffith would be the more difficult of the two to see out of the pavilion background.

Whereas both were fast and formidable Griffith, indeed, seemed the harder to play. Having taken only one tail-end wicket at Old Trafford he was fortified here by getting Edrich with his first ball, caught by Murray, the keeper, from a faint tickle outside the pads.

The score was 20 for two when the game was continued after lunch, Dexter 16. When he was out an hour and three minutes later it was 102, Dexter 70. The 82 runs had come, in fact, off 15 overs, Barrington's share being an inconspicuous but, of course, highly valuable 20.

In Australia Barrington was accused, reasonably enough sometimes, of neglecting short runs and of seeming impervious to his partner's needs. This, I suspect, was chiefly a reflection of his intense concentration.

But to-day no one could have seen a single more quickly, or been more solicitous about allowing the other man the bowling. Seeing Dexter in such form he gave him his head.

The cold details were that when Dexter reached his 50 only 11 overs had been bowled since he reached the wicket and he had received 49 balls. Dexter has all the strokes, and most of them we saw, but those that really roused the crowd were the hooks off Hall and Griffith and also the driving of these fast bowlers.

Where everyone else was so pressed for time that they were mostly reduced to hurried jabs and prods Dexter had the leisure to drive with almost a full swing. The mellow crack of the bat might have been heard in St. John's Wood Road before the applause erupted and echoed round the crowded arena.

When Griffith, his shirt glistening wet, at last took his sweater, Sobers succeeded him and fired off his fast and fastish left-arm stuff over the wicket. The angle is unusual and Dexter had misconnected once, before he perhaps played slightly across a good-length ball and was lbw. So departed the captain, having received 75 balls in all, hit 10 fours and batted an hour and 20 minutes.

England v West Indies, at Lord's, 20–25 June 1963. West Indies 301 (Kanhai 73, Solomon 56, Trueman 6 for 100) and 229 (Butcher 133, Trueman 5 for 52); England 297 (Barrington 80, Dexter 70, Titmus 52 not out, Griffith 5 for 91) and 228 for 9 (Close 70, Barrington 60). Match Drawn.

CHAMPIONS!

Having brought his fellow West Indians together in a new
unison, Frank Worrell chose this moment to retire.
Daily Telegraph, *27 August 1963.*

THE OVAL, Monday

West Indies cricket to-day had its finest hour since the great victories of 1950. That was a 'first time' and so has a special place in history. But in 1950 England were weak. Now whatever faults can be found in Dexter's side he has just returned from fighting a drawn series in Australia.

England have been beaten only once in nine years in a rubber on their own grounds. The West Indies have won by three matches to one: a richly deserved win and they can fairly claim at this moment, pending the visit of the Australians to their islands in the spring of 1965, that they are the best-equipped and most powerful side in the world.

The averages tell, so far as the series just ended is concerned, a revealing story. Where England had one bowler consistently effective, their opponents had four. Where one English batsman averaged more than 35, the West Indies had four who did so.

But figures do not say how much more versatile and complete was the side that Worrell commanded. Nor do they underline the intangible but invaluable part played by the captain himself.

Frank Worrell leaves the scene tonight a figure of dignity and charm and withal a great leader of whom Barbados, the island of his birth, and Jamaica, that of his adoption, may be equally proud.

I have not known a better series than this in an experience going back now, it is rather sad to think, a quarter of a century. Nor have I known, looking round all the Test-playing countries, a better captain.

England v West Indies, at The Oval, 22–26 August 1963. England 275 (Sharpe 63, Griffith 6 for 71) and 223 (Sharpe 83); West Indies 246 (Hunte 80, Butcher 53) and 255 for 2 (Hunte 108 not out, Kanhai 77). West Indies won by 8 wickets.

CURIOUS LETTER

I was playing for the Free Foresters against Eton Ramblers at the home of Henry Blofeld. I was fifty-six and still turning the wrist, if not the ball, in a style rudely described as 'holy rollers'. You may well wonder, gentle reader, what point of resemblance this fellow found in my bowling to remind him of the Demon King of Potters Bar UDC.

19 September 1963

Dear Mr. Swanton

Being a friend of the Blofelds I had the pleasure of watching part of the cricket match last Sunday at Hoveton. Seeing you bowling reminded me of something I have been meaning to tell you about a match which may be of interest to add to your other stories. In 1937 playing for Wrotham Park C.C., which I captained, v. Potters Bar U.D.C., our fast bowler R. Ketteringham took all 10 wickets of the Potters Bar XI for 0. We did not play high class cricket and Potters Bar U.D.C. were dismissed for 9! Even so, Ketteringham's 10 wickets for 0 is somewhat outstanding.

Yours sincerely
C. Fellowes

STARS IN THE EAST

It was something of a rush to plan and make all administrative arrange-ments for this tour during the 1963/64 winter: it was, of course, a venture quite impossible to repeat today. Gary Sobers' five wickets in five balls was the individual high spot of the tour, while I was specially proud, naturally, of the victory at Calcutta against what was more or less the Indian Test team except that Pataudi was touring with us. I had the pleasure of handing over the profit of £1,000 to the Tunku Abdul Rahman, Prime Minister of the Federation, for the funds of the Malayan Cricket Association.

My team was: A. C. D. Ingleby-Mackenzie (captain), R. Benaud, T. B. L. Coghlan, M. G. Griffith, R. A. Hutton, S. E. A. Kimmins, I. M. McLachlan, Nawab of Pataudi, S. M. Nurse, J. D. Piachaud, N. C. Pretzlik, S. Ramadhin, G. S. Sobers and K. A. Taylor. The Cricketer, April 1964.

'If you want to do something useful, you'll take a side to Malaya,' said a friend casually one day last autumn. The thought germinated awhile, and when I decided to try and act on the idea – and to expand it – I found a wonderful degree of co-operation from good folk with Anglo-Malayan interests in the City, as well as from the cricket com-munities of the Far East. In three months or so the financial stability of the operation was guaranteed, the programme was arranged, and the players collected.

The first of our six places of call was the charming island of Penang. The opposition were quickly disrupted by Seymour Nurse, who opened the game by making 88 in four minutes under the hour, after which

McLachlan, a married man of five days' standing, played as well as I have ever seen him. Thereafter in Malaya we always had a good deal to spare, although stroke-making was seldom easy on the reddish pitches, generally short of grass, that tended to dust and powder.

The performance of the All-Malaysian national side (on its first appearance under this title) at Kuala Lumpur over the Easter weekend was up to the best University traditions.

This spectacular game was just what was needed to whet local appetites for cricket, and it was gratifying to learn that the ten thousand spectators over the two days was the most that had been seen there. At Singapore the crowd had been enthused, among other things, by a brilliant 114 from Pataudi, and a stylish innings by Taylor. Now we were reinforced by Sobers, who henceforward with either bat or ball or both was never out of the picture.

On Easter morning, amid a cup-final hubbub, Sobers was bowled first ball by what to him was an off-break, perfectly pitched and flighted by Delilkan, a Singhalese doctor from Penang, who with the Shepherdson brothers, da Silva, and Ranjit Singh represented the best class in the Malayan cricket we encountered. In the afternoon came Sobers's revenge. He had his first victim caught at short-leg off the fourth ball of his first over, the second was lbw, the third went the same way as the first. 'Hat-trick.' Batsmen 5 and 6 were clean bowled by the first two balls of Sobers's second over, and that, incredible to relate, was five in five. Furthermore No. 7, late like his predecessors, was only just able to edge the next ball on to his pads and clear of the stumps.

It was fine bowling, and one's only regret was that it might tend to portray Malayan cricketers to the world, and perhaps to themselves, as rabbits. This they certainly are not, and if Sobers's assault was too much for them let them be sure it might well have demolished men of greater experience.

His new ball speed is authentically fast, and he keeps the ball right up thus giving himself every chance of getting through with the late swing. Having seen his effect on the best Indian batsmen on a perfect wicket at Calcutta I am fortified in the view that Sobers today is the most dangerous new ball bowler playing.

Hong Kong like Malaya has its wicket troubles, the difficulty there being primarily lack of water. At Kowloon, where the Colony strength was gathered against us over the weekend, the captains agreed to the pitch being watered on the first evening to give it a better chance of lasting the next day.

We were further strengthened now by the arrival of Benaud. At Hong Kong, as in Malaya, the administration had been efficient and our various hosts in all the places kindness itself. Hospitality was equally, or even more, prodigal at Bangkok, a fact which the manager noted with somewhat mixed feelings looking ahead to Calcutta.

However he need not have worried. It was appallingly hot – 106.8 the first day and never out of the nineties thereafter, with the humidity likewise ninety plus – but the Commonwealth side stood it fully as well as their opponents. Sobers, Nurse, and Benaud especially showed astonishing stamina, while the fielding, under the captain's encouragement and example, sparkled as though it were just a crisp, dry English day. It would be hard, incidentally, to find a better off-side trio in support of spin bowling than Pataudi, Taylor and Nurse. Griffith's 'keeping should be noted also. He had six victims in the match, missed nothing, and drew praise from all.

Nurse, of course, with 241 runs to his name for once out, had a wonderful triumph, after which it was the assault by Benaud on Nadkarni that paved the way to victory. Otherwise I must leave the score to speak for itself, adding only the necessary assurance, needed nowadays where games of this character are concerned, that the cricket was absolutely hard and straight, with not a cheap run or anything given away. The play was never devoid of incident, and there was an admirably impartial crowd of, in all, around fifty thousand.

Borde's declaration at lunch (the days' play were limited to five hours because of the heat) left Ingleby-Mackenzie's batsmen three hours to make 243. We calculated, correctly, that with three drink intervals to come and a probable rate of 17 overs an hour this meant scoring five runs an over. That was the rate achieved, and the winning hit came with ten minutes to spare.

And so next morning, the 33rd and last, to London, all very weary from 18 days' cricket, twenty thousand miles in the air, a multitude of new friends met, many parties attended, and with memories of people and places to last a long time. The younger players returned surely better and more complete cricketers, and, praise be! our treasurer, John Haslewood with a four-figure surplus. Most important of all we contrived (apparently) to leave a string of satisfied hosts behind. On behalf of everyone in the party I cannot thank them enough.

An Indian XI v. E. W. Swanton's XI at Calucutta, April 11–15, 1964.
Indian XI 348 (Nadkarni 78, Borde 69, Poddar 54, Sobers 6 for 63)

and 215 for 8 dec. (Sardesai 59, Hanumant Singh 58); E. W. Swanton's XI 321 (Nurse 106, Sobers 123, Chandrasekhar 6 for 103) and 243 for 3 (Nurse 135*, Benaud 69). E. W. Swanton's XI won by 7 wickets.

END OF INNINGS

Retirement it was, and high time too.
The Cricketer, *27 August 1965.*

These Notes seem to have developed on unusually personal lines, and they seem destined to end this way, as I must now tell the story of a notable innings with which I was closely connected recently at Harrow. I have seen some pretty good batting since writing in the last issue. There was, after all, Graeme Pollock's great innings at Trent Bridge, and Colin Cowdrey's hundred there – and for that matter his 99 not out on an awkward wicket at Dover against Gloucestershire – and some very fine play at Hove on the part of Suttle and Walker. But without making invidious comparisons none of them was much more admirable of their kind than the innings played by John Woodcock, cricket correspondent of *The Times* for the Arabs against Harrow Wanderers.

The Arabs were up against quite a modest Wanderers' score of 185 when Woodcock opened the innings. But while he stayed firm and scored freely enough from the start partners came and went with depressing frequency. In the end time as well as wickets were a factor when the cricket correspondent of *The Daily Telegraph*, aged and over-weight, made his nervous way to the crease. If only he could play reasonably straight and push the odd single or two, Woodcock would hit the fours and pull the thing off. True, he hadn't held a bat all the summer, having played several times without finding it necessary to go in. But it was a good wicket, surely very like the one he and Billy Griffith had made a lot of runs on here a few years ago. It shouldn't be terribly difficult.

Difficult? The miserable fellow found it not so much difficult as impossible. The bat had no middle at all, it merely gave an occasional sign of possessing some edges. The agony lasted some minutes before there came the fatal, inevitable rattle and the end came with the score 172 for eight, with Woodcock taking out his bat for 94, a heroic innings beautifully judged – if only he could have found a partner of ordinary competence at the crisis. As I write, his wretched colleague of the *Telegraph* is making an agonizing appraisal of the situation, facing the moment of truth. Yes (he has looked it up), he and Griffith did make 'more than a hundred in fifty minutes' for MCC against the boys, and he was even actually bowled trying for a six that would have given him his hundred. But that in fact was in 1952.

One thing was certain. The plastic spectacles hadn't been much use. He bought them a month ago, having missed a straightforward catch at mid-off that left the most perfect facsimile of the Butterflies' colours on his chest: crimson, purple and black. Now he had collected the same colours slightly lower down through missing a slow full-pitch. What now? Is it to be a graceful retirement (as his wife has long advocated) and perhaps a broad direction of tactics from the pavilion? It looks much like it.

PART SIX

1966–1975

1966–1975

If the previous decade had seen cricket in transition, this period, between '66 and '75, saw it establishing new formats. One-day cricket made an entrance and then walked to centre stage. The Gillette Cup had already started in 1963 and its success in drawing the crowds made further similar competitions inevitable. And so was begat the John Player Sunday League in 1968 and four years later the early season Benson and Hedges. Sponsorship was now part of the scene and marketing – low key, in retrospect – was the name of the game.

If the period seems piebald in the mind's eye – the balance-sheet of any era contains credits and debits, of course – it is perhaps because the contrasts were so marked. The Brian Close time-wasting incident, for instance, retains a clarity just because legislation has had to be put in place to defeat such a tactic. So does the riot in the Second Test between the West Indies and England at Kingston, Jamaica in 1968 because it was among the first and worst of its kind. The recent World Cup game at Eden Gardens, Calcutta between India and Sri Lanka, which had to be stopped because of crowd interference, brought it all flooding back.

The happier moments, too, have their place, although the retina image of good news is not always as bright. Tony Lewis leading England to victory against India at Delhi with an undefeated 70 on Christmas Day 1972 is an example. And earlier that year, four of the five Tests against Australia under Ray Illingworth's captaincy were, as Jim says, 'among the best I ever saw'.

As often happened, a stand by Swanton against unpalatable behaviour on the cricket field was in evidence. Incurring his wrath was the attitude of the Ashes-winning side of 1970/71 in Australia, also led by Illingworth, and subsequently endorsed by the Cricket Council's admonition. A broadcast encounter on 'It's Your Line', chaired by Robin Day and begun when Illingworth was not even aware that Swanton was listening, makes compelling reading. The England captain's favourite party-line at that time was, 'Jim is such a snob, he doesn't even travel in the same car as his chauffeur.'

But the overriding issue of this decade was, as will easily be remembered, the D'Oliveira affair. The emanating thunderclaps never seemed to cease. During the 1956/57 tour of South Africa Jim had seen at first hand the change in attitude in the country. At first, after coming to power in 1948, the ruling Nationalist Party had trodden carefully, but now were certain of their position. Jim abhorred apartheid and therefore had declined to go on the subsequent 1964/65 tour of South Africa. By 1968 he led the way in calling for a reform of the MCC after they sought compromise and avoidance on what seemed to many a matter of fundamental humanity.

His reaction surprised some who saw him only as an archetypal Establishment figure. But, as is obvious in these pages, Swanton has never been slow to tilt at windmills regardless of their position on the campus.

A few years earlier, in 1966, Jim edited, with the help of John Woodcock, a tome entitled *The World of Cricket*, the most comprehensive coverage of every branch of the game on the library shelves and an invaluable reference book for devotees. It was a massive undertaking and demanded much of his time and concentration. He also took off his pads in club cricket after scoring some twenty-seven hundreds and taking around 300 wickets. His last game was for his beloved Arabs against the Greenjackets – he did not bat. The decision to call it a day had been taken after a game against Harrow Wanderers, but he has told that story himself.

The 1974/75 tour of Australia was Jim's last outing as the cricket correspondent of the *Daily Telegraph*. The fire-eating, ferocious little Sports Editor of the paper, Kingsley Wright – a Yorkshireman to boot – told him to 'go on as long as you like – pick your own time for retirement.' As Jim had been nominated for the MCC Committee in 1974 with election likely the following year, he felt at sixty-eight years young that that time had arrived.

The Ashes were lost, but the Final Test at Melbourne was won by England by an innings. Jim was bowing out after 270 Tests. His lasting memory of the occasion was of Colin Cowdrey in a sun hat, leaning on a barrier, signing autographs. There could have been few more appropriate recollections.

Of course, it was not the end, more a new beginning. But all that comes later.

D. R. A.

MY DEAR LORD SOCKEM

My old friend Leonard Crawley was inclined to fire off missives such as this – quixotic, completely individual, sometimes penetrating, at others off-beam, spelling idiosyncratic (always 'peices'). I was on envelopes, in conversation, to my embarrassment 'Lord Sockem' because I am supposed to have said, in relation to Daily Telegraph *remuneration, 'I sock 'em for expenses' – a calumny, needless to say.*

Bury St. Edmunds, Suffolk
21st April, 1966

My dear Lord Sockem,

I was so glad to hear of your reappearance at Sandwich from friends who were at the Halford-Hewitt and have either telephoned or called here in the last two days. I have been suffering from gout, an appallingly painful affliction.

Your only occasional pieces in the *Daily Telegraph* from Australia during six winter months are no doubt responsible for the current rumour that you are to retire. But if this is true – and I have heard it here, there, and elsewhere, I do hope it is not on the grounds of ill health, and only because you have put enough by to feel secure with Ann in your lovely home at Sandwich.

I always say you are the best sporting broadcaster I have ever heard. I do hope that if it is true that you are contemplating giving up journalism, you will retain your association with BBC. You give us the picture we want to hear of an interesting day's play and if it has been a dull one, we can always turn you off when you become boring.

I am returning under separate cover your copy of Cosmo Gordon Lang which has taken me a long time to read, but I have thoroughly enjoyed it and the references to my family.

Many of the Archbishop's utterances, and passages from his speeches and his sermons have stuck in my mind, and ought to improve my pathetic little attempts at English in the *Daily Telegraph*.

Unfortunately, Crawley and Golf are always on an early page and as long as the stuff is in time, nothing else matters. I no longer care; all I want is employment.

What are you going to say about Griffith? You must take one side or the other, regardless of your health.   Yours ever,
Leonard

FRANK WORRELL HONOURED AT THE ABBEY

Memorial address, 7 April 1967.

In this ancient Abbey church, which enshrines so much of the history of England and of the British Empire and Commonwealth, we, gathered here today, are taking part in a unique service. Here, where the most famous have been buried, and the lives of the greatest commemorated, we are assembled to mourn for, and to pray for the soul of Sir Frank Mortimer Maglinne Worrell, a cricketer. It is making history to open the doors of the Abbey for the passing of a sportsman. My privilege and responsibility now is to try and give you such a picture of the man as will explain why in their wisdom the Dean and Chapter of Westminster have allowed us, his friends and admirers, from so many parts of the world, to pay our last respect in this glorious, awesome setting.

Frank Worrell was born at Bank Hall on the outskirts of Bridgetown, Barbados, on August 1st 1924. His father was a sailor, and so it came that when his mother emigrated to America he was brought up by his grandmother. It was from the roof of her small wooden house, adjoining the ground of the Empire club which has produced so many of the best Barbadian players, that he watched his first cricket. It was this environment no doubt that fired his ambition and gave him models of excellence to follow.

While he was learning to be a cricketer he was also growing up as a Christian. There is perhaps scarcely a firmer stronghold of Anglicanism in the whole communion of Canterbury than Barbados – a fact that perhaps adds a little more to the appropriateness of this service. Frank sang as a boy in the choir of St Michael's Cathedral, and ever after had a great love of church music. A pleasant story is told by his brother-in-law of how some years ago in Lancashire they both attended the three hours' service of devotion on Good Friday. After the service Frank complained there had not been enough hymns, and so they went home and played some more on the piano and sang.

The foundations of the Christian philosophy that governed his life were laid then as a boy. As a cricketer he grew up fast. At the age of only nineteen he scored 308 not out against the great rivals across the water, Trinidad. Here in fact was a prodigy, whose succession to the West Indies team when war ended, and Test Matches were played again, seemed an automatic thing. He was soon being hailed, in company with two other young Bajans, Everton Weekes and Clyde Walcott – all three born close to one another and in the space of 18 months – as a great player. This is not the occasion to speak either of his technique or of his achievements on the field, except perhaps to say this – that cricket, like any other art, is an expression of character, and there was always about Frank's play a grace, a dignity, and an unrufflable serenity that reflected the man.

But Frank had set his eyes on horizons beyond the cricket field. He came to Lancashire to earn his living as a professional in the League, and at the same time to take his degree at Manchester University. He warmed to Lancashire (and in particular to Radcliffe, where he played), and Lancashire warmed to him. His twelve years there made him the most fervent of Anglophiles, and so he remained. It was a Lancastrian, George Duckworth – that shrewd, humorous, lovable man – who, I think, first saw in Frank the special qualities of leadership. At the early age of twenty-six (ten years before being honoured by his country), he was captaining with much promise a mixed Commonwealth team, mostly of men a good deal older than he, managed by Duckworth in India.

When at last he was named as captain of the West Indies, on the tour to Australia in 1960, the appointment was accepted by the rest of his team, if not by him, as a challenge to his race. Under the subtle knack of his personality difference of colour, island prejudices, seemed to melt away. The tour of Australia was a triumph both on the field and off it, ending, as everyone will remember, with a motorcade through the streets of Melbourne lined with half a million cheering people. Three summers later he brought the West Indies team to England for a tour that enthused the sporting world no less than the one in Australia. He retired from playing after this, and in the New Year of 1964 received the honour of knighthood.

For the last three years of his life he was, of course, a national hero, but in bearing that difficult mantle he lost none of his modesty, none of his warmth. It is, of course, a deep sorrow that by the workings of Providence he has been taken away with such suddenness when it seemed that he had so much more to contribute in areas outside sport: in social fields, and in particular in the life of the University of the West Indies. He had made a deep mark already in Jamaica as University Warden (with a seat also in the Jamaican Senate). Since last year he had been Dean of Students in Trinidad. In both these islands the civic authorities had utilised his influences with young people and his readiness to identify himself with them. He had not worked in Trinidad for long but it was a measure of the affection he attracted that four chartered aeroplanes were needed to fly mourners to the funeral in Barbados.

No doubt, in course of time, he might have served as representative in one or other of the Caribbean territories in the very highest office. He was a Federalist, nearest whose heart was the unity of the West Indian peoples in all their diversity. Myself, I believe he harboured a special ambition to help bring on that branch of the University in his native Barbados which is now building, and on the site on which he is buried.

He had a warm, understanding heart and a sort of sleepy charm that endeared old and young alike.

He was essentially a bringer-together by the sincerity and friendliness of his personality; a sporting catalyst in an era where international rivalries too often grow sour and ugly. In the television age men famous in the world of games have a formidable influence, and strange figures are sometimes magnified into heroes. Frank Worrell was the absolute antithesis of the strident and the bumptious, of, so to speak, the great-sportsman-who-is-not. It is his example – and that of many of his West Indian cricket contemporaries – that has helped so much towards an appreciation and an admiration for his countrymen in England and throughout the Commonwealth. One of his opposing captains in an appreciation of him wrote that however the game ended, 'he made you feel a little better.' Which isn't a bad epitaph. No doubt he made many of us feel a little better, from the youngsters in Boys' Town at Kingston to Sydney hoboes on the Hill.

Have I pictured a paragon? Well, he certainly didn't look the part and would have been horrified at the very thought of a tribute such as this. He was gay and convivial, and though his convictions were deep and sincere they were never paraded. Yet, just as England brought cricket to the West Indies, the West Indies in return, I believe, has given us the ideal cricketer. When His Excellency the High Commissioner was reading those haunting Beatitudes just now the thought came: whom do I know who has fulfilled them better? May God rest his soul and give consolation to his widow and daughter. And may his example live with us.

RIOT STOPS PLAY

The police made one vital miscalculation. The wind was blowing from the scene of the riot towards the pavilion and stands. All were affected, including Lt. General Oliver Leese, President of MCC and my wife, Ann. The meeting of the Jamaican Cabinet, several hundred yards away, had to be suspended. The press got off with bearable discomfort: it was the only box I ever worked in which had an air-conditioning unit. England were odds on to win before the riot: in the extraordinary post-riot atmosphere they came near to losing. The rubber was won by England in the next Test, following Gary Sobers's declaration. Daily Telegraph, *13 February 1968.*

KINGSTON, Jamaica, Monday

Police used tear gas to break up a riot by spectators which halted play in the Second Test match between England and the West Indies at Sabina Park, Kingston, today.

Trouble began when the West Indian batsman, Basil Butcher, was given out, to make the score 204 for 5 in the West Indies second innings with 29 runs needed to avoid an innings defeat. There was uproar and bottles began to fly on to the pitch. Colin Cowdrey, the England captain, was struck on the foot. Cowdrey courageously walked to the boundary fence and appealed for calm. His move was in vain and bottles continued to fly.

Police carrying plastic shields to fend off the bottles moved into action. Gary Sobers, the West Indies captain, joined the appeals for peace and both he and Cowdrey had to retreat.

Parks behind the wicket had just caught Butcher left-handed and low from a leg glance. It was a lovely catch that Butcher could see better than anyone. He walked before Sang Hue, the umpire, had given the decision.

Nothing happened until Holford, the next batsman, got to the wicket. First a few bottles, then a larger number, arrived from the popular side.

Cowdrey at once-appealed to the crowd. There were, perhaps, five minutes when, with Sobers and the England players and police confronting the rowdy section, it seemed that the outburst would peter out.

Sobers shouted: 'Butcher was out.' But those bent on mischief were past hearing.

Suddenly more bottles were thrown from another corner on the same eastern edge of the field. More police, first with shields and then with tear gas, ran from their assembly point.

The order to throw the bombs was given and the crowd broke in panic and made off on to the field and out of the ground.

Typing this with more than a whiff of tear gas making things unpleasant in the Press box, one is confused by the events.

The England team and the umpires reached the pavilion before order was finally lost. The pitch at one moment was being freely run over and the crowd shouted: 'Sang Hue no more.'

After a meeting between officers of the board, Cowdrey and Mr. Leslie Ames, MCC manager, and an inspection of the pitch and outfield by the captains, it was stated that the game would be resumed at four o'clock.

If necessary the time lost – which I estimate as 70 minutes – will be made up on Wednesday morning.

The England team and the not-out batsmen came out at four o'clock with the danger area threequarters empty of spectators and many police among those who remained.

Yet a small fusillade, reputedly from outside the ground, held up play for a further five minutes.

Then D'Oliveira delivered the last three balls of his fateful over. For the moment at any rate the game was on again.

At close of play the West Indies were 258-5 (25 runs ahead).

West Indies v England, at Kingston, 8–14 February 1968. England 376 (Cowdrey 101, Edrich 96, Barrington 63) and 68 for 8; West Indies 143 (Snow 7 for 49) and 391 for 9 dec. (Sobers 113 not out, Nurse 73). Match Drawn.

ENOCH, ENOCH!

Letter to the Editor of The Spectator, *10 May 1968.*

Sir: In a recent letter to the *Daily Telegraph*, Mr Patrick Wall, MP, seemed to applaud Mr Enoch Powell's infamous speech as a clarion call to Britons who have a pride in their country.

Within the last few days an Indian student at Highbury has been set upon, kicked and slashed, by four sixteen-year-olds chanting 'blackman, blackman, Enoch, Enoch.' A respectable West Indian citizen at Wolverhampton celebrating a family christening has been attacked without provocation and injured by people also invoking the name of Enoch, the prophet. 'Enoch dockers' at Westminster have been putting their boots into students on the ground.

Are we to explain this sort of behaviour as some sort of twisted expression of national pride?

Many will echo Mr Wall's cry for leadership of a kind that will kindle 'those principles that made us great' but what has this aspiration to do with a bloodthirsty, hateful speech, lacking a single compassionate phrase towards fellow-members of our Commonwealth, which has so fanned the flames of ignorance and prejudice as to bring about such episodes as these?

If 'Enoch' knew what passions he was about to unleash, he was guilty of an act that was the complete negation of patriotism. It is possibly more charitable to suppose that his frothy speech was a bid for future political power which, pray God, he may never achieve.

If 'Enochism' were ever to win through there would surely be a migration from this once-great land of white as well as black.

E. W. Swanton

FIELD-MARSHAL MONTGOMERY ON CAPTAINCY

I first went down to Isington Mill at the invitation of Monty in March, 1959. He wanted to know the reasons for the humiliating defeats just suffered by Peter May's MCC team in Australia. I grave him a brief résumé of the tour before he announced that the waging of Test Matches, indeed success at all levels of cricket, boiled down to leadership. Thereupon we lunched well and he showed me over the two caravans, his and Rommel's. He had lived in these from Alamein to the surrender on Luneberg Heath. He slept in the more elaborate German one, only surrendering it to the King and Winston Churchill.

Over the next ten years and more we exchanged letters about English cricket, but the great man (who had been a decent player at St Paul's and Sandhurst) never strayed from a simplistic view that everything depended on leadership. During that period no England captain won his approval.

FROM : FIELD-MARSHAL THE VISCOUNT MONTGOMERY OF ALAMEIN
K.G., G.C.B., D.S.O.

ISINGTON MILL
ALTON
HANTS

TEL. BENTLEY 3126

17-7-68

My dear Jim

I hope you will write a book on the present Test series: England v. Australia. It is needed — from you.

Cowdrey is a magnificent cricketer — the best bat in the world today, and a superb slip fielder. But he has a great deal to learn about generalship. In a battle it is captaincy which counts; a Test match is a battle; it is a battle when the British Lions play South Africa.

In England's first innings what was the point in going on to make 409? Cowdrey had a team packed with bowlers. I suggest he should have declared at 300 plus and then loosed his bowlers at Australia — trusting to a bit of _luck_ to get them out. Instead, he played for safety; maybe he wanted some of his batsmen to make centuries, but that is bad.

In my profession you cannot expect _luck_, and don't deserve it, unless you are _bold_. It is the same in cricket. If Cowdrey had been _bold_, and remembered the English climate, he might well have won the third test before the rain came at 12.30 p.m. on the last day. What are your views on that?

yrs. ever
Montgomery of Alamein

MOMENTOUS WEEK IN HISTORY

England halved the rubber with Australia, Basil D'Oliveira, the South African-born Cape-coloured resident in England, having played a memorable innings of 158 which should surely have clinched his place for the forthcoming tour to South Africa. When, on Tom Cartwright falling out, D'Oliveira was named in his place the South African Prime Minister Dr Verwoerd declared it was a political decision and denied him entry. Thereupon MCC cancelled the tour. It was an unhappy note on which the Club handed over authority to the Council which later became controlled by the counties. Daily Telegraph, *4 September 1968.*

It is no ordinary week wherein England win a home Test Match against Australia, an MCC side is chosen for South Africa and almost universally condemned, and the great Club itself brought into disrepute.

When, also, a West Indian cricketer playing for Kent scores 155 runs between lunch and tea, and another, an hour or two later, as if, having heard about it and being determined to put the young man in his place, promptly hits six sixes in an over.

Lighter matters first. Having seen as much of Gary Sobers' cricket as most since he first emerged as a shy 17-year-old against Len Hutton's team in Barbados 14 years ago, I put very little beyond him. If anyone were to beat Alletson's ancient record he would obviously be the man.

The thing I most wanted to know about this slaughtering of the medium-paced Nash was the direction of the strokes, and those who, like me, could find no description in the reports will be interested in the following detail which comes first-hand from O. S. Wheatley, who was enjoying it all from the field of play.

Sobers was batting with his back to Mumbles Bay on the curiously shaped (and capacious) St Helens ground, Swansea. The first six over long-on cleared the wall and smacked against a pub in Gorse Lane. The second went to mid-wicket, and apparently connected with another pub a little down the road.

The third landed among the spectators at long-off, the fourth similarly at mid-wicket. The fifth was the one that Roger Davis at long-off caught before falling over the boundary line, and the last and biggest again flew over mid-wicket down a side street towards the town hall, and was not recovered until next day.

Young Nash was bowling medium-paced 'cutters' – that is to say he was aiming to bring the ball across from off to leg to the left-hander, and he was turning the ball enough to be bowling round the wicket.

He had been economical to that point, and I am assured that 'it wasn't at all a bad over!' Most of the leg-side strokes were hit with orthodox violence off the back foot.

According to Wilfred Wooller, the Glamorgan secretary, he had been batting only 31 minutes for 76 when at the end of this momentous over, Sobers declared.

The hero of the 155 between 2.10 and 4.20 p.m. (170 in 175 minutes all told: five sixes, 24 fours) was, of course, John Shepherd, likewise of Barbados. And I expect that when the news of this *tour de force* got to Sydney and Melbourne, there will have been many sighs over this young man's omission from the West Indies team due there late next month, just as there must have been in South Africa over the absence of Colin Milburn. One way and another this has not been a great year for selectors. Even in these containing days batting aggression wins matches and spectators still have an old-fashioned liking for seeing the ball hit.

In a thoroughly daunting post-bag on MCC's choice (or rather on their non-choice) a reader from Clifton makes this pertinent point: 'We, as coaches of the young, are asked to breathe into them a spirit of adventure and a sense of joy. Yet here are our own mentors choosing honest craftsmen and passing over the men of inspiration.' The reference, of course, was to Milburn and D'Oliveira.

Those who have had their fill of the D'Oliveira matter – and I have some sympathy with them since, other considerations apart, it is so lowering to the spirits of those who love cricket – must credit me with having covered quite a bit of space without a specific mention of the name.

Yet, if a continuing spate of letters were not sufficient evidence that the cricket public still seems to be thinking of little else, it is enough to move among club players, as I am glad to say I have been doing since the Test Match, the happy memory of which has been so sadly submerged.

I have scarcely met anyone, nor have I had a single letter, that has attempted to make a case for the selectors. One reader seems to sum up a general feeling when he writes of 'The grotesque casuistry of the attempt to explain the omission of D'Oliveira on cricketing grounds.'

It was this attempt on the part of the chairman to justify what had been done that was for many about the last straw.

To say that there were 'several better batsmen' after a Test innings of such a calibre; to assert on the one hand that the South African pitches are expected to be grassy enough to suit Cartwright and on the other that D'Oliveira's bowling did not come into consideration: this in the language of ordinary followers was merely adding insult to injury.

This setback in esteem comes at a time when the control of cricket is just being established on a constitutional basis for the first time, and has been put in the hands of an MCC Council on which the committee of the Club has a considerable representation.

As a cricket historian I believe that the game has generally been wisely and selflessly guided from Lord's, and that its collective judgment comes well from scrutiny over the span of a century or more. There are, however, moments that call for reform in all institutions, and such a one must surely have arrived for MCC.

CUTTING VERSE

Daily Telegraph, *30 April 1969.*

I must acknowledge with thanks a prompt verse sent by the Lancashire bowlers following my remark on Monday that their hairstyles would not have suited a sergeant-major. The following is to be sung, they say, to the tune 'All Through the Night':

> *Seven days have come to stay,*
> *Poor owd Jim.*
> *This is why our hair's this way,*
> *Poor owd Jim.*
> *Barber left us, you remember:*
> *Hair cutting begins September.*
> *So till then you must surrender.*
> *Poor owd Jim.*

Well, well, that must almost entitle Kenneth Shuttleworth, Peter Lever, John Sullivan and Barry Wood to claim poetic licence. I take the point about their hard-slogging seven-day week, but shudder to think what they will be looking like by the end of the season.

The best I can offer as an inducement to the first to take four wickets in a Sunday innings is, if it would be acceptable, a trim, shampoo and set.

SOUTH AFRICAN TOUR CALLED OFF

During the 1969–70 winter the Springbok rugby football tour to Great Britain was accompanied by scenes of perpetual disorder and violence. In January 12 county grounds were attacked on the same night in a concerted anti-apartheid action. Shortly afterwards it was announced that the South African cricket tour would be reduced to 12 matches played on 8 grounds. The evidence of the Springbok tour still in progress made it increasingly apparent that cricket matches would be still more vulnerable to disruption. The counties agreed that they would play on artificial pitches if necessary.

When the season began the Cricket Council were still determined to proceed with the arrangements, despite the most widespread opposition. The TUC advised its members to boycott the tour. The Prime Minister appealed for cancellation. A Commons motion was signed by 51 MPs of all parties. On 14 May an emergency debate on the tour issue took place in the House of Commons. I had been coming gradually to the conclusion that in the heat of conflicting political pressures the chief loser would be cricket. I therefore wrote, following the parliamentary debate, that I thought the tour should be called off.

Edward Heath won the election. As I was showing pleasure at the results at the Election Night party at the Savoy, the then Deputy Editor of the Daily Telegraph *expressed surprise saying, 'Oh, I thought you had gone over to the enemy.'* Daily Telegraph, *15 May 1970.*

Listening to the House of Commons debate on the South African tour, I was chiefly struck by the ironical paradox of the party of controls and centralization saying that it was cricket which must make its own decision, while the party of personal initiative and free enterprise was urging that the tour must be cancelled, if at all, by the Government.

With an impending election in everyone's minds it was inevitable, without any belittling of the quality of much that was said, that both the batting and bowling side were playing with a close eye on a declaration.

MCC and the Cricket Council have access to the best brains representing every aspect of the problems surrounding the tour. It is their duty to see the tour within the whole spectrum of international sport, and to take account of the known effect, for instance, on the Commonwealth Games, and of the anticipated effect on community relations. But, above all, it has surely to judge what is best for cricket itself; in the short term as regards the conditions under which the games will be played, and in the longer term as regards the future of international cricket.

One can well understand the temptation of cricket authority, pressurized as it is being, to react defiantly to threat and virtual blackmail. One can appreciate the attitude that says: 'If we give in here, where does it end?' (But *that*, if you like, is a political not a cricket question.) One can sympathize wholly with the view that the atmosphere has been further embittered by the 'free to demonstrate against' speech for which many in the cricket world may never forgive the Prime Minister. One can understand, not least, the widely held view of sporting people who want to see a fine team pitting themselves against England, and are indignant at the prospect of being deprived. (Very few, however, have yet implicated themselves by buying tickets for the Tests. I suspect many normal patrons are intending to watch from the safety of their television screens.)

The Cricket Council, however, I believe must rise above the misrepresentation of motive, the vilification even of the less scrupulous of their opponents and must weigh the balance of evils. If they do this in the light of the facts as they are, and of the likelihood of violence and of the division of the sporting world into colour camps, I sincerely trust they will have the moral courage to follow the advice of men with such credentials as Sir Edward Boyle and Laurence Gandar, to name but two, and call the thing off.

Mr Gandar has changed his views within the last few months, and so have I, for, I suspect, similar reasons. After many misgivings, I felt before the situation had reached its present pass that perhaps the risks were worth taking. I believe now they are not, and that the consequences might well do irrevocable harm to cricket. Most of the players likely to be concerned, and many responsible administrators, are now of this opinion. There would be no joy in the tour for them, and certainly not for the South Africans. Nor could the games be a conclusive test. Note the cricket considerations again, as distinct from the political.

If I be accused of vacillation, I would say that the person who sees this agonizing issue in absolutely clear-cut 100 per cent terms is surely either extremely clever or very stupid. And I would presume to remind readers that for the last year and more, in the *Daily Telegraph* and also in the South African press and in *The Cricketer*, I have pressed for a multi-racial tour party, sufficient to make two sides, to come over together.

There would certainly have been non-Europeans good enough for inclusion in a party of, say, 30 fulfilling First XI and 'A' fixtures simultaneously. On the analogy of the South African Olympic decision in 1967, such a project would have been within the law, and it would have been irrefutable evidence of white goodwill.

What an infinitely melancholy thought that if such an initiative had been taken we might have been looking forward to the tour with pleasure and in comparative peace of mind!

The Cricket Council reaffirmed, after the Commons debate, that the tour should go ahead. However, on 21 May the Home Secretary, Mr James Callaghan, requested them to withdraw the invitation 'on grounds of broad public policy', and the Council complied. The Prime Minister referred to was Mr Harold Wilson.

A CASE FOR GREIG

Tony Greig had not played for England at this point. He did so against the Rest of the World in the next match, was chosen for that winter's tour of Australia and ultimately captained England before transferring his allegiance to K. Packer.

This was the only letter I remember ever having written to a selector in favour of a player.

24 June 1970

E.W.S. to Mr A. V. Bedser

Dear Alec,

I don't know how you're placed at Nottingham, but I'd much like to know your thoughts about Australia if you could spare an evening – either Thursday or Friday. The alternative would be an hour during the match, whichever suits you better.

Meanwhile with all due diffidence let me make a point or two regarding Tony Greig on the grounds that I saw him on hard wickets in the West Indies on the Norfolk tour, and had a fair chance of estimating what he might do in something like Australian conditions.

I think his potential is pretty considerable in that he is a fine natural athlete and strong as he could be. He bowled 12 overs right off in the Barbados heat and pretty quick with the new ball (Old was hurt and couldn't play), and he gave little away. He's got a good change of pace, which on these wickets is very useful, as I don't need to tell you.

I mention his bowling first only because you said at Lord's you thought he was rather wild. As a bat he's not terribly consistent, and seems to be getting out of a bad run after starting the summer very well. But at his best he hits the ball mighty hard, and uses his reach to hit off the front foot between mid-wicket round to extra-cover.

Not least he's absolutely top-class in the field anywhere – I see he's got 20 catches for Sussex, mostly in the slips to the quicks. I'd have thought if he replaced the third quick, batting at no. 6, say at Trent Bridge and Edgbaston, you might find the all-rounder you must be looking for – or one of them.

You may be aware of all this – or you may dispute its accuracy – but I know one can be unlucky going to look at players, and I thought it just possible you and the others might have been so with him. Anyway this for your eye alone, and as I say with due diffidence.

Sincerely,

Jim

SACKCLOTH FOR THE ASHES

Daily Telegraph, *20 February 1971.*

SYDNEY, February, 1971

England have the Ashes back, the victorious captain has been carried from the ground by his team, the technical post-mortems have been held, and the question remaining is: What sort of a game is Test cricket going to be after Sydney 1971?

The first thing for the Test and County Cricket Board to examine is the future relationship between the manager and his players, including the captain. In the past the key figure has always been the captain, with the manager putting up the diplomatic façade and handling all the heavy administrative detail that attached to a touring party, to say nothing of the necessary burden of Press relations.

Here, despite the loyalty of D. G. Clark to his captain, their complete incompatibility of outlook has been distressingly plain for all to see. Without a rigid contract specifying his overriding authority and with accepted pains and penalties for breaches of discipline such, for instance, as fortify football managers, Mr Clark has had to endure a heart-breaking lowering of standards both on the field and off.

The 1946/47 tour gave me a liking for Australians and a respect for their tough but essential fair-mindedness which has made some of the happenings of this tour hard to bear. To some at home who might say: 'Ah, but Illingworth has only been taking them on at their own game,' I would say: 'You haven't been here, and I expect that you don't know Australia.'

It is admirable that what has been palpably the better side should have won the Ashes, but it could have been done just as certainly, if not more so, without a surly, unlikeable attitude by a few members of the team to opponents – and umpires.

Before the last Test ended – and before the communication had been received by the secretary of the Australian Board of Control – a Sydney evening paper printed verbatim what it alleged was a letter by the England captain, complaining about 'the unfair tactics' of umpire Rowan in issuing the warning (the third of the tour) to Snow for intimidatory bowling.

The captains automatically make a report on the umpires at the end of matches anyway, and what reaction, if any, the Australian Board makes to this letter that Illingworth admits leaking to the Press I do not know. But it could make a telling counter-blow through the proper channels.

As to relations between players and umpires I would just quote from a reliable source the comment that the language on the field during this series was 'simply terrible.' If Illingworth's precipitate letter does not provoke Det.-Insp. Lou Rowan to include in his statutory report on the last Test a frank appraisal of umpire–player relations he will be showing a wonderful restraint.

I believe the players in the heat of battle need protecting against themselves. I think I might reward them to some extent in relation to profits. I would give them the best in accommodation and general comfort. But I would demand 100 per cent effort and rigid discip'ine as their side of the bargain.

As to the number of Test matches, I agree thoroughly with Illingworth when he says that the man who advocates seven Test matches 'wants shooting.' He says rightly, I think, that five is the ideal, one in each centre, and there would seem an excellent solution at hand to compensate Melbourne and Sydney, which, on every other visit, get a second Test match.

The one-day international match is a thing of the future – not to supersede Tests, of course, but to run in complement. The 46,000 crowd in Melbourne should have made the way plain for a series of five one-day games, sponsored of course, and alternating between Melbourne and Sydney and avoiding close contact with Test matches.

EXCHANGE WITH ILLINGWORTH

An extract from the BBC archives.
'It's Your Line', BBC Radio 4, 13 April 1971.

ROBIN DAY: Good evening, this is Robin Day and It's Your Line tonight to a sportsman who will be honoured next Monday at a celebration banquet at Lord's – Ray Illingworth, England's Captain on last winter's victorious, dramatic and sometimes stormy tour of Australia, the tour which won back the Ashes for England after twelve years but a tour also which stirred some heated controversy about the way the game was played and about Ray Illingworth's captaincy. The gloomy verdict of one pundit was that this was a tour which damned international cricket. After the angry incident during the Final Sydney Test one of our veteran cricket correspondents wrote, 'By openly questioning an Umpire's verdict Illingworth showed a singularly bad example to cricketers everywhere.' On the other hand, according to one Australian columnist, Illingworth showed more guts and commonsense than has been shown by anyone in this entire series. But what is your opinion, because It's Your Line tonight to Ray Illingworth, whether you think of him primarily as a Captain who led his team to victory in this series or as the Captain who led his team off the field at Sydney after those beer cans began to fly.

EWS: *I chanced to be listening and rang in, rather to his discomfort after he made the following comments:*

ILLINGWORTH: Some of the press you do see quite a bit of but in actual fact it was perfectly true what I said that from the start of the tour until the finish of the tour I don't think I saw Jim Swanton at all; in fact I think the only time I saw him was when I pulled up at the traffic lights and he was in the car next to me.

Jim Swanton doesn't stay in the same hotel as the rest of the press boys, he stays on his own somewhere and this is probably the reason we never saw him. Most of the press did stay in the same hotel as us but Jim didn't.

[*Later in the programme*]

DAY: ... and now Mr E. W. Swanton. And that I expect is *the* Mr E. W. Swanton whom we were talking about earlier, the distinguished and veteran cricket correspondent of the *Daily Telegraph*, known widely as Jim Swanton. Is that *the* Mr Swanton?

SWANTON: Good evening Robin Day.

DAY: Good evening.

SWANTON: I'm answering your invitation.

DAY: Oh how fine of you to call in, and I'm sure that Ray would like to talk to you as he appears to have not talked to you very often in Australia if his report be accurate. You're calling from Sandwich, go ahead with your question or comment Jim Swanton, please?

SWANTON: Well, my comment is this. Ray said that he didn't see me on tour. Now there's an implication in that. I see something of all players on tour. I didn't see a great deal of him but I'm just going to ask him about one or two times when he certainly met me. I'd like to say first though, that I'm an old'un now, on my seventh tour in Australia, and I never think that young or youngish cricketers like to be bothered too much with the older generation. I'm generally there if they want to listen to me, if my experience and reminiscence is of any interest, but I rather wait for them to come to me. But I was in fact with the team in four of the Test matches in the same hotel. He said that I wasn't in the hotel with them in any of the Tests – I was there in four – but if he is listening, as I take it he is, I'd like just to ask him three questions. In the first place, Ray, do you remember that when the team was chosen, I said to you ... I'm sorry, when the Captain was chosen, I said to you, 'Well, Ray, I hoped myself that Colin Cowdrey would be chosen. I thought that he did a wonderful job in the West Indies when he returned, having won the rubber, and I thought it was his prerogative to be chosen, but now you've been chosen, I'll do the best I can and I wish you well' – do you remember that?

ILLINGWORTH: Yes, that's correct – at Headingley.

SWANTON: That's right it was at Headingley, yes it was. Now do you remember that on our arrival at Brisbane, we had quite a long talk and you were kind and told me a little bit about what had been happening on the tour up till that point, because I didn't get there until just before the First Test?

ILLINGWORTH: That was the first day you arrived in Brisbane, yes.

SWANTON: That's right. Do you remember that I congratulated you as warmly as I possibly could on the excellent performance in winning the Fourth Test at Sydney and I did so in the Hotel Windsor at Melbourne where we were both staying?

ILLINGWORTH: I can't remember that particular occasion, Jim, no. But I'm not saying you didn't stay at the Windsor. It's probably one hotel you did stay in.

DAY: Jim Swanton, Robin Day here. I think the main point being made by Ray in his earlier answers was not any personal point against you but the fact that you were a cricket-writer who, on the whole, remained a bit remote from the players and therefore perhaps didn't take the trouble to find out about what the cricketers were doing and why in their games. I'm summarising it badly, but I think that's what he was getting at. Is that right, Ray?

ILLINGWORTH: Yes.

DAY: Now what about that, Jim? That was the general point. However often you talked to each other.

SWANTON: Well, I think that the critic has got a difficult job, just as the player has got a difficult job in his relations with the critics. What I think is that I try to make as close a touch as will give me an idea of what they're thinking, what lies behind what they're doing, and although I didn't see very much of Ray, I did see something of him, including the questions I put to him at the last Press Conference which I'm sure he hasn't forgotten. But there were sixteen other members of the team, or fifteen and the manager, and I regard myself as being the best judge of how much to see of them all.

DAY: Well thank you for calling, Jim, but just before you go, I'd like to know whether Ray would like to ask you a question, because it's rare that we get a critic of your standing and a cricketer of his standing.

ILLINGWORTH: Well, there is one piece I would like to . . . you wrote a summing up on the tour, Jim, and you did write that there'd been a lowering of standards on and off the field, and I wasn't very impressed with that for the amount I did see you on the tour.

SWANTON: I said there was a lowering of standards. Yes, I did say that, Ray, with very great reluctance. It's no pleasure to anybody like myself who loves to see England win and nothing else, to see certain of the things that went on. I thought I'd never hope to see an England Captain threatening or seeming to threaten by wagging his finger at an Australian umpire with twenty or thirty thousand Australians looking on. If the game is going to come to this sort of pass where the umpire is going to be openly challenged on the field, I think that the end of cricket in the Test Match sense is really pretty near. If, for instance, you'd done that sort of thing in the West Indies, such provocation would almost certainly – you've been talking about the West Indies – it would almost certainly have literally brought the house down.

DAY: Now Ray Illingworth, do you want to add to your explanation of why you did that?

ILLINGWORTH: Well now, Jim knows why. Does he think the umpire was right on that occasion?

SWANTON: Did I think the umpire was right? Well, I think that the umpire must always be right, and he must always be respected by the players. I know all about tensions and that sort of thing, but I've been watching Test Matches for longer than I care to remember. I've seen some two hundred odd of them, and I've never before seen a captain resort to that.

ILLINGWORTH: No, It's probably very true, that you've never . . . captain's spoken his mind before.

SWANTON: We've had a great many captains who've spoken their mind very well, Ray. Don't imagine that because you're a York-

shireman and tough, you're the only person who can speak your mind.
ILLINGWORTH: Oh no, I don't imagine that at all.
SWANTON: I think that there were a great many of them before that.
ILLINGWORTH: Well, we shall see.
SWANTON: Douglas Jardine for a start.
ILLINGWORTH: Ah, well, I don't go back that far, Jim.
SWANTON: No, well there you are – I have the advantage of you.
ILLINGWORTH: Yes, you're quite right there.
DAY: Well, E. W. Swanton, thank you very much indeed for responding to our invitation to call in and to have it out a bit with Ray. You haven't convinced one another, but it's been nice hearing from you and perhaps the matter will come up again. I only just go back to Jardine, but I'd better not admit that.

FAIR END TO A GREAT SERIES

*By winning the last Test Australia halved the series. England,
however, retained the Ashes, with honour all round.*
Daily Telegraph, *17 August 1972.*

The climax of the Fifth Test match fully lived up to all that had gone before. It was anyone's game right up to the last half hour or so of its five and a half days – until, in fact, Paul Sheahan and Rodney Marsh, in their utterly different ways, took final command. When the last day began, Australia, requiring to add a further 126 to their 116 for one, needed only a trouble-free start to make the rest a formality. When Stackpole, that admirable but fortunate fellow, was missed by Hampshire at first slip in Arnold's first over without a run added, it seemed as though his luck was going to hold to the end.

Yet just before half past eleven first Stackpole, then Ian Chappell, then Edwards, were all got out within the space of five runs, and suddenly the target looked a mile away.

Sheahan and Greg Chappell added a priceless 34 for the fifth wicket, but when the latter left the last five wickets still needed 71 with the ball now occasionally lifting and regularly turning on this hitherto impeccable wicket.

Nothing but the straightest of bats and the quickest reaction to the unexpected would have availed now against Underwood, while Greig, with two wickets to uplift him, was bowling with rare menace at the other end.

Happily for Australia they found in Sheahan the man for the occasion. Where everyone else had needed a load of luck he met everything with the middle of the bat.

Leaving temperamental requirements out of the matter I rated Sheahan's innings of two hours 20 minutes the technical equal of anything done in the series by either side – which in practice I suppose, means the two hundreds made by Greg Chappell at Lord's and the Oval.

In the last phase Marsh also batted with rare judgment and discretion, only hastening at the end when his eye was truly in and a mistake would probably no longer have been disastrous. Thanks to him the series ended with a thoroughly appropriate flourish.

Writing as one who has had the luck to see somewhere around 240 Test matches, I can safely say that for prolonged excitement, and the perpetual ebb and flow of fortune, I have never seen a better. One will recall it with the Lord's Test of 1930, and that against the West Indies there in 1963.

If the quality of the play has certainly been variable, the high peaks have been memorable indeed. All in all it has been a classic which has done untold good for cricket. In perfect weather (Saturday afternoon excepted) it has been watched by more than 120,000 people paying £71,435, both records for the Oval.

But then this has been a wonderfully fine series altogether, for which we have every cause to be grateful, as also for the fact that it has been shared at two matches apiece.

Almost everyone who has seen all five Tests this summer seems agreed that a drawn rubber is the fairest result. Indeed there is only one respect – and that a very important one – in which the picture could have been improved, and that is if Illingworth had not been injured and compelled to watch this final day with his ankle swollen and sore.

Would Australia have won if Illingworth had remained on the field and able to bowl? If it is a profitless question, it is an intriguing one none the less. Underwood and Illingworth in harness with a bit of dust flying would have been twice as dangerous as one operating alone. Spinners are complementary, and in the hour after tea on Tuesday before he turned his ankle over Illingworth had Stackpole and Ian Chappell stretching uncomfortably, and the old Australian off-spin bogey raising its head once more.

There was also the matter of the handling of the England side. Edrich found the job thrust upon him in unenviable circumstances, and cannot fairly be judged by Illingworth's circumstances.

It was strange, however, that from 32 for one to the end, England's premier bowler Snow was given only one over. Again, if a gamble were to be taken with Parfitt's off-spin it would have been better taken when there were more than 47 runs to play with.

Let it not be said that Underwood failed at the pinch. Even without the help of Illingworth he must have demolished batsmen of lesser spirit and quality than those who brought victory to Australia.

England v. Australia, at the Oval, 10–16 August, 1972. England 284 (Knott 92, Parfitt 51, Lillee 5 for 58) and 356 (Wood 90, Knott 63, Lillee 5 for 123); Australia 399 (I. M. Chappell 118, G. S. Chappell 113, Edwards 79) and 242 for 5 (Stackpole 79). Australia won by 5 wickets.

SOBERS – BY BRADMAN

I must try and get this film re-circulated.
Daily Telegraph, *5 October 1972.*

At Melbourne last New Year, Gary Sobers played an innings of 254 for the Rest of the World against Australia which used up the superlatives of all the critics lucky enough to see it.

In particular, it was eulogised by Sir Donald Bradman in a phrase which echoed round the world: 'This was probably the greatest exhibition of batting ever seen in Australia.'

From the greatest of all modern *batsmen* to the greatest of all *cricketers*, this was the ultimate tribute.

I now hear that Sir Donald has amplified his appraisal to the extent of providing the commentary for a 35 minute film of the innings, made for the *Melbourne Herald* group of newspapers from the tele-recording. It is called 'The Gary Sobers Special.'

I hope I have written enough to excite practical interest, for there has not been a moment during my time when the principles of the batting art were in greater need of emphasis. There is no finer exemplar than Sobers at his best; and, whether in books or in private talk, no more lucid theorist than Bradman.

Any innings by Sobers illustrates, to my mind, the elementary and vital message of showing the bowler the face of a vertical blade right through the arc from the moment that the wrists are uncocked at the start of the downswing. No hurried jab across the line from a minimal backlift but a full, rhythmic pendulum swing of the bat, whether in attack or defence.

At times last summer I watched depressed as lively bowling and the usual athletic fielding were confronted by little more positive than fast-footed stabs, interspersed when the scoreboard demanded, by fevered heaves or sweeps to leg.

There were, of course, exceptions and not all provided by the overseas players, even if such men as Barry Richards, Asif, Clive Lloyd and Greg Chappell come early to mind.

Greig had the bowlers wringing their hands not infrequently in the Test matches, while Denness played an innings to remember in the Canterbury Week. Owen-Thomas's off-driving in the University match might have belonged to the vintage age of Cambridge cricket.

I saw Ealham win a match for Kent by swinging the bat lustily from the shoulders, while even Lloyd's tremendous batting in the Gillette final did not altogether submerge the orthodox method and vigour of Hayes.

In less exalted circles, two hundreds on the Arabs' tour, one by Clive Williams (joint headmaster of Ashdown House), the other by Mark Faber, for purity and power of stroke, were in the classic mould. At Eton, anyway, they are evidently still taught to bat.

Such are a few of the pleasanter recollections of a bumper season kept bright by weather which, in our corner of the world, is still warm and sunny enough for cricket.

No doubt if it is too early to be complacent about the future of first class cricket. At least, however, for reasons which are well enough known to close followers, we may now assume a feeling of confidence which would have been hard to maintain a year or two ago.

The first-class game has been greatly refreshed both financially and in terms of public interest and support, and, if the pattern of county cricket is still in transition, the TCCB can today negotiate with their friends, the sponsors, from a position of greater strength than hitherto.

What they must aim to achieve is a system that is both viable and capable of maintaining the English standard of play that will ensure Test sides of high quality, holding their own at home and abroad. At the moment, the chief need is to breed and encourage batsmen – and, of course, spin bowlers. But that is food for another day.

INDIAN CHRISTMAS PRESENT

A happy, trouble-free tour. (India won the five-match series 2-1. All three Tests in Pakistan were drawn.) Boycott and Snow both declined to tour. In his prime Boycott missed thirty Tests in three years and, in all, three tours. Daily Telegraph, *28 December 1972.*

I have eaten Christmas Day lunches of divers kinds and in divers places at the call of cricket, but when most are forgotten I shall remember with nostalgic happiness that at the Ferozshah Kotla ground at Delhi. There, sitting in the sunshine, enjoying bread and cheese, two oranges and a bottle of beer, I surveyed a scoreboard that showed England with four wickets down, needing only 12 runs for victory. After a morning's cricket begun in acute anxiety and finally quite dominated by the two Tonys, Lewis and Greig, the issue was conceded by our colleagues in the al fresco Press-box.

It added savour to the occasion to receive the felicitations of the Indian cricket writers, some friends and some unknown, just as when the formalities had been completed the England team were congratulated in their dressing-room by Ajit Wadekar and his men. There had been tension enough in all conscience during the more dramatic phases of this supremely eventful, low-scoring match, but at the end there were no hard feelings.

The Indian reaction to what was a wholly unexpected defeat has been of unstinted praise for the English performance, the only note of criticism being reserved for the local cricket administration whose ineptitude seems to be a general byword.

Lewis was named man of the match, Greig batsman of the match, while two others apiece of the several sponsored prizes went to Arnold for bowling and to Wood for fielding.

Going down the list of the side one can add some sort of tribute to one and all, not forgetting Donald Carr's managership and the healing powers of Bernard Thomas, whose official title is assistant to the manager and physiotherapist. There has never been a medical man in whom a team had such confidence.

At Newlands, Cape Town: I made the first cricket commentaries in and from South Africa with the MCC team of 1938/9.

Miss Daphne Surfleet before she became Mrs Richie Benaud: the perfect secretary who, with Irving Rosenwater in the early 1960s, helped put together the 1st edition of *The World of Cricket*.

August 1955, on the roof of the Oval pavilion for the Test against South Africa. The T.V. commentary team was Peter West, EWS, Brian Johnston and the scorer and statistician Roy Webber.

Stalwarts of Trinidad and West Indian cricket on the field and off, Gerry Gomez and Jeffrey Stollmeyer, April 1961.

Our house, Coralita, looked out on to the 9th hole of Sandy Lane Golf Club. The *Daily Telegraph* and *The Cricketer* had to be satisfied.

The plush side of cricket-writing. At Half Moon Bay, Jamaica, during the MCC West Indies tour of 1960. *From the left facing camera* Mrs Frank Rostron, Ian Peebles, Ron Roberts, EWS and wife: *opposite them* John Woodcock, Raman Subba Row and (now) wife Ann, John Goddard, Gerry Gomez and Mrs Rex Alston.

At Kuala Lumpur, Easter 1964: with Viscount Head (High Commissioner), Ian McLachlan and the Nawab of Pataudi.

Colin Cowdrey (1956) and Colin Ingleby-MacKenzie (1961 and 1964) captained EWS's XI on overseas tours, but here having played against the Arabs in 1976 for W.F. Sales's XI at Wellesley House.

EWS's XI v. A West Indies XI at Trinidad, *Sitting*: Bob Barber, Everton Weekes, Colin Ingleby-MacKenzie (captain), EWS, Ray Lindwall, Peter Walker, Abbas Ali Baig. *Standing*: Nawab of Pataudi, 'Bomber' Wells, Harold Rhodes, Ossie Wheatley, Ian McLachlan, Bob Gale and Alan Smith.

Yes, the position of the top hand is crucial: Denis Compton helps his fellow cricket-writer at the Authors v. Publishers at Vincent Square, June 1958.

One more for the Arab scrap-book.

With Ann and our best man, Ian Peebles, at Lennon's Hotel, Brisbane, November 1958.

Not the approved finish: an occasion rather above my station.

That's much more like it: Henry Longhurst, fellow-lodger in the Temple, scratch golfer, author, journalist, and ace T.V. commentator.

Henry Kendall, Ann Swanton, Jimmy Pittock and Baba Beck at Royal St. George's, 1955. Permit Holders versus The Ladies.

After the OBE investiture, 1965. With Ann and my sister Tina Langdon.

The launch of the first *World of Cricket* at Melbourne in January, 1966: the Prime Minister of Australia, Sir Robert Menzies, with Doug Walters, who 8 days before his 20th birthday had scored a hundred in the first Test and was about to score a second.

Old Cranleighan R.F.C. dinner 1963: clockwise from EWS (President), H.P. Jacob, H.C. Catchside, Sir William Ramsay, S.C. Griffith, anon, D.A. Emms (Headmaster), C.O'N. Wallis, Wing-Cdr. J. Lawson, D. Crichton-Miller.

Canterbury Week 1993. Two ardent cricket-lovers. The Right Hon. John Major comes to support his county, Surrey.

More cricket at Canterbury: Archbishop Runcie umpires at an interlude of the 1988 Lambeth Conference. In the centre the Bishop of Liverpool, a.k.a. David Sheppard.

Barclays World of Cricket, 1986: The Game from A to Z: encyclopaedic, heavy, the weight shared with George Plumptre, Editor (right), and John Woodcock, Consultant Editor.

Brian Lara at Wormsley in June 1994, the glow of sudden fame still bright. Modest charm was the first impression.

Ann and Jim shared forty years of contented married life before her death in 1998

Paul Getty's love of cricket has found perfect expression in Wormsley.

The way Denness is batting it should not be long before he joins the ranks of the scorers of Test hundreds. His 35 in an hour, ended a bit unluckily when a leg-hit that was going for six found Viswanath standing in the one spot which gave him the chance of a catch, was the innings that put the pitch and the task ahead in proper perspective.

Amiss was another who is making batting – though not yet, unfortunately, catching – look a rational art. Cottam bowled well in the first innings, and there are hopes that his injured foot will be recovered for the second Test beginning on Saturday.

Knott's 'keeping to the spin (and for that matter Engineer's also) was as admirable as ever, and it was noticeable that it was to his wicketkeeper that Lewis usually turned for comment and advice.

Underwood and Pocock played a full part with seven wickets between them in the second innings on a good pitch that allowed them only an odd inch or two of turn. As to Fletcher, one can only applaud his cheerfulness in adversity and add that he was caught off his glove in the second innings from one of the few balls that misbehaved.

I expect that the side for Saturday will be unchanged, assuming Cottam passes fit, but if replacements are needed they can be found without damage to its over-all balance in the persons of Roope, who fielded admirably as substitute, Old, Tolchard, Gifford and Birkenshaw.

These last two, giving practice against spin to the England batsmen in the nets, probably bowled as many overs as Underwood and Pocock in the middle.

This small item gives an important clue to the result of the game. England's success was due basically to sensible planning and the complete co-operation of all concerned.

Untried in Test cricket himself, Lewis could not have commanded such an unstinted response from last summer's side which were so impolitely christened 'Dad's Army.' No individual performance by Boycott or by Snow could have been nearly so valuable as this.

In several respects, Lewis's beginning has parallels with that of F. G. Mann, who also captained England in his first Test match, in South Africa in 1948/49. Mann turned defeat into victory and so won the rubber by making a hundred in the Fifth Test.

On the evidence of Delhi, Lewis has the character and the skill to do something similar, though let us hope the need does not arise.

India v England, at Delhi, 20–25 December 1972. India 173 (Abid Ali 58, Arnold 6 for 45) and 233 (Solkar 75, Engineer 63); England 200 (Greig 68 not out, Chandrasekhar 8 for 79) and 208 for 4 (Lewis 70 not out). England won by 6 wickets.

SIR ROBERT MENZIES

The first paragraph of this letter about calling my own tune refers to my coming retirement from the Daily Telegraph. *At sixty-six I was then beyond the normal retirement age, but my Sports Editor, Kingsley Wright, said I could pick my own time to give up. I had a natural successor in Michael Melford, Cricket Correspondent of the* Sunday Telegraph, *and it was arranged that he should take over from me after the 1974/75 tour to Australia. There was a thought that I should write articles for* The Sunday, *but this came to nothing – which was much for the best, since it would probably have delayed my election to the MCC Committee and in consequence my work on the Indoor School project.*

My friendship with Bob Menzies developed when as Lord Warden of the Cinque Ports he spent part of the summer at Walmer Castle. He was a large man in every way, a great Anglophile of natural kindness and sharp wit. He had had a severe stroke in 1971, which completely crippled him physically but left his mind unimpaired. Thus he spent the last six years of his life in a wheelchair.

SIR ROBERT MENZIES
9 Collins Street
Melbourne C.1 Victoria
Telephone 63 9463

13th July, 1973

My dear Jim

It was good to hear from you. I am happy that you are able to call your own tune with your paper and thus not over-exert yourself as you approach the time you are thinking of retiring. Perhaps before too long you will get your 'swap' with the *Sunday Telegraph*.

By the way, please excuse me for not thanking you for 'Sort of a

Cricket Person' which was so kindly signed and sent to me. It came when I was in hospital and I did not realise I overlooked letting you know. I read it with great interest and enjoyed it very much.

We both join in sending our love to Ann and you,

Yours
Bob
(R. G. Menzies)

GREIG'S FINEST HOUR

Few innings stick more vividly in my mind than Greig's.
Daily Telegraph, 2 December 1974.

Tony Greig has done many fine things in five years as an England cricketer, but nothing in point of quality or temper to better his first hundred against Australia and incidentally the first made for England in Brisbane since Maurice Leyland in 1936–7. On Saturday, coming in with four men out for 57, he was fortified by the solidarity of Edrich. Yesterday the burden reverted to him, and splendidly he bore it against an Australian fast attack that called for a high degree both of courage and technical proficiency.

Greig's height helped him to play the short ball down, both defensively and often with great force. He did not hook, preferring to sway out of the way of the short ball. But he played all the other shots and for five hours built his sixth Test hundred, stinging the fingers of the off-side fielders, embodying defiance with every hammer blow of a bat weighing around three pounds.

It was all very heartening and when he came in to a great reception from the 20,000 that is near the capacity of this smallest of Australian Test arenas Greig and the England side could reflect that thanks to him it was still anyone's match.

The second day belonged to Australia, just as the first had been England's, and the character of the cricket had a lot in common, with the fast bowlers doing most of the work and runs generally hard to come by.

The action was inevitably slow (12 eight-ball overs an hour) but the intensity of the struggle on another hot, cloudless day, with a southerly breeze to temper the heat, continued to grip the crowd.

There was, however, an important difference between the two attacks in degree, if not in kind, for where Willis and Lever when fresh were fairly fast, Thomson and Lillee in their opening spells were much more so. Indeed England have not been confronted by such speed at both ends since Hall and Griffith were at their peak. It was a daunting experience which threatened at its height to demolish the innings. Happily, however, the need found the men in Edrich and Greig whose respective efforts could scarcely be overpraised.

Knott lasted almost an hour before cutting into gully's hands. Lever was soon taken at first slip but Underwood now played like a real batsman, announcing himself with a four through the covers off Walker that anyone would have been proud of.

The eighth wicket lasted over lunch and almost saw Greig to his hundred. However Chappell brought on Walters, often a useful change bowler, and Underwood was undone by the slower pace giving a low catch to mid-off from his first ball. His share of the stand of 58 was 25.

Greig reached his hundred in the grand manner with the second of two cracking cover-strokes off Lillee, celebrated it with two more powerful hits off Walters and then chanced once too often.

The English tail could not quite match Australia's but, after such a start, 265 was at least a reasonable muster.

Australia saw their next job as to consolidate and so accurately did England – and particularly Underwood – bowl that in the final 2½ hours they scored as slowly as they had done on the first morning.

Wally Edwards, after being hit on the cheek by Willis, was caught behind, while Ian Chappell was very well caught by Fletcher at slip, diving to his right in Underwood's first over. Thereafter, Underwood conceded absolutely nothing.

Australia v England, at Brisbane, 29 November–4 December 1974. Australia 309 (Chappell (I. M.) 90, Chappell (G. S.) 58) and 288 for 5 dec. (Chappell (G. S.) 71, Walters 62 not out, Edwards 53); England 265 (Greig 110) and 166 (Thomson 6 for 46). Australia won by 166 runs.

LAST REPORT

A much abbreviated version of my last match report before retirement as Daily Telegraph *Cricket Correspondent. The summer of 1928 had seen the first, in* The Evening Standard. *The reporting thus totted up to forty-one English seasons and twenty-five overseas tours, some long, some less so.*

February 1975. England not only gained their consolation victory, but they did it in the end with an emphasis that to anyone who has seen the series through was very surprising. The general view before play began was that if Peter Lever was fit to bowl there was just about an even chance of the last seven Australian wickets being got in sufficient time for the necessary runs to be made. Yet Greg Chappell was supported when play began by three other highly reputable bats, while England have found the Australian tail highly obstreperous all the way round from Brisbane.

As it was, Lever rose from his bed and gave the attack the edge it had notably lacked on Wednesday. Arnold bowled a particularly good spell when the ball was still red first thing to dispose of Edwards and Walters, while Greig did not the least important act of the day when he held one back a bit and caught and bowled the obdurate Walker. It was Arnold who produced perhaps the ball of the match to bowl Walters, pitching leg stump and hitting the off – just as Alec Bedser was inclined to do on this pitch a quarter of a century ago.

Lever performed what was, in effect, the *coup de grâce* when he found a break-back of rare quality to bowl Chappell immediately after he had reached his hundred, and when Australia still wanted four runs to make England bat again. Chappell was eighth out after a chanceless, and all but faultless, innings that had lasted four hours ten minutes. A couple of overs later it was all over, without another run scored and with upwards of three hours to spare.

Australia had started the day at 274 for 3, 103 runs behind. At lunch they were 364 for 6, after which the last four tumbled for nine runs. In all, they lost 7 for 99. When lunch came, Chappell wanted four for his hundred. He still wanted them when Walker was caught and bowled by Greig, and he saw his last substantial support disappear. A glance for four gave Chappell his due reward and the final *dénouement* swiftly followed.

The loss of Lillee on Sunday, after he had bowled only six overs, was naturally a crippling loss to Australia. There can be no telling whether the England batting could have backed up Lever's great bowling on Saturday if Lillee had lasted the game, but it must be remembered that both Denness and Fletcher, the chief scorers, overcame their difficulties against speed to the extent of very good innings in the Fifth Test in Adelaide. They certainly batted excellently here.

The win, without altering basic conclusions about the series, certainly puts it in much better perspective and it must hearten England's leading players for the forthcoming four-Test rubber in England. It can be seen, too, as a deserved reward for a captain and team who have withstood their disappointments and kept their spirit in spite of much ill-fortune.

My last sight of Melbourne Cricket Ground was an impromptu little gathering on the outfield in front of the banner reading 'MCG fans thank Colin – six tours'. The central figure, wearing a large straw sun-hat, was signing endless autographs, posing for photographs and exchanging friendly talk with young and old in the way that has made him as popular a cricketer as has ever visited Australia.

Australia v England, at Melbourne, 8–13 February 1975

AUSTRALIA

I. R. Redpath c Greig b Lever	1	c Amiss b Greig	83
R. B. McCosker c Greig b Lever	0	c Cowdrey b Arnold	76
I. M. Chappell c Knott b Old	65	c Knott b Greig	50
G. S. Chappell c Denness b Lever	1	b Lever	102
R. Edwards c Amiss b Lever	0	c Knott b Arnold	18
K. D. Walters c Edrich b Old	12	b Arnold	3
R. W. Marsh b Old	29	c Denness b Lever	1
M. H. N. Walker not out	20	c and b Greig	17
D. K. Lillee c Knott b Lever	12	(11) not out	0
A. A. Mallett b Lever	7	(9) c Edrich b Greig	0
G. Dymock c Knott b Greig	0	(10) c Knott b Lever	0
Extras b 2, l-b 1, n-b 2	5	b 9, l-b 5, w 4, n-b 5	23
Total	152		373

FOW: 1–0 2–5 3–19 4–23 5–50 6–104 7–115 8–141 9–149 10–152;
  1–111 2–215 3–258 4–289 5–297 6–306 7–367 8–373 9–373 10–373

Bowling: *1st inns:* Arnold 6–2–24–0; Lever 11–2–38–6; Old 11–0–50–3; Greig 8.7–1–35–1; *2nd inns:* Arnold 23–6–83–3; Lever 16–1–65–3; Old 18–1–75–0; Greig 31.7–7–88–4; Underwood 18–5–39–0

ENGLAND

D. L. Amiss lbw b Lillee	0
M. C. Cowdrey c Marsh b Walker ..	7
J. H. Edrich c I. M. Chappel b Walker	70
M. H. Denness c and b Walker.....	188
K. W. R. Fletcher c Redpath b Walker	146
A. W. Greig c sub b Walker	89
A. P. E. Knott c Marsh b Walker ...	5
C. M. Old b Dymock.............	0
D. L. Underwood b Walker........	11
G. G. Arnold c Marsh b Walker	0
P. Lever not out	6
Extras b 4, l-b 2, n-b 1	7
Total	529

FOW: 1–4 2–18 3–167 4–359 5–507 6–507 7–508 8–514 9–514 10–529

Bowling: Lillee 6–2–17–1; Walker 42.2–7–143–8; Dymock 39–6–130–1; Walters 23–3–86–0; Mallett 29–8–96–0; I. M. Chappell 12–1–50–0

Umpires: R. C. Bailhache and T. F. Brooks
England won by an innings and 4 runs.

PART SEVEN

1975–1996

1975–1996

R etirement is but a word and yet Jim has not quite discovered what it really means. For he has never taken up what Dr Johnson referred to as its 'soft obscurities'.

Having left the *Telegraph* in the spring of 1975, he continued to work for the paper and has done ever since. In that time Swanton has opined on the letter pages and in the editorial columns, but it is with the sports features that he is still read with regularity; particularly so from 1989.

When in the second half of the 1970s the Packer affair disrupted world cricket, Jim was vociferous in opposition. He once memorably described the Australian tycoon as 'the anti-Christ', later modified to 'the anti-hero'. It was a reminder, if any were needed, that he views issues distinctly. He is an authoritative voice, if you like, the headmaster, dealing for the most part patiently with often unruly pupils skipping around the playgrounds in uniform white or rebellious colours. And, in fact, the academic analogy is not inappropriate, as he once considered a career as a schoolmaster.

Not everyone smitten by the lordly tone has liked it. At various times he has been called 'overbearing', 'pompous', even 'papal', although the latter perhaps is a sort of compliment. During a cricket commentary, white smoke was seen billowing from a distant chimney. Pressing the off-air switch, John Arlott turned to his fellow colleagues in the box: 'Ah, I see that Jim has been elected Pope!'

If anything has been missing from recent years, it is Jim's masterly summaries on both television and radio. That beautifully produced brown, treacly voice with ecclesiastical overtones was and is compelling. Those précied reviews remained in one's mind long after the action of the day had disappeared: idiosyncratic and quaint words and phrases that were cherished by everyone, but were all his own – 'chary', 'so to speak', 'and there it is'. And on one occasion on camera when some buffoon in his sightline was oblivious to his work and distracting him, an admonitory, 'Now, look here . . .' A friend of mine, hearing the Swanton vowels for the first time, remarked that it reminded him 'of a great-uncle with a partiality for brown Windsor soup and gentleman's relish . . .' And who was it who reckoned his eloquence had a 'Theophrastic touch'?

Possibly because Jim has worked consistently for over fifty years for a Conservative broadsheet with a big C, it has been assumed that his attitudes are always those with a little one. All right, he has enjoyed being involved in the sanctums of influence and also keeping company with those of social standing, but it is there that he has often been a lone supporter of the radical viewpoint. In other words, he has fought battles from within as well as on the press pages.

In these last two decades he has been a member of the MCC Committee from 1975–86; Chairman of the Working Party before the building and of the Indoor Cricket School, 1977–83; Chairman of the Arts and Library Sub-Committee at Lord's for three years and still involved in its affairs. In 1990 he was elected a life Vice-President of MCC, the only non-past President to be so honoured with the exception of Sir Donald Bradman. He was President of Kent in 1981 and one of the curators of the county club; but, certainly more important than any of this, what might be thought of as Grand Panjandrum has been a faithful public championing of cricketing standards in times of rapid change throughout a long working life.

He has also been a constant advocate for Caribbean cricket and has spent part of nearly forty winters in Barbados where he has owned property; he was therefore a natural choice to pen the history of the world-famous Sandy Lane Hotel. He is, as well, an integral part of Sandwich in Kent and is in his twentieth year as President of the local cricket club. If one ignores the predatory traffic, Sandwich is a surviving bastion of olde worlde England, seemingly remote from the callousness of inner city, flush with evocatively-named byways such as Rope Walk, Knightrider Street and Holy Ghost Alley. Again, as a member of the club – in this case, golf – Jim was an obvious choice to give editorial advice and a written introduction to the *History of Royal St George's*.

The Cinque Port of Sandwich boasts three medieval churches, St Clement, St Mary and St Peter – now embodied as one. Jim was Churchwarden of St Clement's for ten years and takes a continued interest in parochial matters. In 1987, as a prelude to the Lambeth Conference of the following year, he provided a layman's sketch of *The Anglican Church* from its origins to the present, with a foreword from another keen cricketing churchman, Robert Runcie, then Archbishop of Canterbury.

In 1991, he went to South Africa and in a broadcast speech welcomed them back into the cricket community after the years of isolation. There were meant to be seven hundred and thirty people present at the dinner but, as Jim told them, one could not make it, so reminding him of the 1930 Test Match at Lord's where the Australians accumulated the same total. 'Unfortunately, nobody could find a figure 7 to put on the Tavern scoreboard . . .'

In this year of writing, 1996, he was given a standing ovation in the Long Room at Lord's at the Jubilee Dinner of the Cricket Writers' Club of which he was one of the founders. His recollections, delivered with urbanity and humour, of times before many of the company present were born, had hard-to-impress fellow luminaries listening intently.

As we approach the final part of this foray, let us now picture Jim in his study at Sandwich, from where the Crusades left centuries before. His wife Ann can be heard playing seductive piano in the drawing room, his secretary Doreen is busy with correspondence at the typewriter, and Valerie has just brought a cup of coffee – the Swantons have always had staff. At his desk, Jim is busy composing his latest article proclaiming the virtues of non-intimidatory bowling, or of not questioning umpires' decisions or of much else that aligns to correct behaviour both on and off the field of play. His concerns are good for cricket and cricket needs him to be concerned. Long may he continue to be its guardian.

D. R. A.

THE MAGIC AND MENACE OF FAST BOWLING

Many fast bowlers have bestridden the stage since 1975, but I would not put any above Lindwall, though the West Indians, Holding and Marshall run him close. Sportsweek, *Quarterly Issue, November 1975.*

When I was asked by an Indian editor to write a piece on some modern fast bowlers I gave, so to speak, a wistful sigh on his behalf. How much is it to be desired that India should produce a couple of good, strong fellows capable of making Englishmen and Australians and West Indians hurry their strokes, and take swift avoiding action now and then. How satisfactory if for a change the boot were on the other leg!

As it happens my earliest memory of India on the cricket field envisages two such, for either of whom Indian cricket would give its eyeteeth today. That first side labelled All-India which came and charmed the world of English cricket in 1932 had Amar Singh taking the new ball at one end, Mahomed Nissar at the other. Amar Singh, it is true, was brisk rather than truly quick but, with his strong, lissom build, a truly magnificent bowler. Nissar by contrast was genuinely fast, and *Wisden* tells how in all matches the pair of them took 226 wickets between them in that far-away English summer.

Mind you, both England and Australia know what it is to make do without extreme speed. The Australians were short of it when England descended to Bodyline under Jardine, while after the war, Ken Farnes having been killed, England were utterly without anyone with pretensions to pace. In 1948/49 on MCC's tour of South Africa England scarcely needed to stand back from start to finish.

Australia in the first post-war decade could call upon Lindwall and Miller, and it was no coincidence that they carried all before them. They had a fine all-round side, of course, but it was that sharp spearhead which was the basis of their strength. For three rubbers England had no effective counter. Then, within a year or two, first Brian Statham popped up in Lancashire, then Fred Trueman the other side of the Pennines. Peter Loader, not quite so good but a man who would have been welcomed with open arms not long before, joined Alec Bedser, Jim Laker and Tony Lock to give Surrey the perfectly balanced all-round attack, while tales began to come in of a youngster from the far north who was striking sparks from the sluggish Northampton pitch. This was Frank Tyson, who on very little in the way of solid evidence was picked for Australia in '54 and, after a depressing start, suddenly found a new degree of pace and in three successive Tests swept through the enemy and secured the Ashes for England.

Frank was not a classic fast bowler in the mould of Lindwall or Larwood, Trueman or Hall. But he had several prime virtues in ample measure. He was broad in the shoulders, long in the back, well developed round the rump and, not least, he had physical strength and a great heart. No ground was too hard for him. In fact the harder the better apparently, as he pawed the turf with his spikes, endeavouring to propel himself towards the crease with all possible momentum. I've never seen anyone bowl faster than did Frank in those few crucial weeks on either side of the 1955 New Year. But I wouldn't say that both Lillee and Thomson in certain spells may not have been his equal in Australia a year ago. I say Australia because the pitches there were so much livelier than we saw in England last summer. Lillee was assuredly the better man of the two, and often the faster, or so it appeared from the pavilion. I've never seen a faster *pair* than this – for it must be remembered that Statham, though a model in many ways, was a fair way behind Tyson in terms of sheer miles per hour.

Fast bowlers are much to the forefront just now, and I confess that, though happy and busy in my retirement, I should have enjoyed to see something of the series this winter in Australia with Lillee and Thomson on one side and Andy Roberts no mean counterweight on the other. What a showing this young West Indian put up on the easy-paced Indian pitches last winter! One hopes only that he won't rattle himself to bits, for he is a relatively small man without the 'cushioning' of his rivals. Still, if it comes to that both Harold Larwood and Gubby Allen were of much the same build, and they both were just about as quick as they come.

Who was the best of them? Well, even I never saw Richardson or Kortwright or Kotze or Knox, and Gregory and McDonald together only as a fourteen-year-old, though I watched the latter for Lancashire later and saw him uproot Don Bradman's stumps (at Liverpool) the only time he ever bowled against him. Macdonald was an artist, marvellously light on his feet, who in later life used his utmost pace only sparingly as a latent threat. Some of his contemporaries – such as are still alive – might well plump for him; but as for me I haven't seen the equal of Ray Lindwall, who wasn't just a very fast bowler but one who on a fine rhythmic action built the arts of swing and pace-change: change of length, too, with equal command of the yorker and the bouncer. My accolade goes to him.

MERCHISTON WIN THE HEWITT

The largest golf tournament in the world – contested by the Old Boys of sixty-four schools, each side comprising five foursomes – enlivens each spring in our breezy corner of East Kent. The Halford-Hewitt Cup has been played at Royal Cinque Ports, Deal since 1925. The neighbouring links of Royal St George's are also nowadays used for the first two of the four days. Country Life *called on me [15 April 1976], I suppose, because their regular writer, Pat Ward-Thomas, was covering the Masters at Augusta.*

A new name, that of Whitgift, so nearly came to be inscribed on the Halford-Hewitt Cup last Sunday evening on the noble links of the Royal Cinque Ports, for at half way Merchiston, who won six years ago, were up in three matches and all square in the other two. Thereafter it was Whitgift who made most of the running and they were rewarded with two wins, the Hedges brothers getting home at the 21st against J. C. Briggs and G. T. Russell. This was thanks to a lovely 3 iron to the green by Peter of Walker Cup renown, in the top match, while P. Souster and N. Durance overcame another brotherhood, that of the Zuills, A. M. and J. A. S. at the 19th. This was after Durance had holed from ten yards on the 18th to keep the game alive.

So in the end the ancient Hewitt recipe was repeated, with all depending on the last match. There was little in this all the way, and they came to the 18th all square. From what I saw it seemed that Michael Grint was the hero here. At the short 14th after Ian Caldwell (another Walker Cup player) of Whitgift, had holed from eight yards for a three, Grint from not much closer followed him in for a two. Neither side found the last green, Whitgift ending below the bank while Merchiston were just through. The third stroke was not distinguished on either side, but Grint from fully seven yards holed out once more, whereupon poor Garment's ball, from an almost identical distance, missed by a couple of inches. Perhaps it was the presence of the Chief of the Band of Brothers Cricket Club, his father-in-law Oliver Grace, as his caddie, that tilted the balance in favour of Grint – but possibly I am biased.

The Halford-Hewitt's long history of close, agonising matches was lived up to after two rather uneven semi-finals. In the first Merchiston beat Radley led by Ted Dexter, whose only defeat this was, by 4-1; and by the same score Whitgift overcame Bradfield, another good evenly matched side also led by a Cambridge golfer in Brian Chapman.

This was one of the more benevolent Halford-Hewitts in terms of weather, which got progressively more genial right through to Sunday afternoon. It was all a great change from the biting east winds of 1975. This time it blew gently from the prevailing south-west quarter, making the long home stretch at Deal a tough test certainly, but not a cruel one. The sun shone, and the larks sang their heads off, and all was right with, at any rate, this little corner of the world.

Present sides tend to be younger than of yore, but at least one venerable survivor was seen again, T. Dilkes Page partnering Freddie Brown for the Leys. The very oldest, E. C. (Bunny) Millard, of Lancing, dropped out this year having by absence abroad missed only three times since 1927. 'Pretty good effort', said I, 'he must be nearly 70'. 'Nearly 70?' came the reply 'He fought on the Somme!'

Loyalty such as this is the very essence of the Hewitt; to see surging youth is wonderful, but pray Heaven it does not all come too terribly professional. Touching this, in one important respect there was a highly welcome improvement. Every competitor was given a printed reminder that a foursomes match ought to take approximately two hours and a half 'and should certainly not exceed three hours'. The committee on the course had to chivy a few slow-coaches but generally speaking the hint was taken.

INTIMIDATION UNPUNISHED

Twenty years on the situation is no better, though we have seen nothing quite so frightening as this assault on Close and Edrich by Roberts, Holding and Daniel under Lloyd's captaincy at Old Trafford in July, 1976. Letter to the Editor of the Daily Telegraph, *15 July 1976.*

Sir – The condemnation of the West Indian bowling on the Saturday evening of the Old Trafford Test by Mr Michael Melford was fierce indeed, and surely all the more effective coming from such a temperate critic.

On the evidence of television the West Indian fast bowling in this session of play was about as disgraceful as was that of the Australians at times on the last MCC tour, especially when egged on by 'The Hill' at Sydney. If English bowlers have been less at fault of late it may be because the captain has had less fire-power at his disposal; but in fact England were warned for intimidation at Brisbane in November 1974–75 before Lillee and Thomson had bowled a ball in the series, as they had also been several times in Australia in 1970–71.

Short fast bowling is, of course, more dangerous – and correspondingly more contemptible – when aimed at less proficient batsmen, as for instance the bouncer from Holding that flew past Underwood's head in the first innings. I equated that with the first ball bowled to England's No. 11, Arnold, by Lillee at Sydney that narrowly missed his face before flying over the wicket-keeper for four byes.

The object however is the same, to whomever such bowling is directed – to frighten the batsman, or at least unsettle him. As such it contravenes Law 46 which enjoins the umpire to deliver two warnings, and for a further offence to instruct that the bowler be taken off and not allowed to bowl for the remainder of the innings.

The International Cricket Conference when they meet next week at Lord's with this explosive subject on its agenda have to face the fact that the ultimate sanction has *never* been applied, and to ask themselves whether in the tempestuous atmosphere of modern Test matches any umpire would dare to apply it.

All the evidence is that umpires are perfectly prepared to give decisions on matters of inches and fractions of a second, but that they are, and always have been, far too reluctant to deliver judgments with moral implications, for instance on throwing and time-wasting in addition to intimidation.

In times past (except in the bodyline episode) captains could generally be relied upon to see that the players in their charge obeyed the spirit of the game. Now they are often either unable or unwilling to intervene, with proper effect. So much the worse for the poor umpires, and for the game itself.

In my view the ICC have on their hands the most difficult problem since the throwing debate of 1960. If they decide that a law embodying a penalty that can scarcely be applied is in need of revision, what change can they recommend to MCC, the law-makers?

Meanwhile, in order to lessen the danger of a fatality, and to prevent a further erosion of goodwill, could the umpires not persuade themselves that one clear bouncer an over should be the maximum rather than two – which is said to be the accepted number, though it is sometimes exceeded without demur?

E. W. SWANTON
Sandwich, Kent.

MCC, BRIEFLY

This digest of Club history was written for the brochure announcing the opening of the first MCC Indoor School in 1977. I was privileged to have been closely concerned with the building of it and chaired its Management Committee until 1983.

Within the memory of most of us Marylebone Cricket Club, in a rapidly-changing world, has changed less than most of the London and the England around us. I nearly wrote less than other comparable institutions, but if we know our cricket history even passably well there is no near-parallel to the Club, exclusive and autocratic in its early days according to the fashion of the times, which has evolved in a gradual and in a for the most part orderly, decorous way until here we are within just a decade of its bicentenary.

It was in 1787 that, Thomas Lord having provided the nobility and gentry of the White Conduit Club with a headquarters ground (the first of three within a mile or two of one another) within the borough of Marylebone, they changed their name to the appropriate title that is now universally shortened to MCC.

As the game became organised, cricketers began to look to Lord's for a lead in administration, but they seldom found MCC eager to intervene. Middlesex certainly began to play their matches at Lord's – and so are celebrating their centenary of the event this summer – but, it was not until 1901 that Francis Lacey, the recently-appointed secretary of MCC, wrote to the counties suggesting the setting-up of an Advisory Committee to administer the affairs of county cricket.

'Ben' Lacey, who on his retirement became the first man to be knighted for his work for cricket, was a young barrister when he took over at the turn of the century, and Lord's and MCC were more businesslike concerns from that moment. The present pavilion, which surely symbolises to perfection Victorian prosperity and the place of cricket in an ordered, seemingly unchanging world, was as it is today; but little else round the perimeter of the field or of the Nursery remains.

The authoritative role of MCC likewise increased, though again the prodding came from without. It was the counties who persuaded MCC to set up the Board of Control for Test matches, and it was the Melbourne Cricket Club, its namesake who occupied a parallel position to MCC at least within the state of Victoria, urged it to undertake responsibility for choosing and managing English tours to Australia. Now at least, if not before, MCC could be described as a private club with a public function, and Plum Warner could say of them that 'they reign but they do not rule.' The Imperial Cricket Conference (the 'I' not changed to International until the 'sixties) is another of the institutions which MCC agreed to administer.

Such was the Club to which, after playing two summers of qualifying matches, I was duly elected in the mid-'thirties. I like to think that for a young cricket-playing member MCC was at its best between the wars. One had all the net practice one wanted, for that matter places in most of the out-matches one could get away to play in – some two hundred of them, a number slightly increased today. With a membership of little more than 6,000 the pavilion never seemed uncomfortably full, and there was among the staff from gate-man to secretary a pervading unique sense of friendliness. (The waiting-list, except for young cricketers brought forward out of their due turn, was upwards of thirty years, by the way, which meant that the membership seemed to change very little, and the regular habitués tended to know one another. With today's numbers this is patently impossible.)

By this time, of course, MCC were sending teams to every part of the world that flew the Union Jack. Except from Australia they and the counties asked no profit. If one said that here was a benevolent autocracy in action the accent was much more on the adjective than the noun.

Since the war economic necessity and the stress of events have precipitated great changes. Now the cost of new buildings, and latterly the crippling effects of inflation, have given the membership graph much the steepest rise in the club's history. Associates have been taken in, and today around 18,000 members rather than 6,000 have the privilege of wearing the colours of MCC.

While numbers have been building up in this way, the historic functions of MCC by contrast have diminished, and much that they themselves were prevailed upon to initiate they have been chiefly instrumental in handing back. The old Advisory Committee has become the Test and County Cricket Board, run by the counties for the counties; the diverse work being done for club, league, and school cricket – including the movement organised after the war for encouraging boys of all classes and having every sort of facility (or none) to enjoy the game, which was first known as the MCC Youth Cricket

Association - has been drawn together under a new body known as the National Cricket Association.

So there are three bodies, the TCCB, the NCA, and MCC itself, and all supply representatives in more or less equal proportion to the Cricket Council, which is now the game's official ruling body. I wrote at the start of this essay that MCC has changed less than most that surrounds us today, and I repeat it as a testament of faith in the essential kinship and common affection that bind those who love cricket. Yet if we are realistic we must recognise that necessity has expanded MCC to a degree that is not without risk. MCC is an institution of much power. It is still the law-maker. To a considerable degree it holds the purse strings of English cricket as the owner of the ground whence so much of the Test profit comes, to say nothing of the cash for the Finals of the great competitions.

Cricket has need of MCC in these practical ways, but its various composite parts need also a body which can exercise its old traditional role of wise and friendly counsellor – not wholly disinterested, of course, in these days of economic stringency, but to a degree at least above the heat and dust of battle.

OH DEAR, SIR!

To the Editor   Stanmore, Middlesex
The *Daily Telegraph*   July 1956

Dear Sir,

D on't you think that the time has arrived for your cricket corre-
spondent to be quietly disposed of, stuffed, and placed in the Long Room with the curved bats, the sparrow, and the other freaks of the noble game?

Yours etc.,
L. T. Sainsbury

5 March 1978

Dear Mr Swanton,
I emigrated to New Zealand in 1957 and recently acquired a paperback copy of your excellent book *Sort of a Cricket Person.*

I was amazed to see a letter quoted on page 286, written by me in 1956 and addressed to the Editor of the *Daily Telegraph*. I would like to assure you that it was meant to be witty but in cold print I realise that it could well be offensive.

For many years I have enjoyed your authoritative writings, comments and books (when I can obtain them) and so you need spare no sympathy for the poor fellow concerned!

I would like to assure you that no offence was intended at the time and would appreciate your assurance that none was taken.

With kind regards,
Yours sincerely,
L. T. Sainsbury

IAN PEEBLES REMEMBERED

Ian Peebles and I – his full Christian names were Ian Alexander Ross – lodged together, at first with Henry Longhurst, through most of the 1930s. I am Godfather to his son Alastair and he was our best man. It was therefore given to me to deliver the address at his Thanksgiving Service at St James's, Piccadilly.

There was a thread that ran through the life of Ian Peebles which it seems to me can be well expressed in the phrase: happiness through friendship. Almost everyone took to Ian and, though he was far from undiscriminating, he generally found it easy to like people and had a knack of fastening on to the best in them – the most amusing side perhaps, or some special interest or attribute – and making the most of it. He also had almost the best memory of anyone I ever knew. He remembered faces and people and things about them, both serious and funny, and so achieved that difficult and necessary art which John Masterman described as keeping friendships in good repair.

In short he was a captivating person and one can trace this wonderful gift of his from his boyhood up. Being mad about cricket, he contrived, aged fourteen or so, when Leicestershire were playing Scotland at Uddingston, where his father was the Presbyterian minister, to meet George Geary and Ewart Astill. These two staunch fellows, more than twice his age, became and remained firm friends for life.

Determined, after leaving Glasgow Academy, and following a brief trial of the job, that the Bank of Scotland was not for him, he decided to come south and try his luck as a cricketer. Aubrey Faulkner, that great coach, not only took him on promptly as his secretary and perpetual bowler but shared lodgings with him. Ian worked two and a half years at this – for £3 a week.

When he was nineteen he played under the captaincy of Plum Warner, who was so impressed by the young man and his promise that he promptly arranged for him to go out to South Africa with MCC, officially (since he had no county record) as secretary to the captain, Ronny Stanyforth. And so it came that this unknown young cricketer, before his twentieth birthday, had bowled for England in a Test Match and amply justified what even in those days was a unique opportunity. He was, incidentally, the first Scot born and brought up in his native country to play for England.

I don't think this is the place to say much directly about his cricket, except to record that in the subtle and demanding art of spin bowling (which he had set his heart on perfecting) he reached the very peak of skill for perhaps three summers before he tore the fibres of his right shoulder, and could never quite summon back the magic. (He went on playing, of course, for Middlesex, and in 1939 captained them.)

But in 1930 he was in a class of his own and there will not be many here in church who do not know the story of his first great duel at Old Trafford with Don Bradman, from which Ian emerged the winner. After fifty years I recall the scene so clearly. When England batted later I happened to be in the Long Room as he walked through to go in, and I saw a figure in clerical dress, his father (a keen and accomplished cricketer, by the way) step forward to wish him luck.

I should add here that the son never acquired that firm adherence to the Church of Scotland that his father must have hoped for. But if he was not a church-goer, he brought with him from the manse the Christian virtues that made him the man he was.

Ian by this time had spent a blissful year at Oxford – but MCC were due to return that winter to South Africa and he was invited. He loved South Africa (as he came later to love Australia and the West Indies). This, as it turned out, meant the end of Oxford. But there was some consolation in this disappointment, as he tells in his autobiography. 'The *Daily Express*,' he wrote, 'did me proud. Under the headline *Cricketer's Sacrifice* their correspondent inferred that I had made a noble gesture in abandoning a promising academic career in the interests of cricket and country.'

Ian's first job in London was evidence of his social gifts. He so impressed the proprietor of Ladbroke's that, though he knew nothing of racing, and so far as I know never went on a race-course, he became – and remained for some thirty years – a director. He also found a powerful friend in the very rich cricket philanthropist, Sir Julien Cahn, who offered to set him up in business in London with a young German kinsman of Cahn's, Hans Siegel, whose family were wine-growers, anxious for their son to avoid the Nazi persecution.

This association was soon interrupted by the war in which they both served, Ian being almost incredibly lucky to escape with his life from a bomb, at the cost of his left eye and permanent damage to an ear and a leg.

Ian did not let even this stop his playing and told with relish a story against himself. In a club match at Lord's he managed to make 50 – whereupon one of those amiable cranks who seem somehow part of the place accosted the *Times* correspondent and said, 'There you are, sir, I've always said it's easier to bat with one eye. This proves it. Peebles isn't very good now, but he's better.' Lord's and all it stood for was very near to his heart – Lord's and especially the Middlesex cricketers of his time.

Soon after the war three things happened to Ian which shaped the rest of his life. First and most important, he became married to Ursula. Secondly, he got down to serious work in a happy and fruitful partnership with Hans Siegel, which enabled him to support a loving wife and family.

Thirdly, he developed his natural skill as a cricket-writer, as a freelance to start with, and then for fifteen years as Chief Correspondent of *The Sunday Times*. As a reporter he was entertaining, as a short essayist with his light and humorous touch he was superb. This writing he expanded into several books; then came three biographies and, not least, with Diana Rait-Kerr, the continuation of Plum Warner's History of Lord's.

When his firm was taken over, and in retirement he found time hanging rather heavy on his hands, he got down to an autobiography and told his story simply, modestly and, of course, with winning humour. Winning quite literally, for *Spinner's Yarn* won the Cricket Society's award for the book of the year 1977.

By now the worst of all diseases had begun its work. He bore the pain, the discomfort, the weakness with a resignation that was wonderfully cheerful, fortified by Ursula's devoted care, and the many visits and letters of his friends. He even went on writing when he felt able, for *The Guardian* now and for *The Cricketer*.

Ian had an active and inquiring mind and there are several hobbies and interests I have had no time to touch on. But most things were second to cricket – cricket as an art, and as a philosophical expression, with all its opportunities for chivalrous rivalry and fellowship. It was his most illustrious opponent, Sir Donald Bradman, who wrote this to Ursula after his death: 'At all times there was a serene gentleness, a lurking sense of humour and a soft expression which were appealing. Of all my English friends there was nobody for whom I had greater admiration or affection.'

Ian's outlook on life is expressed well enough surely in those well-worn lines of Belloc's:

> From quiet homes and first beginnings
> Out to the Undiscovered Ends
> There's nothing worth the wear of winning
> But laughter and the love of friends.

Ian said of Lionel Tennyson (of whom he was very fond) that when he entered the room everyone smiled. And so they did when they saw Ian.

WHY CHAPLIN TOOK TO BASEBALL

*I met Chaplin at a party at Mrs Blanche Blackwell's house in Jamaica. They have recently got round to a form of recompense when there is no play at a Test Match.*Daily Telegraph, *12 February 1985.*

The grim phase 'No play guaranteed, no money returned,' displayed at the entrance to every first-class ground, has always been an offence against common justice as well as an evident affront to public relations.

My mind goes back to a question asked me once by Charlie Chaplin late in his life when he was reminiscing about Tom Hayward, Bobbie Abel, Tom Richardson and other Surrey heroes of his Kennington youth.

'Tell me,' he asked, 'have they got around to giving a rain-check yet?' As a young comedian playing at a Nottingham music-hall he had gone to Trent Bridge to watch his team, splashed out half-a-crown on a stand seat, and seen not a ball bowled. The injustice had rankled for upwards of half a century. 'So I had to go over to America and watch baseball,' he added.

BODYLINE – A CARICATURE TOO FAR

This was a contemptible Australian film wherein every English portrayal is a gross caricature. A Letter to the Editor of the Daily Telegraph, *13 June 1985.*

Sir – Mr. R. Fairclough's comprehensive letter (June 12) has relieved me of the need to explain to those who read the sadly-mistaken leader of June 6, headed 'We were not guilty,' the true nature of bodyline bowling.

It need only be added that when MCC had digested the evidence after the team's return, and also in the light of an attempted continuation of the tactics by Notts, they issued a specific ruling against 'direct attack' and promised the umpires full support if they found it necessary to invoke the Unfair Play law in this regard.

But may I take this opportunity of suggesting a few of the respects in which the Australian-made film disparaged Englishmen involved, rather in the manner of other films and books alleging to portray the fall of Empire?

Douglas Jardine, deluded, dauntless, trapped in an untenable situation of his own device, was far from the Nazi-ish ogre whom no team would have tolerated for a minute. Harold Larwood, shown with a snarl on his face, never hated anyone, and nor did Bill Voce – two good men led astray.

Gubby Allen never threw the ball back at his captain when asked to bowl. His attitude to Jardine is conveyed beyond argument by the letters home to his father, excerpts from which can be read in my recently-published biography.

Plum Warner was a small, bald, abstemious, soft-spoken man, not a largish hard drinking, finger-wagging fellow alternately blubbering and blustering.

The most ridiculous caricature of all was of Lord Harris, a universally-respected man of awesome dignity, rather than a many-chinned blimp not apparently above a spot of blackmail – this is a fictional episode with P. G. H. Fender that is contradicted by history.

Fender did not resign the Surrey captaincy to allow Jardine to proceed from that to the captaincy of England. In 1931 Jardine led England while Fender was still leading Surrey.

And poor Mr Fender! Fancy living to 92, as he has, and being portrayed as one of the more outrageous characters by P. G. Wodehouse!

E. W. SWANTON
Sandwich, Kent

BELITTLING OF THE ARCHBISHOP

A letter from the heart, to the Editor of the
Daily Telegraph, 30 November 1985.

Sir – Miss Joan Whatmough must have been flattered to see her letter (Nov 27) with its offensive belittling of the Archbishop of Canterbury and her allegations of a 'rapidly disintegrating Church' leading your correspondence columns.

It is inevitable, no doubt, that the Establishment as represented by the government of the day, the Church of England or, for that matter, the MCC should be used by the disaffected as a cheap Aunt Sally. And loyal Anglicans in particular have been long inured to insult. Most of it comes, though I do not suggest so in this case, either from professed agnostics or others with little or no knowledge of the Church, its formularies or its worship.

In the five years since his enthronement, the Archbishop as *primus inter pares* within the world-wide Anglican communion, has travelled widely and assiduously to listen, to learn to inform and to preach.

As to external relationships, those with the Roman Catholics – as witness the Papal visit and the conclusions of the Anglican–Roman Catholic International Commission – and with the Orthodox, thanks to the archiepiscopal triumvirate of Ramsey, Coggan and Runcie, have never been more cordial or promising.

At home, faced with problems, some inevitable, some surprising, he has stood surely as four-square defender of the Church of England, Catholic and Reformed. Within our own diocese, I sense that all who have met him have found a man of our times, compassionate, approachable, and spiritual above all.

Of course, the Church of England has difficulties and divisions to face, as, according to the Acts, did the Apostles themselves. But we may hope that they are debated in the spirit of that 'unity in fellowship' of which the Queen spoke at the opening of the General Synod.

E. W. SWANTON
Sandwich, Kent.

SALE OF TWO CENTURIES

An ample windfall for MCC, and evidence perhaps that the old Club was moving with the times. Christie's Review of the Season 1987.

The sale by Christie's of 845 items in the possession of MCC at Lord's on 13 April was a landmark in the world of cricket from several angles. Throughout its history Marylebone Cricket Club has been inclined towards ambivilence in its appreciation of the memorabilia of the game, the books and pictures, the implements, and all that can be generically classed as cricketana. Although many objects, including paintings, pre-date the foundation of MCC in 1787 the Club's sole possessions all but a century later were two pictures, one of them admittedly by Francis Hayman.

MCC were fortunate at this point in the interest taken in all things artistic by Sir Spencer Ponsonby-Fane, a man steeped in the public service. He was private secretary in turn to Palmerston, Clarendon and Granville at the Foreign Office. It was he who brought back from Paris the Treaty that ended the Crimean War. He was imbued all his long life with a deep love of the game. Ponsonby-Fane, Treasurer of MCC for thirty-six years from 1879 until his death in 1915 aged ninety-one, acquired pictures and drawings, persuaded his friends to donate, and commissioned works on MCC's behalf. With the expansion of the game more and more objects of historical importance found their way to Lord's.

As to a library, a gift of books was accepted from a Capt. H. B. Sutherland in 1893, so the Committee decided there was no need for a library 'at present' – in the age-old dismissive phrase of Committee minutes. It was the generous and unfettered offer of her husband's library in 1944 by Lady Cahn, widow of Sir Julien, the furniture millionaire (who had himself acquired most of it by purchase from F. S. Ashley-Cooper), that put MCC in almost fortuitous possession of the most complete collection in the world at that time. MCC have since provided themselves with the most worthwhile of the mass of cricket writing.

In future, it is safe to say, the importance of the artistic and literary side of our possessions will be more respectfully regarded by even the more philistine elements of the membership, seeing that by the auction sale of 'selected objects' from the *reserve* collection MCC are the richer by £290,000. Thus it was far from a selling-off of the family silver, to borrow the late Earl of Stockton's phrase. The object was to build a fund in order to keep the main collection in good repair and to be in a position to acquire any such desirable item as came on to the market in future.

The expectation hovered around £100,000. Christie's thought that might be on the low side, yet they were surprised as well as gratified by the result, and the fact that at the end of an eleven-hour non-stop sale their team of auctioneers – nine in all – had found a buyer for every one of the 845 objects in the catalogue. It was said to be Christie's longest ever day.

So what went for what? Well, the pattern was set right away when Henry Wyndham, of MCC and Christie's, no stranger to the new ball, totted up £1,000 or more for each of four water colours by Frank Reynolds which first appeared in the 1922 summer number of *Punch*. This was some three times above the mean of the estimates. Soon a small eighteenth-century painting showing a curved bat was fetching £6,500, and Eleanor Hughes D'Eath's eighteenth-century copy of a boy, Lewis Cage, at the wicket after R. A. Cotes, £10,000. This proved to be the top score of the day.

Printed cotton handkerchiefs, as always, were popular. Without offering any normally on display the Club were willing to part with a commemorative handkerchief in purple depicting a game at the White Conduit Club at Islington just prior to MCC's foundation, with the Laws of the Noble Game making a frame around the borders. This went for £7,000 to the syndicate who are constructing the Bradman Museum at Bowral, Sir Donald's birthplace. Generally speaking, the earlier the date the higher the price.

Bats and balls of every age, description, size and weight were offered in profusion. The oldest bat, mid-eighteenth-century, and much the heaviest at 5lb. 5oz., made of oak, curved an bowed with humped back, a rather ridiculous looking object, was sold for £5,000. Others of slightly later date, made at Ickham, Kent, stamped with the ducal coronet of Buccleuch and almost black, also attracted lively attention. The autographing of bats was common in W. G. Grace's day, a Gunn and Moore signed by him and many others of the Golden Age realising £1,500. Balls were less popular, although the one used in the first Test wherein South Africa beat Australia, the seam almost flush with the leather, went for £750.

A few of the objects on view were as bizarre as some of the prices realised: none more so than the 'cream wool tennis shorts inscribed P. F. Warner' which went for £140. They had been unearthed by the Curator, Stephen Green, from a dark corner of the courts.

When all is said and done the personality which dominated the proceedings was that of W. G. Grace, the man who in a career spanning over forty years (1865–1908) did much more than anyone to transform a country pastime into the national summer game. The writing was on the wall of his first visit to the wicket when a pen and ink caricature of W.G., black-bearded, sun-hatted, estimated at £100–120, realised £1,000. A series of pen and ink sketches by Harry Furniss went for £3,000, a crude pen and ink likeness in a frame carved with wickets, bats and balls for £2,200.

The best-known photogravure of Archibald Stuart Wortley's painting of W.G. at the wicket, signed by subject and artist, the market price for which has recently been around £200, went for ten times more. W.G. scored four figures in all his first six innings: the forty-odd items in which he featured added up to £24,030. Needless to say, numerous remembrances of W.G. remain to decorate the pavilion and the Memorial Gallery, a man whose humanity with its quirks and foibles still stands out as clearly as his massive achievements with bat and ball.

Everyone was too weary to enjoy the full culminating irony. The head and skin of a tiger shot on an MCC tour of India went for £2,000. The marksman was C. S. Marriott, an admirable bowler but one of the worst batsmen ever to put on pads for England. (He is one of the few men in history who have taken many more wickets than they scored runs.) That tiger must have been as sleepy as were those who had sat for so many hours weighing up and bidding for what Mr Michael Sissons, the Chairman of Arts and Library, succinctly described as 'an attractive rag-bag of oddments from the pavilion basement'. Cricket, surely, and all appertaining to it, has a fascination for its devotees to which the world of sport has no parallel.

CHURCH MILITANT

This booklet appeared serially during 1987 and 1988 in the Parish Magazine of St Clement's Church, Sandwich. The Lambeth Conference, embracing the bishops of the twenty-seven Provinces of the Anglican Communion, meets every ten years at Canterbury. I thought it worthwhile to picture the traditional roots of the Church of England from which so many others have spread. His Grace the Archbishop, Dr Robert Runcie, kindly wrote a Foreword, and purchasers within the parishes of the Diocese of Canterbury gave £1 per copy for the Church Urban Fund.

Since I wrote, the General Synod of the Church of England in 1992 voted to sanction the Ordination of Women, achieving the necessary two-thirds majority by a margin of two votes. This was followed by the secession of several hundred priests headed by Dr Graham Leonard, the former Bishop of London, and an undisclosed number of laity. Anglicans, both Catholic and Evangelical, determined to uphold the ancient teaching of the Church, have come together in movements known as Forward in Faith and Affirming Catholicism. Here are the opening paragraphs of my essay.

The year of the Lambeth Conference with its great company of five hundred bishops from the twenty-seven Provinces of the Anglican Communion seems an appropriate moment to attempt to sketch the historical beginnings of the post-Reformation Church of England, and thus to show how from its purely English beginnings it has expanded over the last two centuries into a vast world-wide brotherhood. It extends today from Alaska in the west across the continents to the Philippines in the east, and in latitude from the Hebrides of Scotland down to the extremities of Africa and Australasia: nearly seventy million members in 164 countries.

These many Churches, autonomous though they are, form a family which is united by what the *Encyclopedia Britannica* calls 'a common loyalty to the Archbishop of Canterbury and by an agreement with the doctrines and practices defined in The Book of Common Prayer, a 16th Century liturgical book whose roots lie in the early history of the Christian Church in England.'

Note that the author here underlines the fact that the basis of our Prayer Book derives from the early, undivided Church established in England many centuries before the Reformation. The mother Church of the Anglican Communion is nevertheless the Church of England, so called from the time of King Henry VIII's dispute with the Pope and his consequent declaration in the Act of Supremacy of 1534 that he was 'the only Supreme head of the Church of England'.

With the Roman link thus broken, what then was the character and status of the Church that emerged? It is fundamental to Anglican theology of whatever particular complexion that, as the Apostles' Creed proclaims, the Anglican Church believes in 'the Holy Catholic Church'. The Nicene Creed more specifically speaks of our membership of 'one Holy, Catholic and Apostolic Church'. As we recite Sunday by Sunday, Anglicans derive directly from that divine institution founded by Jesus Christ himself, and perpetuated by Him when He said to His Apostles, 'Go ye, therefore, and teach all nations . . . teaching them to observe all things whatsoever I command you.' (Matthew 28.20)

THE INIMITABLE GUBBY

One example of his nerve and thoroughness: as a photographic liaison officer between the Army and RAF he elected to fly over the Ruhr in the rear gunner's seat of a bomber to assess enemy anti-aircraft fire in action. The crew had a very narrow shave at the hands of a Messerschmidt as they came home. Daily Telegraph, *1 December 1989.*

Sir George Allen, universally known as 'Gubby', who has died aged eighty-seven, had a stronger influence on the world of cricket and for a longer span of years than anyone since the 4th Lord Harris.

Allen played the first of his twenty-five Tests in 1930. He captained England both at home and in Australia; was elected to the Committee of MCC in his early thirties; and served the Club as both Treasurer and President, as well as on successive committees for more than fifty years.

George Oswald Browning Allen was born in Sydney on 31 July 1902, of a family with deep roots in Australia. His great-grandfather emigrated in 1816, was the first man in Australia to serve his articles as a solicitor there, and founded what today is the oldest legal firm in Sydney. Gubby's father, Walter, brought his family to England in 1909, and at the outbreak of the First World War joined the Metropolitan Special Constabulary, eventually becoming Commissioner and earning a knighthood.

From his private schooldays at Summerfields, Oxford, young Allen showed that he had cricket in the blood. When Eton and Harrow resumed their rivalry at Lord's in 1919, Allen was run out in the first over on the first morning without receiving a ball. However, things turned out well for him – as they generally did – in the second innings, his 69 not out helping Eton to an easy victory. He was lucky in having for a housemaster C. M. Wells, formerly of Cambridge and Middlesex, who ran the cricket, and for a coach the celebrated George Hirst.

By the time their mettlesome protégé left Eton, his promise as a fast bowler, with a beautiful action and late out-swing, was clearly recognizable, whereas he was correct and determined as a batsman.

Allen walked into Hubert Ashton's powerful Cambridge side of 1922 and his nine wickets in the University Match for 78 runs sped Oxford to an innings defeat. After two years he left Cambridge for the City, where he became a successful stockbroker, and thereafter became his own brand of amateur, playing never even half a season for Middlesex and, despite this, reaching the top of the tree as an all-round cricketer. Commuting, so to speak, between the Stock Exchange and Lord's, he rarely failed to make an impact for Middlesex whenever he turned out, either as batsman or fast bowler, or both. His performances generally spoke for themselves, but the Allens and the Warners were close friends and Gubby was lucky to have a powerful friend at court in Sir Pelham, who was either a Test selection chairman or cricket correspondent or even both.

The first of his twenty-five appearances for England was against Australia in the famous Lord's Test of 1930 when, substituting for Harold Larwood, he bowled expensively but, with A. P. F. Chapman, made 125 for the sixth wicket in the second innings. The following year he and L. E. G. Ames against New Zealand at Lord's combined in a stand of 246 which is still a world record for the eighth wicket in Tests, both making hundreds.

His choice for D. R. Jardine's MCC team in Australia in 1932–3 was strongly criticized. Yet he was one of the successes of the tour, taking 21 wickets in the Tests and averaging 23 with the bat. It is a matter of history that although entreated by his captain to do so he declined to bowl 'Bodyline', and was always frank in his disapproval of it.

Allen first led England in the 1936 series against India, in obvious preparation for the captaincy in Australia the following winter. After winning the first two Tests there, England were defeated in the following three – thanks chiefly to some phenomenal scoring by Bradman.

Just as Allen's leadership in Australia before the war had come in for the highest praise on all counts, so it did again in 1947–8 in the West Indies, even though Allen was now forty-five and, with a weak side, MCC could not match the emergent brilliance of the 'three Ws', Worrell, Weekes and Walcott. He was a model touring captain in that he took infinite trouble over every member of his side. At his best Allen was a valuable Test all-rounder, a fast bowler whose speed stemmed from a perfect action, a sound bat, and excellent close fielder. He took eighty-one wickets in Tests at an average cost per wicket of 29.37, and made 750 runs, averaging 24.19. His first-class record was: 784 wickets at 22.24; 8866 runs, average 28.05, including ten hundreds.

Allen's most notable feat was in 1929 at Lord's when he took all ten Lancashire wickets for 40 runs, this after arriving late on the field (by arrangement, naturally) and so missing the new ball. In county cricket at Lord's it was a unique feat, and so it remains.

The Lord's Committee Room was the scene of his work for cricket from 1932 to 1985 – an unprecedented span interrupted only by the Second World War. In 1963–64 he was President, and from 1964 to 1976 held the Club's key post of Treasurer.

An amateur in the most complete sense on the field, Allen was very much a professional in committee. No one had a wider knowledge of every facet of cricket politics and administration. No one was better briefed, nor, it should be added, more tenacious in his opinions. He had more time than most, and he could show infinite patience in order to win his point. It was sometimes whispered that the easiest way to get a thing through was to persuade the *éminence grise* that it had been his own idea. There is no doubt he could be difficult. Likewise it generally had to be admitted in the end that 'Gubby is probably right'.

Allen was the chief instigator of the national post-war movement in cricket for the involvement and teaching of the young. This was hitherto an uncharted field, but now there are associations covering every area. It led to Allen's authorship with H. S. Altham of *The MCC Cricket Coaching Book*, a best-seller for many generations.

When England and Australia were very much at odds over the perilous issue of throwing after the MCC tour of 1958–9 it was Allen who, with Sir Donald Bradman's eventual strong co-operation, devised a successful formula for eliminating the 'chucker'. He performed no more vital service than this. Not the least of his labours was his seven seasons' chairmanship of the Test Selectors from 1955 to 1961.

Allen was not only a shrewd judge of a cricketer but he was also, on the testimony of all who served with him, an admirably fair and thorough chairman with a flair for finding the man for the occasion. In all he did there shone his great devotion to the game and helpful, unfailing friendliness to all cricketers.

He was awarded the Territorial Decoration and the American Legion of Merit in 1945, appointed CBE in 1962 and knighted in 1986. Gubby Allen never married. His family said he was always wedded to cricket.

TEST REFEREES

It was (now Sir) Colin Cowdrey's initiative which in 1991 resulted in the ICC, despite opposition, accepting the revolutionary concept of referees to fortify umpires in international cricket. Five years on few close to the scene would argue against them. Daily Telegraph, 2 April 1990.

Colin Cowdrey, the chairman of the International Cricket Council, has flown to Barbados to watch the fourth Test and no doubt to acquaint himself further on West Indian and TCCB affairs in the light of the current Test series.

Before he went, he left me in no doubt of his hopes that the ICC at their next meeting in July will move to strengthen two contentious items in the Unfair Play law, time-wasting and misbehaviour on the field.

As I have pointed out, the umpire's sanction in the event of a breach in both cases is restricted to warning and report. Do they not need to be provided with stronger teeth, and if the Test countries decide so, will they agree to amend their match regulations accordingly?

These are the sort of matters which will test Mr Cowdrey's diplomatic skills. It was the recognition that in the modern game difficulties are seldom far below the surface that impelled the ICC to appoint a past president of MCC prepared to stand as chairman for four years rather than the hitherto traditional one.

But, it will be said, can the umpire be saddled with even more responsibility than the poor fellow is carrying already? It is a good question, and the idea is being mooted that a referee, a distinguished old cricketer acceptable to the authorities of both sides as a man of impartial judgment, might be appointed to oversee every Test match. If all went well he would have no part to play. In the event of crisis he would be at hand to fortify the umpires in their duty.

To some this will seem a revolutionary, far-fetched notion, to others welcome evidence that every plan is being considered to prevent the conduct of cricket slipping further downhill.

Lastly, a reminder to all who at home will be straining to hear and see the Barbados Test: if the incessant Greig–Boycott TV duet drives them to distraction they can turn off the sound, let the picture speak for itself and pick up what they can from the crackle of Radio 3.

When Stewart came in at that crucial moment, both for his side and himself, in England's second innings, Greig cried in a strident crescendo: 'I'll tell you what – his heart will be pounding a bit.'

Shades of Howard Marshall! Come over, Richie Benaud! Our Geoffrey says some perceptive things and could be acceptable under different direction if he could be persuaded to talk half as dogmatically, and half as much, leaving the viewer now and then with his own thoughts.

'The golden pause', forever associated with Henry Longhurst, is the essence of TV commentary, on cricket as on golf.

REAGAN ON CRICKET

Daily Telegraph, 22 December 1990.

It was an honour to meet former President Reagan at the recent Saints and Sinners lunch and a surprise indeed to hear from him a cricket story about the archetypal actor of English patrician parts and one-time distinguished cricketer, Sir Aubrey Smith, doyen of the English community and of Hollywood CC in the 1930s.

Aubrey Smith, in his middle 70s, was still playing when Ronald Reagan began his film-making. When a new man came in to bat, Mr Reagan said Sir Aubrey sent the fielders out to 'the very edge of the park'.

The batsman was quickly out and when Sir Aubrey was asked about his field-placing, he said: 'Why? He was the best batter in England in '09.'

There was no time to swap my favourite Aubrey Smith story. The old man dropped a catch in the slips, then another. General unease. Annoyed, he summoned his man to bring his spectacles – which he did, no doubt on a silver tray. Down went another catch. Real embarrassment now – until he exclaimed: 'Damn, the fool's brought my reading-glasses!'

Sir Aubrey Smith was in his prime in the late 1880s. He was no chicken in '09, and was still turning out at Hollywood in the 1930s when seventy-plus, the doyen of the English film colony there.

GETTY'S GLORY

Mr J. P. Getty is giving untold pleasure each summer to a rich variety of cricketers, hundreds strong, wearing the colours of club, university, county and England and playing the game as it was meant to be played, strenuously, fairly and amicably on his lovely ground at Wormsley. Daily Telegraph, *August 1992.*

John Paul Getty II, of the American oil dynasty, is a man whose riches are matched by his benevolence. As a resident Anglophile who has subscribed unobtrusively to many good causes, he received six years ago from the Queen the accolade of knighthood: still a citizen of the United States, his KBE has to be honorary.

How did cricket come into his life? Well, in the 1970s he and Mick Jagger became Chelsea neighbours. As they made one another's acquaintance, the pop star switched to cricket when it was shown on TV and Mr Getty found himself perforce watching 'this ridiculous game with its pin-ball scores'.

That lucky meeting was followed by another when he and G. O.

Allen – Gubby, later Sir George – were fellow patients at the London Clinic. A warm friendship sprang up with Mr. Cricket himself. 'Gubby's devotion to cricket was total. He was a great man and I loved him dearly.'

From this association, which stimulated the lives of both during the remaining years of Gubby Allen's life, first sprang Mr. Getty's massive contribution to the rebuilding of the Mound Stand at Lord's, which was opened by the Duke of Edinburgh at the beginning of MCC's bicentenary year, 1987.

Until the former died, the names of Sir George Allen CBE and J. Paul Getty KBE were inscribed together on the door of Mound Stand Box No 3. This is where Mr. Getty entertains at the big matches, adjacent now at the Nursery End to the Compton and Edrich Stands, to the building of which he was also a handsome contributor.

Cricket has had its patrons since it emerged from the rustic simplicity of its beginnings in the villages of the Weald. As it won the interest and affection of a wide variety of men, the game gathered airs and graces.

In its modern, sophisticated form it has appealed to the most improbable people and, in that he was born and brought up in California into a family with little in the way of sporting predilections, you might say that Mr Getty was among the unlikeliest. Yet apart from a deep love of music in all its forms he is also a distinguished bibliophile, and cricket has always had a strong affinity with music and literature.

Since he is rising 60, Mr. Getty in his love affair with cricket is clearly making up for lost time. This summer he has added to his innumerable financial benefactions the bringing into use of his newly-laid private ground, a perfect oval in an idyllic pastoral setting in the Chilterns, literally on the Buckinghamshire–Oxfordshire border. MCC, properly enough, were the first opponents and the sixth and last match of J. Paul Getty's XI has now brought the Wormsley season to a close.

Has Mr. Getty enjoyed this extension of his cricket experience, I asked him. 'It has been for me the happiest summer since my boyhood,' he said. What first attracted him about this strange English game so far removed from baseball? 'Its complexity and endless variety. There is an inner excitement about it even when it is superficially boring. There are so many different skills, such a diversity of tactics.

'As an American I had supposed that baseball was the more strenuous and demanding game, cricket by comparison a pastime of softies. Not so, I discovered. Baseball, on the contrary, is simplistic, draughts as compared with chess.' They are Mr. Getty's words, not mine. He uses conventional phrases about cricket, the team game, as a character builder.

Mr. Getty's devotion to the game does not blind him to its problems and dangers. He dates a decline in the spirit in which top-class cricket is played to the Packer intrusion – 'the worst thing that ever happened. Every cricketer is entitled to a decent living wage and future provision but there should be a limit to commercial exploitation.

'I loathe the thought of coloured clothing and am much distressed by the TCCB decision to adopt it with the absolutely unnecessary white balls and black sight-screens. I'm horrified by things like this that cheapen cricket. Every retrograde step should be fought.'

Mr. Getty's concern is such that I asked him how he viewed the prospect of cricket in the 21st century. 'I don't see it surviving very long as the game that has been handed down, except at local level. The limited-over game is threatening to become halfway to baseball.' Pray heaven this proves too pessimistic an estimation!

The first thing one sees on entering Mr. Getty's London flat is a framed photograph of W. G. Grace. He is represented at most sales of cricketana and has a discriminating and varied collection of pictures and objects as well as a select cricket library.

Music and cricket predominate in an awesome collection of cassettes and videotapes. He answers with a chuckle the question of how he acquired his set of *Wisden*. 'It came from Robert Maxwell's office at the Daily Mirror [for a brief period Maxwell owned the *Wisden* copyright]. No doubt it was just filling shelf space.'

EXIT IAN BOTHAM

As I write Botham, the complete individualist, has been very properly rejected as a Test selector by the TCCB. The best service he could leave to the game, I suggest, would be to provide a commentary on a film of the model bowling action of his prime, with another of one of his great innings, probably his tremendous 118 against Australia at Old Trafford in 1981. I mean, of course, a knowledgeably edited version showing the defensive strokes as well as the fireworks. Daily Telegraph, July 1993.

S ince Ian Botham first donned an England cap 16 years ago everything about him has been, as they say, over the top: his feats of
glory on the field, his excesses off it.

Many among senior generations are too sentimentally attached to
the modest heroes of old to appreciate the Botham style. But if the
swagger is not for us, as he leaves the first-class scene, we must
acknowledge the greatness at his best of a lion-hearted all-round
cricketer.

In the lissom days of youth and in early manhood his command of
late swing as a bowler, his eye and strength as a batsman, and his
exceptional reflexes in the field made him an awesome all-rounder; and
when time and life-style gradually took their toll the basic orthodoxy of
his methods – learned, by the way, as a teenager on the Lord's
groundstaff – kept him going almost if not quite to the end. Only one
all-rounder surely stands ahead of him as of all others, the incomparable Gary Sobers.

THE GREATEST

Daily Telegraph, 26 March 1994.

F orty years ago a slim, loose-limbed youth of 17 made his way to
the crease in the electric atmosphere of Sabina Park, Jamaica, to
play his first innings for the West Indies.

The score, unbelievably, was 110 for seven. They were all out for
139: Gary Sobers at No 9 made 14 undefeated. In England's innings
of 414 he took four wickets for 75 with slow left-arm spin. When the
West Indies batted again the youngster made 26 and though he had
been chosen chiefly as a bowler, talent of a high order was plain to
see. (England, thanks to Trevor Bailey's inspired bowling on the first
day, won by nine wickets, so halving the rubber – a recollection to
cherish in 1994).

Such was the first of Sobers' 93 Test matches wherein he built up a
monument of achievement secure in its pre-eminence: 8,032 runs at
an average of 57.78, including 26 hundreds; 235 wickets at 34 each;
110 catches: this despite the fact that of all great cricketers none was
more indifferent than he to figures and records.

For just 20 years he decorated the Test scene in his inimitable way, an all-rounder of unparalleled versatility, completely unselfish, and with an unquenchable urge, whether batting, bowling in any of his three styles, or fielding, to attack – and, in so doing, of course, to entertain. He was always conscious of the game's obligation to give pleasure, yet was the reverse of a show-off. He allowed his cricket to speak for him. And speak it did, all over the world.

Barbados could not have a better ambassador than its most famous living son. Where so many modern heroes have shown feet of clay, Sobers has never swerved from the principles of sportsmanship and fair play in which he was brought up, and which became second nature to him. He has always been a modest winner and a cheerful loser, an ideal model for young and old.

In his *Sir Gary*, one of the best of all cricket biographies, Trevor Bailey traces his subject from earliest beginnings, brought up frugally among a family of six by a saint of a mother in a small one-storey wooden house. Gary was only five when in January 1942 his seaman father went down with all hands in a ship bringing supplies to Barbados.

There was no lack of neighbourhood father-figures to encourage his passion for cricket, but it was a white one, Wilfred Farmer, then captain of the police team, later to be Commissioner for Police in Barbados, who spotted him in a softball game, and, impressed by the lad as well as by his cricket, recruited him into the police band. The police played in the BCA League from which the Barbados team was chosen: at the age of 16 he was picked to play for his country against the touring Indians. He took seven wickets in 89 overs of slow left-arm spin for a match return of seven for 142. Installed in the island team with the three Ws, Worrell, Weekes and Walcott, his call to the Jamaica Test followed a year later.

When, many years afterwards Sobers, staying with Bailey in Essex at the time, heard that Farmer was in hospital he took the next train to London to see him. Characteristic though this was, I would mention here that he has always been remarkably unconscious of colour, making friends among men and women regardless of their skin. He was equally at home among his family and contemporaries in Barbados or in his five-year captaincy of Notts or when his all-round virtuosity was bringing the Sheffield Shield to South Australia.

He has been lucky in the close friendships which have always been necessary to his carefree, gregarious nature. Until his death, Sir Frank Worrell (who recommended that Gary succeed him in the West Indies captaincy) kept a very close eye, especially after the death of Gary's boon companion, Collie Smith. Gary was driving on a journey from Lancashire to a charity match: he was unhurt in the crash, Collie was killed.

In 1969 he married a charming Australian, Prue Kirby, and they had two sons. She was a stable factor in his life for the best part of 20 years.

There has never been a cricketer who apart from outstanding quality as batsman and fielder could offer three bowling methods according to what the situation demanded. He soon added wrist-spin to his orthodox style and in the Central Lancashire League with Radcliffe, then began to bowl over the wicket at speed with the new ball. The late in-swing, coupled with the ball that drifted away, made him and Alan Davidson of Australia for some years as dangerous opening bowlers as any in the game.

Sobers' activity in the field, however valuable, was nevertheless secondary to Sobers at the wicket. His 365, the highest Test score, against a weakened Pakistan attack, was notable for stamina and concentration but not typical in that his other big innings against the best bowling were shaped more specifically to the needs of the side.

He rates with particular pleasure the 163 not out with which he and his young cousin David Holford (105 not out) pulled the Lord's Test of 1966 out of the fire. The point always remembered about that record partnership of 274 for the sixth wicket, is that he gave confidence to his inexperienced partner by allowing him a full share of the bowling.

When the South African tours to England and Australia were cancelled in 1970 and 1971, Sobers captained powerful Rest of the World sides in some of the best cricket seen in both countries. His heartfelt opening address at Lord's to a mixed side of five West Indians, five South Africans, two Pakistanis, an Australian and an Indian revealed a diplomatic awareness that bound his team in a spirit they found unforgettable. Gary was in his element in all respects and at Melbourne some months later played an innings of 254 which Sir Donald Bradman described as 'probably the best ever seen in Australia'. The Don later wrote: 'With his long grip of the bat, high backlift and free swing, I think, by and large, Gary Sobers consistently hits the ball harder than anyone I can remember.' So spake the oracle.

Equally crucial to the picture, of course, was the most rigid of straight bats in defence. The only possible chink in the armour, as I saw it, was a reluctance to move either foot very much when he first came in. I usually wanted to see a spinner confronting him early on.

Among pictures in the mind was a stroke off Jeff Jones of Glamorgan in a Bridgetown Test. Jones achieved a fast bouncer to which Gary jumped and with both feet off the ground cut to the square boundary like a rocket. At Dover for Notts against Kent, having taken 11 wickets in the two innings, he batted in appalling light, to win the match against time. Sobers scored the fastest 100 of the season in 77 minutes without a false stroke; it was dark when he finished and the fielders had been lucky to escape without injury.

There were two phases to his Test captaincy, the first highly success-ful, the second not so, and it was a relief when he was succeeded by Rohan Kanhai. He inspired by his example and was a shrewd tactician, but by the 1970s after nearly 20 years of almost continuous all-round cricket winter and summer, he had lost his zest for the job.

Sir Garfield Sobers was not only the most captivating and glamorous of cricketers. In Bailey's words 'he has, quite simply, been the greatest of all time, the most complete all-rounder ever'. That is my judgment without reservation.

THREE SENTIMENTS

On diverse themes, the Abbey service to Brian Johnston, South Africa's readmission to the ICC and the significance of Allan Border's retire-ment. Daily Telegraph, 16 May 1994.

The best statistic of the season so far is 2,500, that is to say the 2,000 or more who thronged Westminster Abbey for the celebration for Brian Johnston's life plus the 500 who applied for tickets in vain. What other personality and what other game could have brought together such a company? The whole occasion was an evocation of what senti-mentalists like me call the fellowship of cricket.

The same phrase in a very different context occurred to me when I read of the appointment of Steve Tshwete as Minister of Sport in Nelson Mandela's cabinet.

Three years ago he and Ali Bacher, on the eve of the formation of the United Cricket Board of South Africa, took a distinguished party of us to a huge field in Soweto where hundreds of boys were learning the basics – and a few lucky ones being shown how to do it by such heroes as Sir Garfield Sobers and Sunil Gavaskar.

If it had not been for the diplomatic skills of this recent co-resident with Mr Mandela on Robben Island (15 years, much of it in solitary), South Africa would not have been welcomed back into the International Cricket Conference so swiftly.

Although on his mission to London Mr. Tshwete pleaded South Africa's case to the High Commissioners of all the Test-playing countries, only England, Australia and New Zealand at first gave support.

John Major wrote to all the Caribbean Prime Ministers and it was only when the West Indies were won over that the Asian trio came off the fence. It would have been deplorable if the impetus had been lost, for the renaissance and continuing spread of cricket in South Africa is the best thing that has happened to the game for years.

Allan Border was a cricketer whose battling characteristics were worthy of respect. Readers of this column will not, however, expect me to regret his retirement, which had to be the first step in any effort towards the restoring of acceptable standards of Australian behaviour on the field.

With a tour of Pakistan due, we should all wish well to Mark Taylor, the expected successor as captain. The Board chairman, Alan Crompton has recorded, at last, an official determination to improve things. But I wonder that anything less than a crusade at all levels of authority will achieve much. Persistent sledging and pressurising of umpires runs deep throughout Australian cricket.

THE UGLIEST CLOUD

Intimidation, of course. A limit of one bouncer an over (as annually proposed by England) would at least put a brake on excess. Daily Telegraph, *21 September 1994.*

The ugliest cloud in the sky remains the preponderance of fast, short-pitched bowling in Test cricket. So long as intimidation is tacitly accepted by those most closely concerned, namely umpires and captains, attacks will lack balance and the arts of spin bowling will remain submerged. I will not repeat myself on this issue since readers know my views well enough, except to deplore the International Cricket Council's recent decision to allow two bouncers an over (a third of the total of all balls bowled) instead of the continuation of a maximum of one per over to each batsman, as proposed by England, supported by Sri Lanka. Bob Wyatt, still in favour, as I am, of a line midway down the wicket with penalties against balls pitching short of it, reminds me that he first advocated this at an inquest at Lord's following the Bodyline Tour in 1933.

Sir Stanley Jackson in the chair expressed his disagreement, saying that if the game were played in the right spirit no line would be necessary. 'I quite agree,' said Bob (Douglas Jardine's recent vice-captain), 'but is it?' The question echoes still. These columns contained a no more significant comment this summer than Mark Nicholas's withering condemnation: 'Cricket was not meant to be a game of intimidation or violence . . . and an international body that encourages the use of two bouncers an over is risking the misguided education of another generation.'

Sir Donald Bradman, in a letter written on his 86th birthday, while recognising the evil of intimidation, is reluctant to pronounce. The great man, sharp in mind as ever and as nimble with the pen as with the bat, reserves his severest scorn for the front foot bowling law, 'foisted on the world against Australia's wish'.

How about the ICC calling a meeting in Adelaide to hear on this and other issues the shrewdest mind in cricket?

'W.G.'

Enough said! This is a shortened version of my Daily Telegraph *anniversary article in May 1995.*

He was accounted the best-known man in Victorian England, with the possible exception of the Prince of Wales. Arguably, more column inches have been written about him than any sportsman in history. Who else is recognised by his initials alone after more than a century?

As time passed the most luxuriant of black beards, which had ornamented his features from early manhood, added a patriarchal touch to the legendary figure of Dr. William Gilbert Grace.

There were many milestones in the phenomenal career of W.G. – naturally so, since the game as we know it evolved around him in a span of unparalleled length between his boyhood emergence, aged 16, in 1865 and his 58th birthday on July 18, 1906. This latter event he celebrated by playing a final innings of 74 in the last of his 85 encounters for the Gentlemen against the Players.

Yet of all his achievements, none made such an impact on sporting England as that which began a century ago tomorrow. 'A colossal personage' bestriding the world of cricket, as Bernard Darwin pictured him in his classic biography, W.G. in May 1895 was seemingly long past the zenith of his powers.

The Champion was said (retrospectively, maybe) to have struck a wonderful vein of form; but he carried a lot of weight, and he was nearly 47.

In his first first-class match of 1895, for MCC against Sussex at Lord's, starting on the ninth of the month, he made 13 and 103, the latter being his 99th first-class hundred. Against Yorkshire at Lord's he had to make do with 18 and 25.

And then to Bristol in the Whitsuntide match against Somerset, the old enemy: for the only recorded time, as he neared three figures W.G. was palpably nervous. So was his old Somerset adversary and friend, Sammy Woods, who at last relieved the tension with a leg-side full pitch which was duly despatched for the 100th hundred. At this point the next in line, Arthur Shrewsbury, had made 40 hundreds. That goal achieved, on a day so bitter that the snow settled on his beard, the Old Man plundered on to 288. The runs were made in 5½ hours, during which, the Somerset wicketkeeper said, he had allowed only four balls to pass the bat.

With two matches remaining, the hitherto unthinkable goal of a thousand runs in May was now within his sights. At the Oval, playing for England against Surrey in Walter Read's Benefit Match, Tom Richardson bowled him for 18. On the 30th Gloucestershire came to Lord's to play Middlesex, W.G. needing 153. He won the toss, began slowly, bothered by a slow bowler he couldn't quite 'get at', but surely the runs came and amid a tumult of cheering the target was reached.

His 169 gave him 1,019 runs in 22 days. It had been a sunny May of good pitches (they were good by then) but think of the journeys, by train and horse-drawn cab: from Bristol to Lord's, back to Bristol, to Cambridge, to Gravesend, to London for the Oval and Lord's. He also bowled 45 overs (five balls) in one innings, 42 in another.

It was to be more than 30 years before Walter Hammond reached 1,000 in May, 1927, as Charlie Hallows of Lancashire also did, in 1928. It has never happened since, though several (including Don

Bradman twice) have reached the goal having started in April.

Now came the avalanche. MCC and Gloucestershire started testimonial funds, as did *The Sportsman*. Even more significantly, the *Daily Telegraph* launched a shilling fund which raised 100,000 shillings, £5,000. The sum total was, according to Darwin, 'an honest pot of money £9,073 8s 3d' – equivalent to more than £500,000 today.

So, was W.G. an amateur? Strictly, of course, the answer is 'no'. When he took Lord Sheffield's team to Australia in 1891–2 he was paid £3,000. A unique crowd-puller from youth up, he always made himself available for the professionals' benefit matches, receiving liberal expenses for so doing. Such matters were elastic in Victorian days. Everyone knew that W.G. was not a man of property, as were most amateurs then. He was a country doctor, who employed not one but two locums to take care of his practice when he was playing cricket. He was 30 when, in 1879, he won his diploma and became the parish doctor in a poorish quarter of Bristol called Stapleton Road. He answered his patients' needs for 20 years until, at the turn of the century, he moved to Crystal Palace to found the London Counties Cricket Club.

W.G.'s career divides into two parts, punctuated by the threat to English supremacy which came with the arrival of the first Australians in 1878. By then his all-round skills and personality had completely overturned the age-old supremacy of the professionals.

His rise to maturity was such that he was first chosen for the match of the season, between Gentlemen and Players at Lord's, at the age of 17. When, three years later, he made the first of his 15 hundreds against the Players – 134 not out (out of a total of 201) – he also took 10 wickets for 81 in the match. In his physical prime, already bearded but still slim, he regularly took a hundred wickets with his steady medium pace.

On the rough pitches of 1871 he scored 2,390 runs with an average of 78, more than double that of the next man. In a hot week of August 1876 he made more runs in seven days than any man before or since: 344 v Kent at Canterbury, 177 v Notts at Clifton, 318 not out v Yorkshire at Cheltenham, 839 in three innings, once not out.

Yet without fresh fields to conquer, matrimony and medicine might well have won the day but for the Australian challenge. When he took his first side on a largely missionary visit to Australia in 1873 he encountered in his colonial cousins a competitive outlook akin to his own.

In the first of all Tests in England, at the Oval in 1880, W.G., inevitably, contributed 152 to a hard-won victory. Thereafter, he was a talisman in the recurring battles until at Trent Bridge in 1899, now coming up to 51, he duly and sadly made his exit.

What manner of man was W.G.? Well, on the basic elements of his character there was complete unanimity: he was modest and utterly natural, and he had a wonderful kindliness. These qualities did not however inhibit his loquacity on the field. 'He always wanted his pound of flesh', wrote Darwin, but 'he bore no malice, when he did not get it. . . . He had not the particular kind of sensitiveness that shrinks from an argument.'

Darwin, who knew him well on the golf course in later life, describes him as a spontaneous, unaffected countryman with an invariable kindness, 'except', as one of his most devoted friends has observed, 'that he tried to chisel them out lbw.'

There was a family legend that in my pram I saw W.G. The fact is that in the summer of 1907, when I was a few months old, he made 140 against Forest Hill, the club of which my father was treasurer. He was there and my mother would have been helping with the teas.

What I very distinctly recall is playing in my young days with quite a few men who had played with 'the Old Man': substantial fellows with red and yellow MCC sashes holding up their trousers. They all talked of him with affection.

IZ LEAD THE FIELD

Amid the stresses of the 1990s the 150th anniversary of the founding of I Zingari seemed an appropriate occasion to salute the whole wide spectrum of wandering club cricket and its quiet upholding of sporting standards. This Daily Telegraph *article [24 October 1995] originally contained also the name of the Yorkshire Gentlemen, whose President gently reminded me that they have a full fixture card of home matches at Escrick Park where I have myself played. Mea culpa!*

Early in Queen Victoria's reign after a scratch team raised by one William Bolland had played a match at Harrow School, he and three others drove back to London and took supper together.

By the end of a convivial evening they had decided to start a wandering cricket club. What should they call themselves? At this, R. P. Long, made slumbrous by claret and port, exclaimed 'the zingari, of course', and promptly dozed off again. *I zingari* in Italian simply means the gypsies. Next day the founders informed 21 of their friends that they were members. Shortly afterwards they were portrayed bedecked in the distinctive colours of black, red and gold.

The year was 1845 and so it is that tonight at the Savoy Hotel more than 300 Zingaros of widely assorted generations will celebrate the club's 150th anniversary. The governor of IZ, the old captain of Middlesex and England, F. G. Mann, takes the chair, and speeches will come from Field Marshal Lord Bramall, a wartime captain of Eton, and Vice-Admiral M.P. Gretton, now representing NATO navies in Brussels. Both were cricketers of quality within the restrictions of their distinguished Service careers.

There are resident clubs, notably in the towns and villages of the Weald, whose foundations pre-date I Zingari. I recall playing in the bicentenary week of Sevenoaks Vine back in 1934. Clifton CC in the West Country claim their birth in 1752. Looking north, the game had early roots in Nottingham and Sheffield.

IZ, however, are the first of the purely wandering clubs, the forerunners of countless more, whose foundation in the last half of the 19th century went hand in hand with a general explosion of cricket activity: towns and village clubs sprang yearly into being, university, college, hospital, business house clubs, now in the wake of the emerging county clubs both first-class and minor.

I Zingari were unique from the start in that, unlike all others at that time, they encouraged amateur bowling, employing no professionals.

Yet, before the County Championship grew in size, their strongest side, fortified by such early Test heroes as A. G. Steel, Alfred Lyttelton and F. S. Jackson, could hold their own in the first-class arena at Lord's, Canterbury, Scarborough and even in India.

The Free Foresters, who originated in the Forest of Arden, 11 years junior to IZ, kept the flag of amateur cricket flying high as a first-class side against Oxford and Cambridge until fairly recently. The Foresters are credited, incidentally, as the initiators in 1861 of white coats for umpires. One of their batsmen complained he could not see the ball against the dark suit of the umpire, who was promptly provided with a nightgown.

Of the many other peripatetic clubs who closely followed the lead of IZ and are still active were the Harlequins and Quidnuncs, composed of Blues and near-Blues of Oxford and Cambridge; also Incogniti, who have traditionally had a strong Service flavour. No special associations attach, as their names imply, to the Nondescripts, Stoics, Frogs and Cryptics, all of whom were in the field before the First World War.

So were the clubs who wandered through specific named counties and received visitors therein on private grounds. First came Band of Brothers of Kent. Towards the West they went for alliteration in their choice of title: hence the Hampshire Hogs, Somerset Stragglers, Gloucester Gypsies, and Devon Dumplings, North of the Trent are the Derbyshire Friars, the Gentlemen of Cheshire and Northern Nomads. Countrywide are more such. As to school old boy clubs, Eton Ramblers, founded in 1862, led the way, since when there is scarcely an independent school which has not sprouted an old boy club.

What the prosperity of every sort of club depends on is, of course, the devotion of a few officers to do the necessary work behind the scenes. In this no club can have been luckier than I Zingari in their secretary for 40 years, Sir William Becher, to whom a presentation will be made tonight. Despite progressive deafness from a war wound, he has been the life and soul of the club over this long span. Not least he has spotted and encouraged the young, so that it is far from true today, as once perhaps it tended to be, that there is a safe single to an IZ cap.

The important point about these wandering clubs was – and still is in the 1990s – the standard of sportsmanship in playing the game and socially afterwards, members being elected after a probationary period.

There will be those who scoff at elitism of this sort. I would maintain, however, that such clubs generally broaden and enrich the club scene and are popular opponents. Moreover, there is evidence that some players tire of league cricket when it becomes too dour and cut-throat, preferring the ethos of the wanderers, to whom the winning means a great deal while the game is being played – and afterwards nothing at all.

MUSIC AT LORD'S

In the perfect setting of the Long Room Julian Bream provided an enchanting evening. He entered to much laughter accoutred with pads, bat and gloves and wearing a Free Forester cap. Daily Telegraph, 3 October 1995.

On Thursday Julian Bream takes his guitar to Lord's cricket ground for what is properly billed as a unique evening. The Long Room, through which every character of renown has passed for a century and more, has seen dinners, a ball, an auction and, when the adjacent synagogue was bombed in the war, Sabbath services, but there has never been a classical concert. Bream is an especially appropriate performer in that he is one of a distinguished company of artists whose cricketing appearances in the Lord's Taverners XI – in his case playing in white gloves to protect his hands – have brought in large sums for the charities which the Taverners exists to support.

The affinity between cricket and the arts, and notably music, goes back to the game's beginnings. John Nyren, historian of the Hambledon Club, which was the 18th-century cradle of cricket, tells how the great cricketer John Small, on his way to a concert with his double-bass, 'like a modern Orpheus beguiled a wild bull of its fury in the middle of a paddock'.

Cricket-lovers have always taken for granted that their sport is likewise an art and as such attracts artistic people. The link seems natural to them. Neville Cardus, who doubled as music critic and cricket correspondent of the *Manchester Guardian*, of course personified the connection, forever using musical analogies in his romantic presentation of the game and the players. Enthused by style and personality rather than technique, he had nevertheless served during the First World War as assistant cricket professional at Shrewsbury School. His friends, the great conductors Sir Thomas Beecham and Sir John Barbirolli, patronised Old Trafford.

There have been Test cricketers with musical pedigrees, starting perhaps with a First World War casualty, Colin Blythe of Kent and England, an artist to his fingertips whether with ball or violin. Maurice Allom, who took four Test wickets in five balls, had played the tenor saxophone as a Cambridge undergraduate in one of the early jazz bands, led by Fred Elizalde.

The greatest batsman of the modern game, Sir Donald Bradman, once made a piano recording of a piece called *Bungalow of Dreams*.

In the August after leaving school, Tony Lewis, later to be captain of Cambridge, Glamorgan and England, received simultaneous invitations to join the Welsh Youth Orchestra as a violinist and to play in the last two county matches of the season. He opted for the latter, confined himself to university orchestras and for many years presented classical music programmes on HTV.

Several present-day musical celebrities take the field in the Taverner cause with unstinted zeal if varied degrees of skill. The versatile Richard Stilgoe, composer, among other things, of a popular musical for children is said to purvey telling lobs. Eric Clapton, Nigel Kennedy, pianist Howard Shelley, conductor Nicholas Cleobury and ex-Rolling Stone Bill Wyman are others who don flannels in the summer. It was Mick Jagger who introduced J. Paul Getty to the game.

The master of ceremonies at the Lord's concert epitomises supremely the connection between cricket and music: Sir Timothy Rice, lyricist, chairman of the Foundation for Sport and the Arts and withal a member of the MCC committee.

MISS MOLLY HIDE

In its early days the figure-head of women's cricket.
The Cricketer, *November 1995.*

When the Women's Cricket Association, founded at Colwall in 1926, began to spread its wings in the 1930s it was clearly in need of a figure who would be respected in the public mind as, one might say, the acceptable face of Women's Cricket. Molly Hide, handsome, dignified and an outstanding player filled the picture to perfection.

One day on the Saffrons ground at Eastbourne she mentioned sadly to me how difficult it was for the press to take women's cricket seriously. Knowing how susceptible was Plum Warner, founder and editor of *The Cricketer*, to feminine charms I invited her to meet him at Lord's over lunch (2/6 a head in the MCC dining room for him and me, 3/6 for her!). By the end of it the ladies had a regular foothold in this magazine.

At the Oval in 1937 I saw Miss Hide lead her braves on to the field against Australia, agonized as poor Betty Snowball was run out for 99, and admired the cricket played by the talented and stylish triumvirate of Myrtle Maclagan, Snowball and Hide. Thereafter I could but follow and admire from afar, largely through the writings of her contemporary and close friend Netta Rheinberg.

As with Michael Atherton, captaincy improved her play. In the Antipodes in 1948/9 she made five hundreds and topped both batting and bowling averages. On her retirement after 17 years as England captain, like a good trooper she worked to put back into the game something of the pleasure she had had from it.

KENT'S 'HOPPER'

Just two items from the 'Hopper' Levett saga.
Daily Telegraph, *7 December 1995.*

W H V Levett, who has died aged 87, was in the tradition of outstanding Kent wicket-keepers, six of whom have played for England.

'Hopper' Levett made his mark in the 1930s, as understudy to Leslie Ames, the Kent and England wicketkeeper. Levett stepped in when Ames was away or when back trouble allowed him only to bat. He appeared four times at Lord's for Gentlemen against Players and was chosen in 1933 for D. R. Jardine's MCC tour of India, where he played in one of the Tests. Loquacious, cheerful and good-natured, Hopper Levett added to the pleasures of the day wherever he went; and for Hopper the game continued in the bar after stumps were drawn.

A story is told of his taking the field one morning after a particularly sociable evening. The first ball flew past his motionless form for four byes. He dived full length to make an aerobatic catch off the next, remarking as he regained his feet, 'Not bad for the first ball of the day.'

He was the focal point at Lord's in a scene of great hilarity when Jim Smith, a renowned hitter, smote the ball completely vertical, to a stratospheric height. Shouting 'Mine!', Hopper focused underneath, at first rotating slowly and then with increasing speed until he lost balance and landed, his legs in the air, just as the ball fell yards away. It was some time before order was restored.

RETURN TO SOUTH AFRICA

Prospect articles often make sad reading after the event: this is
a melancholy example thereof.
Daily Telegraph, *October 1995.*

A little over four years ago, in Johannesburg, I had the pleasure of being present at the dissolution of the old racial cricket authorities and the inaugural meeting of the United Cricket Board of South Africa. That same evening mine was the privilege of speaking words of welcome at a great dinner of celebration attended by 700 cricketers of every age and colour, including famous names from every Test-playing country. Major change was in the wind, though the miracle of Nelson Mandela's bloodless election victory had yet to happen.

Dr Ali Bacher and his colleagues had worked fast, and they continued to do so. Helped by the determined diplomacy of Sir Colin Cowdrey, chairman of the 1991 International Cricket Council, they achieved an immediate return to the body which their predecessors had formed, in company with England and Australia 80-odd years before, and from which they had been excluded on the departure of South Africa from the Commonwealth in 1961.

Every overseas tour of an England Test team has an impact for better or for worse on hosts and visitors alike; but a special significance surely attached to the one that is about to begin, the first by an official team from this country since M. J. K. Smith's MCC side of 1964–65.

In those days, as from its beginnings, cricket was the game of the English-speaking South Africans, rugby football that of the Afrikaners. There were periods when, despite having to draw from such a restricted field, South Africa were a match for England and Australia – and in the middle and late 1960s, immediately before the general antipathy to apartheid brought down the curtain on international sport against South Africa, more than a match.

Over the span of history, however, South Africa inevitably had the worst of it: England had won 46 Tests to their 18, Australia's margin was 29 to 11, seven of those 11 gained in the Republic in successive series between 1966 and 1970.

Today, the overall picture is much more favourable to South Africa in that many more Afrikaners now bring their aggressive philosophy to the game while the generation of black and coloured boys, introduced to cricket since apartheid ended, will surely soon be competing for places in the national team.

For these youthful cricketers the England tour, covering 14 different grounds from Johannesburg to Cape Town, will be the game's shop window these next three months: that for Michael Atherton and his team is their challenge and their opportunity. an extent which at moments may test their self-discipline, they will be on parade both on the field and off.

A COURSE FOR HEROES

This is a shortened version of my Introduction to the History of Royal St George's Golf Club, published during the summer of 1996. The title is a quotation from the sporting writer Peter Lawless, a war correspondent killed in 1945 at the crossing of Nijmegen Bridge.

The history of our Course and Club strikes an opening note of adventure rewarded. The tale is a romantic one from the moment of our Founder's mounting of the Norman Tower of St Clement's Church and his discovery of nature's golden gift before his eyes.

There, stretching out to the sea, was the promised land, a vista of rolling dunes that Providence can only have intended for a golf links. The quest of Dr. Laidlaw Purves was over, and one can surely see the satisfaction of a mission accomplished as he looks down on us from John Collier's superb portrait on the wall of the St George's dining room. He had sought a links course in southern England after the Scottish model, and he had found it.

The Doctor came, he saw and he conquered, designing among the sandy, wind-swept humps and hollows the course whose general shape and character in 1996 are remarkably akin to his original design upwards of a century ago. Dr. Laidlaw Purves was a pioneer in the heyday of Empire, with the zest and sublime self-assurance of the Victorian age. Intolerant perhaps of interference, a 'difficult' colleague maybe, he nevertheless emerges a striking figure who built what was swiftly hailed, as it surely stands in its modern form today, the sternest of tests, indeed a Course for Heroes.

Five years from its foundation St. George's was staging the Amateur Championship, and in 1894, after seven years, the first Open Championship ever played in England. Another two years and Bernard Darwin, many decades later to become our President, was disporting himself round Sandwich in the University Match, resplendent in red coat and light blue collar with the arms of the University in gold and ermine on the pocket. Arthur Balfour, soon to become Prime Minister, was a member: his enthusiasm for golf gave added distinction to the growing game and to the Club. Membership by the mid-'90s had risen to 600. A prestigious future was fully assured.

It has been a rare pleasure for me to exchange, so to speak, the wicket for the tee and to have had some subsidiary part in the making of this book. As a member of tolerable seniority, I would say in conclusion that in all the most important respects the Club and the course, thanks to recent Captains and Committees, seem to be in admirable shape. The 1993 Open, with its brilliant play on the part of the world's best, testified to the enduring quality of the links which remain a magnet for all sorts and conditions of golfers both from home and overseas. The clubhouse is unpretentiously comfortable, and from steward to caddiemaster members and guests are admirably served by the staff. Above all, there is surely a general amiability about Royal St. George's which makes for affection as well as pride in what the Club is and what it stands for. Why then should we not look forward in confidence to the millennium and beyond?

EARLY MENTORS

I wrote for the seventy-fifth Anniversary number of The Cricketer *[May 1996] an article on cricket-writers of my time. For this last selection of my work it is surely fitting to salute those elders of the craft who laid down sound foundations in the years between the wars and whose friendliness to this young scribbler will be an abiding memory. These are the opening paragraphs.*

In the summer of 1925, the first of my tyro years as a sporting journalist, I was introduced by my father to an elderly figure who, hearing of my ambition, wished me well. We were outside the entrance to the press box at The Oval, and he was Sydney Pardon, no less, editor for some 34 years of *Wisden Cricketers' Almanack*. I had had the luck to shake hands – as it turned out, shortly before his death –

with the father of modern cricket writing, the man whose word had been followed and respected in the daily press and in the annual Almanack associated with him since the prime of W.G., the early Test matches and the growth of the County Championship in the 1880s: I write 'modern' out of respect for and in relation to those whose heroic prose immortalised the Hambledon story, Nyren, Mitford and Pycroft along with the later researchers, Haygarth and Waghorn.

The influence of Pardon in our craft of cricket writing can scarcely be exaggerated since he founded the Cricket Reporting Agency which, under the broad umbrella of Reuters and the Press Association, covered the daily and evening press from the days before there were signed reports and men invested with the dignity of 'Our Cricket Correspondent'.

By the middle and late 1920s Colonel Philip Trevor, CBE (regularly so designated) was operating for the *Daily Telegraph*, Plum Warner, our *Cricketer* founder, and R. C. Robertson-Glasgow for *The Morning Post*, Neville Cardus in *The Manchester Guardian* and at first (anonymously) A. C. M. Croome for *The Times*. Just as importantly, the *Wisden* editorship remained, as indeed it did until 1981, in the responsible hands of successive partners of the CRA (familiarly known as Pardon's); first it was Charles Stewart Caine, then Sydney Southerton, briefly W. H. Brookes, and finally Hubert Preston and his son, Norman.

Pardon's descendants came not from the famous schools nor were they players of repute, though Southerton was son of James who played in the first of all Tests, in Australia in 1876/77. There were, however, no more rigid upholders of the game's traditions, and the degree to which they were trusted can be gauged from *Wisden's* obituary comments at their decease from such MCC figures as Lord Hawke, Warner, 'Shrimp' Leveson Gower and Billy Findlay.

The quality and discernment of these agency writers was epitomised by Southerton's masterly appraisal in the 1934 *Wisden* of the Bodyline affair. It should be required reading today for any serious historian. Halcyon times, we may think, with the politics, such as they were, in safe hands and the play day by day intelligently reported.

From Crusoe's pen came rippling humour and from Cardus the high-flown imagery, rich in musical allusion, which recruited a new public to the game. A lighter touch came from William Pollock in the *Daily Express* and H. J. Henley in the *Daily Mail*, the latter a large and cheerful fellow who assuaged the discomfort of a war-wounded leg with a free intake of beer.

SURRENDER TO THE LURE OF MONEY

S IR – As your rugby football correspondent for nearly 20 years after the war and *Evening Standard's* for a decade before it, I read of the state of affairs in which the Rugby Union has enmeshed itself with a mixture of incredulity and anger.

It is almost unbelievable that the committee of the English governing body, whose ancestors administered the game from its foundation in 1871 onwards for the benefit of its constituent clubs, should have surrendered so abjectly to the lure of money as to provoke the other three Home Unions to bar them from the International Championship.

The Rugby Union is to meet its counterparts of Scotland, Ireland and Wales at Cardiff tonight in a belated effort to avert the rupture of relationships and to save those annual matches which from the first have been the summit of ambition for the players and the spectacular high points for millions.

As things stand at present, top-class international opposition will apparently be confined to France and possibly one or more of the three major nations of the southern hemisphere whose seasons coincide with the English summer. England's programme would be dictated and watched only courtesy of Sky TV within Rupert Murdoch's worldwide sporting empire. Goodbye BBC.

I do not pretend any longer to close involvement in the game. I am however confident that the spirit of camaraderie, fostered by voluntary workers in their thousands which made it the tough yet uniquely sociable exercise it was, has not been wholly lost.

I have it on the highest authority that upwards of 90 per cent of the clubs in the membership would vote against any contract which threatened the Five Nations championship. Every past president of the Rugby Union opposes, if helplessly, the current arrangement.

Twickenham debenture-holders are equally unhappy. By their back-door deal those responsible have betrayed the trust of good men and true who ruled the game in which most of them had played. They tell me there are too many millionaires today on the Rugby Union committee. I don't remember any.

All popular games are at risk from hard-headed business interests which tend to override the instincts of the old players. A concluding irony: amateurism is a dirty word in the modern media.

We have, however, just seen the Open Championship, the highest expression of golfing skill, run to perfection by a purely amateur body, the Royal and Ancient Golf Club of St Andrews. A pity some of them could not be present to sort things out at Cardiff this evening.

E. W. SWANTON
Sandwich, Kent

Envoi

E. W. SWANTON

The publisher has airily suggested that the appropriate signing-off to this seven-part serial should be a prophetic look at the future of cricket up to and following the millennium, coupled with any contribution I foresee for myself. It is a pleasure to renew with Richard Cohen a happy association begun in the days before Collins was swallowed up by Mr Murdoch. I hope that I have, in reasonable degree, fallen in with this tall order; but as to my own involvement I cannot tempt Providence by saying I hope to do more than help to guide my own Arab club, and to enjoy the cricket and the company in the amiable environs of the Committee Rooms of Lord's and Canterbury.

*

The future of cricket! Those of my distant generation, and of others who played the game a while after we had retired from the field, cannot but be apprehensive of developments in the years ahead. The fear is not that cricket as a game of that name will decline in public interest and support. The many millions who were enthralled by the recent World Cup, and the many millions it generated in the currency of the nations involved, would seem to ensure that the instant limited-over edition is and will remain the popular recipe. And it is foolish to be snooty about it. One-day cricket calls for many of the basic skills, though some in much lesser degree than the authorised version. Close finishes are frequent and they can be almost unbearably exciting. It's good melodramatic theatre.

Its fundamental limitation, however, is that it denies one of the two essential objects of the game as they have been pursued for centuries, namely for the batting side to score runs and for the fielding side to take wickets. The arts and skills of the game have developed around this simple basic conflict.

No longer is this so. Under limited-over regulations the bowler who bowls his maximum ten overs for 20 runs without taking a wicket has probably served his side better than if he had had two or three for 45. The side which in its 50 overs scores 250 for few wickets or even none is defeated by opponents who pass them with nine wickets down. After the first few overs the rôle of the bowler is normally purely defensive, the fielding captain's tactics likewise. We may see thrilling fielding: speed and throwing are all. But the bowling virtues are diminished.

*

In my view the standard of bowling from top to bottom of the game in England is depressingly low, and I hold the proliferation of one-day cricket from the beginning of the 'seventies chiefly to blame. What has changed is the general psychology of the bowler. The old 'uns knew they had to bowl the enemy out before they could take their boots off.

Other factors have also affected the attitude of the first-class bowler. The covering of pitches, which started in 1981, deprived the game, according to the Editor of *Wisden* in that year, of 'a part of the very heritage of English cricket – a drying pitch and a sizzling sun'. That extreme apart, full covering, denying the turf the gifts of nature, has helped to make for a dull surface, lacking in life. Nor has the jump from three Championship days to four encouraged bowlers to attack. Unless they find a pitch to give real help they are inclined to plug away with little thought or experiment, waiting for the batsman to commit some indiscretion.

I believe that most of the retired county cricketers now in their sixties and beyond – especially perhaps those of Yorkshire and Lancashire whence I have always looked so much for cricket wisdom – would largely agree with this analysis.

As to the effects of so much one-day cricket on English batting technique – and remember that a county's chief batsmen play almost as many one-day as first-class innings – the style of play has led to lessening of respect for orthodox principles. Coaches must take considerable blame here, many of them far too keen on endless physical fitness routines at the expense of net practice. The best way of getting fit for cricket is to bat and bowl in the nets, and, of course, to catch and throw. Was it not Winston Churchill who, inspecting troops in the war and being told by an exercise-fanatic officer, 'Must get them fit, sir,' asked, 'Fit for what?' I think I still see sufficient Test and county cricket to judge that there is far too much hitting across the line of the ball rather than through it, and as for the sweep shot in its varieties, it is surely overdone.

To moderns inclined to think otherwise I would ask this: how do they account for the lack of great English batsmen and bowlers coming through since the plethora of one-day cricket, covered pitches and the four-day formula became the order of the day? If they are thinking of such names as Ian Botham and the three Gs – Gower, Gooch and Gatting – all were already spreading their wings before I retired as Cricket Correspondent in 1975.

*

If the real game is under threat from the one-day variety – and in some countries even Tests only draw moderate gates, state and provincial games much fewer – everything must be done to make it as attractive as possible. Again, I wish I could seem less of a Jeremiah, but much of Test cricket is anathema to me because of the intimidatory bowling in plain defiance of the law which the umpires, necessarily fortified nowadays by a referee, are there to administer. The game is being regularly brutalised by bowlers of sufficient pace to frighten batsmen right down the order, and the latter, protecting themselves to the hilt, seem increasingly resigned to it all. The over-rate struggles to reach fifteen an hour, and, with the bowler officially allowed two bouncers per over by the ICC, the spectator is paying more and more for less and less in the way of positive stroke-play. (England in calling for a maximum of one per over seems to be a lone voice.)

Spin and the more subtle arts of bowling in Tests and all first-class cricket are accordingly at a discount: England take eight bowlers to South Africa, six varying from fast to medium-fast, with one orthodox left-arm spinner and one who alternates between off-breaks and medium-pace.

The International Cricket Council cannot now be dismissed as the toothless body it once was. It has its own secretariat and, thanks largely to Sir Colin Cowdrey's initiative, it imposes a Code of Conduct on all its members: it just needs to impress itself more forcefully on to the world scene.

*

At the moment of writing the future structure of English cricket is a matter of conjecture. The Cricket Council, TCCB and NCA are over-due to be absorbed into a broader English Cricket Board which, work-ing through County Boards, will be responsible for the governance and administration of the whole game. It is to be a stream-lined, gradu-ated system representing all levels from school and village upwards. It should clearly be a move in the right direction, even though it is nothing for the average cricket lover, be he or she player or patron, to get excited about. Nor can we hope that England will necessarily in conse-quence ascend swiftly from their modest international position to the top of the tree. The only sure way to win a Test match is to take twenty wickets – of 720-odd played by England only one has been won following an opponent's declaration – and in the present state of English bowling that is likely to occur only if our attack happens upon distinctly helpful conditions.

I hope that the latest enquiry does not fall for any of the radical nostrums fashionable at the moment. English cricket is reckoned regularly to be at the cross-roads unless we happen to be holding the Ashes, and some very curious remedies have been thought up by past Inquiry Committees, tried and discarded. The most drastic 'reform' which has some serious and influential advocates is the proposal to divide the Championship into two divisions. One can see the objective of concentrating the quality and maybe improving the standard of a few sides, but it would be at the cost of diluting the interest, the member support and loyalty of nine counties. It is not as if there was anything like a natural dividing line. All the major counties contribute their own characteristics and flavour: why, over the last thirty years eleven of the seventeen (excluding Durham, only admitted in 1992) have won the Championship. Warwickshire are top dogs at the moment; three years ago they were sixteenth. In 1992 Worcestershire were seventeenth; the next year they were runners-up. A two-division Championship would give the richest counties – broadly speaking the ones with the privilege of staging Test matches – an undeserved advantage. It would inevitably lead towards a full-scale transfer market, with some clubs probably facing bankruptcy.

Two sensible moves to increase competitiveness are operating this year, the reward of three points for a drawn match and an increase in Championship prize money from five counties to nine. Motivation is a word nowadays much used. How determined is the average player to reach the top? Would a nationally-run Academy after the Australian model stimulate ambition as well as refine technique? I would hope the new authority will consider such a scheme. At the same time motivation to succeed must be a matter of degree, and it is a fact of life that the average young Englishman will not be inspired to the same pitch as a Brian Lara, youngest of eleven in a poor family subsisting in the citrus country behind Port-of-Spain. Readers may have gathered from these remarks that I would like to see the three one-day competitions reduced by one and, whatever happens, I hope the new Board will insist on white clothes, banishing coloured clothing. The TCCB have never had a popular mandate for 'pyjamas'. Polls undertaken have

indeed shown a large hostile majority to what was a marketing gimmick weakly let through by top executives themselves strongly averse
to it.

*

But enough – too much maybe – of cricket problems and politics. My
concluding note must be of deep thankfulness for my life in cricket,
for all that it has brought me in so many ways. Old men forget, Duff
Cooper thought, and of much this is mercifully true. But so deeply
happy are many cricket recollections that for me they remain wonderfully clear. The luckiest thing I ever did was to found the Arabs. We
celebrated our Diamond Jubilee, courtesy of Mr J. P. Getty, last summer on his lovely ground at Wormsley, and I am deeply grateful for
friendships in every generation. I can go back even before the first
Arabs of the 1930s to favourite cricketers of the 1920s whom I came
to admire not only on the field but subsequently off it: to paraphrase
Francis Thompson,

> As the run stealers flicker to and fro – to and fro
> Oh, my Hobbs and my Woolley long ago.

Fond memories too of so many grounds and places: Barbados and
Adelaide, the Oxford Parks, Fenner's at Cambridge, the Saffrons at
Eastbourne pre-war, Beckenham on either side of it, Trent Bridge,
much-lamented Bramall Lane and the Oval, each with an atmosphere
all its own; St Lawrence, Canterbury, most gracious and beautiful of
county grounds.

Lord's, however, is for me a place apart, a home from home, hal-
lowed as only the richest of histories can make it, both a symbol of
the past and, surely, a pledge for the future. I have known Lord's,
of course, from several aspects, first and always as a reporter, as a
probationer, as a member privileged to play there, as serving on Committees dating from the late 1960s to the present, and finally as a Life
Vice-President with the privileges that go with that great honour.

From such a fortunate perspective my opinion may be rated as of
limited worth. Nevertheless let me express the estimation that over the
sixty years of my membership MCC has never been in such good shape
as it is today. A collection of men of high ability and distinction – to
mention names would be invidious – have been in office in recent years
and, if annual general meetings, dinners and the mood at great matches
are true guides, their commitment is reflected in the membership generally. As to the ground itself, we may surely be thankful that the

rebuilding of so much of the accommodation has not changed its character. Lord's is still a cricket ground, not a stadium.

Since the devolution of authority in 1968 the relationship between Marylebone and the TCCB, of which it is a constituent member, has not until recently been as harmonious as it might, indeed should have been. Thankfully the difficult days are over and I hope and trust that the men who are shaping the future Board appreciate the experience and co-operation which the Club is able and anxious to provide. I rate as highly auspicious in this and all respects the key appointments recently made of Lord McLaurin as Chairman and Tim Lamb as Chief Executive.

*

It is the truest of axioms about cricket that the game is as good as those who play it, to which should be added surely those who guide and administer it. Those who play it respond to positive leadership: the captain must be the clear boss, responsible for the spirit and attitude of his team, from the England eleven downwards. Behind the scenes I would suggest the time is ripe for some fresh blood: such names as Acfield, Barclay, Lloyd, Graveney, Nicholas occur to me as being men of sound instinct and ideas. If the traditional game is to be preserved and to flourish it is the forties generation who must see to it. Good luck to them!

E.W.S.

PART EIGHT

1996–2000

The End of the Innings

This is where *Last Over* finished. Jim let it be known (without, it must be said, being overly dogmatic) that it was his last book. He, however, was not one to disappoint those (myself among them) who confidently predicted that *Last Over* was only a rehearsal for such an event. Sure enough, in 1999 he needed little persuasion to make a further offering between hard covers with *Cricketers of My Time*. The collection of obituaries he had written over the years included some of the greatest exponents and advocates of cricket throughout the 20th century – as evidenced in the title, *his* time. All but one of the roll-call – George Hirst – he knew personally, either through acquaintance or friendship.

In this final phase of his life, Jim was as industrious as ever, continuing to write regularly for the *Daily Telegraph* and occasionally for *The Cricketer* magazine. The issues of the day which exercised both his mind and his pen were addressed with his usual acuity and, for the reader, with the same sense of overview. His ability to encapsulate – not a word he would have used – conflicting arguments and then, within a few paragraphs, to give reassured judgement, was that of a revered member of the High Court. Whether his concerns were mismanagement of the England side; the evils of sledging; the new framework of first-class cricket; or the loss of amateurism in 'rugger', Jim opined. His views were those of the old-fashioned purist, but he readily acknowledged new fashion and sought to find an acceptable way to marry the two. In his 'Personally Speaking' column, he doffed his cap to the household names of long ago, the recent past and the heroes of today. He relished the genius of Lara and Tendulkar, admired the adventure of the Sri Lankans and had confidence in the state of 'varsity' cricket. He also frequently bemoaned excessive short-pitched fast bowling and general unsporting behaviour. He recalled the past with affection and looked to the future without pessimism. He even explored an act of forgiveness of Japanese brutality during the Second World War. From *The Cricketer* are memories of tail-enders who signally failed to inconvenience the scorers and on the domestic front are reflections for the *Sandwich Society Newsletter*. With the arrival of the new Millennium, he signed off publicly and most appropriately by fronting a series of articles in the *Daily Telegraph* on 'My Sporting Century'. Inevitably, with a knock as long as his – over seventy years writing mostly about cricket – there are a few strokes which cover the same ground, but any repetition does not pall. There is, instead, a sense of disbelief that he did not make his own hundred, and a far greater sense of loss that he is no longer around to tell us what to think.

D.R.A.

CLASSIC CASE OF MISMANAGEMENT
19 January 1996

'It is absolutely wrong for managers to criticise players in public.' This was the reaction of Peter Edwards, the secretary of Essex when, a few days before Devon Malcolm burst into print, I talked to him about Ray Illingworth's derogatory remarks concerning another England cricketer, Peter Such.

There can surely not be any sort of sportsman concerned in a team game who would not agree with Essex's experienced and much respected secretary. The operative phrase, of course, is 'in public'. What is said in the privacy of the dressing room is a different matter altogether.

It is a great pity, even if it is understandable, that Malcolm has voiced his grievance against the England manager in violation of his Test and County Cricket Board contract, so exposing himself to disciplinary action. It is the sort of publicity the game can do without.

The one mitigating aspect of the affair is that it must bring to a head the propriety of the comments on players in his charge which Illingworth has been making ever since, directly after his appointment as chairman of selectors two years ago, he started firing unwelcome comment across the Atlantic at the England team in the West Indies.

As soon as England got down to practice in South Africa last November Illingworth and his bowling coach, Peter Lever, began belittling Malcolm, the hero of the victory over South Africa at the Oval and the one bowler whom the South Africans feared, alleging he did not co-operate in their desire to change his action. Lever talked of him as a cricket 'nonentity' and the manager reportedly told the press. 'He wouldn't frighten you, let alone the South Africans.'

It is not for a critic far away to suggest they were necessarily wrong to try to bring Malcolm's delivery more square-on, dangerous though it is to tinker with the mechanism of a mature fast bowler, not necessarily ill-advised provided it could be done quietly and with the bowler's co-operation. In the event the exercise became a classic case of man-mismanagement as to which, in the angry words of Kim Barnett, Malcolm's Derbyshire captain, 'the South Africans must be laughing their socks off'.

Illingworth's demeaning remarks about Such were contained in a long interview published in the *Daily Mail* on Christmas Eve. He was reported to have said in answer to a question why he was not chosen for South Africa. 'He is a very soft person. He is frightened to death when he bats against quick bowling.'

What does that sort of talk do for the morale of a keen cricketer? Mr Edwards, not unnaturally incensed, incidentally gives contrary evidence. He says that three summers ago at Chelmsford, Such and John Childs put on a rapid 79 for the last wicket against the speed of Malcolm Marshall, of Hampshire, in the match that settled the County Championship for Essex.

In the same interview the manager was asked whether he saw in advance of the Test the notorious Edgbaston pitch. No, he had asked Fred Titmus to look in, but 'Fred is not one to make positive statements. He waffles.' So much for the views of his fellow selector.

Illingworth may well say he is misquoted, and on occasion I'm sure he is. The general impression of outspoken criticism in print of all and sundry is, however, beyond argument. If anyone is going to be charged with bringing the game into disrepute, where might it not end?

England's tour of South Africa was an ill-starred affair in two respects for which no blame attached to the England players or management on the spot. First was the unprecedented rainfall which ruined the first Test and restricted practice: second was the inadequacy of the early opposition provided. All of this militated against a party of sixteen getting acclimatised and into form.

The umpiring, judging from afar by Sky TV, was variable. 'Does it not often seem to visiting sides that the umpiring goes against them?' I once asked Don Bradman. 'No,' he said. 'not often, *always*.'

That said, mitigating factors must give way first to congratulations to South Africa – a sentiment in these one-eyed days little expressed. Their ground fielding and catching touched tremendous heights, their bowling (apart from emphatic reservations as regards 'intimidation') was altogether stronger and the batting adequate enough to cope with an attack which lacked persistent control and, in the two Tests when Illingworth was absent, essential variety. Cork, until he became over-tired in the one-day extravaganza, was the only exception.

At each critical point, except when the England captain was playing his long heroic rearguard at Johannesburg, it was South Africa whose spirit seemed the stronger.

The sorry fact is that only three of the England side have emerged with reputations enhanced: Jack Russell, Dominic Cork and, of course, Michael Atherton. In parenthesis it was sad that circumstances denied John Crawley, England's youngest player, the chance of advancing his claim as a regular Test batsman.

Most of the South Africans contributed valuably, and they have priceless finds in their two youngest, Shaun, the copper-nobbed son of Peter Pollock, and the charismatic coloured 18-year-old wrist-spinner with the unbelievable action, Paul Adams.

The most distasteful thing about the tour to me was the complete ignoring by umpires and almost completely by the critics of the Intimidation Law 42. Christopher Martin-Jenkins, who tells me that none of the umpires involved in the series gave even a first warning to any bowler, described how at Cape Town 'Donald then completed the demolition . . . peppering Peter Martin with four short balls in five. The fifth was fended off with a glove from in front of his face.' Caught short leg.

At Port Elizabeth in the previous Test it was also Martin to whom Donald went round the wicket, bowling two balls fast and short and a third which was prevented by the helmet visor from striking him in the face. A fast bowler only goes round the wicket, at any rate to a tailender, to hit him or induce a catch from a stroke in self-defence; in short, to frighten him.

Yet what was Geoffrey Boycott saying on Sky TV? A brilliant piece of bowling, we were told, Donald's best over. On another occasion, Boycott said how much he would have liked to test himself against South Africa's pace. If he had done so, I dare say his point of view might have been different. He batted bravely enough against the West Indian fast bowlers when he returned from self-imposed exile, but one cannot forget that while continuing to captain Yorkshire he opted out of Test cricket from 1974 to 1977. England had to tackle two series against Lillee and Thomson and one against Holding, Roberts and Co without their best batsman. It took him a while to get to the sticking point.

'None of us likes it, but some of us show it more than t'others,' said another great batsman, Maurice Leyland, in days when the short fast ball was usually just a variant. What sickens me is that umpires, critics and the players themselves are accepting the alien philosophy that 'anything goes'.

Of Atherton himself, a stoic in this respect, Richard Hutton wrote in *The Cricketer* that his great saving innings was played 'in the face of some ferocious bowling which stretched to the full his technical efficiency as well as frequently threatening life and limb'.

Thus the once beautiful game is being brutalised. I have run out of space, but there are remedies and I trust the International Cricket Council will address the matter again at their summer meeting. Meanwhile, thank heaven the Indians will be with us, displaying the various arts of the game as they habitually do.

JAYASURIYA LEAVES INDELIBLE MARK ON WINTER OF CONTENT
1 May 1996

How better to begin another summer's periodic scribbling than to salute the popular newcomer to the game's elite? For most of us surely the victory of Sri Lanka over Australia in the final redeemed the World Cup, though England's sorry eclipse may have prejudiced our judgement.

Mark Nicholas and Peter Roebuck in the 75th anniversary edition of *The Cricketer* saw plenty of merit in the cricket generally while deploring the administration.

What was so refreshing about the Sri Lankans was their unsophisticated approach and likewise a batting technique based on first principles which was in evidence right down the order.

On current form not even Brian Lara is more entrancing to watch than Aravinda de Silva. One-day records are here today and gone tomorrow, but Sanath Jayasuriya's fastest-ever 50 against England in 30 balls must secure a place in *Wisden*. (In all his 14 fours and three sixes and eight oddments added up to 82 in 44 balls: unforgettable stuff.)

Under Arjuna Ranatunga they kept their cool admirably. What a moment for him and for the man managing quietly behind the scenes, Duleep Mendis. It was Mendis who captained Sri Lanka to a moral victory on their first Test appearance at Lord's in 1984.

Sri Lanka have been invited here for only two late August Tests since then, a ration which the TCCB have justified, not with complete conviction, on financial grounds. It must be said, however, that they have given monetary help to visits home and away both by 'A' and under-19 teams.

What now, one asks? The answer is that before the World Cup they were invited here, number of Tests unspecified, in 1998 when South Africa are due and also in 2002. They will in addition be over, of course, to defend the World Cup in 1999.

Touching again on *The Cricketer*'s anniversary, and as its president declaring an interest, I congratulate the editor, Richard Hutton, on achieving a nice balance between reflections on the past, coverage of the topical and distinguished views on the future.

Deeming it not improper after thirty-three years to publish his father's personal papers, the editor has moreover brought off two distinct scoops.

There are four letters from Sir Pelham Warner, in 1953 in his 80th year, concerning the make-up of the MCC team to West Indies for which father Len had already been appointed captain; and there are long extracts including frank reports on all his players and critical comment on the political scene in the islands and the attitude of the West Indian cricket authorities towards their visitors.

Those familiar with my tour book, *West Indian Adventure*, will know that the picture of events therein and the conclusions therefrom differ considerably in some respects from Sir Leonard's. I have, however, always stressed that MCC made what was always going to be a difficult assignment much more so by denying him not only the manager he had asked for, S. G. Griffith, but any full-time alternative. To have appointed C. H. Palmer player-manager, subordinate on the field and technically the No. 1 off it, made for a situation unfair to both parties.

As it happened I was well abreast of the situation, having been asked by the MCC treasurer, H. S. Altham, on my way to a Roses' Match at Sheffield to ascertain who the captain would like as his manager. 'I'd like the Colonel,' he said, much to my pleasure for I thought him the ideal choice. Recently appointed an assistant-secretary of MCC, the club decided he could not be spared.

It makes a nice change to be able to quote Ray Illingworth with warm approbation. In the aforesaid issue of *The Cricketer* he says: 'I doubt if we will go back to three-day championship games, though I still think that length of match on uncovered pitches is the right thing. People learn a better technique than on the more stereotyped pitches today.'

Verb. Sap. But with the future pattern of county cricket controversial to say the least perhaps retired cricketers, nearly all of whom would rejoice to see the old order restored, need not completely despair.

The new England set-up with a 'supremo' replaced by a coach is surely a move or two in the right direction. If anyone can help Michael Atherton and his teams to show evident enjoyment in their cricket and as coach imbue not only technical help as required but a leaven of humour it is David Lloyd.

David Graveney, I would say, has both the experience and temperament to make a good selector and though it might not have been an ideal arrangement for him to have combined the posts of secretary of the Cricketers' Association with chairman of selectors for a summer he would no doubt have coped satisfactorily with any conflict of interest.

With authority and the media in all its diversity overlapping nowadays in various directions men not infrequently must have to think hard as to where duty lies. No doubt the Cricketers' Association president Jack Bannister will have done so when by barring Graveney, their secretary, from accepting the chairmanship of the selection committee the way was cleared for its continuation by Ray Illingworth with whom Bannister was collaborating in his biography.

There are any number of precedents for a current player to serve as a selector, as Graham Gooch has been chosen to do: Brian Sellers, Norman Yardley, Wilfred Wooller, Doug Insole and A. C. Smith to name a few. There have even been at least three selectors persuaded by their colleagues to play again for England – and, incidentally, with notable success in each case: Freddie Brown, Cyril Washbrook, and the immortal Wilfred Rhodes.

The work of selection involves hours and days of quiet, at times perhaps unobtrusive watching in liaison with a chairman guiding itineraries to see that teams and likely candidates get fair attention. How five counties (reputedly) considered Ian Botham a suitable candidate defies comprehension.

To clear up one point before leaving the subject, Illingworth has been quoted as saying he as chairman has the right to a final say. It is true that at his appointment last year the right of veto on grounds other than cricket last held by the chairman of the TCCB was transferred to him. It does not mean that if his four fellow-selectors, Atherton, Lloyd, Graveney and Gooch wanted one cricketer Illingworth could on technical grounds nullify their choice. In fact, as generations of selectors have told me, a consensus is almost invariably reached without a vote. One who has been a witness of many meetings indeed says he never remembers a vote being taken.

A warm note to end on: the Bedser twins, Alec and Eric, are justly proud to have been recent recipients of a single gesture in the shape of an official luncheon in their honour at Parliament House, Sydney. It was given 'as a token of the esteem in which they are held as Honorary Australians for over 50 years'.

A whole Test team of Alec's opponents most of whose wickets he took more than once graced the occasion under the chairmanship of the former Governor of New South Wales, Sir Roden Cutler, VC.

BUSY ENGLAND ARE ON TRACK FOR ONE-DAY RETURN
22 May 1996

No sooner are England's winter adventures concluded and the post mortems digested (or otherwise) than the new cycle of international matches is upon us. For the leading players there is no let-up and in their case, though *not* for the run-of-the-mill county player, the cry of 'too much cricket' is valid enough. They embark tomorrow on a summer programme of three one-day internationals and three Tests against India, followed by three Tests and lastly three of the one-day variety against Pakistan.

The first point to make about the 13 names from whom the England XI will emerge at the Oval tomorrow is that whereas other countries charge their regular Test team with the responsibility for one-day fixtures the England selectors, on the contrary, have announced that this is specifically their pick for one-day purposes.

This may be a valid strategy, perhaps, in that in an era when great cricketers who would choose themselves for England simply have not been produced over these many years, the alternative can only be to find substitutes with the mental toughness and relish for the limelight to advance their claims at a higher than county level.

One of the three new men whose temperament has impressed good judges is Ronnie Irani, a hard-hitting bat; but can a man be seriously thought of as an England all-rounder whose career record is 60-odd wickets at almost 40 a time? Mark Ealham's all-round record is more evenly balanced without being exceptional. As a fielder he is not too far below his brilliant father, Alan.

The third newcomer to big cricket is Alistair Brown, a notable striker of the ball, who had the luck to be blossoming as opening partner to his captain on his home pitch. My feelings about Mr Brown are somewhat ambivalent in that although we share the same birthday, in the 1996 *Cricketer's Who's Who* he has stated a preference for coloured clothing. Perhaps TCCB's Chairman Silk (or almost any other old player) will have a word with him about that.

More to the point he must enjoy the considerable confidence of the selectors to be preferred to the left-hander N. V. Knight, of Warwickshire, who on Sunday scored a pertinent 134 off 104 balls: balls, by the way: in my book postmen make deliveries. I dignify him with his initials since the riveting *Who's Who* delcares he has these three nicknames. Stitch, Canvas and Fungus. Does this say anything about the tight-enclosed county circuit, or is someone pulling editor Richard Lockwood's leg?

Of the remaining three names among the thirteen which may have evoked surprise Matthew Maynard, 30, is a dangerous one-day stroke-player, as is Neil Smith. In his tenth season he has taken just over 200 wickets at 38 runs apiece. However, he came out of the World Cup ahead of some with bigger reputations.

Chris Lewis has more natural talent than any contender for an all-round place, and in 27 Tests has enjoyed days of success. The doubts about him are concerned with fitness – he played only four days' cricket last year – and attitude. He greatly disappointed both Leicestershire and Notts. Now he is one of four Surrey representatives among the thirteen and has started the season well enough.

The least satisfactory feature of the new selectors' first effort is the utter sameness of the bowling. Whereas the World Cup illustrated the value of spin, the England thirteen include five right-arm fastish bowlers with only Smith aforesaid and the periodic off-spin of Graeme Hick. Mention of the latter is for me a melancholy reminder that if

Worcestershire and the selectors and Hick himself had seen eye to eye five years ago there were the makings of a true off-spinning England all-rounder.

The best news on the thin spin front is that Min Patel, who had a disappointing 1995 after an auspicious 'A' tour of India, has recovered confidence and form to the tune of 15 wickets in three innings against Lancashire and Essex. He would seem the best slow left-armer at the moment, and it helps his case that he is a lovely mover in the field with as flat and fast a throw as anyone, and no mug either with the bat.

Frankly one cannot be over-sanguine about England's immediate prospects, at any rate in the Tests, with the standard of bowling as it is, but there is surely a silver lining in the likely new regime. I recently found Michael Atherton in buoyant and cheerful form and much encouraged at the prospect of working with a Barclay–Lloyd partnership.

From P. D. Reddy, one of the Madras cricket family. I hear that Madras CC, the oldest club in India, are celebrating their 150th year and are marking the occasion by publishing their history.

I used to hear much about cricket at the Chipauk ground from C. P. Johnstone, who, for many years, was a prop and stay of the game in Madras. I fear, however, that my pathetic little story about him is too flippant to interest Mr Reddy though it may raise a smile from a cricket widow or two. Con Johnstone used to play for Kent when on leave from India, taking with him a wife whose interests lay very much elsewhere.

My old friend installed his lady in the stand at the Rectory Field, Blackheath, before playing one of his finest innings in the great derby match against Surrey. Putting on his Cambridge blazer he went expectantly to join her but searched the stand in vain. Behind it they had taken the hay off the football field, and there he found her fast asleep under the haystack. She hadn't seen a ball bowled. Odd how such trivia sticks in the mind.

RECALLING SOME RABBITS, FIRST-CLASS AND OTHERWISE

The Cricketer, *September 1997*

There is a fascination surely in the extremes of quality, the marvellously good and the wondrously bad. Let us here concern ourselves with the rabbits. I am thinking, so far as first-class cricket is concerned, of bowlers who have been rabbits with the bat; also of club cricketers who were just rabbits full stop.

In the former category we in Kent can boast quite a full hand, so to speak, in three excellent bowlers who all took many more wickets than they made runs. There was that extremely tall practitioner of seam and cut, Norman Graham, who in a career between 1964 and 1977 took 614 wickets and scored only 404, at an average of 3.84. Before Graham we had C.S. Marriott, always known (though he was not in holy orders) as 'Father'. He was a high-class spin bowler who played once for England, in 1933, and took 11 for 96 against the West Indies: but he was a real duffer not only with the bat but in the field.

In spite of this, and strangely enough, he was greatly acclaimed as a coach, who as a master at Dulwich produced a succession of fine players including Hugh Bartlett, S. C. (Billy) Griffith, Denys Wilcox, Trevor Bailey and Tony Mallett. Father Marriott between 1917 and 1933 took 711 wickets but made only 574 runs. I saw perhaps his most useful contribution with the bat for Kent at the Oval in the local Derby against Surrey, and recall it because of the gradual change of expression of that most dramatic of cricketers, P. G. H. Fender. When Marriott came to join young Gerry Chalk, Bill Fender, having taken the last five wickets for very few, clearly enjoyed the prospect of taking his sixth and last to win the match. By six o'clock, which found the rabbit somehow still in residence and the game saved, Surrey's famous all-rounder was far from smiling. I can hear the laughter now as the unlikely hero returned to the dressing room.

Our prime Kentish rabbit of modern times, though (1975–1990), was that popular fast bowler, Kevin Jarvis, whose final figures were 404 runs at 3.59 and 674 wickets at 29 runs each. There was a time when Jarvis might have finished his career taking two wickets for every run scored. However, he finally played a few matches for Gloucestershire where the air seems to have suited his batting rather better than that of his native county to the extent of his average rising from 0.34 points to 3.25. But most dogs have their day and Kevin like Father briefly had his, likewise against Surrey and at Canterbury. In a crucial B & H match Kent with nine wickets down needed four to win, Kevin being required to face the last over from Sylvester Clarke, as fast a bowler as any in the Championship. At this crucial moment our rabbit contrived that most delicate of glances which, finding the narrow aperture between right leg and leg stump, and just eluding the keeper's dive races to the boundary, leaving the long-leg fielder sprawling. There are sarcastic names for this stroke, such as the Surrey cut and the Harrow drive. In fact it is the modern version of *the draw* portrayed by gentlemen in top hats.

Confining himself to post-war players who have taken more wickets than they have scored runs, and have taken upwards of a hundred wickets, archivist Robert Brooke lists 17 names, four of them Test cricketers: Bill Bowes, Eric Hollies, David Larter and 'Hopper' Read. Of these the first two were, of course, leading bowlers over long spans who were not encouraged to stay long but could often do so in a crisis. I recall Eric once denying the Gentlemen a rare Lord's victory. Of the others eight men have career averages under four, the lowest being the lanky Frank McHugh of Gloucestershire who took 276 wickets at 24, but props up the batting with 179 runs at an average of 2.63. That would seem the lowest figure within moden times. There used to be more bowlers without any batting pretensions than there are today, led perhaps by Fred Morley of Notts, of whom it was said that when he came out to bat the Trent Bridge horse located himself between the shafts of the roller.

So much for what one might call high-class rabbits. But I recall also certain oldish fellows who, in my young days when full scores were printed in *The Cricketer*, used to appear going in last for MCC and never as they say, troubled the scorers for very long. They were men of means who kept up their trousers by wearing red and yellow sashes and did a useful job managing sides of otherwise reputable and often distinguished cricketers. In the red books which until after the war have full scores of every MCC match whether at Lord's or elsewhere – hundreds of them, as now – the name of H. D. Swan appeared just above mine in the annual batting averages of 'Gentlemen and Professional'. His tally of runs for the season ran neck and neck with the number of matches he played, though not-outs sometimes enabled his average to arrive at as much as 3. 'Swannie' used to field ponderously at mid-on, very straight, and he maintained an expression of aloof detachment as the ball whistled past the welts of his boots. He travelled as a purely honorary manager of the MCC side which Harold Gilligan took to New Zealand and Australia in 1929/30. He rates as the worst cricketer I ever played with, though there was little to separate him from another MCC manager of the same kidney, Captain T. H. Carlton-Levick. He, too, was a self-appointed tour manager, who can be seen squatting in front of an MCC side to the West Indies or Canada, a trim figure wearing co-respondent's shoes and a blue cap of his own design with the letters MCC picked out in white. When war came Carlton did a valuable job for the Club transferring the pavilion pictures to the country and at the end organising their return.

Talking of indifferent cricketers playing with their betters, the outstanding case in cricket history was surely that of the Midlands furniture millionaire, Sir Julien Cahn, who between the wars not only owned and played on his excellent grounds, one at West Bridgford, Nottingham, the other at his house, Stanford Hall at Loughborough, but also took sides all over the world. He played regularly in England for his side and sometimes abroad, as for instance in Canada, USA and Bermuda in 1933 when I had the pleasure of touring with him. He was just a man of hospitable instincts who loved cricket and the company of cricketers, several of whom he employed in his business.

Julien's natural skills were scarcely existent. However, he wore pneumatic pads which the butler solemnly blew up, and he knew to keep front pad and Gunn and Moore closely aligned. So it was not only difficult to bowl him out, but he was responsible for many leg-byes, and the convention was that his umpires, John Gunn and 'Tich' Richmond, forgot to signal them. Moreover he sometimes went in early and club opponents were inclined to be happy enough for him to stay, so as to limit the scoring at one end. His bowling consisted of donkey drops which were hit for enormous sixes, but occasionally mis-hit, producing spectacular catches in the deep.

'How is Sir Julien bowling this year, John – up and down I expect?'
'Not so much oop and down, I'd say as to and fro.'

His XI played several three-day matches each summer, mostly on his city ground against touring Test teams (other than the Australians) and a few of the counties. He played six first-class matches, three of them in a sort of Indian summer coming up to his 53rd birthday in 1935. Against the South Africans he made 5 not out, against

Leicestershire he actually delivered 17 overs and took 0 for 115, and against Lancashire in an otherwise well-contested match (and his last), going in No. 11 he made his top score of 17. How all concerned contrived those 17 must have been a wonder. Julien gave great pleasure to thousands of cricketers of every race and degree. He was at once the most prolific patron of cricket between the wars and comfortably the worst-ever first-class cricketer.

TENDULKAR BEARS OUT COMPARISON WITH BRADMAN
12 June 1996

What with an England Test win, the appointment of T. M. Lamb to high office, the excitement of B & H semi-finals, working parties hard at it (we hope) aiming to see our once-glorious and beautiful game in true perspective, an invasion of Lord's tomorrow by ladies and the June Test there following next week, it's all go, as they say.

It is no satisfactory Test match when in ideal weather only four men – in this case Hussain, Srinath, Tendulkar and Atherton – can exceed 55, and if Warwickshire cannot produce a better pitch than this they will be lucky to remain on the Test rota, let alone have the honour of opening the Ashes series as they are due to do when Australia are here next summer. These last three years, Edgbaston have finished 17th, fourth and 17th again in the TCCB's pitches table of merit.

The more credit, then, to Nasser Hussain, who needed some luck to survive, as anyone would have done, against the admirable Prasad and Srinath. There is class and a sound method in Hussain as there certainly is in John Crawley, who had the cruel luck to be named and then omitted. As to Tendulkar's beautiful hundred, it will only not have surprised those who read Sir Donald Bradman's recent comment, made on television, that 'he plays very much as I played'.

There has been no sign at the several low points of recent years of any lack of confidence by the England XI in its captain, yet nothing solidifies team spirit like a victory and Atherton's side showed every manifest sign of being pleased with themselves, a very different-looking bunch from the downcast also-rans at the Cape.

David Lloyd can be relied on to keep them buoyant and cheerful, a reflection of his own nature: his problem may rather be one of restraint. I have been an admirer of young Dominic Cork since he made a magnificent 92 not out in the 1993 B & H final, and he is today plainly the best of England's medium-fast battery. His enthusiasm within limits is fine, but the aggressive histrionics when he has either taken a wicket or has thought he has are altogether too much of a good thing. They are a bad example to boys especially, but indeed to all cricketers who ape what is done in front of the cameras.

It happens that next Tuesday sees the launch by Richard Cohen Books of *Uncorked*, the diary of his last cricket year: a catchy title notwithstanding which I venture to hope that he now corks it up a bit – without going too far of the way with Harold Larwood. That great fast bowler expressing astonishment in his latter days at all the back-slapping antics at the fall of a wicket said, 'We just sat down and waited for the next bloke.'

On the same theme, I can't resist retelling the remark of the son of the toughest of Tykes, Arthur Mitchell, when asked what his father would have thought of a particular over-spill of emotion: 'I don't think he ever kissed mother.'

In parenthesis, those who sigh for more conventional – if you like, more old-fashioned – behaviour on the field could find it, I feel sure, tomorrow, when Lord's stages the Women's Cricket Association's one-day international between England and New Zealand. MCC are welcoming the opportunity to open the pavilion to ladies, members being allowed to introduce up to four guests of either sex. Entrance to the ground is £2, for juveniles £1.

The appointment of Tim Lamb as the chief executive-designate of the TCCB and shortly of its successor the English Cricket Board, should be approved by cricketers and lovers of the game everywhere, for he has wide credentials and a lively mind.

His experience as a player embraces Shrewsbury, Oxford, Middlesex and Northants, and at 42 he still turns his arm over to good effect. He was a county secretary with Middlesex before becoming, in 1987, cricket secretary of the TCCB. In this capacity he has travelled the Test cricket world organising in advance tours at all levels run by the board.

At his initial interview, Lamb touched on the permanent dichotomy between cricket and marketing when he said he welcomed business within a game as opposed to the game within a business.

The shift in the governance of cricket to a broader-based board overseeing the whole game rather than just the professional side of it has taken longer than was hoped, but David Morgan, chairman of Glamorgan, tells me that his working party hopes the new administration may be operative from the 1997 new year.

The face of English cricket will not be transformed in a hurry but opinion, I hope and trust, is moving towards the view that the crucial thing is to halt the slide in the techniques of both batting and bowling.

It is axiomatic that batting standards are governed by the quality of the bowling and contemporary bowling is so poor and so deficient in spin that batsmen can get away with minimum regard to orthodox principles. This point is strongly made in the current issue of *The Cricketer* by R. T. Simpson, an England batsman of the classical school and a stalwart of Notts cricket ever since his retirement in the 1960s. His spirited polemic should be required reading by all first-class cricketers and by all coaches everywhere.

'Modern efforts to play fast and slow bowling are appalling and make me shudder,' he says. A strong back-foot player himself, he condemns the premature forward lunge, the 'cross-bat cow-shot', and other strokes across the line of the ball.

Simpson's thesis is echoed in *Ted Dexter's Little Red Book*, a slim volume that shows that tremendous and tireless cricketer in ripe form, full of keen observation and topical comment on the players of today and yesterday. Both lay a good portion of the blame for the state of affairs on the habits of one-day cricket.

From David Rayvern Allen's *The Cricketer's Quotation Book* I select this tailpiece: 'When we were living in Sydney, a friend told me that one night while she and her husband were making love, she suddenly noticed something sticking in his ear. When she asked him what it was, he replied. "Be quiet, I'm listening to the cricket."'

CLASS OF '96 BRISTLE WITH DEFIANCE AFTER THE DEFENCE OF HQ
17 June 1996

A hundred years ago this week, a century before the first of this summer's two Lord's Tests begins, against India, a crowd without parallel in England assembled at Lord's to see the first day of the Test match against Australia: 25,414 paid at the gate, members bringing up the total to almost 30,000.

England had won the Ashes at home three years before and had since retained them by the odd match of five in a memorable series Down Under. Patriotic feeling had been stirred by these successes, and crowning all anticipation was the presence once more as England's captain of cricket's majestic father figure W. G. Grace. His triumphs of the previous year, 1895, the thousand runs in May and the 100th hundred which inspired an outburst of public acclaim, had raised W.G. to the height of a national symbol.

Here he was, coming up to his 48th birthday, massive, bearded, opening the England innings as he had been doing since that first Test at the Oval 16 years earlier, and making a solid 66. By the way, W.G. in this summer played 54 innings, scoring 2,135 runs with an average of 42.4, and for good measure bowled 553 overs and took 52 wickets. Who says our modern heroes play too much?

Retrospectively, this Lord's Test of 1896 appears as no ordinary milestone. 'It was W.G.'s last Test at Lord's; it was the last of the three-Test series, before the addition of Trent Bridge and Headingley to the rota of the Oval, Lord's and Old Trafford brought the number of Tests on each Australian visit to five. Above all, this was the scene of the last-but-one victory over Australia at Lord's in 100 years, the only other being 'Verity's Match' on a turning pitch after rain in 1934.

The match was dramatic in the extreme. Harry Trott won the toss for Australia on a perfect pitch, whereupon the great Surrey bowlers Tom Richardson and George Lohmann dismissed them before lunch for 53. By close of play, thanks to W.G., Bobby Abel (also of Surrey), who made 94, and the Hon. F. S. Jackson, with a brilliant 44, England had run up 286 for eight.

The crowd far exceeded the rudimentary seating and, to the discomfort of the Australians, encroached on to the field of play. They impeded Joe Darling from catching Jackson on the on side whereupon, according to *Wisden*, he 'palpably gave away his innings', immediately putting up a catch in the same direction. *Noblesse oblige,* indeed.

Writing in the *Daily Telegraph* before the Lord's Test against Australia in 1956, I speculated whether such a gesture might then be repeated, and imagined Keith Miller (then on his last tour) reacting as Jackson did. Forty years on, the gesture probably seems just endearingly quixotic.

The crowd on the second day was half that of the first, chiefly, thought *Wisden*, because the result was considered to be a formality. But Australian fighting powers had been underestimated. In a defiant partnership, Syd Gregory and his captain made hundreds in their side's second innings of 347, and when rain overnight made the wicket difficult on the third day, England had to struggle hard before winning by six wickets.

MCC members alone can have watched the play in comfort, secure in the noble pavilion built six years before which stands unchanged today. By the time the next Australians came in 1899, the club had put up the Mound Stand. They had also appointed a notable secretary in Francis Lacey, of whom it was said that he dragged the MCC into the 20th century.

Cricket was on the march in Queen Victoria's last decade, with other names such as Jackson and Stoddart getting ready to take over the leadership from W.G. and with a talented, responsible professional nucleus in support. This, so to say, was the springtime of the Golden Age, shortly to be adorned by such commanding figures as C. B. Fry, Jessop – 'the Croucher', J. T. Tyldesley, Archie MacLaren, Sydney Barnes, Wilfred Rhodes and the inimitable 'Ranji'.

Those looking out behind their moustaches in the accompanying photograph were household names: Stanley Jackson, under whom, before he went off as Governor of Bengal, England in 1905 swept to triumph over Australia, the captain heading both batting and bowling averages; and Andrew Stoddart, who led England at rugby as well as cricket.

The tall figure at the back, William Gunn, of Notts, founder of the famous bat-makers Gunn and Moore, and uncle of Test cricketers George and John Gunn, was also a double international as outside-left for Nottingham Forest. He was the first professional to be elected to his county committee, being followed in that distinction by the man on his right, J. T. Hearne, of Middlesex, prince of medium-pacers (more than 3,000 wickets) along with Lohmann. The latter, a master of the bowling arts who actually took 112 Test wickets at 10 runs each, is seated on W.G.'s left. A tragic figure, he seems to be showing perhaps the beginnings of the tuberculosis from which he died five years later.

Above Lohmann is Tom Hayward, mentor of Sir Jack Hobbs, who brought that greatest of professional batsmen from Cambridge to the

Oval. At his feet is Bobby Abel, diminutive in size but formidable in accomplishment, who was tending his sports shop outside the Oval when I was a junior member of Surrey. The stalwart Richardson is deservedly seated, having bowled 58.3 five-ball overs in the match and taken 11 wickets.

Note how W.G.'s physique outstrips them all – which brings me to the beard. This 1896 Test was *probably* the scene of the most famous ball ever bowled, the one by Ernest Jones that went through his beard. I raise the doubt because there is conflicting evidence. P.F. who became Sir Pelham Warner, in his history *Lords 1787–1945*, says that the first ball of England's first innings was very short and very fast. J. J. Kelly, the wicketkeeper, 'lost sight of it in Grace's beard and it went to the sight screen'. Lord Harris, in his reminiscences, confirms the ball, the place and the occasion and adds that it also touched the top of the bat handle – which, of course, probably made it a chance to the keeper.

The great Harris's word was law. Yet Charles Fry, in his autobiography *Life Worth Living*, declared that the encounter had taken place previously at Sheffield Park. He was playing for Lord Sheffield's XI there, as was Jackson, who went in first with W.G. and, according to Fry, said likewise 'What the hell are you at, Jonah? Or alternatively 'What, what, what?' cried W.G. Both versions agree on the immortal reply, 'Sorry, doctor, she slipped'. The question never to be answered is whether she slipped twice.

Fry says that W.G. emerged from the Sheffield Park match black and blue. What is not in dispute is that Jones was mighty quick. He seems also to have been something of a rough diamond. Asked at a reception whether he went to St Peter's, the leading Adelaide school, he replied: 'Yes, I drive the dirt cart there every Monday'. Our Australian cousins had their characters too, that fine day at Lord's a century ago.

RAY LINDWALL: OBITUARY
25 June 1996

Ray Lindwall was a fast bowler from the classic mould whose partnership with Keith Miller formed an attack which under the shrewd captaincy of Don Bradman secured and maintained Australia's pre-eminence in those crowded post-war years.

Both Lindwall and Miller were formidable figures, their strong physiques toughened in the hard school of Australian Rules Football, when together they burst on to the Test scene with great effect against W. R. Hammond's MCC side in Australia.

Ray's approach to the crease from a run no longer than the 22 yards of a cricket pitch was a model of balance and control, a quiet few paces culminating in longer strides and maximum power at the moment of delivery. The upward thrust of his left arm was followed by a rather lower swing of his right arm than the text-books advocate.

He quickly developed the varied skills of a fast bowler, and in particular became a master of pace change. His standard balls were the outswinger and the break-back. But in 1952, during a season with Nelson in the Lancashire League, when the league players found his outswinger literally beyond them, he perfected the inswinger and thus completed a better armoury than any other fast bowler in history.

The perfection of his method, and a rigorous attention to physical fitness, enabled Ray to maintain his form beyond normal retirement age. He was in his 40th year when, under this writer's managership of a Commonwealth XI, he embarked on a 9th and final tour and gave a last object-lesson to cricket-lovers in the West Indies.

Lindwall reached the peak of his speed in Australia's tour of England in 1948. With 27 Test wickets, and Bill Johnston also with 27, plus Miller's 13, England were sadly out-gunned.

In the last Test at the Oval Lindwall took six for 20, England being bowled out for 52. Under F. R. Brown England were also over-shadowed in Australia in 1950–51. In 1953 it was the threat of his top pace that helped to undo the best batsmen. By then the complete artist, he took 26 more Test wickets on that tour; but England, with Alec Bedser at his best and stronger batting to support Len Hutton and Denis Compton, discovered what it was to win again. At long last the Ashes were regained and in Lindwall's last two series against England they were retained.

When Australia paid their first visit to West Indies in 1955, team-work and the all-round form of Miller and Lindwall were largely instrumental in their victory, despite the record of 500 runs in a series by the current ICC chairman, Sir Clyde Walcott. In England in 1956 Lindwall and Miller had their last fling together, but two years later, at the end of an MCC tour marred from the English viewpoint by several suspect Australian actions, Lindwall was brought back for the last, and his last, two Tests. The cynics greeted his swansong as that of the last of the straight-arm bowlers.

Seeking satisfactory employment away from Sydney, Lindwall moved to Queensland for his final five years of Sheffield Shield cricket (from 1954 to 1959) and captained that state with distinction. A friendly, ever-popular man, a natural sportsman of transparent integrity, he had all the qualities of leadership. In the mid-1960s he joined his wife, Peggy, in what became and still is a leading florists in Brisbane.

His name will never fade among the hierarchy of fast bowlers, and many would echo the opinion of Sir Pelham Warner, and several of Lindwall's distinguished contemporaries, who rated him the greatest of them all.

OXFORD AND CAMBRIDGE
FACE FIRST-CLASS FUTURE
3 July 1996

With attention focused on the 151st University Match taking place at Lord's, I can reassure friends of Oxford and Cambridge cricket who may have been worried by the latest suggestion that their first-class status might be discussed at next week's International Cricket Council meeting. Countries, not the ICC by rule, determine which of their fixtures are to be first-class and the Test and County Cricket Board are making no move in this matter. The older universities are still nurseries of talent, if less so than in times past and earnest efforts are being made within both to accommodate the scholar-sportsman.

The ICC for their part have plenty of international issues for consideration, such as Sri Lanka's claim to greater Test participation, the eternal intimidation headache, plans for the next World Cup and, not least, the choice of a new chairman if Sir Clyde Walcott is not to continue.

The Lord's Test is a focus without equal for cricketers old and young, eminent and obscure and, as such, an important showpiece of the modern game. Sadly, the most interesting cricket between England and India, with Anil Kumble making a partial return to his best form, was in front of the sparse attendance on the last day. Prior to that, the game fell somewhat short of the occasion.

We could admire especially the skills of Srinath and Prasad, the grit and concentration of Russell, the beautiful innings of Ganguly – notice how completely still he stands as the bowler's arm comes over, how smoothly he moves into the stroke – and, not least, at lunchtime on the Saturday the now traditional excellence of the Christ's Hospital band.

Thank Heaven, by the way, for the presence of both Ian Salisbury and Min Patel in the thirteen for Headingley: five medium-fast bowlers operating in rotation is simply not an attack.

I incline more and more to think that the most serious threat to all cricket everywhere is behaviour on the field. In conversation at Lord's, a schoolmaster told what difficulty he had in restraining his boys from talking and clapping and generally gesticulating. Their opponents were often aggressive and noisy: why could they not follow suit? I heard of a southern league in which there had been three punch-ups. A young friend with experience of the Surrey and Western leagues tells me that he infinitely prefers the spirit and atmosphere of the latter.

In these columns a fortnight ago, Matthew Fleming, our lively Kent cricketer who is deputy chairman of the Professional Cricketers' Association, wrote of the 'fine line' between acceptable aggression – which is to be encouraged – and unacceptable over-aggression, which brings the game into disrepute.

'The image of our game is all-important for its future.' These are welcome sentiments coming from a contemporary player and, as it happens, they are strongly echoed by the doyen of critics and one of the game's most illustrious figures. In *The Appeal of Cricket*, published last year and now available at £7.99 in paperback, Richie Benaud begins his broad survey of the modern scene with a withering first chapter concerning Australian behaviour in South Africa on their tour of 1993–94: in particular of Merv Hughes and Shane Warne, against whom the Australian board chairman, Alan Crompton, moved with decisive promptness and effect. What Warne did was 'to scream abuse at Hudson as the batsman walked from the crease.'

Benaud gave full marks to the umpires, Barry Lambson and David Shepherd, the latter of whom 'immediately called Allan Border over and his body language was unmistakable, holding Border responsible for the actions of his team.' The former Australian captain went on to say he always considered himself responsible for the actions of his team, as is laid down in the laws and also repeated in the ICC code of conduct.

Those who, reading my reintroduction of this subject, may well have thought this was an over-emphasis by a hoary old has-been will,

I hope, have pondered it afresh in the light of these endorsements. When the English board eventually start operations, they would do well to print for circulation wherever cricket is played the text of Law 42.1: 'The captains are responsible at all times for ensuring that play is conducted within the spirit of the game as well as within the laws.'

From Michael Atherton to the humblest village captain. Nuff said.

Let me strike an infinitely more cheerful note. I have had a soft spot for the Oratory School ever since my old friend D. C. F. Burton (Yorkshire captain 1919–1921) coached them to four successive victories over Beaumont at Lord's in the late 1930s despite the place being almost devoid of boys. It seemed an annual miracle. Nowadays they have plenty of boys and in recent years have more than recaptured the former tradition, having won no fewer than 45 matches out of 60 over the last three years and lost only one.

There is an outstanding all-rounder named Steven Tomlinson who has averaged 90 this term and last year, aged a bare 16, played for Wales Under-19 and also won the British Under-18 Real Tennis Championship. They have a real tennis court at the Oratory and also an indoor cricket school regularly inhabited, I am assured, during the winter. Enthusiasm and sound coaching are clearly the keys. Bradfield and Stowe are among the stronger schools met, and the fixture list is due to be strengthened.

Christopher Martin-Jenkins recently shed light on the ever-growing opportunities for cricket at all age groups for boys in the summer holidays, organised by dedicated people. I hear of a new youth festival due in the last week of July by the Schools Cricket Association of that minor county of rich traditions, Norfolk. To have a distinguished old player involved is, of course, a bonus and this enterprise is the work of Richard Jefferson, the Cambridge and Surrey all-rounder of the 1960s who has taken early retirement from school teaching in the equally noble cause of cricket coaching.

I have had some applause, by the way, for my use of 'balls' rather than 'deliveries', which are made by postmen – and, for that matter, milkmen and midwives. Another dislike is for decently accurate bowling to be described as 'mean': a complete misuse of the word which the dictionary describes as 'ignoble, ungenerous, stingy. One reads of a sweater being referred to as a jumper – ugh! Aren't jumpers for feminine use? The superfluous use of 'on' before a score is a regular irritant first introduced, I think, by *Test Match Special*. What's wrong with 'Smith was 24 when missed by Bloggs,' etc? Ah well, we are spared the old-time journalese: the crimson rambler is no longer sent speeding to the confines. The modern jargon does, however, grate a bit.

ALAN McGILVRAY: OBITUARY
18 July 1996

Alan McGilvray was the most professional of commentators in that he was essentially a meticulous communicator of fact, sticking to the ground rules approved by ABC and BBC producers without much in the way of personal gloss. His commentaries were nevertheless instantly distinctive because his Australian intonations were almost whispered into the microphone, too quietly sometimes to be heard by his colleagues in the broadcasting box.

He and I were brought up in the school wherein the unforgivable sin was to be late on the stroke. The prevailing wisdom was that the listener had to be given a mental vision of the bowler's run up, delivery and the batsman's stroke as they happened. This gave a regular pattern to which comment was added.

It might be added that the pace of commentary used to reflect the bowling of 20 overs an hour: the modern rate of 15 an hour means there is more time to be filled up.

Alan never adapted to the looser, more relaxed and often jokey style of *Test Match Special*, and to that extent some found him a difficult colleague. There was, for instance, little rapport between him and John Arlott. As Trevor Bailey observed: 'McGilvray was a very good commentator *and* a very good cricketer, and it jolted.'

David Rayvern Allen in his biography of Arlott quotes McGilvray: 'He [Arlott] was a good commentator in his own way, but he didn't give the score or the card. You should give the score three times in a six-ball over. He had a different technique to mine, more intimate, but he didn't care about the Aussies not listening – a lot of what he said was way above their heads.'

Alan was wholly reliable as regards fact, and he had the prime virtue of complete impartiality. He wanted to see and describe good cricket:

but for his accent there was no telling which team was closer to his heart. Personally I found him easy to work with, and I had the greatest respect for his judgment.

Alan was a firm traditionalist: the attempted takeover of international cricket by Kerry Packer was anathema to him, and he deplored the deterioration in the game's spirit that followed.

A man with great pride in his calling, Alan nevertheless brought upon himself a crowning disappointment to which it was unwise afterwards to refer. At Brisbane in December 1960, thinking Australia was sure to win the First Test against West Indies, he arranged the commentary periods so that he could catch an early aeroplane back to Sydney.

When he got there he heard the news that the 500th Test match had ended in the first-ever tie – a commentator's dream that would have suited McGilvray to perfection. The final stages of the match were obviously a highly taxing exercise – so much so that the ABC commentary by the local man of the thrilling last over is never repeated.

In the 1930s, before McGilvray gave a genuine Test commentary, he was involved by a commercial company in a synthetic broadcast for listeners too far away from the cricket for the live transmitters. The exercise involved a studio, plan of the ground, a continuous stream of cabled information and an effects man to synchronise sound noises with the commentary thus realistically manufactured. The similitude was such that the unsophisticated audience of those days thought they were listening to the real thing.

Alan McGilvray came first to England with Don Bradman's Australian team of 1948 and thereafter followed all Australian Test tours home and away until the visit here of 1985 when David Gower's team recovered the Ashes by three matches to one.

Ode to E. W. S.

'Jim's the boy' brave Camrose said
'To get our readers out of bed.
We'll put him on a sticky wicket
And make him commentate on cricket.'

Two fifty Tests have now been played
At which our Scribe, so sound and staid,
In tones episcopal has tried
To keep his audience goggle-eyed.

At close of play on B.B.C.
His views, portentous as can be,
Censure those who've erred and strayed
From ways in which they should have played.

Friend of Governors, Lords and Kings
Authority on all sorts of things
Let's raise our hats with much finesse
To cricket's own E. W. S.

Celebratory verses after Jim had covered his
250th Test Match in 1973. Author unknown

HERE'S HOPING FOR PEACE
IN A TEST SERIES TO RELISH
24 July 1996

All was sweetness and light when last evening MCC entertained the Pakistani team to dinner at Lord's. Under the leadership of the handsome Wasim Akram they are a fine-looking bunch of young men; like their predecessors, well endowed with national pride. Their manager, Yawar Saeed, is an old player well acquainted with the English game from three years with Somerset in the 1950s and happily unacquainted with the arcane world of modern cricket politics in the subcontinent.

With several past series in mind, the hope must be that neither side's enthusiasm over-spills. As to that it is much to the good that, as Michael Atherton has remarked, he and his opposite number are not only Lancashire colleagues but friends, as also is England's coach, David Lloyd. The world will be watching them.

One looks forward especially to seeing Saeed Anwar, a newcomer to England with three attractive hundreds to his name already, and Inzamam-ul-Haq, who has developed into a formidable player since he came here as a fledgling in 1992: also, our old adversary Mushtaq Ahmed, who keeps the wrist-spin flag flying in support of Wasim Akram and Waqar Younis.

It could even be that Pakistan may field spin at both ends, for against Kent over the weekend Saqlain Mushtaq, reputedly only 19, looked a highly promising off-spinner with some hint of flight and variety. It stands to reason that England will have to be at their best to beat Pakistan in a rubber for the first time since 1982. May the occasion inspire them!

The visit of the Pakistanis to our lovely Canterbury in perfect weather drew around 9,000 to the match. It acted as an agreeable aperitif to Canterbury Week which, in the era of the four-day game, now consists of one championship match. It starts a week tomorrow when Kent, strongly in the running for the championship, play Worcestershire, presumably including Graeme Hick.

Much the oldest and most famous of Weeks, it is in its 155th year but this is the 150th anniversary of the St Lawrence Ground, which has been a place of pilgrimage for lovers of Kent cricket since 1847. The best part of 20 tents will ring the field from the sight screen to square leg; on the first three days, bands will play, womenfolk will enter for the hat competition and the staff will sprout buttonholes on the Thursday, which by tradition is Ladies' Day.

When David Acfield's committee deliver their proposals for the future shape of first-class cricket, I hope they will feel able to put right the annual irritation of the void of 10 days without championship cricket at the heart of the season in mid-July. Sixteen of the counties are left idle, while the remaining two contest the Benson and Hedges Cup final. It was especially galling this time since the barren period coincided with the start of the most beautiful weather of the summer. The two fixtures involving the finalists (assuming the Benson and Hedges is to continue in its present form) would need to be accommodated later. Admittedly some flexibility in fixtures would be called for, but there need be no insuperable difficulty.

For a diminutive 13-year-old at Lord's to make 75 (one more than the rest of the side together) and 44, and to take eight wickets for 97 in a two-day match which his side won by two runs, is the stuff of schoolboy fiction. It happened, though, exactly 50 years ago next week, the match being between Tonbridge and Clifton and the boy Colin Cowdrey.

Looking back, his chief memory is of terror at being kept on with his very slow, flighted leg-breaks when Clifton's last pair needed only three runs to win. In fact, the youngest boy to play at Lord's showed his nerve by bowling a maiden, whereupon the 10th wicket fell at the other end.

This was the first of Cowdrey's five years in the Tonbridge XI, in the last of which he not only averaged 79 with the bat but took 47 wickets. Four years after that, at Melbourne, he was making the first of his 22 hundreds for England.

What a pity, by the way, that Cowdrey's bowling was not in adult life taken seriously. Unfortunately for the prospect of this, when he started with Kent Doug Wright's career had seven years still to run, and Cowdrey's spinning skills withered from neglect.

MCC have commissioned a portrait of Sir Colin and the artist, Bryan Organ, is delivering it appropriately to mark the anniversary to the president Sir Oliver Popplewell, during the Test match.

BOWLING HEROICS MAKE UNIQUE DAY
17 September 1996

Old men forget, as one is sometimes reminded. I can only say that in 70 years of watching first-class cricket, I can recall nothing quite like the events at the St Lawrence ground yesterday.

At lunch, and for 44 minutes afterwards, Hampshire were apparently strolling to victory and Kent were almost resigned to a championship place of fourth or fifth. Suddenly, at 143 for one, Martin McCague sent the off-stump flying – and the scorecard records Hampshire's catalogue of disasters, completed by Matthew Fleming.

McCague bowled as fast as anyone I have seen since Devon Malcolm spreadeagled South Africa at the Oval three years ago. Dean Headley, after missing the month of May, has had great days, as has Mark Ealham. McCague, however, has been the backbone of Kent's attack all summer. At 27, this formidable fellow, 6ft 5in and upwards of 16st, has reached his peak. What might 1997 and the challenge of Australia bring forth from all three of them?

As to hat-tricks, Howard Milton, Kent's archivist, tells me that in 149 years of history, there had been only two Kentish hat-tricks on the St Lawrence ground, one each to Tich Freeman and Doug Wright. Now McCague's yesterday, plus two of Headley's astonishing three, makes three more on the ground in a few weeks.

Has there ever before been two Kent hat-tricks in the same match? The answer is yes and no. At Oxford in 1959 D. M. Sayer, a Kentish bowler playing for the university, did a hat-trick against the county, for whom Fred Ridgway riposted with another the *same day*.

PRODUCT OF LORD'S RANKED WITH BEST
15 October 1996

John David Benbow Robertson, universally known as Jack, who has died at Bury St Edmunds aged 79, was a batsman of high pedigree whether opening the innings for Middlesex or England, and in his years of retirement he was a distinguished coach.

Robertson and Sid Brown had just established themselves in the Middlesex XI at the onset of the Second World War. Yet six years later they were able to build up a partnership as prolific as almost any in history: thirty-four times they put on a hundred together, so paving the way for the famous duo, Bill Edrich and Denis Compton.

Robertson's batting was in the classical mould, very much after the elegant style of a senior product of the Lord's nursery, J. W. Hearne. He was, however, a more robust edition: one cannot imagine 'Young Jack' plundering Worcestershire for 331 not out in a day, as Robertson did in 1949 at Worcester, nor making a hundred before lunch as he did twice.

In English cricket this 331 has only been exceeded in a day three times: C. G. Macartney made 345 for the 1921 Australians against Notts at Trent Bridge, K. S. Duleepsinhji (wearing a sweater) 333 for Sussex against Northants at Hove in 1930 and two years ago came the 390 which Brian Lara made, bringing his score to the highest-ever 501 not out on the last day of the drawn match between Warwickshire and Durham at Edgbaston.

Robertson went on two tours with MCC, to West Indies in 1947–48 with G. O. Allen's injury-stricken side whose averages he topped, and to India in 1951–52. At Port-of-Spain his admirable 133 saved the match.

At home his path was blocked by the association of Hutton and Washbrook as England's opening pair. However, when Washbrook was unfit for a Lord's Test against New Zealand Robertson went in with Hutton, made 26 and 121, and was omitted from the next match because Washbrook was able to play.

Such was the strength of England's post-war batting that Robertson played only twice in home Tests.

It is as a county cricketer of the top flight, and a notable contributor to Middlesex cricket during its ascendancy under R. V. Robins that he will be remembered.

In his career he made 31,914 runs (average 37.50) and his 67 hundreds included one against every county – a satisfaction not afforded to more than a handful in history. He was Middlesex's coach from 1958 to 1968.

With his modest manner and gentlemanly disposition, Robertson was ideally suited for the coaching of youth. He did splendid work at Lord's and elsewhere for the National Cricket Association, and was about his duties when taken gravely ill at Eastertide 1982.

His oesophagus was removed, and he spent four months in hospital. Thereafter he was an invalid rarely free from pain, tended by Joyce, his wife of 56 years. They had one son, Ian.

Last summer he was taken to Cambridge to see Middlesex play the university and to watch once more his youthful pupils, notably Mike Gatting and Mark Ramprakash.

SURPRISE, LUCK AND CROFT ARE ENGLAND'S BEST BETS
7 May 1997

The sun never sets on cricket, as Plum Warner first remarked many years ago, an aphorism even more literally true today than ever. The top players are caught up in a continuous circus which surely calls for some regulation by the International Cricket Council.

Yet the high hopes in an English spring are perennial, and this year there is that special expectation, which heralds the coming of Australia and the prospect of yet another fight for the Ashes.

It is 10 years since Mike Gatting, in Australia, retained the Ashes won here two years before by David Gower, and results since have been too depressing to mention. On the evidence of the respective bowling resources it would be foolish to deny that once again the odds over a six-Test series strongly favour Australia.

It might be different but for Shane Warne, and if any England bowler other than the admirable Robert Croft could aspire to the steadfast quality of an Angus Fraser, let alone a Botham or a Bedser. Yet surprise is the essence of cricket, and luck a permanent element. The better side, thank heaven, do not always win.

The crowds who will fill every Test seat and the untold mass of followers everywhere would surely be satisfied if England played with courage to the utmost of their capacity *and* if they showed a cheerful and generous spirit.

One of the hopes for the new season with the Australians in our midst must be for a general condemnation and action against sledging. The Australians were not the originators of this foul habit of verbal abuse but it has been for many years endemic in their cricket. I hope too that England show a more acceptable demeanour than was apparent at times during the winter, especially in the matter of appealing.

Cricketers, especially young ones, take their cue from what they see on the box. The eyes of the cricket world will be on this Ashes series, which will be genuinely acceptable only if the captains, the umpires and the referees all play their parts in making it so.

George Mann and E.W.S. no doubt remembering the time when, as Middlesex opening batsmen, one nearly ran out the other at Fenners

Even presidents came under the Swanton scrutiny . . .

Two nonagenarians comparing their adjacency to W.G. Grace, with Roger Knight, Secretary of the MCC, enjoying the conversation. Jim was a babe in a pram when Grace played at Forest Hill, whereas Primrose Worthington, Grace's granddaughter, actually sat on his knee and plaited his beard . . .

With Ann at Buckingham Palace, having received his CBE, 1994

Sharing a conversation with John Major and Tim Rice

Old comrades from the Bedfordshire Yeomanry who were Japanese prisoners of war.
The reunion took place in August 1992 at Sir Paul Getty's ground at Wormsley

(*Left*) The 1939 Wisden Almanack re-bound in remnants of gas cape and glued with rice paste by Foster & Gould (POWs) Bookbinders in Nakawn Paton, 1944. Jim carried this cherished volume with him throughout the war. Each POW in Siam, as it was then called, was allowed to borrow it for only twelve hours at a time, such was the demand
(*Photograph: Briony Allen*)

(*Right*) The fading purple Japanese 'not subversive' stamp can be discerned at the top left of the title page. On the left facing page is the inscription 'Major E. W. Swanton R.A., Hut 44 nr. Paton'
(*Photograph: Briony Allen*)

Just spruce and dandy! Jim's study is on the ground floor to his right

A view of the garden from Jim's study window

(*Right*) A benign perception . . .

(*Left*) 'Some caddy' – E.W. aged 91 at Royal
St George's
(*Photograph: Mark Williams*)

'Now, this should be your stance…'
A lesson to aspiring youngsters at the
Lord's school

(*Below*) Wheathampstead CC v.
E.W.'s XI, 18 May 1952, including
Brian Johnston, Peter May, Cuan
McCarthy, E.W.S, 'Gubby' Allen, John
Warr, Chris Winn, Ian Bedford, Harry
Altham, Billy Griffith and Michael
Melford

Once more unto the breach, dear friends!

(*Below*) Giving some fielding practice at Berbice in 1961

(*Above*) With Archbishop Robert and Lady Runcie in the garden at Delf House

(*Above*) With Trevor, the lifeguard at Sandy Lane, Barbados

(*Right*) Outside Canterbury Cathedral after the memorial service in March, 2000 (*Patrick Eagar Photography*)

Talking of behaviour, it is 20 years this week since news broke of what turned out to be the most serious assault on the game's accepted values in its history. My recollection of the events of May 1977 is specially clear because after a Thursday's play at Canterbury, Len Maddocks, the Australian manager, with two of his side, came to dine with us at Sandwich.

It was the last happy evening poor Maddocks spent on the tour, for two days later at Hove he learnt that all but four of his team had signed secret contracts binding allegiance to the brash, over-bearing media tycoon, Kerry Packer. There followed the sorry chapter of fractured loyalties, friendships broken, Test cricket played by skeleton sides while the rebels competed in so-called 'Super Tests' against one another.

After two years, a commercial compromise between the Australian board and Packer allowed him television rights on condition that his World Series Cricket ceased to compete with the established game. There is an inclination now in some quarters to say that Packerism was perhaps not such a bad thing as players became better paid. In fact, in England and Australia, improved salary scales were in train anyway.

I have been looking up contemporary comments on WSC in 1977–79. Tony Lewis told *Sunday Telegraph* readers that more bouncers than he had ever seen were destroying the best batsmen. Henry Blofeld wrote of 'despicable' fast bowling. Tony Greig, of the Packer camp, with implicit approval said bowlers were dishing out an unprecedented amount of bouncers at the 'rabbits'.

When the Packer circus ventured to the West Indies, riots occurred in three of the countries visited. At Georgetown, the pavilion was looted and records destroyed. The modern evil of intimidation had its roots in the brutalising of cricket under Packer. I once, by the way, won a £10 cricket wager from his father, Sir Frank, owner of several newspapers in Sydney, who was a genial fellow in comparison.

What memories spring to mind at the news of Denis Compton's passing. For all his 17 Test hundreds, my clearest picture is of his 76 not out in the Lord's Test of 1938 when, on a pitch made difficult by rain and sun, and with Hutton, Barnett, Edrich, Hammond and Verity out, and only 76 runs on the board, he stood, a cool, debonair youth of 20, between Australia and victory, confronting with consummate artistry the spin and lift of O'Reilly and the high speed of McCormick. He used to say it was his best innings – when he remembered.

As a relief from much pain and general ill-health in his last years he could still relish the company of such great friends as Colin Ingleby-Mackenzie and John Warr; but he who had given so much to so many could no longer find pleasure in life. To those old enough to recall the late 1940s there was never such a sporting hero.

Wilfred Wooller was another glamorous figure in the world of games for whom I had much admiration. By an ill-fated chance a letter he dictated to his wife congratulating me on my birthday a few days before he died did not reach me until afterwards.

He recalled a friendship going back 60-odd years to his freshman days at Cambridge when he and Cliff Jones led the university in a glorious era on the rugby field. Wooller and Tony O'Reilly were the greatest three-quarters I ever saw, and the break by Wilf which in 1935–36 brought about that most thrilling victory over the All Blacks at Cardiff was the most exciting memory of all of us who were there on that famous day.

As a cricketer he must be accounted one of the two makers of Glamorgan, building on, after the war, the foundation made before it by Maurice Turnbull. He was a belligerent captain – a shade too much so at times – and in particular a pioneer in the aggressive use of catchers round the bat. His winning of the championship in 1948 was a nine-day wonder.

ENDLESS APPEAL IN BURNING ISSUES OF A CLASSIC CONFLICT
2 June 1997

The Ashes! To anyone attracted by the history of cricket – which is to say most lovers of the game – the story is endlessly fascinating. Which were the strongest teams? Who were the best captains? What were the greatest matches? And so on. I am lucky enough to have followed the ebb and flow of success and failure since the Oval Test of 1921 wherein England, under Lionel, the future Lord Tennyson, fought a favourable draw against one of Australia's most powerful sides, led by Warwick Armstrong, who had already retained the Ashes.

This first recollection of a match where the Ashes were not at stake brings me to say at the outset that although the urn and the Ashes are symbolic of the ancient continuing battle, every encounter is a high event regardless of them. Some of the greatest games indeed have been played after the Ashes had been regained or retained. This was so in 1902 when at the Oval, after Jessop's wonderful hundred, Hirst and Rhodes got the necessary 15 runs together for the last wicket. Leonard Hutton's monumental 364 in 1938 was made after Australia had secured the Ashes.

England, after the last war, lost 11 Tests over three series before what we called the Elusive Victory at Melbourne in the fifth Test of 1950–51 came as a vast relief as though a reproach had been wiped away. Again, English relief was the keynote, also at Melbourne, in 1974–75 (at the end of my eighth and last reporting tour of Australia) when victory by an innings and four runs did much to assuage the early batterings of Lillee and Thomson.

From the first there was about Tests between England and Australia a special savour, the relish of raw colonials tweaking the lion's tail. Over the century and more, despite the population disparity, it has happened more often than not: 111 wins to Australia, 90 to England, with 84 matches drawn. On Thursday at Edgbaston yet another series gets under way, the 68th since the first confrontation at Melbourne in 1876–77.

The oldest recollections are generally the clearest, and the picture remains sharp of A. P. F. Chapman's recovery of the Ashes at the Oval in 1926, of his ushering forward, as they made for the pavilion in advance of a vast, cheering crowd, the 48-year-old Wilfred Rhodes who had played his first Test under W. G. Grace 27 years before. Rhodes and young Harold Larwood had each taken six wickets apiece, but the brightest glory belonged to Hobbs (100) and Sutcliffe (161) who had with utmost skill weathered the attack on a pitch made horribly spiteful by an overnight storm.

I was lucky in that the first Test I ever reported was a classic almost beyond compare wherein 1,601 runs were scored at Lord's inside four days and young Don Bradman's 254 set him on a pinnacle where he has remained ever since. Australia won by seven wickets, thus breaking the sequence of six successive victories by Chapman (despite his own 125), a record no captain is likely to challenge. The Lord's Test of 1934 is a landmark because it denotes England's only victory over Australia at Lord's since 1896, and that gained only because Hedley Verity with 14 wickets in the day took utmost advantage of a pitch made difficult after weekend rain.

The peak of national jubilation after the war was, of course,

England's regaining of the Ashes under Sir Leonard in the Coronation year of 1953, the first of three series won before a horrible descent Down Under in 1958–59. Three series out of four were halved in the 1960s before Ray Illingworth's side brought the Ashes home in 1970–71.

The Packer intrusion and attempted takeover of Test cricket scarred the two series at the end of the 1970s, since when the one perpetually recalled to revive English spirits is that of 1981 marked by the heroics of Ian Botham and Bob Willis. England's winning of the Ashes in 1985 under David Gower established his greatness as, I think, the best English left-handed bat since Frank Woolley, after which Mike Gatting achieved a well-fought success in Australia in 1986–87.

When Australia won a consolation victory in the sixth and last Test they were celebrating the end of a barren run without precedent of fourteen Tests against all opponents, a statistic which perhaps discounts, if only slightly, England's dismal showing in the four subsequent Anglo-Australian rubbers which we trust may be about to come to an end.

To ponder two of the questions I posed at the outset, perhaps the best-equipped England side in Australia was that of 1928–29. In batting order it was Hobbs, Sutcliffe, Hammond, Jardine, Hendren, Chapman, Larwood, Geary, Tate, Duckworth, White. At home I doubt whether the XI that won at the Oval in 1953 has been improved on: Hutton, Edrich, May, Compton, Graveney, Bailey, Evans, Laker, Lock, Trueman, Bedser. This might have fought a rare battle with the 1948 Australians: Morris, Barnes, Bradman, Hassett, Miller, Harvey, Loxton, Lindwall, Tallon, Ring, Johnston. As to leadership, Chapman, Brearley and Illingworth commend themselves especially on one side, Bradman (after the War), Benaud and Ian Chappell on the other. But in such a field they can only be invidious choices.

I expect it may be thought that, while I discount the dire episode of Bodyline, my preferences favour the past as no doubt do those of most in the sere and yellow. There have been fine England cricketers of late if no recent sides of the old quality, up to and certainly including Michael Atherton. Forgive me if I paraphrase Francis Thompson's lines:

As the run stealers flicker to and fro,
Oh, my Hobbs and my Woolley long ago.

ATHERTON HONOUR TIMED TO REFRESH
LORD'S NOSTALGIA
18 June 1997

It is a rare luxury that England go into a Lord's Test against Australia one up in the rubber. Can they break the long tradition of Australian supremacy at Lord's? There is no doubt that our visitors will be very much on their mettle and equally that England's present confidence and attitude will not easily be surrendered. For many the nostalgia of the moment is refreshed by the honours awarded to Michael Atherton and his illustrious predecessor, Colin Cowdrey.

Australia's record at Lord's since W. G. Grace brought England to victory in 1896 is one of the unlikeliest and most unaccountable of sporting legends. Of the 24 subsequent matches they have won 11 times, England once. Detailed scrutiny does slightly relieve the picture in that of the 12 draws, Australia held an advantage in only one, England certainly in six. In 1968, for instance, in a rain-ruined match, captain Cowdrey declared at 351 for seven: Australia out for 78 and in the follow-on 127 for four.

Australia also followed on when Hedley Verity spun England to victory in 1934. There will be a few of us looking on tomorrow able to recall how after hundreds by Maurice Leyland and Leslie Ames had brought England to 440, Australia had replied with 192 for two before the weekend rain. Bill O'Reilly always said it never occurred to them that they would not make the 99 more they needed with eight men left. As it was, against Verity's spin they failed by seven runs.

Those seven runs decided the match, for sun had made the pitch more awkward after lunch and O'Reilly and Clarrie Grimmett (who had taken 19 wickets between them in Australia's win by 238 runs in the first Test) would probably have reaped a harvest. As it was, Verity's 15 for 104 will be a permanent monument to one of the nicest men who ever played.

The England captain's OBE as he prepares to lead England for a record 42nd time is due recognition of his endurance through stress and toil into a happier situation tomorrow than he has known hitherto. Ever since his highly popular captaincy for two years at Cambridge he has been a leader his own generation have admired, whether in victory or defeat.

It was just four years ago against Australia at Lord's that, when his place was far from sure, he showed himself a thoroughbred with a chanceless innings of 80 and 99 spread over eight hours.

One natural leader of outstanding guts faces another tomorrow. With so much in the balance and facing a desperate situation in all respects, who can withhold the utmost admiration for Mark Taylor's innings at Edgbaston.

Although Colin Cowdrey's life peerage is to be understood as a voice in the Lords for recreational sport generally and schools sport in particular, it is, of course, cricket which can enjoy the reflected glory of the first-ever such honour: Knights, yes, Lords hitherto, no.

In the decade since his presidency of MCC in its Bicentenary year, he has been the quiet, persistent diplomat, working always to preserve what can surely be called, without excess of sentiment, the fellowship of cricket against all the various modern evils.

The idea of referees for international matches and the Code of Conduct by either of which they can fortify the umpires, were his conception.

These, with help from others, and notably Sir Clyde Walcott, were steered through an initially sceptical ICC. It needed the intervention in the nick of time by John Major, briefed by Colin, which brought South Africa back into the ICC fold before the formal abolition of apartheid in 1991. As president of the Lord's Taverners he has worked hard to attract funds for helping cricket clubs and schools and providing transport for the disabled.

The MCC Cricket Sub-Committee under Cowdrey's chairmanship is currently addressing itself to the acute problem of excessive and sometimes continuous noise around the bat.

As the law and ICC regulations stand, the umpires can intervene only if they consider the talk to be intimidatory.

As president of their association, the new peer knows the mind of the umpires when he says: 'They have no wish to add to their function by issuing yellow and red cards. They point out that in the first paragraph of the Unfair Play law, captains are held responsible for the conduct of the game.'

Talking of which, a change is surely due whereby captains at the end of every match report to the Board on the conduct of umpires. Is it not plainly fair that umpires, if they wish to do so, should report on the captains? Noise on the field in all grades of cricket is a pressing subject to which I intend to return.

There is no topic in the game more emotive than coloured clothing. It was introduced in Australia along with white balls and black sight-screens as an accompaniment to night cricket and floodlights. It was introduced here by the TCCB marketing department for the Sunday afternoon 40-over league as a purely commercial gimmick to sell replica shirts, with accent on 'the kiddies'.

Every poll among the watching public has strongly denounced it, nor have I heard it taken up at any other level of English cricket. White remains the universal uniform. Among discriminating followers 'pyjamas' are a switch-off.

I have an idea for the attention of the ECB. For the 1999 World Cup which they are hosting here and for AXA on Sundays, assuming it is decided to continue with the competition, why not a coloured shirt with white trousers? The effect would be distinctly less offensive: we could have a red ball and a white sight-screen – no more pads of purple or pink. I wonder whether the idea will elicit the same official response as when I suggested that sight-screens might be green rather than funeral black: 'Afraid we never thought of it.'

At the risk of denting my no doubt Blimpish reputation, let me add that in these days of anonymous helmets for batsmen and even fielders, I would not be averse to numbers on the backs corresponding on the score card.

Following my recent mention of Andrew Festing's Conversation Piece of famous cricketers which, lacking Geoffrey Boycott's portrayal, hangs in the museum at Lord's in the *Fine Art of Cricket* exhibition, I am pleased to hear from both artist and cricketer that they are due for a sitting this very day.

They are busy people, Mr Festing the more so since he is still less than halfway through a giant conversation piece of members of the House of Lords. He plans to add the figure of the trenchant TV critic when the exhibition closes at the end of the summer.

LADY BRADMAN: OBITUARY
17 September 1997

Lady Bradman who has died at Adelaide after a long illness aged 88, was the wife of Sir Donald Bradman, the great cricketer, and was aptly described in Charles Williams' biography of her husband as 'an Australian heroine in her own right'.

Those who have been at all close to Don Bradman and the world of cricket over their long married life will echo the description.

Jessie Bradman led a life of unswerving devotion, returned in full measure by a man who, though splendidly equipped as a cricketer, yet suffered recurring ill-health, partly, it was thought, psychosomatic, when his constitution became overtaxed. Subservient though she chose to be, she had a mind and will of her own. 'She is my best critic,' he said, 'and my best friend.'

Bradman's impact on the game from his first triumphal tour of England in 1930 to his retirement in 1948 lifted the shy young country boy from Bowral, New South Wales, to a dangerous pinnacle. All at once, he was the popular Australian idol, a situation for which neither his background nor nature prepared him. Although, from the first, meticulous in fulfilling what he regarded as the obligations of his position, Bradman jealously guarded his privacy and keenly resented any invasion of it.

In the early 1930s, young as he was, pulled by competing interests in an era of deep economic depression, Bradman stood in special need of a sympathetic, level-headed wife. He found her in the pretty, dark-haired, blue-eyed companion of his schooldays, Jessie Menzies.

The Bradman and Menzies families had been friends from the couple's childhood. While Don was making his first hundred for Bowral High School, Jessie was winning a gold medal for needlework. Jessie's father, James Menzies of Mittagong, was a bank manager, and his daughter was an employee of the Commonwealth Bank when Don caught up with her again in Sydney.

They became engaged in November 1931 and were married on April 30 1932 at St Paul's, Burwood, on Sydney's outskirts. Canon E. S. Hughes, president of the Victorian Cricket Association and a well-known patron of the game, came up from Melbourne for the ceremony. The bridegroom was 23, the bride younger by 15 months. A crowd which broke police barriers and stood on pews to get a better view gave Jessie a first experience of what she was in for.

Likewise, the compensations of fame followed in the shape of a cricket tour in the New World. The funding for this enterprise, organised by Arthur Mailey, depended on Bradman's presence. He agreed, if Jessie came too. It was an extended honeymoon too concentrated for comfort, but a broadening adventure under the guidance of Mailey, cricketer, artist, writer and loveable bohemian. They travelled by boat via New Zealand and Honolulu to Vancouver and the Rockies, played matches down the east side of Canada and the USA, returning west to Winnipeg en route home. They had celebrity treatment everywhere, met the stars of stage and screen. Don finding the time and energy to score no fewer than 3,782 easy runs with an average of 102.

Back home 'the best partnership of my life' began in Bayview Street, North Sydney, 'Our Don' looking out over 'Our harbour' and (newly completed) 'Our bridge'. Tired by his American tour, worried by a struggle with the Australian Cricket Board on the issue of player-writing, and weakened by a dose of 'flu, Don was declared medically unfit for the First Test against England in what became known as the Bodyline Tour of 1932–33. That he recovered his health and maintained his playing reputation through the remainder of that unhappy series owed much to Jessie, who bravely sat through the continuing uproar.

Her responsibilities increased when, in early 1934, Bradman's writing and broadcasting contract ended and he accepted an offer to join the Adelaide stockbrokers H. W. Hodgetts. Leaving New South Wales, the couple started a new life in the quieter environment of Adelaide, building a pleasant verandahed house in the suburb of Kensington Park, which was to remain their home.

The most serious of Don Bradman's illnesses brought Jessie in haste to England at the end of the Australian tour in 1934. Complications following an emergency appendix operation led to a hospital bulletin to the effect that he was struggling for life. 'It's all right, Don, I'm coming,' Jessie cabled, and the P & O delayed their sailing until she could get aboard. Thanks to her message, the surgeon stated, Don turned the corner and the press could put away their obituaries. While spending the first part of a long convalescence, Don was able to show Jessie 'some of the beauties of England'. If he had not been an Anglophile imperialist before, the kindness lavished on them made a permanent impression.

Four years later, Jessie was back in England once more tending an

invalid, this time having come by prior arrangement at the end of the
tour. At the Oval, after Len Hutton had made his record 364,
Bradman took a turn to relieve his hard-worked bowlers and,
ironically, broke his ankle, turning it over in the deep footmark made
by O'Reilly.

A son, John Russell, was born in July 1939, both a relief and a
blessing, for three years earlier there had been a son who lived only a
few hours. In April 1941, there came a daughter, Shirley June,
diagnosed at birth with cerebral palsy.

The war years were a testing time for Jessie, looking after two young
children and, for many months, a depressed husband: Don's health had
broken down after two years of service, first with the RAAF and on
transfer, with a commission, to the Army School of Physical Training.
The ardours of the latter appointment gave rise to such back pains as to
bring about his discharge from the service on grounds of chronic fibrositis. Hard to bear was the taunt that he had exchanged a post likely to
involve contact with the enemy for one where this was improbable. In
Australia the greater the hero, the more intrusive the searchlight.

The immediate post-war years, busy though they were, were some
of the most fulfilling of the marriage so far. Don led Australia with
success against England both at home and away. As head of his own
firm of stockbrokers, he had achieved financial security, and with his
retirement from cricket in late 1948 they could look forward to the
more private home life to which both aspired.

Knighthood in the New Year Honours of 1949, coupled with his
administrative work for Australian cricket, meant that Don would
never cease to be a public figure. Yet the Bradmans' domestic
contentment was scarcely interrupted until, in 1978, Jessie had to
undergo open-heart surgery. In her old age it was Don who mostly
looked after her, and this, despite a mild stroke in 1996, he continued
to do in her last years when cancer had taken a fatal hold.

CAPTAINS MUST COUNTER UNSPORTING
BEHAVIOUR
7 April 1998

A week in the frenetic world of international cricket can be a long
time. In the euphoria of the two one-day matches in Barbados we
rejoiced in two performances of high quality in several respects, albeit

one was narrowly lost; superlative fielding and a splendid sense of mutual confidence carried over from Sharjah; in particular Nick Knight's batting was a revelation which must bring him back into the forefront of Test reckoning.

The colourful St Vincent weekend was a rude awakening because a greatly improved West Indian performance was so ineptly countered. England, of course, have no counterparts to Brian Lara and Carl Hooper. If both are on song over 50 overs their side will almost certainly win. What was so disappointing was the batting technique, especially against the slow bowling shrewdly managed by Lara, timid lack of footwork and the incessant 'working' of the ball to leg rather than hitting straight. The series is lost but let us hope for a worthier epilogue at Port-of-Spain tomorrow.

My intention is to write an appropriate valedictory piece on Michael Atherton's captaincy, and I will come to it. However, the Test series was so unsatisfactory in crucial ways that no one who knew the game in better times, and who saw one Test in person and much of the rest on TV, can withhold judgment.

Integral to all cricket and beyond all else is the pitch, and the undisputed truth is that the only good one from start to finish of the tour was in Barbados: one out of six, though Antigua played well enough after the first day. With so much depending on Test matches, all concerned, and not least the spectators, are entitled to a perfect surface and I trust the International Cricket Council will voice their disapproval and consider penalties in future cases. The best batsmen and likewise the best bowlers have always developed their skills on plum pitches.

The most serious indictment of the Test series, however, was the undue pressuring of the umpires by constant appealing, some of it quite ridiculous. Worst were cases, tantamount to cheating, of gestures calculated to deceive the umpire. Michael Holding, whose shrewd and fair-minded comment on television throughout the series was a model – he was one of what I took to be a generally well-balanced and impartial team of TV critics – wrote from the heart in a *Sunday Times* article entitled 'This Unsporting Life' giving chapter and verse and censuring both sides.

On the same day Dominic Lawson, editor of the *Sunday Telegraph*, who watched the Barbados Test, was equally disparaging.

On my inquiry, Lord MacLaurin, chairman of the ECB, tells me he went along completely with both these articles. 'We have to ask ourselves what sort of a game we are to pass on to future generations, and especially to the young cricketers now growing up,' he said. 'There is to be another of the annual meetings of the captains of all Test countries at Lord's in May prior to the series against South Africa. The captains' responsibilities must be expressed clearly once more. Only the accepted standards of sportsmanship will be tolerated.'

What sort of a game are we indeed passing on? Andrew Longmore's bitter denunciation of school cricket standards in the new *Wisden* underlines the depth and breadth of the problem. Ian MacLaurin added that David Graveney, chairman of selectors, and David Lloyd, the coach, hold equally firm views.

It may be remarked that despite the serious blemishes the two teams, and especially the two captains, remained on friendly terms – which, of course, was very much to the good. The conclusion, however, must be that each side's conduct was tacitly accepted by the other. Lastly, on this matter, my impression was that Barry Jarman, the referee, whose function was to fortify the umpires and do his best to preserve the spirit of the game, was too tolerant.

And so to Atherton: as I watched him announcing his resignation in Antigua after the last Test, even-tempered, managing a smile, unhistrionic, completely in character, my mind went back to the Lord's Test of 1993 against Australia.

His stock was at such a low ebb that when he went to the wicket against a massive score he must have felt this was probably his last chance. Such was the background to the two innings of 80 and 99 wherein he batted over six chanceless hours. But for the slip turning for the third run which would have given him his hundred. England might even have saved the match.

Gooch had already said that he would resign if and when Australia retained the Ashes, Alec Stewart and Mike Gatting being the favoured contenders. Some people now began to think again. Three Tests later, with Australia three up and two to come, the selectors turned to Atherton, and in his second Test as captain England won a handsome if belated victory, the first in 19 Tests against the old enemy.

England proceeded that winter to West Indies and the usual pummelling by speed. Surviving much intimidation, the captain topped the averages with 56. England surrendered the *Wisden* Trophy series 3–1, the victory being the famous one at Bridgetown wherein Atherton and Stewart put on 171 for the first wicket.

Such has been very much the pattern of things throughout Atherton's almost five years in the job. When assessing England's prospects in the West Indies at this new year I ventured to say that the result of the series would depend upon the degree to which England's faster bowlers could match the West Indies' opening attack. In the event the disparity was depressingly wide and conclusive. A captain can only be as successful as the talent under him allows.

The crucial encounter was that of the first of the Trinidad Tests played on the hastily prepared pitch following the fiasco in Jamaica. Angus Fraser, with 11 for 110 in the match, had to face the fact that he was on the losing side. Against the England team of Sharjah the West Indies could not have made 150. Atherton must have known in his heart that the real chance he had had of winning the rubber had then almost certainly disappeared.

Atherton is phlegmatic by nature but as the tour progressed he must have been weighed down by the ceaseless columns of conjecture surrounding the captaincy. Day after day *The Times* ventured into psychological introspection, measuring up Atherton's worth against several candidates for the succession. While England were fighting their long rearguard in Antigua, *Daily Mail* readers were told 'the match is already so far out of England's reach that it has long since become an irrelevance. Its chief purpose now must be as the final exercise in sorting the men from the boys, of deciding which of the handful of candidates will succeed Atherton.' I found myself sighing for the craft of cricket-writing other, of course, than as in the columns of the *Daily Telegraph*.

In certain instances, apart from his regular under-use of the razor, the late captain has disappointed. He even declined, surprisingly and inexcusably, on his last day to apologise for a silly gesture on the field despite strong pressure to do so. Yet over most of his record span of 52 Tests he has been the bulwark of the side, an indomitable fighter giving them a courageous example to which they have responded with the utmost respect and much affection. From his two taxing years as Cambridge captain he has shown an admirable sense of fairness and sympathy, an instinctive leader of men. These have been sterling virtues in the service of English cricket: may he now enjoy his batting with the burden off his shoulders.

MCC MUST RISE ABOVE ABUSE
OF PRESSURE GROUPS
29 April 1998

The result of the MCC members' vote on whether women should be admitted to the club has engendered, as such emotive issues are apt to do, more heat than light. The club's solicitors advised, when the resolution was being prepared, that it could be dealt with as a regulation, requiring only a majority, rather than a rule change, which needs two-thirds of the votes. Happily, the committee commanded the services of legal authorities of the stature of Lord Griffiths, a Lord of Appeal, Sir Oliver Popplewell, the High Court judge, and the eminent QC, Lord Alexander.

The ironical fact is that although all three happened personally to be very much in favour of the admission of women, they nevertheless all advised the committee to require again a two-thirds majority as had been called for in the referendum of 1991. Although the majority of the current committee also favour the admission, they agreed that after 211 years of history, a decision so fundamental demanded something approaching unequivocal approval.

With 55 per cent voting yes, what now? I assume that the committee may want to make a gesture reflecting the newly acquired majority at next week's annual meeting. I voted in favour of the admission of women as an encouragement towards the spread of the game, assuming that some senior members of the Women's Cricket Association with long service would be admitted to honorary membership. There could be a separate list to which were elected young cricketers qualified to play in the colours of MCC against schools and clubs affiliated to the WCA, which, by the way, is in the course of being incorporated into the England and Wales Cricket Board. Seeing that the Lord's pavilion can hold at the big matches only one in 10 of the 18,000 members, women's accommodation could only be strictly limited.

What I hope is that MCC will rise above the abuse of strident pressure groups. There are more momentous matters concerning the welfare of the game which the ECB and the club need to tackle together.

Anniversaries of one sort or another can usually be found to stand exposure to the spotlight; but it is no ordinary year that takes in the

150th anniversary of the birth of W. G. Grace (July 18) and Sir Donald Bradman's 90th birthday (Aug 26).

Within a few weeks, we shall, in fact, be commemorating the two most famous names in the game's history. The Don, fit and well by latest report, must be prepared for a volley of salutes in books and all forms of media. At Lord's, by a happy coincidence, the one-day match between MCC and the Rest of the World serves a double purpose as MCC's contribution to the Diana, Princess of Wales Memorial Fund and a tribute to W.G. on his birthday: two icons in their respective times unique.

Hubert Doggart's impact on the cricket scene exactly 50 years ago is a more immediate milestone. In his first first-class match, he made 215 not out at Fenner's for Cambridge University against Lancashire – and it was the full county attack. No other Englishman had opened with a double hundred, nor has any repeated it until the 18-year-old David Sales made an astonishing 210 not out for Northamptonshire against Worcestershire in 1996, whereupon last summer for Glamorgan in the Oxford Parks, young Michael Powell made 200 not out.

After 15 years as an active president of the Cricket Society, Doggart has just handed over to an equally hard worker in the service of the game, the *Daily Telegraph's* own Christopher Martin-Jenkins. In his 33rd year as president of the English Schools' Cricket Association, Doggart has also done many years as chairman of the Arundel Castle Cricket Club. Altogether he has had a very busy time since, on his retirement as a Winchester master, he became in turn president and treasurer of MCC. It would be good to think that among more recent generations at all levels there is a ready supply of cricketers prepared to pay in service for the pleasure they have had from the game.

By chance, I have a personal anniversary coming up in that I attended my first annual dinner to the touring side as a member of MCC 60 years ago: eight courses to welcome the 1938 Australians, seven speeches, including an agreeable one without a note from young Bradman.

Earl Baldwin of Bewdley, the president, was in the chair. He was not the first or the last Prime Minister to play or be fond of cricket. Clement Attlee, I recall, frequented Lord's and was said to hover round the House of Commons tape machines only to keep abreast of the cricket scores. Harold Macmillan also patronised Lord's and was proud of the batting for Sussex of his late grandson, Mark Faber. Sir

Alec Douglas-Home, Prime Minister in 1963–64 and President of MCC in 1966–67, was, of course, a first-class cricketer, tried as a fastish bowler by Oxford and Middlesex and a tourist with MCC to South America. John Major, announced as president-designate of his native Surrey, played until injured and is a formidable cricket historian.

And what of Tony Blair? Well, my information from a Fettes master of his day is that he was a promising cricketer in the junior colts before he opted for basketball as being more quickly finished. So what price a conversation? My informant remembers the boy as 'bumptious but amusing'.

WE COULD BE GRATEFUL

27 May 1998

If there is one episode of the Second World War, the memory of which provokes feelings more extreme almost than any other, it is the building of the Burma–Siam Railway by Allied prisoners of war.

To some survivors of that experience, the visit of Emperor Akihito not only re-opens old wounds afresh, but also compels them to demonstrate their everlasting antipathy in public. They are a minority among us, I am sure. The majority keep their thoughts to themselves, however vivid their memories, however much they mourn their comrades who either lie in those beautifully tended cemeteries at Chungkai, Kanchanaburi and elsewhere, or are buried unrecorded in jungle graves.

We cannot, of course, forget either the Battle of Singapore or the grim aftermath and, for those in the 18th Division who landed at the eleventh hour, the stigma of association with one of the greatest disasters in British military history added to the disenchantment. We have to remind ourselves of Churchill's verdict: 'The 18th Division, which after three months on board ship needed time to get their tactical feet, had to be thrown into the losing battle as soon as they were landed.'

The circumstances of our captivity need little elaboration, so often have they been portrayed. Conveyed by cattle-trucks from Singapore up the spine of Malaya to the railhead in Siam, we marched for several days towards and into the jungle where the railway had to be built following the River Kwai. It had to be built against time, by prisoners on a diet largely of rice and vegetables, with primitive tools, urged on by blows and curses by Japanese and Koreans giving free rein to the most sadistic instincts. The death toll from dysentery, malaria and beri-beri was inevitable and horrendous, especially among the youngest other ranks. The officers, engaged mostly in camp construction, had the better of it.

Misery, it might be thought, was complete. Yet there is a limit to unhappiness where men are thrown together in misfortune, as one discovered on that first march. We were no sooner enclosed in the jungle than it began to rain cats and dogs. Drenched to the skin, we slipped and slithered on. Our cup of woe, in every sense, might be thought full and brimming over. But, as if spontaneously, a strange thing happened. The men had borne the heat with terrible curses. Now, suddenly, they began as one to sing. Everyone grew cheerful. Perhaps they were reminded of home. I will never forget the look of utter, fearful mystification on the face of our own particular Japanese guard. We were altogether beyond his comprehension – and so, in general, were all Europeans outside the understanding of all Japanese. And vice versa. Besides the language difference, we were as much a mystery to them as they to us.

We cannot forget, but can we forgive? It is remarkable that some of those who suffered must have found it in their hearts to forgive, and to have made their forgiveness public. Of all the actions by POWs that carried the certainty of extreme torture and the probability of death, the most dangerous to those concerned, just as it was of the greatest value to the POW communities in general, was the setting up and use of radio sets. Eric Lomax, a Scot in the Royal Corps of Signals, was detected by the Kempe-Tai (secret police) and, in his book *The Railway Man*, described in relentless detail sufferings so severe that to read them turned the stomach. After many years, he made touch with the Japanese interpreter Nagasi, his chief torturer, who, burdened with guilt, had built a Buddhist shrine to the fallen at Chungkai. They met, and the final chapter sees them with their wives visiting the museum at Hiroshima, where a relation of Nagasi was a victim.

The two outstanding POW leaders on the railway, who constantly risked death and suffered serious injury standing up to the Japanese – Col Philip Toosey of the Hertfordshire Yeomanry and the famous Australian surgeon Col 'Weary' Dunlop – dedicated their lives after the war not only to the welfare of former POWs, but also to reconciliation with the Japanese. J. L. Wilson, the Bishop of Singapore, whose torture in Changi was told by John Hayter, his chaplain, in his book *A Priest in Prison*, exemplified the virtue of forgiveness in his subsequent ministry. The Lord's Prayer makes the Christian's duty plain. In our case, it is hard duty, made perhaps a little less so by such examples.

As one looks back, there is much for which to be thankful. One saw human nature in the raw, and it made for a common bond of fellowship that helped to sustain us until the glad moment came. Let me quote again the summing up of the American wife of an RAMC officer incarcerated in Changi: 'It wasn't unrelieved gloom. I wouldn't have missed it in terms of human experience. It made me grow up; I became a little less self-concerned.'

I would go along with that.

FOND MEMORIES OF FENNER'S COME FLOODING BACK
10 June 1998

High celebrations are afoot at Cambridge this weekend to mark the 150th anniversary of Fenner's. The university will play one-day matches against an XI raised by Frank Fenner, great-great nephew of Francis Philip Fenner, on Saturday and against MCC, the first opponents in 1848, on Sunday.

Roger Knight, secretary of MCC, will lead a side including the great Majid Khan, Russell Cake and Paul Parker. Derek Randall, the university coach, will have Derek Pringle, Nick Cook and some of the best of the Millfield boys coached by Frank Fenner during his 10 years in charge of cricket at the school. F. P. Fenner, who had a tobacco and cigar business in Cambridge and was a playing contemporary of Fuller Pilch and Alfred Mynn, laid out and rented his matchless sward at the request of the university cricketers, who wanted to get away from the hoi-polloi of Parker's Piece. It has been the most fruitful nursery of talent ever since, with the Oxford Parks not too far behind.

The intention of the England Cricket Board to facilitate centres of excellence at anything up to six universities, with subsequent attachment to counties, within the next few years has important implications for all young cricketers. John Carr, the Board's cricket operations manager, visualises Oxford and Cambridge entertaining the counties as usual, meanwhile, with the possibility of Durham

University also doing so if fixture patterns permit.

There are few first-class cricketers or writers who have the privilege of recording the game for whom the name Fenner's does not provoke nostalgic recollection: Bradman on a fresh May morning bowled for a duck by Jack Davies, sleeves flapping, with an off-break that didn't and his walk back with a half-smile amid a disappointed hush: an imperial 185 by Ted Dexter, 105 of them before lunch, against Lancashire, the evidence of which fuelled my criticism of his omission from MCC's selection for Australia a year later: a mere 30 or so by Michael Bushby against Ray Lindwall which evoked high praise from the Australians.

Such pictures come readily to my mind along with – a sharp descent in quality – my one appearance there for Middlesex, 12 and 26, the first innings abbreviated by a monstrous lbw decision by the elderly university umpire which, of course, I accepted without the very faintest suggestion of dissent.

And so to the major feast-day of the summer, the Lord's Test. Frustrating though the Edgbaston climax was, at least the course of the four days' cricket can only have stimulated interest in the series. No one could have responded with better spirit to a critical situation than Jonty Rhodes and though the latter part of England's first innings was altogether too limp, all followed Alec Stewart's obviously positive orders on Sunday.

Michael Atherton's return to form is, of course, a major blessing as also is Dominic Cork's. As to Darren Gough's deflating injury, we can thank the selectors that they played five bowlers. If, as happened at least six times in the Illingworth regime, England had gone in with only four, they would have been reduced to a trio, as I recall happening at Sydney in 1951. First Trevor Bailey had his thumb broken, then Doug Wright pulled a muscle in getting run out, leaving Alec Bedser, Freddie Brown and a raw John Warr to shoulder 123 overs between them. May Alec prove a luckier captain than FRB!

The world will see the latest embellishment to the face of Lord's, the new Grand Stand now complete and due to be officially opened before play starts on Thursday. The Duke of Edinburgh will perform the ceremony, as he did with the new Mound Stand opposite, cutting the ceremonial tape, meeting those engaged on the project, and returning to the front of the Pavilion, where the England and South African teams will be presented.

Former MCC president twice, patron of the Forty Club and Twelfth Man of the Lords' Taverners, the Duke has always kept in touch with the game which he played pretty well, if infrequently, himself. He once delivered an aphorism never more worth repeating than today. 'Cricket can only flourish if it is played by civilised people with the highest standards of sportsmanship and good humour.'

NB: humour.

Watching at Canterbury recently, Derek Underwood reacted with strong disapproval for so serene a personality to an attempted reverse sweep. He suggests umpires ought to disallow it on the ground that the batsman is in effect batting left-handed, which by convention (though not by law) he may not do without informing the umpire. It is a modern ploy which can arouse strong emotions in some of us who ache to see batsmen showing spinners the full blade of the bat.

There are, of course, more pressing cases for fresh legislation, for instance a curtailing of the growing nuisance of spin bowlers, as a defensive ploy, systematically pitching wide into the rough. The fact is that MCC are engaged on a thorough revision, in time for the Millennium, of the last code of laws published in 1980, their working party being under the distinguished chairmanship of the former president and Lord of Appeal, Lord Griffiths, ex of Cambridge and Glamorgan.

BEARDED GIANT WHO TURNED A PASTIME INTO AN INSTITUTION
18 July 1998

D r Henry Mills Grace had a country practice outside Bristol. In 1831 he married Martha Pocock and they had eight children, four of each. A busy man, he loved cricket, taught his boys to play and had the chief hand in founding the Gloucestershire County Club. The last but one child was William Gilbert, known to the family as Gilbert and to the world to this day, though he has been dead 80 years and more, as W.G.

Born on July 18, 1848. W.G.'s early adulthood coincided with a countrywide explosion of interest in games. The railways had arrived to bring to the cities the pastime which had been popular for centuries in the villages of southern England. In London the Marylebone Cricket

Club had had their headquarters at Thomas Lord's ground in St John's Wood since the year of Waterloo. What was needed was a focal figure, and if ever the hour produced the man it did so in this tall, strapping young Gloucestershireman.

His preponderance as a batsman came astonishingly quickly. Gentlemen v Players, Amateurs v Professionals, were the great matches of the year. He played first against the Players at 17, and the Gents won for the first time in 19 years. Thereafter, for many summers, they scarcely lost. When he was 23, on those still rough pitches, W.G. scored 2,739 runs, a figure unapproached for 25 years. His batting average, 78, was twice that of the next man.

I must content myself with the two high peaks of his career, each testimony to his amazing stamina.

In 1876 he made, in 10 days, 839 runs: 344 v Kent at Canterbury (then the highest score), 177 at Clifton against Notts, and finally, what he rated as his best innings, 318 not out at Cheltenham against Yorkshire. Don't forget all the travel, by train and horse-drawn cab and maybe pony and trap.

Then, a veteran coming up to his 47th birthday, he scored 1,000 runs in May 1895, never done before and only twice since, including his 100th hundred. No one else had made as many as 50. Seizing the public mood, the *Daily Telegraph* raised £5,000 in shillings, MCC over £2,000. There never was such a hero: not even, I think, Bradman. Physically so unalike, these two men at the peak of cricket fame had two qualities in common: great determination and great strength of character.

I have perhaps one credential for celebrating this 150th anniversary, for my father was treasurer of Forest Hill Cricket Club, where W.G. made one of the last of his hundreds, 140 to be exact, in July 1907 for London County. My mother helped to preside over the tea pavilion, and I'm sure she would have had me, her six-month-old baby, with her. The Old Man managed and led London County for a decade or so into the new century, living in Lawrie Park Road, Sydenham, just round the corner from my parent's house some years later.

Fifty-nine in July 1907, W.G. carried a lot of weight, but his energy and appetite for cricket and other games were undiminished – he made a thousand runs and took a hundred wickets in club cricket that year. He was a founder of the Bowls Association, and in 1903 at Crystal Palace had captained England against Scotland in the first of all international bowls matches. He had also, when over 50, taken up golf with enthusiasm, as recorded by Bernard Darwin, who played with him in foursomes at Walton Heath. Ever a keen competitor, Darwin records his playing at Rye with his old Australian crony, Bill Murdoch. They had both been in some trouble when Murdoch called out: 'I've played five'. W.G.: 'I've played two less than you'.

In his charming memoir Darwin wrote: 'He must always be doing something, preferably out of doors, and in the nature of a game or a sport.' From youth, he had embraced all the country pastimes. He was a good shot and a skilful fisherman. Though he became too heavy to ride a horse he followed the beagles until he could no longer run. In a London ice-rink, when about 60, he took up curling. His stamina and energy and combative spirit were extraordinary from youth to old age.

It happened that as a young man I played cricket with quite a few who had played with him. Young cricketers of his latter years – and he always encouraged the young – were in the late 1920s only in their 40s. Cricketers went on playing a lot longer then than now, and I can see some of them still, their trousers held up by the red-and-yellow sashes of MCC: Bell, Slater, Grierson, Beaton, Colman, Bridger: names long forgotten. They all talked to me about W.G. and they all spoke of him with great affection. So did C. B. Fry when he and I wrote for the *Evening Standard* in the 1930s. W.G. came across as a spontaneous, cheerful and wonderfully modest companion. Indeed there seems not to be anyone who knew him who was not devoted.

I underline this fondness and esteem because some of the writing leading up to this anniversary has been curiously ambivalent and in the case of an article in the current *Wisden* positively disparaging in parts. Geoffrey Moorhouse, the author, concluded there was 'not that much to Grace' apart from his skills and his devotion to his family and 'one might identify Grace as suburban man incarnate'. To categorise W.G. as suburban in heart or mentality, in the common understanding of the term, is a ludicrous assessment. It contradicts Darwin, Clifford Bax, H. S. Altham, A. A. Thomson and other reputable biographers who all stress that by birth and upbringing, and in his love of open-air pursuits, he was every inch a countryman.

As to there being 'not that much' about him outside his cricket, Sydney Pardon, the great editor of *Wisden*, in his obituary notice in the 1916 edition, painted a rather different picture: 'Personally, W.G. struck me as the most natural and unspoilt of men. Whenever and wherever one met him he was always the same. There was not the smallest trace of affectation about him. If anything annoyed him he was quick to show anger, but his little outbursts were soon over. One word I will add. No man who ever won such worldwide fame could have been more modest in speaking of his own doings.' That is surely a fair assessment from Pardon, the prince of critics. Note the quick temper and its equally quick recovery. 'Won't have it, can't have it, shan't have it,' he once exploded. He and his hot-headed brother E.M., the coroner, were no paragons, but the stories of W.G. stretching the conventions of the game, indeed at times the laws, concerned the exhibition matches, the benefit games for professionals, wherein he was the star attraction, the one all had come to see. He was a way apart from the public school amateur trained to curb his emotions. The crowds loved his robust spirit.

They also loved the full beard he wore from his youth. Beards, it seems, had become popular in the Crimean War, to keep out the cold. Bax wrote: 'There is no more renowned beard in all humanity.' It helped to make him the best-known man in England after another bearded figure, the Prince of Wales, later Edward VII. At the recent opening of the W.G. Grace Exhibition at Lord's one of the eight Grace descendants, his 93-year-old granddaughter, Mrs Primrose Worthington, told us how as little girls she and her sister were allowed to plait the famous beard, sitting on his knee.

Was he truly an amateur? In that he was openly paid for playing, the answer is a clear no. The fact is he had a status of his own, accepted by all and in particular by the MCC, who shrewdly elected him a member when he was 20 and indeed raised their first testimonial for him before he was 30. At the time MCC's authority in the game was under threat from the professionals. If he had joined them, who knows? There he was, on the one hand studying to be a doctor at the Bristol Medical School, intending to follow his father and three elder brothers in the profession. On the other hand, the game was poised to spread rapidly far and wide. It was about to be lifted on his broad shoulders to unimagined heights of public popularity.

For a decade, medicine took second place to cricket. However, in 1879, following an intense period at St Bartholomew's Hospital, the wretched exams were passed. And when, the following year, the first home Test was staged at the Oval, the first English hundred (152 to be precise) was scored by Dr W. G. Grace MRCS, LRCP.

A word about his doctoring: he became the parish doctor of a mostly poor district of Bristol, and for 20 years devoted himself wholly to his practice in autumn and winter. To help him out in the cricket season he employed not one locum but two. He sat up all night with a woman he had promised to see through her confinement – and made 221 not out at Clifton against Middlesex next day. At Christmas, up to 100 of his patients brought two pudding basins to be filled with roast beef and plum pudding. He was kindness itself to the poor and the young, the well-loved father of the parish. This busiest phase of his life ended when some official re-arrangement of the boundaries led to his improving his financial security by accepting the managership of the new London County Cricket Club.

In that June of 1899, aged 51, he played his last Test against Australia. He now gave all his energies to the London County experiment and actually, 41 years after his first encounter with the Players, played just once more – it was the 85th time – for the Gentlemen against them. In an atmosphere of such euphoria as may be imagined and on his 58th birthday he made 74. Until he tired, they said, his batting was like old times.

The last the public heard from W.G. was a letter to the press in August 1914, a few weeks after the outbreak of war, appealing to all cricketers to come to the aid of their country in its hour of need. With two sons serving – Edgar was to become an admiral – he found the slaughter of youth on the Western Front agonising. In October the following year came the stroke from which he quickly died. His epitaph can be written in the well-worn phrase: he found cricket a country pastime and left it a national institution.

THE DON STILL A HUGE HIT AFTER
ALL THE PASSING YEARS
22 August 1998

In his standard work, *A History of Cricket*, H. S. Altham's chapter entitled 'The Coming of W.G.' salutes the emergence of the game from its ancient pastoral roots. The massive achievements of 'The Champion' heralded the foundation of the county clubs and Test cricket against Australia.

While W.G.'s impact was, of course, unrepeatable, there can be little argument as to the arrival of a new era with the coming of Don Bradman. In April 1930, he arrived in England with Billy Woodfull as one of several promising young cricketers in a side chosen with an eye to the future following England's retention of the Ashes by Percy Chapman's MCC side in Australia. Before the end of that summer it was evident that another phenomenon, a champion of a new order was among us.

Of a little less than average height and build, he had the nimblest of feet and the swiftest of reflexes. There was an apparently effortless rhythm about his play, a tireless concentration. He was in every way the complete batsman.

For the benefit of the generations who have been born to the game since Bradman's retirement in 1948, here for digestion are a few facts. His Test aggregate of runs, 6,996, is exceeded among Australians by only three men, the most successful of whom had almost twice as many innings. His Test average is 99.94. only three other batsmen in history have achieved as much as 60. His total of 29 Test hundreds (19 of them against England) has been exceeded only by Sunil Gavaskar, who played nearly three times as many innings. He is the only man who has scored over 300 Test runs in a day. His 974 in 1930 is far and away the most scored in a Test series.

It was in that first of his four English summers that I first saw him. He preferred batting in England, as successive opponents rued to their cost, because the light was softer and the turf more yielding than at home, as the figures below show.

The most detailed analysis of his batting, from his arrival aged 19 to his retirement at 40, is to be found in His Honour B. J. Wakley's *Bradman the Great*, published in 1959. There one may learn not only that he made hundreds (117 of them) in more than a third of his innings, but that of his 338 innings 16 were ducks while 37 were upwards of 200. He was run out only four times, only once after he reached the age of 21. He scored almost half as fast again as his partners. He made all his runs at 42 per hour, and his average stay at the wicket was 2hr 14min. Hedley Verity and Clarrie Grimmett dismissed him 10 times each, Sir Alec Bedser eight. And so on. And so on.

It is possible to imagine that in other circumstances a robust, extrovert young man might have endured, indeed greatly enjoyed, the sudden onset of his fame. Don, of course, was appreciative of the acclaim of the crowds and shrewd enough to realise that the success might enhance his financial prospects. Yet neither his background nor his personality prepared him for his sudden ascent to undreamt heights of sporting stardom.

Australia was at a low ebb, unsure of herself and with high unemployment reflecting the worldwide depression. If ever a country needed a national hero, Australia did and she found it in this unsophisticated country boy. Don had come to England as an employee of a sports goods firm, which on the return of the 1930 team to Fremantle exploited their man for all they were worth. While the ship bore Woodfull's team slowly to the eastern states, he was taken ahead by train, being hailed to his embarrassment by vast crowds and mayoral receptions normally given to returning teams in Adelaide, Melbourne and Sydney. Don, then a non-smoking tee-totaller, had not mixed much with his touring colleagues. Imagine what they thought of him now!

Happily for this all-too-public, all-too-private young man, also awaiting him was his childhood sweetheart, Jessie Menzies. They married in Sydney in April 1932, and she remained his inspiration and companion in all their long life together.

Notice that the marriage shortly preceded the MCC tour to Australia of 1932–33, wherein amid bitter controversy England's bodyline tactics were devised to counter the prolific Bradman of 1930 – devised and succeeded to the extent of lowering an average of 139 to a human 56. The spotlight, needless to say, never left the Don, through the eight Australian summers and three more tours of England that lay ahead.

He was the dominant figure in every series and Australia won them all, except for the one shared in England in 1938. The only brief challenge to his supremacy came with his appointment to the captaincy in 1936. At the end of the 1934 tour of England, he was struck down with a poisoned appendix and for days, threatened by peritonitis, his life was in danger.

In consequence, he could play no cricket in 1934–35 and, Woodfull having retired, the popular Vic Richardson led a successful tour of South Africa in 1935–36. The players, and in particular Bill O'Reilly and Jack Fingleton, were disgruntled when the Australian Cricket Board chose Bradman for the series against the MCC team led by G. O. Allen. After losing the first two Tests, the little man won the remaining three, making 677 runs in four successive innings.

At the Oval in 1938, in the Test wherein England squared the series with their biggest victory, having seen Len Hutton beat his Test record of 334, and with England's score 887 for seven, Don gave himself a bowl with leg-breaks and in the pit formed by O'Reilly's deep footmarks, fractured a bone in his ankle. It was an irony in two senses.

The war years were for Don a sad, frustrating experience. Commissioned as a supervisor in the army school of physical training, the man who had been apparently tireless through all his hours at the wicket broke down completely in the face of the rigorous demands of PT. After several spells in hospital, he was discharged from the army in June 1941. In days when muscular and psychosomatic illness was a less expert branch of medicine, the verdict was fibrositis. There was nothing for it but a resumption of his stockbroking business in Australia.

After so dramatic a mixture of triumph and trauma, Bradman's post-war life has followed a more mellow and fulfilling course. Seeing him in the Adelaide nets, plainly short of fitness after further back troubles, on a cool spring evening in October 1946, I wondered whether, at 38, he could fight his way back to anything like his form of the Thirties. Gradually, much of the old mastery returned, and with it a maturity in leadership which blended and bound a Test side too formidable for England's post-war resources. Now, as not before, he was fortified by the affection as well as the admiration of his side.

So it remained when, after the 10-year gap, Australia toured England once more in 1948. Before a ball was bowled, Don made a broadcast speech so eloquent, so full of feeling for the sufferings of war, yet touched with humour, that the BBC delayed the nine o'clock news so that it could run its course. The immediate result was sackfuls of mail which it could truly be said has been flowing every since. All that fate denied him was the four runs in his last Test which would have left him with an average of 100. In every way the tour was a personal celebration, on the field and off, culminating in one last hundred at Lord's on the eve of his 40th birthday.

Since his retirement, which was immediately followed by knighthood, Sir Donald Bradman has combined continual service to cricket with a full family and business life. A selector almost uninterruptedly until 1971, and an Australian board member likewise with two periods in the chair, his has been the advice most eagerly sought on the game's major issues. There is no better or more readable instruction manual than his *The Art of Cricket*. Jealous as ever of his privacy, he has contributed forewords in plenty, answered (at least until recently) every letter by return, written signatures by the thousand every week.

Today, when the integrity of the game is so much under threat from market forces, the services of old players in the ways open to them is specially important. In this, as in other respects, the Don has fulfilled all demands. He has even seriously considered, and only reluctantly declined, more than one nomination for the presidency of MCC.

When the care of Jessie, his wife, through a long illness from cancer ended in her death a year ago, one wondered how he would face up to life without her. In fact, his resilience yet again answered the call. He resumed playing golf and has beaten his age round the Kooyonga links, and enjoys daily visits from his son John.

On his 90th birthday next Thursday, when a company of 1,300 will sit down to a dinner in Adelaide in aid of Bradman charities, he will be dining quietly a mile or two away, at home with his family.

Bradman's English summers

	Innings	Not Out	Runs	Average	100s
1930	36	6	2960	98.66	10
1934	27	3	2020	84.16	7
1938	26	5	2429	115.66	13
1948	31	4	2428	89.92	11

SRI LANKA'S MARVELLOUS SUCCESS IS WORTHY OF SALUTE
2 September 1998

The subject that is imperative today is the warmest congratulations to Sri Lanka for as conclusive a victory as could be imagined, the details of which to English eyes and ears hold sad, salutary lessons. Our opponents confirmed at the Oval that the uninhibited freedom of their batting, which brought them victory in the World Cup, expresses their enjoyment of the game as naturally at Test level as at any other.

In these sophisticated, deeply analytical days of 'counselling' and over-emphasis on physical fitness their attitude was refreshing to a degree. Nor was it any surprise to those of us who were struck by the great zest for the game at all ages when, during our journeys by sea to Australia, we stopped off for a one-day match at Colombo. As the West Indies and Pakistan have enlarged the Test scene since the war, so now have Sri Lanka to the great benefit of cricket.

As for the performance of Muralitharan, one could only marvel and admire as perfect an exhibition of the art of slow bowling as has ever been seen in this country. Shane Warne is a master of back-of-the-hand wrist-spin. This Sri Lankan uses an extraordinarily flexible wrist to baffle from a model length with constant changes of flight and degree of spin.

The one proper regret English supporters can have is that the pitch produced was almost guaranteed to be of the least benefit to Stewart's fast and fast-medium attack. They have, however, another self-inflicted wound to stomach in the surly comments of coach David Lloyd which once again in defeat have caught him completely off balance.

Let me add one thought for future enlargement in the light of the utter paucity of English slow bowling as emphasised in the winter tour selections. Sir Alec Bedser tells me that when he asked two eminent Australians, Arthur Morris and Neil Harvey, what should be done to improve English cricket they answered emphatically: 'Take the covers off the pitches.'

None of cricket's perennial problems, important though several are, is so crucial as the threat by TV coverage to the authority of the umpire. A week ago Ted Dexter declared in these columns that the job of umpiring Test cricket with honour and dignity has become impossible. The views of a great cricketer still close to the modern game demand all respect and his comment reflects a general depression among followers. But the umpire's function must not be made impossible, for the conduct of the game can only be regulated by the umpires, supported by the captains, and with the ultimate arbitration of the referee.

Cannot the International Cricket Council bring umpires more closely into the scheme of things? They could do so with higher remuneration and full security, with continued National Grid sponsorship if available. The maintenance of their status is essential to preserve discipline on the field, in collaboration with the referee. Let the third umpire continue to decide on camera evidence, close run-out cases, disputed catches and the comparatively minor matter of stops on the boundary. These are measurable matters. Where I believe the bowler's umpire must continue to make up his own mind is on the matter of lbw: as one reader put it, the only camera that matters is the retina in the umpire's eye. Here, surely, his eye and instinct must prevail, the batsman, of course, getting the benefit of the doubt.

If any amateur theorist is sufficiently interested, anyone bowling towards three parallel strings stretched end to end from the stumps may be surprised, for instance, by the fact that a good length ball, delivered from the middle of the bowling crease which pitches on the off stump and pursues a straight course will only hit middle-and-leg. If it swings or turns in it will almost certainly miss leg stump. By contrast, any bias from leg to off has the angle in its favour. It is a matter of geometry.

After which diversion let me add that the ICC must ensure that the list of Test umpires, most of all for series-deciders, is confined to those few who have earned the confidence of players and referees. Such a criticism would have precluded the appointment of Javed Akhtar.

Opinion is sharply divided on the decision of the MCC Committee to seek a third vote and the second within six months on the admission of women to membership. Having voted in favour in February, though my inclination was certainly to allow the dust to settle until the Millennium, I naturally hope the resolution goes through. Tony Wreford and his working party have produced a thorough presentation, the important difference this time being the emphasis on the prospect held out of women cricketers playing under the colours of MCC against girls' and women's schools, universities and clubs. MCC's admirable new ground at Shenley in Hertfordshire would be ideal for this purpose. The stimulus to women's cricket would be reflected in an increase in the number of games-minded teachers to coach in mixed schools both public and state.

The volley of critical letters in last Thursday's *Daily Telegraph* surely emphasised the deep and powerful instinct against political correctness. By contrast, the word from Lord's is that early membership indications seem to be favourable. We shall see.

Need I say that MCC Members and all who know how much the club does for cricket will take for what it is worth the unadulterated insult voiced by a 'fellow' columnist on these pages on Monday.

I write as a long-standing supporter of women's cricket, an admirer of the stately captain, Molly Hide, and one who saw poor Betty Snowball at the Oval against Australia run out for 99. There is a pleasing grace among the best players, and their manners might be a good example to – well, you name them.

IMBALANCE OF ENGLISH SUMMER
26 October 1998

And so to a future wherein the national summer sport will no longer be seen, after more than half-a-century, on the national corporation's networks; when the rulers of the English game have committed themselves to an unparalleled programme of international cricket each English summer; and when money and player-power tend more and more to rule the game.

There was an MCC president, a former county captain with deep cricket roots, who used to sigh that every change within his time had been for the worse.

Without going quite so far as that, one recalls egregious follies perpetrated by would-be reformers aimed at 'brightening' the game. It is hard to believe that England kindly smoothed the path to victory of the 1948 Australians by the availability of a new ball in English cricket every 55 overs.

Fifty-five! (the number is now 80). Later on in county matches they actually banned the follow-on. One could continue.

Let me not be misunderstood. I am far from condemning out of hand the England and Wales Cricket Board's momentous switch to Channel 4 or all the other nostrums put up by sundry sources. However, there is a downside to most decisions made or projected demanding of more attention than they have received. There are, alas, too many writers making their living from the game with no true love for it who rubbish the status quo, yet venture nothing in the way of constructive criticism.

Having shared with the late Brian Johnston the privilege and responsibility of introducing the early years of cricket on television, the switch from the BBC and the future presentation on TV is naturally close to my heart. Equally significant topically, however, is the news that from the year 2000 the ECB have agreed not only to host the increased number of seven home Tests each summer, but to stage 10 one-day internationals in a triangular mid-season tournament.

And whence are coming the cricketers from whom the England selectors are choosing for this plethora of international cricket? From the counties, of course, whose championship will be diminished by the reduction to three weekends free from Tests, internationals and cup finals out of the 14 available in the heart of the summer, plus six at the beginning and end. This would be fewer if the regional idea is adopted. This possible divisional early-season affair, advanced by some good judges, would bring face to face most of the best players, but in a bloodless battle wherein only individual performance mattered. With results immaterial it would be cricket in a vacuum.

The chief executive of the ECB, Tim Lamb, admits frankly that the increase in international cricket, which further imbalances the English summer, was the factor that added many millions to the Sky-Channel 4 contract as from the Millennium.

He points to the fact that all the extra money will be poured back into the counties, both through their development boards and especially for the benefit of those grounds such as those of Hampshire, Durham and Somerset where big projects are underway. There will also be the expensive up-grading of a seventh Test ground. Cardiff? Chester-le-Street? Canterbury? Several have their merits.

As to Sky's coverage of the triangular one-day tournament stretching over a month in June and July, with each country playing the other two concerned *three* times each, the news is that three of the England matches will be played day-night under lights. Lamb underlines the attraction of these games to those coming from work and also to schoolchildren and undergraduates.

Of the 17,000 spectators at Edgbaston for an evening Axa match – three times the average gate – a quarter said they had not seen a county match before. Who can do other than applaud this day-night development bringing new audiences – provided they are not exposed to an overdose of cheap gimmicks?

Reverting to the championship, the England captain, on the eve of his departure to Australia, saw fit to say he wanted not only less cricket but the counties reduced to twelve. The ECB chief executive naturally emphasised that there was no suggestion afoot to reduce the numbers and added emphatically that the ECB management had no plan to decrease the amount of championship cricket. That was a welcome statement, for there are lesser voices singing a different tune. So let me reiterate: the only way for an ambitious young cricketer to develop and exhibit his technique and temperament alike is in the stern, competitive atmosphere of the championship. Lessen his opportunities there and standards can only recede.

There can be few close followers who received the news of BBC TV's complete elimination from the cricket scene in favour of a commercial channel without surprise and shock. To most, I suspect, especially of the older generation, it will be a matter for regret. The average viewer surely felt that the BBC, with its tried and trusted commentators, did the job pretty well. In the favourable post-war climate the BBC undoubtedly played a major part in the great broadening of national interest in cricket, at first chiefly on sound radio but progressively also on TV.

From 1946 onwards Johnston and I perhaps complemented each other on TV reasonably well, I the technical, tactical half, he supplying the more jokey element. At Headingley once I had the mike when a man came into view for a few seconds with a lavatory seat around his neck. I, poor dimwit, could not think of the *mot juste*: Brian, frustrated, would have made a meal of it.

Memory of those early TV days remains fresh. Three cameras we had to play with as against today's twenty or so: No recording, no zoom lens, of course. Cramped space, summaries in the rain – very popular with the viewers they were. Don't repeat what they can see for themselves. Identify when in doubt. Always remember you are talking not to the wide world but to one person at a time – the golden rule for all broadcasters.

Gradually as TV gained in popularity, cricket's claim to air-time became better accepted, the defining moments being, in the summer of 1953: First and foremost the Coronation and then, two months later, England at the sixth attempt, covering all but twenty years, winning back the Ashes at the Oval. Happily we were on air at the glorious moment when the immortal pair, Edrich and Compton, knocked off the runs. Of the 130-odd home Tests before my retirement I broadcast 50 on TV, many on both channels.

When Peter West, Denis Compton and Richie Benaud came on to TV I performed more on what from 1957 became *Test Match Special*. It's an old story how in 1970 the BBC, without a word and to his fury, dropped Johnston from TV work, thus unwittingly allowing him to establish on *TMS* a legendary reputation which culminated in that memorable Thanksgiving in Westminster Abbey.

Let us switch now to Channel 4, which takes over Test cricket following the BBC's final coverage of the World Cup. Whichever production company they choose come in at a highly critical time when advanced camera techniques, illustrated on the screen and visible to players and crowd, threaten the umpires' authority. No commercial deal is more important than protecting the position of the umpire at all levels. In international and first-class cricket the status and security of the umpires is the prime duty of the ICC and ECB.

This brings me to the crucial role of the commentator. The viewer needs – and the game needs – former cricketers of high reputation whose knowledge and judgment are beyond dispute. Tony Lewis, for so long BBC's senior presenter, has retired to assume the presidency of MCC. Richie Benaud has built over more than 30 years a unique standing while David Gower combines a winning personality with the authority of a great player. Nothing would do so much to reconcile BBC followers as to recruit these two famous figures to Channel 4.

If Channel 4 can win younger viewers to cricket as they hope, that's fine; but if they try to portray the tense, drawn-out drama of a five-day Test as essentially 'thrilling and exciting' (to quote their chief executive's unfortunate opening comment) they will drive viewers to retain the picture, cut off the sound and turn for comment to BBC's *Test Match Special*.

COUNTIES FRACTURE CENTURY-OLD FRAMEWORK
5 December 1998

The truest lovers of cricket like to think that the evolving art of our great English summer game survives the crises which from time to time shake its foundations.

Such a one is now upon us and we optimists have to support the new order and encourage what seem to be its possible benefits.

Good things may come which are as yet unknown.

Yet there is no disguising from those of whatever generation with the knowledge of history that the England and Wales Cricket Board have fractured the County Championship which has produced our great cricketers, batsmen, bowlers and all-rounders since before it grew almost to its present size in 1895.

From Grace, Fry and Ranji to Hobbs, Woolley and Hammond: to Hutton and Compton: to May, Barrington, Dexter and Gower: of bowlers from Barnes and Richardson to Tate and Larwood: to Bedser, Laker, Trueman and Underwood: of all-rounders from Rhodes, Hirst and Jackson: J. W. Hearne and Ames: to Bailey, Knott, Illingworth and

Botham. Were they not sufficiently 'competitive'? The hall of fame rolls on.

Lord MacLaurin, the ECB's strong chairman, tells us that the new 'harder-edge competition' will 'raise the game's profile and improve its quality'. One good prospect for two divisions is that it will reputedly enthuse the young. Indeed, we shall all be on the edge of our breakfast chairs discovering whether our favourite county is heading Upstairs or Downstairs. The absence of the best in seven Tests and as many one-day internationals, the crucial chances of weather and pitches, lottery declarations, and the inevitable conflicts of interest between the pull of county and country in the selection of players: these factors surely make this deep gap far from ideal.

Here is a comical illustration. Neither of the last two champions, Leicestershire this year, Glamorgan in 1997, could have won the title, since both, on the previous year's results, would have been languishing in the lower divisions.

The 18 counties are to be treated equally as regards the annual hand-out, without which few could survive. That is one decision to applaud, and here is another. The present registration system limiting the transfer of players is to remain unaltered. No doubt the most important factor was the hidden agenda item, the likelihood of substantial financial sponsorship. The fact that the regulation ordains as many as three up, three down, probably decreases the danger of a football-style transfer market.

I imagine these are things which influenced the almost unanimous vote (15–1 with three abstentions), an extraordinary volte-face from the previous vote, 12–7 in favour of the continuation of the current championship, which will be contested next summer for the last time. On Thursday the MCC, not being directly concerned, sensitively abstained.

What to my mind is a great pity is that the dividing line for the year 2000 is to be drawn on the results of the 1999 championship alone, despite the major interruption of the World Cup rather than taking the average positions over the past two summers and the next.

These large gatherings, attended by so many representatives, are proverbially difficult to control: the more credit therefore to David Morgan of Glamorgan who, my spies tell me, chaired the meeting admirably.

I must revert to the media climate of the last few years (not by any means excluding the 'heavies') before leaving the past and accepting the challenges of the future. If the dedicated, unpaid work of county committees and executives had been acknowledged and been in the interest of their members and loyal supporters, we would have had respect for their opinions. What hurt was the parrot-cry, latched onto by ignorant men eager to criticise, of selfish dinosaurs not concerned with England's interests. What piffle! Richie Benaud with his unparalleled experience of English and Australian cricket, corrected this line of thinking of the counties being just a production line for Test cricketers. He has written that when he played and captained New South Wales his sole ambition and effort was to win the Sheffield Shield for his State. They never gave a thought to selection for Australia. It was the selectors' job to estimate their ability and their temperament.

We all want a strong England team. Of course we do. But Benaud's philosophy must be ours. The championship must prosper on its own if it is to be an effective nursery. There is ludicrous rubbish in the air that the current championship is 'meaningless' and that the two divisions are the panacea which will prevent England ever being bowled out again at Perth for 112.

The worst damage to English cricket was when the decision to cover the pitches scotched the experiment in progress of a championship mixture of some three and some four-day matches. If the covers had been tried for four days and not brought in also for three days, the merits of both over a few seasons would have been tested.

As it was, county captains as a rule mutually decided on two days of sparring and a declaration and hectic chase on the third. Many old cricketers believe that improvement in technique, marred by one-day cricket and bats like logs, and especially the arts of spin, will only return if a measure of covering comes back.

The importance of the umpires' role will become more important as 'more competitive' today means more aggressive – and more intimidation by bowlers. Too many of our young cricketers in or near the England XI, are free to say and write as they like, talk tough, words made foolish as soon as they are uttered. They even seem to take for granted the puerile and offensive habit of sledging, practised almost universally in Australia.

England's improvement will only come gradually. Meanwhile let the present generation of first-class cricketers be aware that they are inheritors of players mostly modest and with a rich brand of dry humour, admired by the public for the men they were. Their instinct was reflected by village cricketers and upwards: that generosity is at the heart of true sportsmanship: in defeat as in victory.

Postscript. Rain at Brisbane, which probably saved England from defeat in the First Test, was no more than a down-payment for the defeats of 1946 and 1950. In the first instance our hopes of saving the game were washed away by rain and hail, the noise of which on the corrugated-iron stand roof seemed to prelude the end of the world. In 1950 Freddie Brown's side bowled out Australia for 228 on a plumb pitch on the first day, one of the best performances I ever saw in Australia. Thereupon England, after torrential rain, had to bat on the most horrible, impossible of pitches. We generally do better at Adelaide.

OXFORD DOORS OPEN TO TWICE AS MANY TALENTED CRICKETERS
22 *January 1999*

Oxford University Cricket Club are the first to bring about a positive response to the English Cricket Board's plan to institute so-called Centres of Excellence, where young cricketers of promise can combine academic courses with the best facilities for improving their game and playing as a unit.

The OUCC have done so in a radical way by opening their doors to the former polytechnic which has become Oxford Brookes University.

The Brookes' standard of entry is more flexible than that of the Oxford Colleges, and thus can more easily accommodate the scholar-sportsman.

In size, the ancient university and Oxford Brookes are almost identical at 15,000 students each, the latter being situated on Headington Hill, the territory of the late Robert Maxwell. The combined XI will therefore draw from double the number of undergraduates, half of them from, shall we say, a friendlier climate.

Oxford Brookes will, of course, have all the facilities of The Parks, and for first-class fixtures the combined team will be known in the plural as Oxford Universities.

While an old Blue whom I told about the new arrangement had recovered from the shock, he said disapprovingly that this would take the pressure off the colleges to relax their entry system.

The response of Dr Simon Porter, the senior treasurer and permanent officer of the OUCC, to this natural reaction was to say that the colleges are unanimous in resisting all *mens sana* appeals. The traditional ideal of the gifted all-rounder, as exemplified by C. B. Fry, H. G. Owen-Smith, J. G. W. Davies, Hubert Doggart, Michael Brearley and many more is apparently 'old hat'. The other day Cambridge turned down an outstanding schoolboy cricketer with four A-levels.

Long gone, of course, are the days when Dr W. T. S. Stallibrass of Brasenose and Philip Landon, of Trinity, vied with one another to secure the best of the public school cricketers. Until recently, however, at least a few colleges found room for the all-rounder: according to Dr Porter no more. With the backing of such recent presidents as Lord Cowdrey, C. A. Fry, A. C. and M. J. K. Smith, the OUCC were motivated by the urgent desire to preserve first-class cricket in its historic and most beautiful setting.

Over the full spread of years no nurseries of talent can compare with The Parks and Fenner's. It must matter to some even in this egalitarian age that there have been 120-odd Test cricketer Blues, of whom 30 have been captains of England, 12 of other Test countries.

What then of the Cambridge response to the ECB initiative? They have not been idle but, as there is no Cambridge near-counterpart to Brookes, Professor Kenneth Siddle, Cambridge's senior treasurer, tells me they are aiming at a broader field, offering the facilities of Fenner's including the coaching to the several East Anglian establishments which now have the status of universities.

What is to happen about Blues? Here at any rate the older generation can be assured that they will be awarded only to members of Oxford and Cambridge, and only they will contest the 155th University Match beginning on June 25. It is by a long way, the oldest first-class fixture in the Lord's calendar. The ECB's director of operations, John Carr, an Oxford Blue by the way and son of Donald, a former captain, confirms the board's thinking as regards Centres of Excellence. 'We want these centres to attract men who will emerge as accomplished cricketers with university degrees,' he says. 'After all, there's life after cricket.'

The six centres will compete with one another, and, in due course, individuals will rejuvenate the counties. There will still be limited opportunities early in the season for some of the centres to play against the counties. I imagine that the concept will be welcomed by the

Professional Cricketers' Association.

John Carr finally sprang a considerable surprise. He tells me that no fewer than 21 British universities have applied to become Centres of Excellence. Most can have only outside chances of being named, for such as Durham and Loughborough have well-established clubs to line up with Oxford and with Cambridge.

However, the field is open and the number is encouraging evidence that, despite rival attractions, cricket still has a place in the hearts and minds of the young.

Many of riper years will regret the decline of Oxford and Cambridge cricket which has brought this state of affairs about, and will fall back on their memories.

I recall on a fresh spring day at Fenner's a peerless piece of batting by Ted Dexter against Lancashire, 185 in all, 105 of them before lunch. Cambridge were generally in the ascendant in the Fifties, fielding sides with four or five – and, one time, six – members of which went on to play Test cricket.

There was a famous day in The Parks when, on an admittedly awkward pitch, Oxford's George Chesterton and Michael Wrigley bowled New Zealand out twice to their only defeat of the tour.

For sheer artistry nothing rivalled the 142 made for Oxford in the post-war euphoria by Martin Donnelly before crowds at Lord's which on the first two days totalled 23,000.

WHEN RUGGER AND AMATEURISM WERE THE NAMES OF THE GAME
8 April 1999

The Five Nations Championship dates from 1905–06 when France joined the four home countries, who had hitherto competed just for the Triple Crown. The game has grown around the annual battles of the five and in this sense alone the 1998–99 season marks the end of an era.

There was, however, a break in the sequence from 1931 until the Second World War because the French understanding of amateurism, to put it politely, differed considerably from that of the home unions. Unfortunately, by a ridiculous error, the announcement of the break as from the next season was made before the France–England match was due to be played in Paris.

Though only 24, I was in my fourth season as rugby football

correspondent of the *Evening Standard* (a very premature appointment) and my memory of the match is vivid enough. England emerged on to the field to a roar of derision which never weakened from the Paris crowd. The referee was Albert Freethy, rated as the best of the day. It was he who had sent off Cyril Brownlie when the 1924–25 All Blacks came to Twickenham and the future Edward VIII had tried in vain to have him allowed back at half-time.

England led in Paris for most of the game until the second of two French drop kicks went over to make the score 14–13 to them and Mr Freethy, gratefully no doubt, blew his final whistle. I can see Peter Brook going over from a line-out and Brian Pope, the scrum-half (now president of Royal St George's Golf Club) scoring what looked a perfectly good try. Both were disallowed. Freethy never refereed another international.

At the dinner afterwards the company sat through a speech by Adrian Stoop, telling of his personal recollection of England's nine tries on that first English visit to Paris in 1906. As it was being translated the glances conveyed the atmosphere: 'The English, these men who have ostracised us, are they human?'

Happily the night was saved by the England captain, Carl Aarvold, a young man just down from Cambridge. Speaking in French, he thanked the home team for a sporting match. He said he always enjoyed playing against France and hoped soon to be doing so again. Uproarious applause! And an elementary lesson in PR for young EWS.

The men of power in rugby football in those days recalled how their fathers had fought for pure amateurism in the 1890s when 22 foremost clubs in Yorkshire and Lancashire had disagreed on the issue of broken time. They formed the Northern Union which became the Rugby League.

Amateurism was their religion but one felt at every club dinner that the sermon on the spirit of the game might have been taken as read. Good men they were, but terribly earnest. Such men as Sir William Ramsay, Cyril Gadney and Gus Walker (otherwise known as Air Chief Marshal Sir Augustus, etc) knew the game as rugger and were no less jealous of its traditions. The Scottish game was run by one, Jock Aickman-Smith who stood out in the 1920s against the otherwise universal numbering of players: 'Our men are no cattle.'

The rugger world of those days was essentially friendly, hospitable, if too hearty for some. The London club players, high and low, trained on their grounds once during the week and most had their fill of beer on Saturday evenings. Twickenham was filled by the clubs at ten shillings a seat, or five shillings (I think) standing at the south end. The South African Springboks, dedicated, large and humourless, swept the board in 1931–32: not so the third All Blacks of 1935–36, who suffered their first defeats. At Cardiff, Wilfred Wooller was the hero in the last moments. It was the most emotional and exciting match of any sort I ever saw. One was wafted back to the Angel Hotel on a wave of pure happiness.

Then at Twickenham England had an emphatic win by 14–0. Alex Obolensky, 'the flying Prince', scored two tries, the second being the famous slanting one which he began on the right wing and ended midway between the goal and the left corner-flag. Alex, whose lunch before a match was reputed to consist of a dozen oysters, was the fastest man I ever saw on the football field, bracketed with the Harlequin and England wing, J. C. Gibbs. The universities loomed much larger on the scene then than now. The England XV contained four Oxonians and one Cantab.

Another difference was the role and status of the Old Boy clubs, the Old Merchant Taylors being at the forefront with the Millhillians and Cranleighans pressing them hard. I touch-judged for the latter when we won at Swansea and when we beat Bath two years running. When, in 1937, England beat Scotland for the first time at Murrayfield (which had opened in 1925) the hero at fly-half was an OC, Jeffrey Reynolds. What did for the Old Boys was the combination of the six-year war break and the great spread of university education.

The game today, which at its best can be so spectacular and exciting, has been made faster and utterly different by two law changes. One law deleted was the need to play the ball with the foot after a tackle, the other was the freedom to find touch from anywhere. A third, if lesser, factor was the composition of the ball. It required much skill and strength to convert a wet and greasy leather ball over the bar from the touchline. To kick goals from anywhere with a plastic ball carefully teed up is a different operation.

The increase in the pace has demanded a higher standard of fitness and stamina, which in turn means many more hours of training. For professional men maybe with young families, this was asking too much. When Captain Henry Rew of the Army and Blackheath went sick on the morning of the match at Cardiff, John Daniell, chairman of the selectors rang Bristol docks for Sam Tucker, a stevedore, who arrived by air in the nick of time. When the stockbroker and the artisan could pack down together, rugger could be claimed as a game for all classes.

Apart from half a dozen or so, the public schools played the rugby rather than the association code and some of their old boys naturally won top honours. But so did the great clubs of the West Country, the Midlands and the North. Today few professional players come from the old background. For better or worse there will be no more Russian princes or Recorders of London (Sir Carl Aarvold) to decorate the scene.

I hear, though, that the match is still only part of the weekend. Saturday nights are not so very different from the old rugger days even if the name of the game is obsolete.

LARA NEEDS PERFECT BLEND
21 April 1999

The season just begun is beset with problems and impending crises, at home and internationally. All the more reason, then, to start this column on a recent event which merited universal pleasure and applause. I mean, of course, the Barbados Test, wherein the West Indies achieved one of the most extraordinary victories in Test History.

I cannot recall a match with more frequent and exciting shifts of fortune, the prime example of the glorious uncertainty which is the oldest cliché in the book. Few crowds can match the Bajans in their knowledge and critical appreciation of cricket – hence Kensington Oval being as full on the fifth day as on the first.

How many Test sides have scored 490 in their first innings and lost the match? According to statistical expert, Robert Brooke, a higher score than 490 has been played by the losers more often than one might suppose, in fact eight times – four involving England.

I saw two instances myself, both at Headingley. The loss to the 1948 Australians was a calamitous failure of will that is still hard to bear thinking of. Bradman, I later discovered had ordered the team's transport to be ready by mid-afternoon; he and Arthur Morris, helped by several unaccepted chances, made 301 together and Australia scored 404 in the day to win by seven wickets.

At Headingley in 1967, England and India both scored more than 500, the former winning easily.

At Bridgetown last month, the result was the more remarkable in the light of West Indies' recent history and that, following the Australians' 490, they lost their first six wickets for 98. But not that of Lara, whose magnificent double-hundred brought victory in Jamaica. Could he conjure another miracle? He did and in doing so gave an enormous fillip to Test cricket, the genuine article.

The modern media must have its heroes and villains, one or the other, and in Lara's case the transformation came in record time. The coordination of eye and limb worked in perfect union, the footwork and suppleness of wrist added up to perfect balance at the moment of impact. I wonder how it is that so many left-handers exude grace and beauty: Sobers, Harvey, Gower and this wonderful little man. Let us hope that he realises at last that such talent calls for responsibility and discretion. The West Indian Board are not yet out of the wood. It will take time for the disgraceful events of that South African tour to be redeemed.

Matthew Engel, the editor of *Wisden*, has for some years advanced the prospect of a world championship of Test Cricket and in the 1999 edition (second on the hardback sales list last week) he prints a *Wisden* world championship table on a points and percentage basis as at the end of February: Australia, South Africa, West Indies, Sri Lanka, India, Pakistan, England, Zimbabwe, New Zealand. The editor describes his involvement as temporary, pending an official programme from the International Cricket Council.

The president of ICC, Jagmohan Dalmiya, has since flown to India representatives from the Test countries in order to promote his own scheme. He calls it pragmatic but one proposal is that the other nine countries will come simultaneously to England in one championship and fight it out between May and September! I am sympathetic with him in that the Asian countries patronise Tests poorly, having been saturated with the one-day games. Let them compete in triangulars at their mutual convenience. I cannot see other countries getting too excited at the world title prospect.

Dalmiya will preside at the ICC meeting at Lord's in the last week of June. Next year he will hand over to Malcolm Gray of Australia.

The fancy names which are appended to each county in the National League are not everyone's cup of tea. But Kent, at least, have settled for a word enshrined in the county's history. The Battle of Britain was fought across Kentish skies by Spitfires and Hurricanes based at a dozen Kent airfields. In 1941, the *Kent Messenger* suggested that in response to a national appeal, county towns and villages should subscribe the cost of a Spitfire, hence the Invicta squadron of twenty-two planes each named after the town which had 'bought' it.

Furthermore, it suits the Shepherd Neame brewers – the club's main sponsors. They have a Spitfire Premier Ale, altogether a title which needs living up to.

More about Kent, with due apologies all round: great things are about to happen at Bearsted, where the cricket club are celebrating the 250th anniversary of cricket on Bearsted Green. No doubt the Wealden villages played one another before that, but 1749 is chosen because in that year Eleven Gentlemen Of Bearsted came to London to meet Eleven Gentlemen of London on the Artillery Ground at Finsbury. The season will start with a dinner at which Lord Cowdrey will propose a toast to the club – and for all I know may lead the dancing.

As it happens, I can celebrate a personal milestone in connection with Bearsted, for exactly 70 years ago I have a clear picture of a locally famous match on the Green between P. F. Warner's XI and the 1929 South Africans.

It was the first match I remember reporting for the *Evening Standard*. Great names there were on both sides: Woolley, Hendren, Tennyson and Peebles for Plum: Herbie Taylor, Jock Cameron, Bob Catterall, Tuppy Owen-Smith against them, plus a character called Osche but pronounced 'Oooch' – a significant cognomen for a fast bowler.

WORLD CUP UNDERLINED INTER-DEPENDENCE OF BOTH VERSIONS OF GAME
23 June 1999

Today and maybe tomorrow marks a very brief hiatus in a summer of vast consequence to English cricket and the worldwide game, for the International Cricket Council are now in session at Lord's.

We await in the next day or two the news as to the England captaincy and to the identity of the new coach and manager; and then, while the four-Test series against New Zealand takes our attention, the 18 counties grapple with one another to determine their immediate futures. Upstairs or downstairs? The answers will not be complete in this longest of all seasons until Dec 19.

The final of the World Cup, won by Australia at the expense of Pakistan, ended as do so many one-day battles in the most overwhelming of victories, a disappointment, of course, depriving the enormous audience of nearly 41 overs of conflict and a whole ration of excitement. Of the 42 matches, only a quarter had close finishes.

For those at Lord's, though, there were compensations such as sight of the first 1999 full-dress picture of the great ground itself. I write as an enthusiastic convert to the media centre. English cricket may be in eclipse but architecturally, as in other aspects. MCC (despite a fractious minority of members) lead the field.

Critics are inclined to mention the pitch only to complain about it, so let me congratulate groundsman Mick Hunt on a true pitch fast enough to enable Adam Gilchrist to snick a six over second slip and withal receptive enough to enable the great leg-spinner to turn the ball the width of the stumps.

Let us admire the genius of Shane Warne and rejoice in the example his art gives to the young, if not what Mark Nicholas has called his 'deafening ego'.

Steve Waugh described the semi-final against South Africa as the best match he had ever played in and I dare say those able to see it on television may reckon, as I did, that they had never seen a better one, this notwithstanding the utter bathos of the last ball, which saw the splendid Klusener and Donald performing like demented boys in a junior house final.

To sum up in a few words, the impact of the 1999 World Cup has underlined the inter-dependence of both versions of the game. Only first-class and Test cricket can produce the best players, one-dayers fully exploit them and give them a world stage.

For many with undying affection for orthodox cricket who are prepared to tolerate the one-day version, the sticking point is the coloured clothing. It infuriates many of the older generation to see, on a sunny day, fielders, from head to foot, in a medley of colours, mostly darkish, umpires dressed as for a funeral and black sight-screens. Purple pads! Has it occurred to the marketing men that, so far as I know, every degree of club in the land down to the humblest village continues to play in white, the traditional uniform of the cricketer for 150 years or so?

The modern game is built on sponsorship and I expect that

advertising on the shirt must be here to stay. But oh, for a sponsor coming forward who ordains coloured shirts with names and numbers, but white trousers and sight-screens and a red ball! No goodwill follower of English cricket will have other than sympathy for the quartet whose responsibility it is for deciding on the captaincy. Messrs Graveney, Gooch, Gatting and the chairman of the England and Wales Cricket Board, Lord MacLaurin.

There is a general move for change in the captaincy and beyond it. As I wrote three weeks ago, Alec Stewart's triple function was too heavy for anyone to fulfil. One alternative, therefore, would be to choose a specialist keeper who can make runs and retain the captain for the New Zealand series. That solution would please those who believe that the team for South Africa in the winter must wear an altogether fresh look.

They no doubt remember that David Graveney, chairman of selectors, has said that failure in the World Cup had its origins in the dispute involving the senior players about financial reward, which persisted almost until the first match. They would hope that from the four Tests a suitable leader would emerge, even one possibly without previous experience. Such were two previous captains who, admittedly a while ago, were highly successful, George Mann and Tony Lewis, now president of MCC.

An almost unanimous press have been flying the same kite with the name of Nasser Hussain thereon. I do not believe the matter has been cut and dry for weeks, though the guess may prove correct.

The performance and personality of the captain of England has a deep reflection among all Englishmen who love cricket. Hussain would bring two vital qualities as a leader, courage and determination. By reputation he is, or used to be, abrasive, insensitive and unduly aggressive.

Those are all disqualifications, which Hussain or any other candidate would need to conquer. We need a generous-minded captain and not least a cheerful one.

Sign of the times: The oldest fixture in the calendar, Eton v Harrow, dating from 1805, the year of Trafalgar, is to be decided at Lord's next Tuesday by limited overs, with a maximum of 55.

JOHN LANGRIDGE: OBITUARY
29 June 1999

Jim and John Langridge were born and brought up in the heart of Sussex at Newick. Jim was well established in the county side as a slow left-arm bowler and steady left-handed bat when John joined him. They formed the third contemporary Sussex brotherhood, with the Gilligans (Arthur – the captain – and Harold) and the Parkses (Jim and Harry). Later in their time came the Oakeses (Charlie and Jack) and the Doggarts (Hubert and Peter).

In due course there followed a second generation of Parkses and Langridges, to add to other Sussex father-and-son combinations, notably the Tates (Fred and Maurice), the Coxes (G. R. and Young George) and the Griffithses (Billy and Mike). More recently the Sussex families' tradition has been maintained by the Busses, the Greigs and the Lenhams; and today with the Wellses (Alan and Colin).

The Langridge brothers operated fruitfully in harness, the scorebooks showing 133 instances of 'c. Langridge Jn, b. Langridge Jas'. John is reported as saying that he habitually stood 'quite two yards closer' to the bat than later fielders.

John Langridge's batting was built on sound principles, correct rather than graceful, ever watchful though not lacking in strokes once the attack had been blunted.

He was an admirable player of fast bowling, happier against it than when confronted by spin: in short, an ideal opening bat.

He was lucky to find himself in partnership at the start of his career with a highly accomplished stroke-maker in E. H. Bowley. His early years coincided with a surge in Sussex fortunes under three admirable captains: K. S. Duleepsinhji, R. S. G. Scott and Alan Melville.

In 1932 Sussex would probably have won the Championship (which they have still not achieved) but for the breakdown in August of their great batsman and inspirational leader 'Duleep'. As it was, they were runners-up three years in succession, as they were again in 1953 under the leadership of the Rev D. S. Sheppard.

Langridge played under 12 different captains, one of them a professional. This was his brother Jim, who was put in charge following a severe internal disturbance in the club in 1950, and who for three years did the job as conscientiously as was to be expected of a Langridge.

John's views on the respective contributions of the amateur and professional elements would have echoed those of most of his contemporaries. He regretted cases in his youth when cricketers on the staff had to make way for occasional players. He also felt strongly that something of value went out of the game with the amateur's official elimination in 1962.

In 1933 Langridge took part in one of the highest of all English partnerships, 490 in a day against Middlesex at Hove. His share was 195 and Bowley's 281.

When John Parks senior took Bowley's place as opening bat the new pair forged another happy partnership, and made three double hundreds together. There were also stands of more than 200 with George Cox, Harry Parks, Alan Melville and his brother, Jim. Not the least extraordinary statistic is his tally of 69 catches in 1955, his last season – only nine short of Walter Hammond's all-time record.

A Sussex yeoman, calm and philosophical of outlook, ruddy-cheeked and keen of eye, John was natural umpire material. He began standing in 1956 and for four years served on the Test panel. In 1978 the Test and County Cricket Board gave him a cheque and silver coffee pot to mark this modest man's 50 years in the game and he was appointed MBE.

He served for two seasons more, including umpiring the second World Cup matches, to bring his umpiring summers to 23.

IF IN DOUBT, GO FOR CLASS
23 August 1999

Almost exactly a year ago at Headingley, England, under the leadership of Alec Stewart, scored a narrow victory by 23 runs over South Africa, thereby winning the series by two matches to one. In so doing they confounded the media and therefore surprised the generality of cricket followers. True enough, it needed only a fortnight or so for the Sri Lankans to show that this was indeed a false dawn, with a victory gained after England had made a first innings score of 445. That was a sobering prelude to the sternest examination of all, a tour of Australia. England won one Test against their opponents' three.

This summer, a thoroughly disappointing World Cup from the English viewpoint has been followed by a series wherein New Zealand have shown themselves to be a team of rare spirit, with two outstanding all-round cricketers in Cairns and Vettori. They must be saluted for a richly deserved success.

Yes, the sad truth is that on the eve of the Millennium, England, which gave cricket to the world, are the eighth country in the order of merit, and with the daunting prospect ahead of a winter tour of South Africa. There are many things amiss with English cricket and no doubt superlatives of derision and contempt will be descending afresh upon Nasser Hussain and the latest version of the England XI, and on those responsible for their selection.

To deal first with the immediate matter of the choices during these next few days for South Africa and Zimbabwe, I hope that those responsible will remember the maxim of the most highly successful selector of my time, G. O. Allen: when in doubt, go for class. That presupposes an orthodox technique. Yet at the higher levels, the balance between innate skill and temperament inclines more to the moral qualities of determination and courage, both mental and physical. Ambition, too, of course is a factor, especially in these days when all first-class cricketers are relatively well paid.

There is no doubt that there was no clear policy of selection at the start of the summer with South Africa in view. It was sad to see the summary departure from David Graveney's committee of the two senior figures, Graham Gooch and Mike Gatting. But, with respect, they should not have been there in the first place. They have been too long identified with failure. Sir Alec Bedser, who was a selector, mostly as chairman and until nearly the end unpaid, from 1963 to 1985, spent 100 days every summer watching county cricket. He and his fellow selectors got to know what each candidate was worth in all respects. It was essential work performed by dedicated men.

I hope the selectors will withdraw from active service good cricketers now in their decline. They must stick with Hussain, who has put spirit and intelligence into the job, but if only for his own sake he should not have an undue voice in selection. Messrs Graveney, the new coach Duncan Fletcher and the well-tried manager Philip Neale can presumably co-opt whom they will.

Those of riper years dislike much they nowadays see on their screens. They hate coloured clothing, regard sledging with utter contempt, and blame those who indulge in it and also those who write about it without censoring it. We deplore intimidating bowling and the pressure put on umpires by dishonest appealing. We think the board should forbid current players from putting their names to articles, nearly all of which are ghosted.

Despite everything, there is, however, a deep love of cricket in this country, and one trusts that better times may be on the way. There is a vast amount of cricket organised for every age group from 11 upwards. The ECB has been in existence only three or four years. Its blueprint for cricket was called 'Raising the Standard' – and who is to say that in time, the title may not be justified?

MARTIN DONNELLY: OBITUARY
25 October 1999

C. B. Fry maintained that Donnelly was at least the equal of any of the left-handers of his own day and since.

He had all the strokes, executed with rare charm and a refinement of timing given only to the great. The one qualification that should be added is that the 1940s saw a relatively low standard of bowling.

Martin Paterson Donnelly was born in New Zealand on October 17 1917 and first came to England as a 19-year-old with his country's Test team of 1937. He finished the summer with 1,414 runs and an average of 37.

On returning home he completed his degree at Canterbury University before enlisting in the second New Zealand Expeditionary Force. He served with the Fourth Armoured Brigade in North Africa and Italy, emerging in 1945 as a major in time to make 100 at Lord's in August for the Dominions against England in what *Wisden* called 'one of the finest games ever seen'.

Donnelly went on up to Oxford, where his exploits attracted much attention. In the University Match of 1946 he contributed to Oxford's victory with a felicitous 142 out of a total of 261. In that year and the next, when he was captain, his batting brought such crowds to the University Parks as were never seen before or since. He made 800 for Oxford in his two years with an average of 65.

Between his two summers he was the pivot of a record-breaking rugger side which scored 53 tries against three. He was slight in build but beautifully balanced, and against Cambridge had a hand in all the Oxford scoring. It was a mature side, all but one of whom had served in the armed forces. Five members of it played for England – including Donnelly, who was capped once (and out of position in the centre) – and two for Scotland.

In cricket Donnelly had a particular partiality for Lord's. Apart from the two hundreds mentioned, in 1947 he made 162 not out in three hours for the Gentlemen against the Players. Two years later for the visiting New Zealanders in the Lord's Test he made 206 and so became the second man – as he was also certainly the last – to score hundreds in a Test and also the two classic matches at Lord's (A. P. F. Chapman having been the other).

Donnelly, topping the averages with 2,287 runs at an average of 61, shared with Bert Sutcliffe, another left-hander, the honours of the New Zealander's unbeaten side on a tour which touched the ideal in the spirit in which the game was played.

Donnelly's happy attitude to games was indeed infectious. He played a little county cricket for Warwickshire but in 1948 was recruited by Courtaulds and soon was sent to Australia where he became a director of the firm and its marketing sales manager.

Donnelly is survived by his wife Elizabeth, their three sons and a daughter.

MALCOLM MARSHALL: OBITUARY
6 November 1999

Of the formidable array of modern West Indies' fast bowlers none was either faster or more highly rated than Malcolm Marshall. In a career for Hampshire between 1979 and 1992, all the foremost English batsmen faced him and a poll among them would probably vote him as the greatest of all.

Of the eleven West Indian fast bowlers who have taken more than 100 Test wickets, only Courtney Walsh (playing in more Tests) has narrowly exceeded Marshall's 376 wickets, and none has taken them less expensively than his average of 20.

Over the international scene, only three others, the New Zealander Sir Richard Hadlee, Kapil Dev of India and Ian Botham of England (all having had longer Test careers), have more wickets to their name.

Of the eleven fast bowlers mentioned, only Sir Garfield Sobers was a manifestly better bat. Marshall made six hundreds including the first for Hampshire against Clive Lloyd, his Test and Lancashire captain, against whom he tended to add a yard or two of speed.

Marshall was not a conspicuously tall man in the mould of Ambrose, Garner and Hall, but slight with the build of an athlete. His great speed derived from perfect rhythm and a flexible wrist. The delivery came as a flowing continuation of his approach, and the ball tended to skid through lower than when propelled by the giants.

A wispy beard and shining eyes gave him a daunting aspect and there were times when his reliance on the bouncer, as in the case of his fast bowling contemporaries, though ignored by the umpires, was frankly intimidating. Usually he kept a full length, so that the ball tended to move either way, before pitching or after.

Off the field he was geniality itself, with a cheerful Bajan humour and a mode of speech which grew, it was said 'liltingly rushed'. His captain and close friend Mark Nicholas could be persuaded to give a highly comical imitation of Marshall-speak. He was fond of soul music and a good man at a party; next morning he was punctilious with his exercises in preparation for the day's work.

Coming in 1979, aged 21, from Barbados sunshine in his first match for Hampshire he took nine wickets despite his introduction to snow. In 1980 he made the first of four visits with West Indian touring sides to England. In 1982 he touched the heights for Hampshire, taking 134 wickets at 15 runs apiece, no fewer than 44 more than anyone else. He bowled 822 overs, also more than the next man. One of his captains said it was often hard to wrest the ball from him. He just loved bowling.

Against England at Headingley in 1984, he broke his left thumb when fielding and so had to bat one-handed. Typically, he chose the occasion to return his best figures in a Test, 7 for 53.

Having completed his Hampshire career he went in 1993–94 to South Africa directly apartheid had been lifted and captained Natal, signing off with a flourish and a batting average of 60.

In his career he took 1,524 wickets at 18 runs each and made 9,863 runs with an average of 24.

Last summer Marshall underwent a serious operation for cancer, but he was finally overwhelmed by the illness. He married only a few weeks before he died.

SIR CONRAD HUNTE: OBITUARY
6 December 1999

Hunte played a leading part under Worrell in the best-ever Test series, Australia v West Indies in 1960/61, which ended in a ticker-tape farewell in Melbourne. Worrell, with the willing co-operation of his opposing captain Richie Benaud, had determined to lead his side in a positive, challenging manner. He was the first black man to captain West Indies on an overseas tour. They, and subconsciously perhaps he himself, were determined to show the world, in particular the West Indies Cricket Board, that in leadership, colour was irrelevant.

During the Australian tour Hunte was recruited by an Australian journalist to the Moral Rearmament Movement, an event which became the turning point of his life.

In 1963 Worrell brought the West Indies to England for what turned out to be another highly successful tour wherein Hunte topped the list with a batting average of 58. On his retirement Worrell was knighted.

The succession, for which Hunte and Sobers seemed the leading contenders, was clearly significant. The Board, it was said on Worrell's advice, appointed Sobers, with a disappointed Hunte as his vice-captain. The partnership lasted for two series before Hunte retired.

Thenceforward for many years he combined coaching and his MR mission. On the overthrow of apartheid, MCC in association with the South African Cricket Board funded the appointment of Hunte as a coach of young Africans with special emphasis on the townships.

Hunte made 3,245 Test runs with eight 100s and an average of 45. He was a charming man, popular wherever he played.

MY SPORTING CENTURY
27 *November 1999*

I was conceived in 1906, the year in which Kent became county champions for the first time, and just about when the left-handed Frank Woolley was starting his wonderful career. In its review of the season *Wisden* observed in its measured prose that 'the colt Woolley deserves more than passing notice.' What would we be saying today of a 19-year-old who within a week had taken eight Surrey wickets, made 23 not out, enabling his side to win by one wicket, and then at Tonbridge, his birthplace, scored the first hundred of his career, against Hampshire, this 'in about an hour-and-a-half', having gone in with the score 26 for three?

The first article I wrote (and the only one to appear under the name of Ernest Swanton) in a weekly magazine called *All Sports* was an interview with Frank. That was in 1926. After I joined the *Evening Standard* in the following year I often saw him bat, until he retired at the end of the 1938 season. I saw my hero as captain of the Players at Lord's, aged 51, make 41 beautiful runs, against what *Wisden* described as 'probably the best fast bowling seen in the match' since Arthur Fielder in 1906 took all 10 wickets for 90. (Kenneth Farnes's analysis here was eight for 43.)

I have indulged myself this far partly to remind the members of that go-ahead body, the Professional Cricketers' Association, who have left out of their Hall of Fame this man who not only scored more runs than anyone bar Jack Hobbs (58,959 with 145 hundreds), but took 2,066 wickets and made a record 1,018 catches. He progressed according to Gerald Brodribb – sadly recently deceased – at a rate of 55 runs an hour. Yes 55.

I owe my fondness for games to my father's warm encouragement. As we lived in south-east London he made me a junior member of Surrey. Thus I saw the Oval Test of 1921 from the dignity of the pavilion: Gregory and McDonald, the great fast-bowling pair, firing away at Philip Mead whose broad bat brought him 182 not out in a drawn match, Australia having already handsomely won the rubber. Earlier than that, in 1919, I had seen Surrey play Yorkshire against whom Donald Knight, going in first with Hobbs, and wearing a Harlequin cap, made a hundred in each innings, and in two days at that, as were all matches in that first post-war summer.

My father introduced me to club rugger. We used, in the early 1920s, to journey on Boxing Day to the Rectory Field where Blackheath, pre-eminent then as just 'The Club', played the Racing Club de France, a match contested in a holiday spirit wherein (I'm almost sure – and who is there to correct me?) the French backs sported close-fitting skull caps, rather like the *zucchettos* worn by ecclesiastics.

In my last year at Cranleigh it was decided, since I had no ambition to follow my father into the Stock Exchange, that my future might lie in journalism. The Amalgamated Press offered 25 shillings a week, a modest sum which I soon augmented by freelance writing for the *Evening Standard*, first on public school sport, followed by columns on club cricket and sports diary items. Luckily for me I entered the field of games-writing when sport at most levels, and especially rugby football, was expanding and press coverage with it.

When I joined the staff of the *Standard* I was expected not only to report cricket but was soon actually appointed rugby football correspondent. If my credentials for this honour were slender indeed, they were no more so than those of my predecessor, whose only qualification was that he had been to school at Rugby.

I found myself among a company of seasoned journalists who turned their hands to whatever was required and were unreservedly friendly and helpful to this youthful newcomer. There was 'Bertie' Henley of the *Daily Mail*, a dear Cockney character with a war-wounded leg and a not unrelated thirst for beer; Sydney Southerton, editor of *Wisden*, whose father had played in the first of all Test matches in 1876; Owen Lewellyn Owen, who functioned simultaneously (and anonymously) for *The Times* as rugby, football, athletics and boxing correspondent, and enlivened many a long train journey with a flow of impossible reminiscences.

Which reminds me: 'Steady on, Owen,' said someone, 'wasn't that the year you were in Peking putting down the Boxer Rising?' But he was never caught out. Not least, there was Colonel Philip Trevor CBE, of the *Daily Telegraph*, always so bylined. It fitted the column width nicely. (Captains and above were apt to parade their rank after the first war.) In the popular papers, journalese of some ingenuity was often the thing: the crimson rambler was being regularly sent speeding to the confines. But there was also much very good writing from such men as Neville Cardus, R. C. Robertson-Glasgow, Plum Warner and Howard Marshall. Apart from a columnist or two, the journalists were strong Establishment men with affection for the games concerned. They would have had no time for the cynicism of some of their successors of today, the constant superlatives of praise and blame, the level of personal intrusions.

The playing, the watching, and the press coverage were coloured by a sporting philosophy derived largely from the public schools. Most games were nurtured therein, and from them came many of the best players. In the period from about 1890 to the First World War, known in cricket as the Golden Age, the England XI usually contained a fair balance between amateurs and professionals.

There was a leaven between those whose performance was their livelihood and those who played for sheer enjoyment, which made for a high standard of play. It was not essentially the case that the unpaid produced a more attractive brand of cricket than the paid. Frank Woolley used to say that he determined from the start that he would bat like the amateurs only better. The mix, which lasted until economic circumstances led to the discontinuation of amateur status in first-class cricket in 1962, was good for both traditions.

It was sometimes said that in my writing I was too partial to the amateurs, and when the news of their abolition came to us in Australia, I found on my desk in the press box a representation of a coffin under the letters RIP. Had I retained too vividly the style and artistry of Donald Knight at the Oval long ago? Not consciously, of course. I yield to no one in my admiration and liking for the average professional. There was dignity, self-respect and humour, from Hobbs and Sutcliffe to Hutton, Compton and beyond. I did, however, recognise the importance of the unpaid element because it was *independent*, under no contract, and so could be the liaison between fellow-players and their employers.

Such a situation is out of the question today, but who will say that the game is not the poorer for lack of the qualities brought to it by the old amateurs? The moderns, by the way, are at a disadvantage here. It cannot be easy to show charisma and enjoyment behind a helmet.

Sport helped morale in the Second World War. Games were played and watched and read about and reminisced about wherever possible. In the Thai jungle my 1939 *Wisden* was in such demand that at one camp borrowers had to be limited to 12 hours each. When war ended there was an explosion of sporting interest. The gates of cricket grounds had to be closed, even for county matches. The BBC enrolled many new adherents by both radio and television. It was a privilege to have a part in that. Denis Compton was a national hero, a pin-up beyond imagination.

When Don Bradman brought to England the Australians of 1948 they paid our recently formed Cricket Writers' Club the privilege of hosting the first dinner in their honour. The BBC broadcast my speech of welcome and the Don's reply. If cricket-lovers had rated him hitherto a somewhat cold, calculating phenomenon, he showed to millions of listeners a nostalgic, sentimental side which brought him sackfuls of mail, justifying the BBC's decision to hold back the nine o'clock news until he had finished. It was the talk of a statesman and one with a sense of humour. Prince Philip, married only a few months before, was also our guest and I like to think that the spirit of this occasion, his introduction to English cricket, laid the foundation of the patronage of the game – and also the playing of it in his young days – that he has shown ever since.

When I became the *Daily Telegraph* cricket correspondent in 1946, post-war increases in readership came despite newsprint rationing. This meant that Test reports even of the Australians were sometimes restricted to little more than half a column. I adopted a three-part reporting pattern which I would recommend to any and every young journalist, whether he is asked for five paragraphs or many.

First, briefly, the basic facts – *what* happened. Next, a critical view – *why* it happened. For many readers that is all they will have time for. One hopes they may read on to discover *how* it happened; a measure of chronological detail to fill in the picture. Whether for readers or giving a summary on sound radio or television that was my formula. What a privilege it was to be following a game one loved, mostly in pleasant places, and among friends. There were good men presenting cricket to the world in my 29 years as *Telegraph* correspondent: Cardus, Johnston, Melford, Kilburn, Woodcock (who has probably seen and reported more cricket on more grounds than anyone), Mailey, Ron Roberts (in the few years before his untimely death), Wooldridge, Robertson-Glasgow is just a selection. Cardus, by the way, was the only man who commanded attention by physically gripping my lapel. His writing was rare entertainment, based on the complete reversal of the aphorism: 'Comment is free, fact is sacred.'

It is difficult for those of us brought up between the wars who respected the sporting ethos of those days to accept the standards of the 1990s. As money rewards continue to rise, so the winning becomes altogether too important. The strain on referees and umpires grows correspondingly greater, as does the responsibility of those in control, the governing bodies.

Yet games can still have a crucial part to play in our modern culture. When the French had touched the depth of unpopularity in their country on the beef issue their rugby players at Twickenham in the World Cup suddenly touched unimaginable heights, applauded by a predominantly English crowd. There never was such a reception. It was surely a memorable triumph for sport.

NONAGENARIAN REFLECTIONS
Sandwich Society Newsletter, *No. 18, November 1997*

As life proceeds I find myself more and more thankful that my wife and I decided some 35 years ago to forsake London in favour of this blessed town of Sandwich. Ann came to know Sandwich before I did, her first husband, George Carbutt, having in 1951 bought a modern cottage in Bowling Street. Happily she kept it on during her widowhood, and we enjoyed it as a holiday and weekend home from the time of our marriage until we moved into Delf House in early 1963.

The charm of Sandwich today, I suppose, derives from its historical roots and, if the phrase does not sound too pompous, a consequent pride of citizenship. This manifests itself surely in the many associations, both secular and religious, which hold our community together, namely your own Society.

I take a reflected pride in the success of two of Ann's activities, the Sandwich Arts Group which Dennis Harle started, and which now attracts, in the safe hands of Pamela Hyne, so many local artists to show their work at the exhibitions in St Peter's Church: and there is also the Little Gardens of Sandwich, the annual Sunday wander round selected gardens initiated by Ann for the funds of the Church and now in the energetic control of Anthea Bragg.

There is scarcely a more thriving institution than the Sandwich Town Cricket Club, of which I have the honour to be president, a mere titular office I hasten to say. We now have a ground on Gazen Salts in addition to The Butts to accommodate junior teams. Turning out four teams on Saturday, two on Sundays and one mid-week, the care of the grounds, the manning of the bar and provision of food, all involves hard work, administrative and physical, by a core of club officers, who freely and willingly give their labour.

Nationally speaking, the jewel in the Sandwich crown is Royal St George's Golf Club, one of the great seaside links of Britain and a focus for golfers not only of these islands but those from overseas. There have been twelve Open Championships at St George's, a larger number than anywhere apart from the Scottish links of St Andrews, Prestwick and Muirfield. Many will regret that the Royal and Ancient have yet to name our next date. Speaking personally I think we would be hard done by if we have to wait beyond 2001. Thanks to the generosity of a former Captain, the late Roddy Hawes, we have a larger surrounding area than any of the other Open venues. Many will recall the 1993 Open (which brought nearly 150,000 to Sandwich) and its thrilling golf on the last day culminating in Greg Norman's victory. Our president, by the way, is a resident of the town, Brian Pope, as also is our Captain-designate, member of the Committee of the Sandwich Society and former Mayor, John Bragg. If anyone is feeling rich – and perhaps looking for a Christmas present – they can obtain from the Club shop or from Nova Bookshop in Harnet Street for £45 the splendid illustrated history entitled *A Course for Heroes*. The book is quite comprehensive. For instance Gerald Watts, our Secretary, introduces the reader to the flora and fauna of the links; one can read of ripe characters such as Tommy Mills, an original member who so fell in love with Sandwich that he booked in at the Bell Hotel for a weekend and stayed until his death forty years later.

I should mention also the Royal St George's Permit Holders' Club, of which I am proud to be vice-president. The Permit Holders form a friendly link between club and town. In return for the right to play at certain times for a nominal subscription its members give willing help on the course on major occasions.

A different sort of link takes the story back more than a century, in fact to the climbing of the Norman tower of St Clement's Church by one Laidlaw Purves, back in 1887. Purves was a Scottish doctor practising in London who scoured the coast looking for a suitable site for a links course. From the tower he beheld that stretch of sandy dunes which clearly was the promised land. No tower, of course, no club!

One consequence of this gloriously lucky happening has been of utmost value to St Clement's Church these last few years and is still so. The PCC of St Clement's in 1994 committed themselves to raising £500,000 before the Millennium for necessary repairs to our medieval church, especially to the tower, and the provision of a new organ, which is now in place and beautifying our services. When the Appeal for this large sum was launched the captain and committee of the club very generously offered the full use of the course and clubhouse on a summer day in each of the five years' duration of the Appeal. As a result of the consequent Invitation Meetings upwards of £10,000 annually has come to our coffers. The total stands, as I write, at around £375,000: in other words, work still to do.

There have been two good developments this last couple of years in the life and witness of our Parish Church. Paul Baldock, our new Organist and Choirmaster, has recruited from very small numbers a fine body of singers to aid our worship. It is good to see the choir-stalls well populated again. A second welcome feature is the establishment of a band of churchwatchers, who now between Easter and Harvest enable the Church to be kept open for most day-time hours of the week. Last year more than 3,000 people from many countries signed the Visitors Book, testifying to the value of this ministry.

I would be grateful for a few more lines in which to register my deep appreciation to all those who helped in any respect to make my 90th birthday such a flattering and extended celebration: not least, of course, the Town and Parish party in the Guildhall, hosted by Mark Roberts, our Rector, and my warm friend, and Ann's, Jonathan Aitken. There were also four Club dinners and we counted 334 cards, letters, messages and telegrams – that was Don Bradman's score at Headingley in 1930! In other words I have been greatly spoiled. *Deo gratias.*

Last but not least it just remains for me to say thank you to our indefatigable Chairman Patricia Lavers and the Sandwich Society who work so hard on our behalf.

E. W. Swanton

GOING TO CHURCH IN BARBADOS
ANN SWANTON

I have sometimes been asked what it is like to go to church in Barbados where we have enjoyed our annual holiday for more than thirty years.

Let me first explain that Barbados is the size of the Isle of Wight with 250,000 inhabitants. The early settlers decided to divide the island into eleven parishes named after the saints. St Peter, St Thomas, St Lucy *etc.* Ours happens to be St James, in which there are some 7,000 parishioners. It was in 1627 the first settlers arrived on the West Coast nearby and built a small wooden church.

This survived for sixty years and was then replaced by the stone building which is used to this day. Baptism, marriage and burial records date from 1693, and the font with its beautifully carved mahogany cover has on it the date 1684. The church silver, chalices, flagons and a large alms plate of nearly twenty-four inches in diameter, dating from 1682, are really beautiful and only displayed at Harvest Festival. This coincides with the annual garden fete held in the churchyard to which more than 3,000 people come. Barbados has always been British, unlike almost all the other islands which have been French, Spanish or Portuguese. The Roman Catholic Church is accordingly not a very strong element. The tradition is strongly Anglican, with nearly fifty churches in all. Our own is full at both the 7.30 a.m. and 9 a.m. Eucharists. The six hymns and a psalm are sung with great gusto by the congregation and choir; one hymn is in real West Indian style and one can see a few hips swaying, including my own!

But there is nothing, as they say, 'clap-happy' about our worship. The Liturgy (which is fairly similar to our own Rite at St Clement's) is performed with great dignity and style. Incense is regularly used, as in most of the other Anglican churches, for the whole diocese is Catholic-orientated. Until recently the priest training college, Codrington, was run by the Mirfield Fathers from Yorkshire.

We always spend one Sunday morning during our stay here at St Mary's in the capital of Bridgetown. This is a much larger church than St James and seven miles from where we stay. We are picked up by a retired policeman who lives quite close and is a church warden. Here the fervour is even greater with a choir of about thirty boys and men in the Sanctuary. We would almost probably be the only white people, and the 'peace' is given to us with such enthusiasm, not only from our neighbours in the pew, but from many outstretched hands from the pews two or three rows behind ours. It is their way of welcoming us. We then get into the policeman's car and are sedately driven at the legal speed limit of 30 m.p.h. being overtaken by all and sundry.

The churchyard at St James, only a few yards from the sea has recently been renovated by a devoted team of parishioners revealing overgrown graves and iron-surrounded vaults of the old white families – the Alleynes, the Challoners, the Lascelles, who came to start sugar plantations.

This touching marble monument on the north wall evokes the style and language of an age long past.

SACRED TO THE MEMORY of Dames Christian and Jane Ael, successively consorts of Sir John Alleyne, women in whose praise economise has to borrow no false colouring from flattery, and of whom no language can describe the loss. With the former he lived six and thirty years of an unspeakable felicity and but little more than fourteen with the latter. In that short period she blessed him with the birth of seven lovely infants, the eldest of which, John Gay Newton Alleyne, a boy of hopes commensurate to the fondest wishes of a father, in thirteen summers was too ripe for immortality, for longer continance on earth. The afflicting intelligence of his death at Eton School, arrived but one day late enough to spare his expiring mother such pains as she was incapable of feeling for her own dissolution; but such as a mournful Erector of this three-fold monument other instability of all human enjoyment for the sake of his surviving children, and, in silent resignation for the wisdom that ordains it must labour to endure.

There is a small relief carving of Eton College chapel to which I was taken every Sunday until I was fifteen, until my father, a housemaster, retired. An added interest for me.

The Harvest Festival, held in February, includes the Church Fair in the churchyard. There are stalls selling all kinds of things – artists selling their pictures, a talented shell artist, food and fruit. To us this seems an unusual time for a harvest festival but one must remember the sugar cane has just been cut, the pumpkins, plantains and pawpaws *etc*, are all in high season and the church is decorated with flowers unlike anything we see in England. Orchids, Heliconias (lobster claw), and crotons are in most professional arrangements; and the scent of these flowers as one enters the church is magical.

So this is Barbados and one of the reasons it is called 'Little England'. It is said that Prime Minister Chamberlain received a cable in 1939, 'Carry on England, Barbados is behind you'. Whether or not the story is true, it is characteristic of the pride and spirit of a people for whom Jim and I have great affection.

The article above, written by Ann Swanton for the church magazine of St Clement's, Sandwich (as was the previous 'Nonagenarian Reflections' of Jim), emphasises their interest in matters ecclesiastical. A close affinity with Sandwich, involvement in community affairs, family events, and for Jim, golf excursions to the local Royal St George's, meant few idle moments.

After Ann's death from a stroke in late 1998, Jim's sense of loss was, needless to say, profound. He continued to occupy himself with his various commitments and was fortunate to have the wonderfully constant support of his housekeeper Valerie Hillier and her partner Peter Knight.

In early 2000, Jim sat in his study overlooking the garden and began to compose a memoire of Ann. It was his last piece of writing. The unfinished manuscript was found on his desk shortly after his death . . .

A Memoire of Ann Swanton
1911 - 1998

the morning of

On [Friday November 20, 1998 Ann drove over to Deal to pick up the frame for a painting of Day Lillies which she had completed the previous day. She also arranged for copies to be made of a recording she had just completed of her own music for sale at the St. Clement's Church fair next day. She went out again into the town to buy a frame for a photograph of me taken by an Indian Woman, Commissioned to illustrate an article about me which had recently appeared, which she much liked, by "the Observer" She met and had a good gossip with Vivien Judd, a friend, Having cooked our lunch she and Hillier Valerie, our housekeeper, took to the Guildhall ([100 yards away]) some shell pictures and a shell-covered side-table for exhibition being held that evening & a Nad pass

[There was nothing unusual about these activities x She always liked being busy, and thanks to the variety of her interests generally contrived to be doing something productive and interesting.

THE LAST INTERVIEW
DAVID RAYVERN ALLEN
The Cricketer, *February 2000*

I met him at the side door to Broadcasting House. He was punctual as always. I was a little late – nearly as always. Waiting for the lift on the fifth floor had taken an unconscionable amount of time. He was suffering badly from a muscular ailment that forced him to rely heavily on his walking stick, but he was, as ever, alive and astute.

The meeting was to record an interview for Radio 4's *Late Tackle*. His final book *Cricketers of My Time* was to be mentioned, naturally, but really the taped conversation was to celebrate his 93rd birthday on 11 February: a salvo sadly premature.

Jim was full of fettle. With his old friend the microphone in front of him there was a chance to expand. No matter that the end result was to take no more than six minutes. I jested about his having to ask permission to stay up to listen to the late-night broadcast and his proximity to W. G. Grace at Forest Hill, when still a babe in a pram: what sort of form was he in? That familiar chuckle: 'I think he made about one or two hundreds after that [on the day that Jim was in attendance, Grace had scored 140 for London County against the local side] but all his hundreds are put together in *Wisden* – I'm sure it's *Wisden*. All the club hundreds as well, such as 400 not out at Grimsby and so on. You see, at Forest Hill where my father was treasurer, they had a special ladies' pavilion where my mother did all the teas and she would never have left me behind – they packed up [the club not his parents] after 99 years.'

The obvious question: how has cricket changed since he first started watching it? 'My dear chap, utterly and completely different. The Laws are mostly the same but the spirit in which it was played was very different, just as people in that era took life rather more easily than they do now.'

In cricket, is there a single Golden Age, or aligned to one's own youth, is it a moveable feast? 'Well, I think it's not cast in stone, but it's generally reckoned from 1890 to the First World War. And, of course, it was one of the best times when there was a sharing of amateurs and professionals; one complemented the other and that made for the best cricket I think.'

We continued with comparisons between one generation and

another and his number-one hero Frank Woolley: 'He made more runs than anybody ever except for Jack Hobbs, but Frank, of course, took over 2,000 wickets as well and for that matter made a thousand and some catches.' Jim then spoke of the formal method of playing being generally accepted, whereas nowadays people do all sorts of strange things, for instance, not keeping the head and bat still until the moment they make the stroke. 'Of course the bowling was different, not as much on the leg side and there wasn't any cheating. I mean by cheating, intimidation by the bowler and sledging – a cardinal sin. Do you know, it's a most extraordinary thing, even some of these chaps who've been broadcasting back from South Africa – they've done it jolly well – they talk about sledging without saying how evil it is. Of course, people lose their rag and people see it on television and it's a very bad example for the young.'

Further comments about his anti-hero Packer; the balance of the spin and fast bowling; Caribbean cricket – the coming of Lara; the incentives for different cricket nations; leadership – bemoaning the lack of amateur involvement; the impact of Grace, Hobbs and Sobers; the watchability of Graeme Pollock, Barry Richards, Duleepsinhji, Patsy Hendren, Wally Hammond – 'Walter Hammond was a little over-praised I think because he didn't play fast bowling very well and also he was a dreadfully bad captain, but he was a very fine, majestic player'; Donald Knight; two-day matches; pros and cons of one-day games; and so it continued. Too soon, it was time to wrap up.

'Jim, you've always been a custodian of the game's traditional values, what are your hopes for the future?' A pause. 'I think it's going to be a great struggle to keep cricket anything like the game that we've known and loved because now television has got it by the throat and we need the money. It needs people at the head of real vision and we want to get back to a much more orthodox way of playing . . . there was a wonderful feeling, fellowship of cricket I talk about. People think I'm rather wet and soft and so on, but there was a wonderful feeling about the game then, which I fear we can never recapture.'

We adjourned to the top floor of the St George's Hotel for tea and scones. Appropriate really: I had always likened Jim's rich, creamy tones to that of a favourite uncle with a partiality for Brown Windsor and Gentleman's Relish. We carried on talking for over an hour. He was looking forward to his forthcoming annual holiday to Barbados.

Continuing studio commitments compelled me to leave. He pressed me to stay: I dearly wish I had. My last sight of him was as dusk was falling. He was sitting still in a high armchair, gazing out of the window over the rooftops of London in the general direction of Lord's Cricket Ground which, along with Canterbury, was very much his spiritual home.

ADDRESS AT FUNERAL OF E.W. SWANTON ON TUESDAY, 1 FEBRUARY 2000 AT ST CLEMENT'S CHURCH, SANDWICH
THE RT. REVD LORD RUNCIE

Jim Swanton died as he lived with dignity and with style.

His masterly summaries of the cricketers who made the 20th century had been published. Impeccably bound, infallibly indexed. He had circulated his 66th New Year letter for the beloved Arabs – packed with detail of games played, courtesies exchanged and wry humour on the evil effect of late night eightsome reels.

He celebrated a last Christmas party of the Millennium with family and friends and just over a fortnight ago was taken into hospital close by the St Lawrence Cricket Ground. There, perfectly conscious, but weak, he received absolution, took Communion for the last time and died the following day.

You could write over those final moments the words of St Paul: 'Godliness with contentment is great gain'.

Of course there is sorrow. It is a sin not to grieve. It's part of love's price; but we are never meant to hug our grief and allow it to overwhelm us; rather to keep sacred a memory and get on with life.

It isn't difficult for anyone in this church to keep a memory of Jim. Others can, and will, pay more comprehensive tributes but it is for me to insert a personal word into the Prayer Book Liturgy which Jim loved so that our prayers may be warmed by his humanity.

We shared together the exhilaration of the immediate post-war years in Oxford. Jim arrived so emaciated from his years in captivity that his father could pass him on a railway station without recognising him. That the cricketer, journalist and commentator who had established himself in the 30s could so quickly revive was little short of miraculous.

There was his innate character – Jim was not a man plagued by self-doubt. Someone who served with him closely during the War described him as 'arrogant, yes; but the bravest officer I ever knew'.

For the rest of his life he bore the mark of the polio he suffered in captivity but hardly ever mentioned.

In the camps he had also embraced the Catholic faith in its Anglican form through the friendship of the Oxford MP, Lawrence Turner. That brought him his lodging at Pusey House, a centre for Anglo-Catholic undergraduates – immortalised in the poems of John Betjeman. Jim, to the end of his days, loved the order, dignity and colour of Anglo-Catholic worship. The sight of him at High Mass amid the candles and incense of Pusey or Margaret Street was unforgettable, lustily singing to his Creator 'Pavilioned in splendour and girded with praise'. But that of course was top-dressing which the superficial may take to be the whole story. Jim had his rule of life and it was methodical, strict, unparaded but for every day. It embraced the hard bits too like penitence and forgiveness, and church on saints' days which sometimes kept his rector up to the mark.

Above all in those Oxford days he picked up where he had left off as an increasingly recognised authority in the world of sport generally and cricket in particular. He loved the company of the young and encouraged cricketers and writers. He enjoyed the University but never pretended to belong to it like a pretentious bore. It was the same in his religion. Jim recognised and respected holiness and the religious orders – he wanted Ampleforth to be here at his funeral; but he didn't pretend that he was himself an ascetic.

In 1946 he embarked on his long career with the *Daily Telegraph*. To their eternal credit they took him up but never took him over. He exacted an undertaking that no copy would be tampered with.

Nor did he flinch from taking a line which was not always supported in other parts of the paper, either about the behaviour of Archbishops or contact with cricket in South Africa in the apartheid years. There was moral courage there and to be rewarded in 1991 at the inaugural meeting of the Non Racial Cricket Board of South Africa. The two guests they wanted for their banquet were Jim Swanton and Gary Sobers. He spoke words of welcome to 700 cricketers of every age and colour.

Jim's style as a writer, commentator and summariser were inseparable from his character – and that was his strength. Arnold Bennett once said, 'You have said sometimes to yourself "If only I could write." You were wrong. You ought to have said "If only I could think and feel." When you have thought clearly and felt intensely you never had any difficulty in saying what you thought: and when you cannot express yourself, depend upon it that you have nothing precise to express and that what incommodes you is not the vain desire to express yourself better but the vain desire to think more clearly and to feel more deeply.'

Jim's clarity of mind and commitment of the heart to cricket were, in my view, unrivalled.

That well-stocked mind was endlessly surprising. His natural habitat seemed obviously the great cricket grounds of the world – hard to beat Colombo – or Canterbury Cricket Week or traditional fixtures Eton & Harrow or Oxford & Cambridge. A short time ago we had an absorbing conversation about Liverpool in 1941 where I was in my last year at school and Jim, a young officer, turned out to play for Bootle in the Blitz. He described how one day they turned up and found a bomb crater on the ground and he had to rearrange the rules. Characteristically he remembered that this rather grey, and in those days slummy, district of Liverpool had its streets named after Oxford colleges and that Liverpool bus conductors would bang the bell and shout out 'Balliol Road'.

Jim also took very seriously his association with the Libraries and the Art Collections of Cricket. For many years chairman of the Library Committee at Lord's and presiding with great care over anything put into the pavilion at Canterbury. Music and art were part of the family that Ann brought when they were married at All Saints Margaret Street in 1958. It was Ann, the golfer, who brought him to Sandwich. Here they made their home and as I have said before from this pulpit, it was a dream ticket. Jim loved the golf club and the game which he was able to play into his 90s. I am told he was a poor golfer and a bad loser but here, as everywhere else, Jim was the first to enjoy such legends about himself.

He was a big man who loved the grand occasion and there were those who said that when he passed the throne of St Augustine in Canterbury Cathedral he cast a wistful glance towards it. But in Sandwich we learn the truth of Chesterton's 'Nothing is real unless it is local'.

Some of Jim's most revealing articles are to be found in the parish magazine. A series on the Anglican Church was bound together into a small book. When I was archbishop and he churchwarden, I can testify that he took more trouble over choosing a new rector than he would for the selection of an English cricket side.

He and Ann were generous in hospitality, befrienders of the young, reconcilers of those at variance. If he believed in something he would back it with enthusiasm and if it required financial support he would give it. Infinitely courteous except to the small-minded, mean-spirited and rude. His glare could always freeze the opposition.

Wintering with Ann at their house in Barbados, membership of the Church of St James there was hugely influential. The rector was given the same deference and loyalty as he gave to his rector in Sandwich.

When I paid an official visit to Barbados I found in my hotel bedroom greetings from Jim and two tickets for the Barbados Oval with the words 'If you don't use these you will be a disgrace to Kent'. An unusually forthright word to his Archbishop.

But there many misconceptions of Jim. That he had no sense of humour was one. He was not jokey, nor could he produce a string of smart stories for a slick after-dinner speech, but he had the sort of humour and wit that put life in proportion. I remember on one of my first nervous visits to Canterbury Cricket Week I knocked a bottle of wine over at lunch and it spilt on the dresses of two lady guests. We all jumped up, only Jim quietly murmured 'this is a moment to think of eternity'. We all know people without a sense of humour. They should never be put in charge of anything. Jim was not of such a character.

Jim also enjoyed the quite mistaken idea that he was a dinosaur who outlived his age. I owe to Matthew Engel the rebuttal of that. His genius was that while many developments in cricket and many changes in the Church gave him pain he adapted to their existence, understood them and commented sensibly on them though he never surrendered his own convictions.

Nothing to my mind is more remarkable than the way in which the solemnity, prickliness and, yes, arrogance that were part of the serious perfectionist gave place gradually to the gentle self-mockery and kindly wisdom which never seemed to fail us.

He kept his high standards; but they were combined with compassion at failure among his friends – public disgrace or personal follies did not mean the end of friendship – it might indeed be heard as the cry for help to stand by them.

I tried to think how to hold together this character to whom I owe so much and whom I both loved and admired. I am haunted by a memory and a quotation. The memory was not so long ago. It was in Jim's home. He told me conspiratorially that he had received a letter from the Don – Don Bradman. He went to a drawer, opened the letter with trembling hands and spread it out for me, 'I don't think it's improper for me to show it to you', eagerly waiting for my reaction as a schoolboy might show me an autograph.

The quotation? It was scrawled in the Christmas card sent to me by a distinguished scientist – 'The enlightened person thinks they can no longer enjoy the stories which so delighted their childhood years; but this is a false notion. We should rather ask whether childhood has not its own particular virtues – a happy trustfulness, a particular candour, an eager expectation of good things to come, which the grown person must retain at all costs if he is not to end up in sterile dogmatism or corrosive cynicism.'

Jim was not childish. He had long since left behind the tantrums and the sulks; but he never lost that child-like quality which Our Lord assures us will be needed for heaven. It explains his faith, his enthusiasms, the loyalties and energy that lay behind the authority, lucidity and measured words and it gives us the assurance we need for the prayers we shall offer commending him to the Lord in whom he put his trust so staunchly.

PART NINE

Jim Swanton Remembered

Introduction

To describe a funeral or a memorial service as 'splendid' may be thought, if not irreverent, at least unfeeling. Yet both the consecration at St Clement's, Sandwich and subsequently the eucharist at Canterbury Cathedral were indeed just that. The good and great and those who did not qualify under either heading came together for one purpose – to remember 'Gentleman Jim'. The pews were packed and the incense plentiful; the words well-chosen and the music in keeping. They were memorable occasions.

Jim had died at the Chaucer Hospital, Canterbury on 22 January, having been admitted some days earlier with serious respiratory problems. Within hours of his passing the news was relayed across the English-speaking world. Back at home, many who were part of those farewell congregations have contributed to the following pages and so have many who were not there. In essence, they are the thoughts of people who knew Jim Swanton or knew of him.

I hope it is not too immodest to sign off with my own favourite anecdote. There was a time when Jim was trying to gather support for election to the MCC Committee. He had enquired of J. J. Warr, that wonderful wit and raconteur and former Middlesex and England cricketer, whether he might count on his backing. 'My dear Jim,' replied John Warr, 'that's rather like asking Satan to put forward the Pope to be Chief Rabbi!'

D.R.A.

LORD DEEDES OF ALDINGTON, MC, PC, DL
*Memorial service address, Canterbury Cathedral,
Wednesday 29 March 2000*

It does occur to me, looking round, how greatly pleased Jim would have been to see so many in this great cathedral today. Himself a most loyal attender of memorial services for his friends, he would have expected a good turn-out. 'I thought it was satisfactory!' I hear him saying. And I start there, because we are today giving thanks for a life that, all talent apart, fairly shone with human qualities.

There was a great cricket writer, said to have written some eight million words about the game, who certainly brought the game closer to every man than anyone of his time. There was the author of 25 books – not to mention the editor of that monumental *World of Cricket*. But this was also someone who stamped his personality on almost everything he did. We greatly admired his professionalism; we enjoyed his small idiosyncracies even more.

Each one of you here will have some portrait of Jim in the mind's eye. Arabs, old and young, will see him on some sunlit cricket field and will remember him as their founder in 1935 – who took the field with them until he was sixty. Others will forever see him in the Long Room at Lord's.

You have to be of my generation to recall that confident voice, bringing the Test match, ball-by-ball, into the home. And there will be a fair number here today with reason to be infinitely thankful for Jim's gift of encouraging young promise. It was there he bridged the years so well. In Jim, youth always found a friend.

Myself, I shall see him always somewhere on the St Lawrence ground, grey suited, IZ or BB ribbon round the Panama, in early days a millboard in hand, imparting cricket gossip from Lord's or Canterbury with the utmost gravity: 'You know of course, that the committee decided last night to dispense with the captain's services . . . !' How could you possibly know? And from whom other than *Jim* would you expect to hear it?

I think of him too at Delf House one Sunday morning, shortly before he died. We sat drinking pink gins, beautifully put together by his housekeeper Valerie, who took such care of him. And Jim showed me the last picture of Ann, his wife, taken in some television show we were in. When she went, and their lives together ended, the sun went down in a cloudless sky.

And then, as his colleagues know, there was willingness always to give sensible professional advice. He knew where everything was in that well-ordered study of his. And until the day he died, he knew where everything was in his head.

We leader writers at the *Telegraph* would ring him on a Sunday afternoon, after some cricketing disaster overseas. 'Jim, we're doing a leader on the death of English cricket . . .' Rather a cagey – 'Oh, I see . . .' 'Have you any thoughts on the subject?' 'Well, yes, I might have . . . you realise, of course, that things were a great deal worse after Warwick Armstrong's Australians toured here in 1921.' After ten minutes of that, you could write quite a decent leader. And every homily decorated with an anecdote.

As his friends know, the war and captivity in Japanese hands had profound consequences for him. It was during a post-war retreat at Pusey House that he found comfort in the Anglo-Catholic faith which from then on deeply informed his life. You cannot seriously discuss Jim and his ways without reference to his deep and abiding faith. Never golf on Sunday morning; always St Clement's. He might well have joined the Church – what a marvellous bishop we lost there!

It was his religion, furthermore, that gave him some deep-rooted principles. His anger, for example, over the D'Oliveira affair in South Africa. Anger and distress. At some point, I remember, South African Breweries asked me to go out and look at what they were trying to do for black sport. Jim was very shocked, and tried to dissuade me.

But there was a positive side to this. Some of you will remember the cricket side he took to the West Indies in 1964 after some disastrous MCC experience there. It helped to make the peace.

And with it all, what fun he was. Whether playing cricket or golf, there was always a little bird perched on Jim's shoulder, piping, 'You gotta win'.

Jim never made the mistake of confusing sportsmanship with being a joyous loser. Nor did winning draw extravagant praise from him. Only a few months back, he drove me round Royal St George's in a buggy, acting as my caddy. It was the B of B match. Goodness, how hard I tried. We won by a short head. And what did he say, as we drove back to the club house in the buggy? 'I thought that was satisfactory!' He would have made a good bishop, but an even better magistrate. The magisterial style. How enjoyable it was . . .

But best of all, Jim Swanton so well conveyed the spirit of games played long ago. Games like the Arthur Dunn Cup, the Varsity match at Twickers – heyday of the amateur – much of it enshrined in the Arabs.

He never repined against modern sport, with its aspects of the Roman circus. But you couldn't keep his company for long without a feeling that he had known another and different world. And, in that sense, he *did* awaken an echo of those lines of G. K. Chesterton's that I have used before. He was:

The last and lingering troubadour to whom the bird has sung,
That once went singing southward when all the world was young.

THE REVEREND MARK ROBERTS

Rector of Sandwich

As a schoolboy, like hundreds of others, I listened to the distinctive Swanton tones from some Test match ground through my earphone on a little transistor radio. These were the same tones still to be heard right up until his death reading the Epistle or leading the Intercessions at the Eucharist at St Clement's, the Parish Church of Sandwich.

For all Jim's fame in connection with the game of cricket, this was only part of the picture. It is no exaggeration to say that Jim's Christian faith and his life as a loyal churchman came to be at the core of his life. So much of this was fashioned in adversity during his three-and-a-half years as a prisoner of war at the hands of the Japanese on the infamous Burma–Siam Railway. As Jim wrote at the end of an article for our parish magazine (*The Signal*) on the occasion of the fiftieth anniversary of V. J. Day, 'If our minds were not led towards the spiritual in such circumstances they surely never could have been.'

Jim, in my experience, was always so self-effacing about that experience. It was perhaps only in that fiftieth anniversary year that he really felt able to talk at all freely about it.

Jim's Christian faith was a Catholic faith in its Anglican form. He was completely at home in and deeply loved this tradition. Pusey House in Oxford where he recuperated after the war had a profound influence. He loved All Saints Margaret Street, where he married his beloved wife Ann, and he had for year after year, day after day the discipline of a clearly worked out rule of life. How I always so admired Jim's loyalty to the Church of England and Anglicanism. This was not always comfortable for him in the light of some recent developments, which frankly he found painful. However, he remained true to his church. Some will recall Jim's booklet on the history of the Anglican Communion written at the time of the 1988 Lambeth Conference, which was sold in the Canterbury Diocese, in aid of the Church Urban Fund.

Since coming to live in Sandwich over thirty-five years ago, Jim's influence in the life of our parish church cannot be underestimated. He was a long serving and distinguished churchwarden and after his retirement from this office he still nearly always managed to find a reason to invade the clergy vestry on every occasion right until the end!

I don't think he always had his own way, although I came to regard selection to read or pray at the morning Eucharist on a Sunday – the rotas for which he organised – as akin to selection for the England Test side! Jim loved his parish church and cared deeply for it. He worked tirelessly and supported so generously its Restoration Appeal. He was instrumental in what we call our 'Churchwatch Scheme', which provides a large team of people to meet and greet visitors, and enables the church to be open for the majority of the year.

As Jim's Parish Priest, I can, as have my predecessors, give thanks for Jim's wisdom, loyalty and great personal kindness. He was a generous host and Delf House, his Sandwich home, was always a special place to be. I still recall how only 48 hours after Jasmine, my wife, and I moved to the parish we were invited to dine with Jim and Ann. The after-dinner conversation in his study I remember to this day was far more gruelling than the original interview for my new job! Somehow I must have passed muster!

The funeral service for Jim Swanton at St Clement's Church on 1 February 2000 was a great occasion. We tried to organise a worthy celebration, and were guided not least by his own extensive notes on the matter. Jim's body was received into church on the evening before. During that evening parishioners and friends took part in a Requiem Eucharist at which the chief celebrant was Father Aelred Stubbs, a monk of the Community of the Resurrection, Mirfield, someone who had become a very close friend when he came to Sandwich a few years ago to lead us in Holy Week.

The service itself was attended by nearly four hundred people, including famous names from the world of sport and politics, together with our own local community. The congregation included John Major, former Prime Minister, Lord Kingsdown, Lord Lieutenant of Kent and luminaries from the world of cricket, eight of whom acted as pallbearers. The superb address was given by Robert Runcie, our former Archbishop. At the end I shared the prayers of commendation with Dom Felix Stephens, OSB of Ampleforth. I believe that Jim would have heartily approved.

At the Eucharist of the Thanksgiving in Canterbury Cathedral the nave was full. Again, much of the service had been set down by Jim before his death. The Dean of Canterbury, Dr John Simpson, presided, assisted by Canon Andrew Hatch, formerly Rector of St James, Barbados, and myself. The Address was given by Lord Deedes, over the years one of Jim's closest friends.

For me Jim Swanton was a remarkable man. It was a huge privilege for us in Sandwich to have shared his life and faith. We miss him greatly. May he rest in peace.

BILLY CARBUTT

Stepson, talking about Jim and his mother

My brother Eddie and I were first aware of Jim on Christmas Day, 1957. My mother had been widowed and he arrived at the house and spent the whole day with us. He'd first admired my mother in the 1930s, when he'd seen her playing on the golf course wearing those sort of square trousers women golfers wore in those days. Then, of course, they got together at the Golf Foundation Ball at Grosvenor House – this was only a few weeks before that Christmas – and they just hit it off. They were married a month or so later at All Saints.

It must have been difficult for Jim inheriting a fully-grown family. After all, he'd been a bachelor all his life and here he was for the first time married at the age of 51. Eddie was living at home at that time and it wasn't easy for him either. My mother naturally, was giving all her attention to Jim and he probably felt a little left out. But we both liked him very much.

And also, of course, he was away an awful lot – during the summer and on tours during the winter. My mother went with him often. And there was Barbados every year.

They were absolutely suited for one another – absolutely right – they gave each other a great deal.

VALERIE HILLIER, PETER KNIGHT AND DOREEN WAITE

Domestically, the Swantons were fortunate in having the services of a secretary, housekeeper, and, what could be termed, a Man Friday. Valerie Hillier and Peter Knight gave wonderful care and support to the family over recent years and lived in a cottage adjoining Delf House. As far as secretarial help was concerned, Jim appreciated the

work of Doreen Waite. Any secretary of Jim's faced an onerous task.
The following is a taped conversation between the three afore-
mentioned and myself:

DOREEN WAITE: I responded to an advertisement in one of the free papers. I didn't get the job in the first interview – I think Mr Swanton thought I was too far away in Folkestone, and he appointed somebody else who only survived half a day with him. I don't think she could cope with him, or he couldn't cope with her; one or the other. And so he rang me up and asked if I was still available, and I came to see him again, and he offered me the job. I've been doing it for fifteen years. Some good times, some bad times.

On the whole they were good. I mean we had one or two little ups and downs as one always does, and if something was wrong he'd always come in and say, 'Now look here . . .', and I always knew then that something was going to be said or he wanted something altered, but on the whole he was a great man to work for, and I enjoyed my time very much. And his book *Last Over*, I said, would be the last one I did with him – if he did another I'd leave – and then he said he was going to write one more. So, I decided I was going, but he said there wouldn't be a lot for me to type, so we got round that one all right. But, on the whole, they were happy years.

DRA: What were his working methods?

DOREEN WAITE: I don't think he had much of a method! He dictated a little bit in the beginning, or some things he'd leave on tape, which was absolutely hopeless because you'd type it and then he'd correct it, so you had to go back again and re-do it. But latterly it was written out by hand, and the writing gradually got worse and worse, but I got better and better at reading it.

DRA: How would you describe him?

DOREEN WAITE: A big man with a big heart, and he would really do anything for anybody. I think a lot of people perhaps found him a little bit aloof, perhaps a bit arrogant, but he was very kind when I had problems and things. I was very glad I had the time working for somebody like that.

VALERIE HILLIER: Everything seems to be on second choice, because I wasn't the first choice for the housekeeper either – someone else had got the job before me, because Peter saw the article about a fortnight after it had been in the paper.

DRA: Local paper was this?

VALERIE HILLIER: Yes, because Peter's local, he's an Ash man, and I was working in London, I'd just been made redundant. But as I say, somebody else had already got the job, but they blew it out I think, wanted more money or something, so I came down for an interview. Doreen actually interviewed me because they were on holiday – I was offered the job and said I couldn't take it without meeting the people. So I came down for a second interview when they came back and actually started in the March six years ago. I was very dubious at first because I worked in the Royal Arsenal in Woolwich, working for a lot of people, and suddenly I was coming down to two. Because if only 50 per cent of 200 people enjoy what you cook that's not too bad, but if 50 per cent of two people don't enjoy it you're in dead trouble! For about the first three months I didn't know whether I would stay because it was so different.

DRA: What worried you at the time?

VALERIE HILLIER: The fact that I didn't feel that I had enough to do to start with, but then the summer came and there was the garden and that was it, Mrs Swanton and I were bosom buddies in the garden – argued about what should go where. Mr Swanton at that time was virtually very much in the background as far as I was concerned, because it was Mrs Swanton that I dealt with. But I thoroughly enjoyed my six years. Obviously I think we got much closer in the last fourteen months, and I still miss him terribly.

DRA: (to Peter Knight) You were obviously there from the outset with Valerie.

PETER: I was, yes.

DRA: I suppose you also got very close to Jim in the last fourteen months?

PETER: I did, yes.

DRA: What sort of things did you talk about?

PETER: Everything I suppose. I'm not a cricket man. I used to spend an hour with him every night, and I'd read a bit about the cricket on the back of the paper so I'd know something if he started talking about it. But apart from that he liked reading, and he liked reading aloud, and, of course, in the later years Mrs Swanton had cataracts, and she couldn't see very well, so he used to read to her in bed at night. So of course when she died and I used to come in here, and whatever he was reading he would say to me, 'Peter, I shall read a passage out of this', and of course that's what he used to do.

DRA: What sort of things did he read? What sort of books?

VALERIE: The last two were Robert Runcie's and John Major's.

PETER: Yes, Lord Runcie's, because he thought the world of him. And of course John Major's was the last book he was reading, and he was a great admirer of John Major as well. But apart from that he used to tell me all sorts of stories about when he was in a Japanese prisoner of war camp.

DRA : Difficult to get Jim to talk about that wasn't it?

PETER : Yes, but he told me about it, and he used to roll a cigarette – I mean, he didn't smoke but they used to roll the cigarettes and he thought this was being really close to the mark. He said, 'And do you know what they used to call it, Peter?' I said, 'No Sir' – Sir – I've never called him Mr Swanton, I don't know why, but I could never bring myself to. 'They used to call it nag's bush,' he said.

VALERIE : It's raw tobacco I suppose, and they used to grow it . . .

PETER : He told me that the bed he laid on in the camp was split bamboo.

VALERIE : And when Mr Swanton told Mrs Swanton she said, 'Jim darling, didn't they give you a blanket?'

PETER : I spent twenty odd years in the army, and the way I felt about him I was kind of his batman – because I used to bath him, and help him dress you know, and he'd be laying in bed reading the paper and I'd go up there and he'd say, 'Go and pour the bath Peter', you know. I didn't work for him. And at the very end, this was a couple of days before he died, we went to visit him in the Chaucer, and the nurse in there said that they wanted to give him a shower, and he wouldn't let them. 'No,' he said, 'my man'll be in tomorrow' – that was me. Anyhow, I got him ready and we were singing ditties together. When I got him in the shower – I was fully clothed. By the time I come out I was wetter than what he was, wasn't I!

You know he was a very religious man – and once I said, 'I don't think I've been christened, you know.' He said, 'What! never been christened, we must put this right.' So, then I had to phone up the rector at Ash, where I come from, and he checked all through the parish records and of course it turned out that I hadn't been.

VALERIE : At the age of 64 you were christened.

PETER : Yes. It was quite important to me really. I've never been a churchgoer in my life, but through him I enjoy it now. I don't suppose I shall become a rector or anything – I'm too wicked for that.

VALERIE : He was a quiet Christian man, he used to do a lot for charities, never openly, always very quietly.

A TAPED CONVERSATION WITH JONATHAN AITKEN, FORMER MP, AT HIS HOME IN WESTMINSTER

JONATHAN AITKEN: Well, I suppose I've known Jim Swanton for the last twenty to twenty-five years of his life when we were neighbours in the town of Sandwich, and Jim, as you can imagine, was a formidable local figure. He first of all knew everybody, and not just the significant and important people but also the butcher, baker, candlestick maker, and really more or less everyone; it's a town of only about 3,000 people. I used to particularly come across this when there was someone in trouble, because Jim would sometimes telephone me as a friend, but also as the local MP, and say could you see so and so at your surgery next Friday?: he's in trouble because of this, that or the other, and he's just been unfairly dismissed by his employers. I think if you see your way to fitting him in and writing a letter to the chairman of the company that unfairly dismissed him it might make a difference. And that was very much Jim the good neighbour: he wasn't just the good neighbour to the great and good, he was the same to those down on their luck and in trouble. And perhaps I could extend that thought about Jim to myself when I got into trouble. It was a time when it had been very easy for anybody to see a bit less of me and be less friendly or less obviously welcoming. Jim took absolutely the opposite view. At the depths of my much publicised troubles he would invite me to lunches and dinners with some of his grandest and greatest friends. For example, I remember he asked me to supper when I was almost a notorious pariah, just after the libel case – I think it was the first social invitation I received. When I was in hiding almost, Jim called up and said, 'Bob Runcie's coming to dinner, would you come?' and so on. And right through my prison sentence he wrote to me. I actually saw him during my prison sentence. It was the last time I did see him, and we had a long talk and a very good one. Jim was a foul weather friend as well as a fair weather one and I think the local community of Sandwich knew him as such: as the quintessence of the good neighbour.

Also in Sandwich he was a very fine man for what might be called good-cause work, in a quiet way. This included opening his garden for charity fund-raising do's. He was that sort of rather old-fashioned, *noblesse oblige* type who thought it was all part of his duty to be a real supportive pillar, in all kinds of ways. Above all, his heart was very much in the Church, and he did an enormous amount. First and foremost by regularly going to services, and secondly by having very high standards about the finer points of ceremony and worship. I think not every vicar had an easy time with Jim, but nevertheless it was not in a negative way. I don't think he ever really enthused about women priests; he certainly didn't enthuse about changes to the Liturgy, changes to the form and style of worship, but he was always a supporter, even though he had reservations. He was a pillar of the Church as well, and to those of us who went to that church regularly it will never quite seem the same without his being there. And he read the lessons beautifully. I remember, particularly, him reading the lesson at Ann's funeral service, and it was most moving when Jim, aged 91, who of course, felt his bereavement with the greatest of pain, but yet acceptance, came up to the lectern and I think everybody's heart was in their mouth – whether he would get through this rather difficult piece of scriptural reading from the First Epistle of St Peter – and he read it in a voice sort of halfway between heaven and earth with enormous feeling and clarity and understanding. But he read many a lesson in St Clement's Church and was a huge lay figure in every sense.

An amusing memory of Jim in the context of the Church: and it's to do with cricket and Jim's encyclopaedic knowledge. There was a prominent local figure, who I'd better not mention by name, but he was a well-known man both locally and nationally, and he died, and it fell to me to give the address. Beforehand I went to see his widow and we talked about what kind of things should go into the address, as one does, and his widow mentioned to me that it would be good if I made a reference to this man's considerable sporting achievements in his youth: he'd been a Cambridge Blue and he had played for the MCC against the Australians in about 1948. And on the mantelpiece there was a little statuette of a bowler bowling, and underneath it it said the man's name and MCC versus Australians, 8 June 1948 or whatever the date was, 7 for 49. So when I delivered the memorial service address, I said in his youth he was a very fine cricketer and one of his finest achievements was taking 7 for 49, MCC against the Australians in 1948. After the service, Jim, who'd been there, said, 'Can I have a word Jon? Very fine memorial service address, but I'm afraid you are gilding the lily. I mean, this chap never took 7 for 49 against the Australians.' And I said 'Jim, I know you're a great fount of wisdom and knowledge, but actually you're wrong here because I went along to the house before and I myself saw the statuette.' Jim was slightly rattled by this specialist knowledge, and hummed and haw'd, and said 'I don't think so'. A day or two later I got a phone call and he said, 'Jon, pop round when you're . . .', so I dropped round and there he'd got *Wisden* open, and this character, who was a bit of a rascal, had indeed played for the MCC against the Australians in 1948 and so he'd been present at the match, but he'd actually bowled very unsuccessfully and taken nought for 98. And this funeral took place 45 years later, so Jim's knowledge of all this was incredible.

I have many other memories of Jim. I introduced him to John Major at Canterbury Cricket Ground, and John Major was not at that moment particularly important – I think he was an Under Secretary for Health and Social Security. Jim was sitting in a box with Leslie Ames, when John Major and Robert Atkins, another MP, and I joined them in the box, and suddenly Jim asked a question of Leslie Ames, and it was something like – and I'm sure I'm getting this wrong – who scored 100 before lunch in Australia in the first innings and then went on to score a second 100 before lunch? Leslie Ames knew the answer, and then asked a more difficult question of the same sort of rather esoteric nature, and Jim didn't know the answer, but amazingly John Major did. And there then developed a quiz, in which both Leslie Ames and Jim Swanton, who had no real idea who this young Minister was, started to ask questions of a very detailed cricketing history knowledge, and John Major answered pretty well all of them accurately, he was the best of the three. And I remember Leslie Ames saying, and Jim agreeing, 'That young man'll go far, you know'. Well he certainly did. And there developed quite a big friendship between John Major and Jim over the years, and John, with a little bit of back-up work from me, was of course instrumental in making sure that Jim got the CBE late in life. And after the ceremony at Buckingham Palace I gave a party here in this room for Jim which was a particularly happy event with family and friends and it was just a very joyful day. Jim was beaming. I've rarely seen him happier. Jim was of course very traditional in all his attitudes to life and receiving an honour from the hands of the Queen was a great day in his life, even though many of us felt the honour should have been a Knighthood and not a CBE.

He enjoyed giving hospitality and receiving hospitality, and was a wonderful guest and a wonderful host. A little known thing about him was that he was frightfully good with the young. He would almost always, at a lunch party or drinks or sitting, draw out a young person and talk to them. All my children loved Jim and looked up to him and revered him. They thought of him as a sort of period piece, mind you. But I remember one very moving moment, Jim came on his own, without Ann, because she was ill, to Sunday lunch at our home just outside Sandwich, and my son William, who was then only about ten or eleven, had known that Jim had been in a prisoner of war camp, and had been very interested in this in a small-boy way, and Jim had never talked to anyone about his prisoner-of-war-camp experiences. We had a good lunch and suddenly William pipes up and says, 'Mr Swanton, did you ever think you were going to die when you were in the prisoner of war camp?' And from that question there followed a series of schoolboy questions, and all of the rest of us shut up as William asked them. And these were questions about his faith in the prison camp, his knowledge and understanding of who was going to die quickly in the prison camp, how he helped people to struggle through and keep their spirits up, and Jim, who never talked about his experiences much before, after that started then to write and talk about them more. But it wasn't a coincidence that a small boy triggered that, because he was so good with the young.

I remember Jim had a very good sense of humour – again rather involving the young. One of my daughters was one of the first girls ever to go to Rugby School, and living in Sandwich there was another figure of Jim's vintage who was called Hubert Snowdon, who was a schoolmaster and Secretary of the Old Rugbeians Association. The Old Rugbeians Association of course had never included any girls at all. I remember Jim playing a sort of practical joke on Hubert Snowdon, saying he'd like him to come into the next room, he wanted to introduce him to a Rugbeian, and then Hubert came in and said, 'I can't see any Rugbeians here Jim, don't be silly', and it was my daughter who'd just become a Rugbeian. But there was lots of laughter with Jim – he was a very solemn and sometimes a bit of a caricature in his old-fashioned pomposity, which was an acquired taste, but if you knew it you loved it. And he had very high standards, and they're always I think standards of excellence but also very high standards of compassion and forgiveness. One area he didn't have a great sense of humour about was when his own team, the Arabs, were involved. The Arabs always used to play Sandwich every year, and I was for many years the sponsor of this match, which simply involved paying something towards the cost of the tents. But anyway, Jim's good humour wore very thin when the Arabs were losing – he was not a good loser. He used to tell people in the pavilion to stop talking when the match was going against them. But he spent a lot of time when the Arabs were not playing, of course, being a total support of the Sandwich Town Cricket Club and bringing on the young players and advising.

DRA: In many ways, he cemented his Christian faith in times of great hardship during the war when he was on the Burma–Siam death railway. It was a time when things were stacked against him, so there's a parallel between the two of you.

JONATHAN AITKEN: Well, Jim and I talked about this once or twice. I mean adversity is often a gateway to a deeper faith. The wonderful example of Jim is that of course his faith grew and strengthened over the years, and I hope mine will too, but he had an absolutely rock-like Christian faith and it was the strongest thing in his life. I mean Jim will be remembered as the great man of cricket, but I think to those who knew him really well one would say that cricket was a very far distant second in his life to this faith. I'm absolutely sure of that. Some months after Ann died, perhaps some weeks, Jim gave his first supper party which was just for four or five or six friends, of which I was one, and no one said anything quite as banal as 'Do you miss her?' but there was some reference to, you know, how much we all missed Ann, and Jim said, 'Oh yes of course. You know the thing I miss most is that we used to get down on our knees and say our prayers together every single night of our lives' – just a sort of glimpse of how deep that faith and how well practised it was. He loved talking about aspects of the current church scene, and faith, and who was a good bishop and who was sound. To a few people who enjoyed these sort of conversations, and I was one, he was just as good on the soundness of bishops' sermons as he was on the cover drives of a batsman in Test cricket. It was a great subject for him.

DRA: It's amazing he didn't write more about it isn't it – more about the Church?

JONATHAN AITKEN: I think because Jim, who was often thought to be rather a pompous and judgemental person on the cricket field, was actually a very humble and non-judgemental person in his faith-life. He was a great life enhancer, I mean whenever he sort of lit up a room it was always fun, and he rather liked the caricatures of himself, especially as he got older, of being the sort of Old Father Time figure who would make pronouncements. I associate him with a lot of wisdom, he'd always say something interesting about contemporary politics, insights into character.

One great annual highlight of Jim's retirement years was Canterbury Week, that very special cricket festival week, and Jim used to really go round the Canterbury ground slightly like an archbishop blessing various boxes and stands, and he'd spend part of the time in the pavilion and exchange greetings and blessings with people, then he'd move on to the B of B tent – Band of Brothers tent – then he'd go to the President's tent and he'd go and talk to the Kent players and give them a bit of advice. This analogy of the archbishop was slightly spoiled by the fact that there were some years when the Archbishop of Canterbury, Runcie, used to come, but he used to go every day for the six days of the Canterbury Week and be a very commanding and formidable presence there. And again Canterbury Week for me will never quite be the same again without Jim.

In my last conversation with Jim – I was still in prison but I was allowed under prison rules out for six hours, and I came back to Sandwich – we talked about imprisonment as an experience which can strengthen and enrich as well as debilitate and depress. And he had an infinitely worse imprisonment than I did, I mean the two just don't compare so I'm not making any comparison, and yet the experience of incarceration and the low moments that everybody feels have some similarities. And Jim was the first to say that in his case, getting through this period and the extraordinary enrichment and strength of his religious faith had been the great turning point in his life. So what you said earlier about whether it was one in mine – well I can't touch the hem of Jim's garment when it comes to either the depths of that experience or the strength of faith that has flown from it, but nevertheless I did feel a great, great empathy with him, and he with me, because in our different eras we'd been through the experience of imprisonment. It was a very deep conversation that we had – a very brief one but a deep one. It was a very good last conversation ending with: (laugh) 'Well I'm sorry I've got to go now, I've got to take my golf lesson and the professional is waiting'! which I thought at 92 was pretty good. I really miss him as I miss few people . . .

G. H. G. 'HUBERT' DOGGART, OBE,
PRESIDENT MCC (1981–82)

(Sussex & England)

I first heard Jim's distinctive voice in 1936. Our Headmaster, Gilbert Ashton, had invited some of the cricketers through to a lawn on the private side of Abberley Hall, and E.W.S. talked to us about the game that we already loved, but did not perhaps, as yet, fully understand. In retrospect, I realised why Harry Altham, who, two years later, taught me my first period as a boy at Winchester, had chosen Jim to carry on *The History of Cricket* that he had begun in so scholarly a way.

When I started to play for Cambridge in 1948, I became aware of Jim's eagerness to encourage young players – and regularly to back Oxford to win the university match at Lord's! We were delighted, in 1949, to beat Oxford by 7 wickets – against the bookmakers' odds and Jim's considered judgement.

In 1950, at the end of the ill-fated Test trial at Bradford, after the uncovered pitch had received an all-night drenching, and I had captained The Rest to a clear-cut defeat, he took the trouble to write to me with wise and winged words. If I remember correctly, the numbered points moved comfortably into double figures!

I saw him at work, at close quarters, on the E. W. Swanton tour to the West Indies, in 1956, when he invited Colin Cowdrey to be captain, and, to balance dark with light blue, me to be vice-captain. Jim had been upset when relations between the England and the West Indies sides, on the 1953–54 tour, had not been as cordial as he would have liked. Our tour party, which included Tom Graveney and Frank Tyson, were to be, as it were, missionaries – in J. L. Manning's immortal phrase, 'to bind the Commonwealth together with Swantonian cement'.

He gave to each match on this tour, as to any match in which the Arabs were involved, the importance that any game of cricket deserved. He would also show consideration for each member of the party. I recall vividly his indignation when one hostess invited all the side to her house – except Gamini Goonesena and Swaranjit Singh. His concern for injustice was also shown – was it not? – in Dr Ali Bacher's invitation to him to the occasion that celebrated South Africa's return to Test cricket.

Two phrases of Jim's on this tour come back to me over the years. One was in transit in Puerto Rico. Colin and I had been resting and came down to find that Jim had been displeased with the service at supper. He had summoned the poor fellow whom he considered responsible and in ringing tones, described him as 'the worst bell-captain in the whole of the Caribbean'.

In the airport buffet at Bermuda, after, earlier, Jim had opened the batting, been hit on the pads when they were 'fairly adjacent', and delivered a stentorian 'no' which could have been heard in the Bahamas . . . and certainly had the desired effect, Jim took over when the service was a trifle slow, crying with the leadership that came naturally to him, 'hands up for hamburgers'.

One of the notable features of Arabs matches through the years was the badinage, directed often in Jim's direction but thoroughly enjoyed by him. It may seem a paradox to those who did not know him, but he both took himself seriously – rightly so for one of his gifts and experience – but at the same time enjoyed the gentle mockery of others, which was apt to touch lightly on his weaknesses.

The Altham family and I owed Jim a great debt, in 1967, for ensuring that the first book of three that *The Cricketer* and Hutchinson would jointly publish because of their subject, and not for profit, was *The Heart of Cricket*, writings by Harry Altham, and about him, of which I was the editor at the family's request. The timing was right and Jim saw it as a marvellous way of showing his appreciation of Harry Altham as a person and as a writer.

We already miss Jim on the MCC Arts and Library, not least for the vigour of his championing – for instance, of the photographic history of cricket in the Indoor School, which John Woodcock and Humphrey Stone brought to reality so successfully. When the Arabs come to Arundel Castle to play the Earl of Arundel's XI in the 2000 season – without Jim's being on the ground to give his captain a well-directed word, it will be like 'Hamlet without the Prince'.

Sue and I will not easily forget the kindness and fun of both Jim and Ann at Delf House, Sandwich, when the highlights would perhaps be the settling of a cricket question from Jim's capacious memory, or, 'to make assurance double sure', from a *Wisden* in his study – and Ann's brilliance on the piano – more Carroll Gibbons than Charlie Kunz, which would set the seal on a civilised and delightful evening.

And then, next morning, there was the joy of going with them to the Holy Communion service in their beloved parish church, where Jim took infinite pains to ensure that 'beauty of holiness' which was so important to him, and where Robert Runcie would later speak so movingly at the funerals of both Ann and Jim.

I shall always remember with gratitude Jim Swanton as writer, broadcaster, cricket philosopher and friend.

TED DEXTER

(Cambridge, Sussex & England)

If Jim Swanton, who died on Saturday aged 92, had been an American, he might well have been called by his initials, E. W. Everyone in cricket knew who E. W. was. He was the establishment voice of the summer game both on radio and through the columns of the *Daily Telegraph*.

I don't remember how long it took me to call him Jim but it was certainly Mr Swanton in the early years. He would have been aware of Dexter, the schoolboy cricketer both at Radley College and in the representative matches at Lord's, mainly as a close friend and subsequently the biographer of 'Gubby' Allen, who helped me so much in my career.

My first real awareness of this impressively large man was when he wrote a letter to the editor of the *Telegraph* after my omission from the tour to Australia in 1958. I had scored 50 on the eve of the selectors' meeting and when they passed me over it was Jim who castigated them most strongly with the memorable description of 'thrice-blinded moles'.

Jim defied everyone's opinion of him as a confirmed bachelor by marrying late in life. Though he never had children, my wife, Susan, has never forgotten the charming way that he played with our two youngsters in the mid-sixties on one of those balmy days at Arundel.

When I did my near five-year stint as chairman of England selectors, I have to say that I crossed swords with his opinions on various occasions and a letter to the *Telegraph* during that period, this time from me, did its best to tear a strip off him.

Not to be put off, he invited me to dinner and reinforced his opinions with a decent bottle of Bordeaux. When, once again, I interrupted by saying that 'I couldn't agree less' with half of what he was saying, there was that familiar 'harrumph' which meant that we had agreed to differ.

Not that Jim was a man to cross, because he always had influence in cricket, through a variety of committees, both for MCC and for his home county, Kent, quite apart from his powerful position within the media. When he retired from full-time journalism, he was able to indulge his considerable enjoyment of the game of golf and I remember his loyal support when I was chasing amateur honours at Royal St George's, Sandwich.

Aged 90, there were two remarkable demonstrations of his undiminished senses. Across a noisy dining table at a charity dinner, the current sports editor of this paper asked him when his first column was due. Jim gave the day and date without even a pause from his conversation.

He was then the main speaker at the jubilee dinner of the Cricket Writers' Club in the same year. It was a *tour de force*, witty, comprehensive and all of it elegantly constructed in simple English. I began to think that I should have given his opinions more credit in those earlier years.

LORD COWDREY OF TONBRIDGE, CBE

(*Oxford, Kent & England*)

Jim Swanton had a gift for encouraging the young. It could be the 14-year-old becoming established in school cricket, or the 18-year-old, on the fringe of county cricket or setting off to university.

He seemed to have a photographic memory recording everyone's progress, and could produce just the right word at the right moment, determined to keep his young protégé working hard to improve. A firm commanding word was always supported with a smile of encouragement. His genuine interest was an inspiration to so many.

When England won the Third Test match at Melbourne in 1955 to go 2–1 up in the series, all English cricket hearts missed a beat in the excitement, for it brought us close to winning a Test series in Australia for the first time since 1933.

Four emerging new names had made their mark in this famous

victory. Frank Tyson and Brian Statham overpowered the Australian batsmen. Peter May and I contributed fighting hundreds.

The morning after the match, Jim went out of the hotel and bought four leather wallets, and presented one to each of us, to mark one of the happiest moments of his cricketing life as a journalist, but to remind us that we had so much more to do for England.

It was a lovely gesture, from the heart, of one who loved the game and took real pleasure when the next generation broke through.

THE HON. GEORGE PLUMPTRE

Author, journalist and lecturer

Jim Swanton gave me my first proper job when I left Cambridge, as his assistant editor on *Barclays World of Cricket*. Thereafter I worked with him as either assistant or editor on a number of books, including his anthology *As I Said At The Time, Back Page Cricket*, and a second edition of *Barclays World of Cricket*, published to coincide with the bicentenary of MCC in 1987.

Suffice to say that working for Jim was an amazing training that has underpinned my subsequent career as a writer and a journalist. Jim set himself very high standards and passed those on to others working with him. The level of professionalism that he taught me to seek as a norm was fantastic.

But without doubt the greatest reward came from the friendship that I built up with him over a period of twenty years. Whether I was working on cricket books or developing another area of my career such as writing about gardens and gardening, Jim's interest and support was never-ending. I came to realise over the years that Jim derived immense and entirely selfless enjoyment out of promoting others and seeing them succeed as I was fortunate enough to be a major beneficiary of this very productive kind of paternalism. In the end it was always avuncular and affectionate, and if I had to evaluate a list of individuals who have helped me along the road E.W.S. would have had a quite unique place in that list, right at the top.

MIKE DENNESS

(Kent & England)

I first met Jim in the late 1950s and it was very fortuitous for my career. He came to talk at a local cricket club dinner at Ayr in Scotland. At the time, I was contemplating trying to get into county cricket, and as he was very much a Kent man he was extremely forthcoming in not only arranging a meeting with Leslie Ames, but also fixing up a tour with Romany CC and an Arabs game at Chatham. Now he didn't have to do that, but he was kind enough to take the trouble, and it helped eventually to enable me to play for Kent. Coinciding with Jim's approach had been the support of Jim Allan, who had also made contact with the county, so it dovetailed well.

I would often disagree with Jim's views when I was Captain of Kent and England but we never stopped having a conversation together. I loved to sit next to him and listen to his memories. He was a wonderful man with a tremendous capacity for work.

MATTHEW FLEMING

(Kent & England)

Jim was the truest possible friend; my greatest ally when I needed him, and my fiercest critic when I deserved it. I have so many fond memories of Jim, at the St Lawrence Ground during Canterbury Cricket Week, at his home Delf House with his wonderful wife Ann or holding court at the Sandy Lane Hotel in Barbados. The one place that sometimes stretched our friendship to its limits was The Royal St George's Golf Club. My abiding memory of Jim was him leaving his buggy on the edge of the fairway and walking sedately through the impenetrable rough to some distant, and previously unvisited, spot where his partner, me, had sliced his tee shot. He was humming as he walked towards me, and he never once stopped humming whilst I pointed out the minute amount of our ball that was visible. He continued to hum as he returned to the buggy to select his club. I followed at a suitably embarrassed distance, ready to advise on club selection and guide him on the not inconsiderable return journey. He walked up to our opponents, stopped humming, inclined his head and said, 'your hole'. With that he started humming again, got back in his buggy and drove off to the next tee, leaving me to retrieve our ball and ponder my inaccuracy.

DAVID WELCH

Sports Editor of the Daily Telegraph

Jim Swanton returned to write regular columns on the cricket pages of the *Daily Telegraph* during the early days of my sports editorship when he was already in his 80s. I never had a moment's regret about asking him to do so.

Regarded by many as pompous and intransigent, he was certainly never guilty of underestimating his own influence. But he brought enormous authority and experience to our coverage and he was a joy to work with.

Only months before his death he immersed himself entirely in a wonderful piece for our series on sport in the Millennium. Indeed, he responded positively whenever asked to contribute – often at very short notice.

He would always deliver on time; with good grace; and with the conviction and insight that made him a 'must' read over so many years.

DAVID FABER, MP

Member of Culture, Media & Sports Committee; MCC and Arab

Among the many heart-warming tributes to Jim Swanton, only passing reference has been made to the huge hole that his death will leave in the world of wandering club cricket. The Arabs, founded with a few friends on a tour to Jersey in 1935, formed a life's work and a life's reward for Jim, to the benefit of all those who have played for and, indeed, against the club. For 30 years Jim played Arabs cricket himself, after which he dedicated himself to running a club who would compete successfully with the most famous names in wandering cricket throughout the world. A glance down the fixture list reveals tours to Jim's beloved Barbados and East Africa, an annual tour of Kent for the past 40 years based around his home at Sandwich and, more recently, an annual match at Sir Paul Getty's beautiful ground at Wormsley.

Members were traditionally recruited among young cricketers, fresh out of school and university. Jim took great pleasure first in watching them play, before inviting to join those whom he felt would play the game not only to the standards he expected, but to his ideals as well. For good measure, a few former Test and county stars were added to the mix – from 'Gubby' Allen to Richie Benaud; Tony Lewis to Matthew Fleming.

In a world where some aspects of the modern professional game were not always to Jim's liking and wandering 'jazzhat' cricket is often derided by the professionals, he did his best to ensure that the Arabs enjoyed the best of both worlds.

Tony Lewis once wrote: 'Jim understands the everlasting truth – that there is no fun to be had from cricket which is played for fun alone'. Winning was always important, but still more was the manner of doing so. The management of the club, the preparation for matches and their successful administration and reporting was every bit as important to Jim as the result itself.

Woe betide anyone who let him down in this respect, as I once found out to my cost. As captain of an Arabs team for the day, I turned up for a match in Hampshire with just seven players, in part due to my own poor organisation. The home team kindly lent us two fielders, but Jim's arrival shortly before lunch sent a shiver down our spines and his realisation as he surveyed the scene before him, that he could recognise only seven of our nine fielders, led to a distinctly frosty lunch and tea. The 'Warnford seven' somehow managed to conjure up a miraculous victory, but it didn't save me from the chop as match manager for the following year.

His annual letter to all Arab members arrived just a couple of weeks ago – the usual eloquent mix of last summer's results, finance, new members, obituaries and potted Arab trivia from around the world. I know that he was particularly proud that an Arab had been selected to captain the England Under-19 team currently on tour. There was also a typically tongue-in-cheek (I think) reference to the annual golf match at Royal St George's, lost last year by a humiliating 12¼–1, half due, in Jim's opinion, to over-training the night before.

Jim's encouragement to any young cricketer was given without favour or discrimination. He would bestow advice on fellow-Arab or opponent alike if he believed they had the best interests of the game at heart. This week there will have been very many cricketers, some still playing, some teaching, others administering or, of course, writing, who will have looked back and remembered his benign but firm influence at a moment in their career.

For the Arabs committee and senior members there will now be the difficult decision of what to do next. It is probably too soon to be sure whether a club who have been so closely identified with one man can carry on successfully without his meticulous attention to their every detail. For my part, I hope that there will be enough of us prepared to carry on the best traditions of the Arabs as a lasting tribute to Jim.

PADDY BRIGGS

Dubai, U.A.E. Letter to the Daily Telegraph

My father was a prisoner of war with Jim Swanton on the infamous death railway in Thailand and Burma. His stories about Jim were many, and always amusing.

With Jim you were always laughing – sometimes with him, sometimes at him (he never seemed to mind). Once he broke his arm and it was placed in whatever passed for plaster in those grim conditions. Not fazed, Jim strode imperiously around waving his plastered arm and directing events in his inimitable way (you can picture the scene).

The POWs pooled their books to form a 'library' of sorts. Jim's donation was the 1940 *Wisden*. His fellow prisoners became lifelong experts on the 1939 cricket season, before (sadly) the *Wisden* had to perish – its pages much in demand for rolling cigarettes.

[*This sounds like a story that has got taller in the retelling. Even if Jim had, in fact, carried* Wisdens *for successive seasons, it is difficult to believe he would have allowed the relatively slim volume for 1940 to be used for such a purpose.*]

RICHARD BOYD

London. Letter to the Daily Telegraph

What I remember best about Jim Swanton, apart from the quality of his writing and his dedication to the game of cricket, was his determination to maintain the highest standards, and his unfailing courtesy.

I wrote to him occasionally to comment on something he had written in the *Telegraph* and without fail I would receive a reply in a very few days, making a succinct and well-argued comment on my remarks – whether in agreement or otherwise – and showing genuine pleasure in receiving the thoughts of a reader.

On the very rare occasion on which he made an error of fact he was very quick with an apology, accepting his mistake. It is so sad to lose such a rare man still in full possession of his mental vigour even at his great age.

TONY O'REILLY, Ph.D.

Former international Irish rugby star. Newspaper proprietor.
Variously Chairman, President, CEO, H. J. Heinz Co. Inc.
Obituary, the Independent

There is a story told about Jim Swanton which captures something of the man. Jim, it is alleged, was shipwrecked on a desert island. After ten days of total solitude he meets another castaway, and his first question is, 'Could you tell me the way to Government House?' I am sure it is apocryphal, but it conveys the purposefulness, and Britishness, and sense of order that permeated his life.

Vivian Jenkins, that doyen of rugby writers, said that when they were together on a cricket tour of Australia, the press corps had to travel all the way from Adelaide to Perth by bus. It involved an exhausting and humid trip across the Nullarbor Plain. Jim would have none of it. He called up the ADC to the Governor-General and managed to get a Royal Australian Air Force plane to drop Jenkins and himself in Perth, while the press corps emulated the explorers Burke and Wills in steamy conditions far down below. Singapore in 1942 was the greatest single military disaster in British history, and Jim had the misfortune to have arrived there just when General Percival surrendered 250,000 men and equipment to the Japanese. What happened to these brave men is unprintable, but captured in part by David Lean and Alec Guinness in *The Bridge on the River Kwai*. Swanton returned from the Second World War five stone lighter and with half his battalion having died during the three-and-a-half-year internment.

I was Jim's guest speaker at Lord's for the MCC at their annual dinner. I said that I admired his British tenacity in the face of incontrovertible defeat, and mimicked an imaginary Swanton broadcast in a Test against Australia . . . 'Bedser comes in from the pavilion end, he bowls, Arthur Morris goes forward, Bedser beats the bat. He has been beating the bat consistently all morning . . . Australia are . . . 211 for no wicket!' He took it, I must say, in very good part.

Each year for over 15 years, I would join him and Ann, his wife, in Barbados for an annual luncheon of delight and recollection. His phraseology was acute, perceptive, and, at times, highly original. I remember asking him about a famous English batsman and his particular style. He reflected on my question for a while and then said, 'No, he was very puddingy' – very puddingy! How delicious and how descriptive.

Great play has been made of his alleged conceits and the belief that he could barely tolerate driving in a car with his own chauffeur, but, in truth, his greatest conceit was his firm belief that certain cricketers, irrespective of colour, class, or creed, were, in his pantheon, simply extraordinary. In that, he was the truest of democrats.

Foremost among these was his belief that the greatest was 'The Don' – Don Bradman, who was the finest batsman the world has ever, or will ever, see. The Don's average of 99 runs per innings in Test matches is still, in the year 2000, fifty per cent ahead of any cricketer who has ever played. If you add Hobbs and Sutcliffe, D. C. S. Compton, P. B. H. May, Brian Lara and the greatest all-rounder of them all, including Keith Miller and Ian Botham, in Sir Garfield Sobers, you begin to see in your mind's eye the team he is probably assembling in another world today.

If he is, it is a team without 'oiks', and with discipline and style. It will, however, probably include Colin Ingleby-Mackenzie as racing tipster and *bon vivant*, if only for the fact that, after he had captained Hampshire to an astounding victory in the County Championship, Swanton asked him what was the secret of his county's unexpected success. Colin replied, straight faced, 'The reason was my unshakeable insistence that the team be in bed before breakfast every morning.'

COLIN INGLEBY-MACKENZIE

Former Captain of Hampshire and President of MCC

I played my first match for Hampshire in 1951, hanging up my pads at the end of the season in 1965. I loved every minute of it.

Jim was a great personal friend, adviser and always wise counsel, with a refreshing sense of humour. In school terms, he always enjoyed being 'mobbed up', if you were brave enough!

My greatest regret was that he was never made president of MCC or knighted. This was one of cricketing's great oversights. Perhaps there could be special permission for a Posthumous Award.

IAN WOOLDRIDGE, OBE

Daily Mail

A curious thing occurred on the lovely Canterbury Cricket Ground in 1963 when Kent were playing West Indies. Proceedings suddenly came to a standstill when Peter Richardson, batting for Kent, complained to an umpire that he couldn't continue amid the incessant booming noise emanating from somewhere on the ground.

Richardson, an incurable practical joker, winked at the umpire and together they walked to what they suspected was the source of the interruption. This was a television commentary box in which at that moment E. W. Swanton was explaining in his deep, mellifluous tones, that any moment now they would discover the reason for the delay.

He looked down to see Richardson pointing directly at him. 'It's coming from up there,' said Richardson. Colin Cowdrey, sitting alongside Swanton, said: 'It's you, Jim, they are complaining about'. Richardson had heard nothing. He'd merely seen Swanton at the microphone and decided to inject a little humour into the proceedings.

E. W. 'Jim' Swanton, author of 23 cricket books and an estimated eight million words about cricket, mostly for the *Daily Telegraph*, was the butt of many such japes. He even laughed when, on a rugby tour with the Old Cranleighans, he placed his shoes outside his bedroom door for cleaning, only to find them nailed to the floor the following morning.

With his impeccable English, his immaculate clothes, his uncompromising denunciation of bad manners, he was seen by a younger generation as pompous. Well, yes, he was. Indeed, there were times when I thought he was wasted as the emeritus cricket writer of our time. He should have been British Ambassador to Washington – Kennedy would have adored him. Johnson would have pulled out of Vietnam earlier and Clinton would have dropped the Lewinsky woman before it was too late.

Many assumed from his patrician-bearing that he was to the right of Margaret Thatcher. He never was. To the dismay of his friends and Lord's he campaigned vigorously against sporting links with apartheid in South Africa. He knew more about privation than most of them, having endured three years of savage Japanese imprisonment after being captured in Singapore. Years later, at home in Sandwich, Kent, he would appear in a dinner jacket and black tie for supper. You could wear a blazer – a T-shirt would have been frowned upon – but Jim would make no apology for his formality. 'In prison,' he said, 'dreams of living like this kept me alive'. In the 1960s, to the horror of the all-male cricket-writing press, he introduced a woman to the Lord's press gallery. He silenced all opposition with a ferocious glare. She was his secretary Daphne Surfleet and today she is Mrs Richie Benaud.

Jim Swanton was generous and encouraging to newcomers to the cricket-writing game. In John Woodcock, until recently cricket correspondent of *The Times*, he nurtured the best cricket writer still living.

On my own first tour to Australia, naïve, inexperienced, and heavily outgunned by formidable opposition, he took me aside one day and said: 'Such little as I know about this game is available should you wish to consult me'.

It was classic Swanton and I consulted him frequently.

RICHIE (*N.S.W., Australia*) AND DAPHNE BENAUD

DAPHNE: 'That's the copy Daphne, don't change anything just because you don't like it . . .'

More of an instruction than an exhortation. Those were the words Jim most often used when handing over his story at the end of a day's play, whether at Lord's or Canterbury or in the north of England. The copy was always perfect, as was the case with the letters I would take from him in shorthand, nothing ever needed to be changed and he was unique in that respect as an employer.

My introduction to the press-box was an interesting experience. I had worked for the BBC Television in Manchester for over four years and now I was to be the first permanent female occupant, with a journalist employer, in an English press-box.

When I followed Jim into the box at the New Road end there was silence, more intense than the usual phrase involving 'deafening'. Other than for a cheery 'Hello Daphers' from John Bromley, who was number two to Charles Bray at that time.

Working for Jim was never dull and punctuality was vital.

RICHIE: We won't see the like of Jim again in the newspaper world, and that's a pity. It is unlikely these days that the listing of the team as an 'intro' would get very far with an editor who lives only for football.

He was a fine journalist, sometimes with his own agendas, and it was a matter of little moment whether or not those coincided with other people's ideas. He was always willing to listen to another argument, but I suspect it was more to be courteous than to indicate any swaying from what he had just set in stone. He was also a frustrated captain and not even leading the 'Arabs' to many victories could ease the pain of defeat with someone else captaining.

In 1964, after the end of the series in Australia, I joined his team in the Far East, meeting up with them in Hong Kong where we played two games, then one in Bangkok and finally one against a near Test side in Calcutta. Colin Ingleby-Mackenzie was captain in Calcutta and on the last afternoon listened diligently enough to the Founder's instructions on leadership that we won the match with ten minutes to spare.

A year or so later Mackenzie was also captaining the Arabs on a short tour around Kent. It involved both cricket and golf and, at the evening function following the golf, Ingleby had apparently been given a bad ice cube. At any rate, he declared himself unfit for the match at Torry Hill and I was dragooned into the captaincy, something I regarded with a certain amount of unease, remembering the explicit off-the-field, non-playing captaincy of Calcutta.

We set the opposition 250 and they looked like winning with an hour to spare. All the bowlers were taking a hammering, I had 0–70 from not many overs and was wishing I had found the ice cube. Jim, with an eye to tactics, had stationed himself by the sightscreen with the wind at his back so there was no chance of his voice being carried away.

When I brought John MacKinnon (occasional left-arm medium) on to bowl, there was quite a clamour from the sightscreen to the general effect that this was the most stupid bowling change he had ever seen. I instructed MacKinnon to bowl left-arm over-the-wrist spin and he bowled them out. Jim was generous in his praise, 'It remains one of the more incomprehensible captaincy decisions I have ever seen . . . !'

Quotes

DAVID GOWER, OBE

(Kent, Leicestershire & England)

The man was a legend in the game, and that's not bad for someone who never played Test cricket.

H. D. 'DICKIE' BIRD, MBE

(Yorkshire & Leicestershire)

International umpire and author

The game of cricket has lost a great friend, and so have I.

PETER WEST

Television commentator and presenter

He had a wonderful innings and was still writing some wonderful stuff right up until the end. He was a wonderful reporter and the best summariser of a day's cricket I have ever seen or heard.

FRED TRUEMAN, OBE

(Yorkshire & England)

. . . the end of an era of great cricket writers . . . I still looked forward to reading what he wrote about cricket in the *Daily Telegraph* even in his old age. I don't think all Yorkshiremen were his greatest favourites but you cannot take away his ability with the pen. He loved the game and lived for it.

MICHAEL PARKINSON, CBE

Interviewer, television presenter, writer

Jim Swanton was not the greatest stylist but he was the most authoritative commentator of the game.

AN EXTRACT FROM THE
DAILY TELEGRAPH OBITUARY

His imperiousness gave rise to many an anecdote. At one time Swanton was summing up the day's play at a Test match, when some boys starting making faces at him from behind the camera. 'Will you behave yourselves,' he exploded, in the middle of his broadcast. The outburst brought him letters from mothers all over the country, congratulating him on disciplining their wayward children.

Those who worked for Swanton – they included Christopher Martin-Jenkins, a successor at the *Telegraph*, John Woodcock, later cricket correspondent of *The Times*, and Hugh Massingberd, the great obituaries editor of the *Telegraph* – all experienced chastening moments.

Martin-Jenkins recalled being sent to a pub to get his master a gin and tonic, only to discover that neither lemon nor ice was available. 'Have you told them who I am?' thundered Swanton.

Though always an apostle of fair play, Swanton did not believe that frivolity had any part in cricket. Once, when he was batting in a charity match, the more irreverent members of his side felt he had been in for long enough, and sent in the West Indian all-rounder Gerry Gomez to run him out. Gomez pushed his first ball towards cover, shouted 'Come on', and set off. 'Get back!' boomed Swanton imperiously, declining to budge. Gomez was run out.

JOHN ARLOTT, OBE

Commentator, broadcaster, writer, poet
The Guardian

Arlott of course died in 1991. This obituary was written for the Guardian *during the 1980s.*

E. W. 'Jim' Swanton was one of the most capable and respected cricket writers of his time. He wielded most influence as cricket correspondent of the *Daily Telegraph* from 1946–75. He also edited and wrote books on the game and, for many years, broadcast about it. His was a traditionalist approach to cricket; his standards were high and he never hesitated to speak out against any abuse of its values.

Swanton had broadcast running commentary on cricket for the BBC as early as 1934, and, when he returned from war service, he took it up again. He was an outstanding summariser, coming on at lunchtime and close of play with a shrewd and well-balanced ad lib account and evaluation of the game. His deep, rather fruity voice and style conveyed authority.

In all, he made 20 Test tours – to Australia, the West Indies, South Africa and New Zealand – and wrote books about several of them. He was also joint author (after its first edition) of the authoritative *A History Of Cricket*, and general editor of *The World Of Cricket* (later *Barclays World Of Cricket*). A founder member of the Cricket Writers' Club, he was its chairman for the first two years. As a speaker he was sometimes weighty, but invariably sound and considerate of his audience.

Tall and powerfully built, he was also a useful batsman at club level, and in three pre-war matches, for Middlesex against Oxford and Cambridge universities, he scored 67 runs at an average of 13.40. In 1935 he founded the wandering club known as the Arabs, and made several tours with them, to the West Indies, Malaya and the Far East.

Fastidious about his clothing and his car, Swanton was essentially a serious man with little sense of humour. In his early professional days he was often autocratic, fussy and even pompous. Indeed, the name 'Jim' was bestowed on him as a humorous reference to 'Gentleman Jim, the Journalist'. To this, his own players proved an admirable corrective, pulling his leg until he came to accept it with a slightly wry smile. He was, at bottom, shy and most anxious to be liked.

Swanton ensured accuracy in his reports by engaging a series of assistants, and often, too, a scorer, so that when, like every cricket reporter, he was forced to turn his head away from the play, someone else took care that no event was missed. Indeed, it is probable that he was the most thorough, reliable, and accurate cricket correspondent of his period.

He was not an imaginative recorder of play in the manner of Neville Cardus, and he had no striking turn of phrase. But he was a sound, professional journalist who wrote lucidly and without affectation. His judgement and values were sound and he always maintained a historical and moral perspective. In the D'Oliveira affair, to the horror of some of his *Daily Telegraph* faithfuls, he eventually came down on the side of the angels, and firmly against the South African government.

Swanton was loyal; he could be generous; and, beyond his autobiographical title, he was very much indeed a cricket person.

MATTHEW ENGEL

Editor of Wisden Cricketers' Almanack

E. W. Swanton's autobiography, *Sort of a Cricket Person*, was once misprinted with the second 'S' missing. This caused widespread amusement in cricket press-boxes; we could all picture Jim as a Latin American dictator.

TED CORBETT

The Scotsman

His writing influenced both cricket's law-makers and the selection of teams, and as recently as five years ago Ray Illingworth, former chairman of selectors and team manager, described him as 'the fairest and most influential commentator on our game', after Swanton had criticised some controversial aspect of Illingworth's return to the England scene in charge, many years past his best.

Although his *Who's Who* entry has him down as playing cricket for Middlesex from 1937 to 1938, he did not play much above club level. Nevertheless, Swanton was capable of telling England captains how they should play the game. Many of his critics thought that the title of one of his books, *As I Said At The Time*, told more about the author than the contents. He could be pompous and old-fashioned; 'I can say without fear of contradiction that I have never in my life quoted the words of a player and I pray I never will,' he said at a meeting of the Cricket Writers' Club which he helped to found in 1946.

One day at Lord's he was found in the chair that had been reserved for the Queen after the traditional meeting with the two teams at the second Test. 'I'm not sure that he thinks even that seat is good enough for him,' was the comment of one of his contemporaries.

SANDY STRANG

The Scottish Herald

Formidable, magisterial, authoritative, Swanton was the doyen of cricket writers. 'A titan, the voice of cricket before Arlott and Johnston,' as Christopher Martin-Jenkins rightly declared, he was '*A Sort of Cricket Person*', his autobiography's neatly understated title, who saw cricket as 'one of the saner relaxations of a weary world'.

He rose to rightful prominence declaiming, in those slow, deep, mellifluous tones, his lucid, trenchant, daily close of play Test match summaries. He cut a rather sinister figure, more than a trifle deranged, a King Lear without the self-doubt, as Simon Barnes reminisces, marvellously. A man of legendary work-rate, extending to 23 books and eight million words, he was an uncompromising stickler for high standards in everything. Occasionally prone to pomposity, he could afford to laugh when he heard for the umpteenth time: 'Swanton is no snob: he is quite prepared to travel in the same car as his chauffeur'.

To Donald Trelford is ascribed the lovely tale of a famous English Test cricketer who made front-page headlines following a romantic involvement with a barmaid. Trelford braced himself to ask Swanton, acknowledged guardian of behavioural mores, whether he reckoned that standards had slipped since the allegedly halcyon good old days.

Swanton paused gravely before responding: 'What this episode reveals, I fear, is the sad decline of the English barmaid'.

ROBERT HUDSON

Former Head of BBC Outside Broadcasts and commentator

Jim Swanton was a master of the art of summarising a day's play, but even masters find life difficult when they don't know how much time they will be allowed.

Very often – and at Lord's in particular – the clocks on the ground were in disagreement, both with each other and with GMT. Also, if an over could be started even fractionally before 6.30, it would be bowled and Jim's five minutes time allocation would suffer a further setback. For all these reasons one would sympathise with Jim's exasperation, as his carefully prepared, and very important points about the day's activities had to be jettisoned one by one. Fortunately he usually had a further five minutes on the air, later that evening, from a local studio, so all was not entirely lost.

Jim had the enviable ability, born out of long experience, to put his finger on the key moments of the day's play. The ball-by-ball commentator can become bogged down in detail and lose sight of the bigger picture; Jim would restore the balance for his late night audience, which would often include the commentators themselves, anxious to find out what they had been talking about!

As a commentator he was perhaps less at ease – particularly as on one occasion, when his allocation of twenty minutes consisted entirely of maiden overs!

Through all that he did at the microphone, there shone a deep love and knowledge of the game. Cricket lovers, listeners and watchers will be saddened by his death and cricket will be the poorer for it.

PETER BAXTER

Producer, BBC Test Match Special

It was part of the ritual of the day. As the close of a day's Test cricket approached, a presence would arrive in the radio commentary box. The passage of this day's events was about to receive the Royal Assent which would set it properly in its place in history. Jim Swanton would give his summary of play.

He would come armed with a thermos flask which he would set down on the commentary desk with his notes, after a courteous, 'Do you want me here?' to the young producer. He would probably have to endure an irreverent comment or two from Brian Johnston, either on the air or off it. 'Always fourth form, Johnston,' he might protest, with a long suffering and almost avuncular smile. The jacket would come off and be arranged on the back of the chair, revealing braces that would in themselves be far too tempting a target for the commentary-box prankster.

While the commentator, entrusted with the last twenty minute session, aware of the preparations for the end of his day's work, was describing the final overs, Jim would be reaching across to receive Bill Frindall's scorecard and make sure that it was understood that he would be reading it out at close of play.

Two more things were required of the young producer: stopwatch set on the precise clock time and a card inscribed in large figures with the time he must finish, would be set down in front of him. There was an instruction for the young producer, to be repeated every evening until the great man was sure of him. 'No signals!' This was delivered in a tone that brooked no discussion. Not for Jim the indifferently manicured finger raised before his eyes to indicate that he had a minute to go.

'Now, with his summary of the day's play, here's E. W. Swanton of the *Daily Telegraph*.' And he was away. Until that hand-over he would not be sure of how long he would have to do. In those days play finished at 6.30, but if a fast bowler began an over thirty seconds before that, the nominal nine-and-a-half minutes could be greatly cut. Hence the insistence on his prop: 'I shall begin by reading the scorecard,' he would intone. This could be read through, with or without comment, setting the pace of his summary with consummate skill.

Sir Jack Hobbs, seen leaving Lord's early on a Test match day, explained that he would be all right if he could hear Jim Swanton's summary. It was a brilliant factual summary of events. Nothing left out and opinions delivered only in passing if relevant – and, of course, if the unforgiving stopwatch permitted. It was delivered with no more than the odd note to prompt him. And his final great gift to the young producer – he always finished bang on time.

HENRY BLOFELD

Commentator and writer

All of us in the cricketing media owe Jim Swanton an enormous debt. In writing and broadcasting he pioneered a path we've all tried to follow. His authority and knowledge will be badly missed and those of us lucky enough to have played for his own club, the Arabs, will have seen him at his best – and at times, at his most intolerant too! He was a great and good friend.

BEN BROCKLEHURST

Chairman and owner of The Cricketer

When Jim wrote his first autobiography, those of us working on *The Cricketer* thought we should suggest an appropriate title. Two were sent: one was *Wind on the Willows* and the other was *Pomp and Circumstance*. For some reason both were turned down and he preferred *Sort of a Cricket Person*.

We had him to stay in Lefkas, Greece in a very unsophisticated seaside village. Jim appeared the first morning on the beach immaculately dressed in Bermuda shorts and an enormous Panama hat and a brightly coloured golf umbrella. The Greeks were amazed – they hadn't seen such a formidable figure since Ulysses.

Shortly after I had been elected to his Arab Cricket Club he rang me up and said, 'I want you to play in a certain match' and I said, 'Jim, I am sorry I can't, I am already playing that day and I can't let them down.' A week later he rang again and said, 'I expect you on the ground at eleven o'clock.' When I repeated what I had said before he seemed most surprised. It seemed that his wishes at all times were paramount.

A well-known Sky television cricket broadcaster and writer came to *The Cricketer* Cup final where people are normally pretty smartly dressed. He, however, was wearing a very smart white shirt with no tie and black trousers. All Jim said to him was, 'Which part of the ground do you work on?'

TONY LEWIS

(*Cambridge, Glamorgan & England*), *television presenter and President of MCC, 1998–2000*
The Cricketer

E. W. Swanton of the *Daily Telegraph* – not so much a by-line as the most important cricket title since the Second World War. Many have aspired to it.

If Jim's accession to the job in 1946 was fortuitous – he was available when the *Telegraph* found itself without a cricket correspondent mid-season – he soon made his columns the seat of authority.

Cricket was his serious love, the embodiment of honourable conflict and personal conduct. In the 1930s he played first-class matches for Middlesex against Oxford and Cambridge Universities which meant that he had played enough skilful cricket to understand the game's complexities but not enough to become sanguine or sceptical as former Test players sometimes do. He always kept closely in touch with the club game.

Whatever shocks befell the game in his lifetime, whether it was the imposition of coloured clothing or the current fracturing of the County Championship, both of which made him snort with disapproval, he still maintained eternal trust in the game itself and never backed down from his self-appointed role of *fidel defensor*. He was writing columns for the *Telegraph* and *The Cricketer* clearly and powerfully, right to the end.

We were close friends but he left me with one contradiction. He insisted that his life had turned on luck, but I have never known anyone do so much planning and preparation. His research was impeccable. For example, after a day's play against his much-loved Kent at Dover I went with some Glamorgan players for dinner at Jim's home, Delf House in Sandwich; captain Ossie Wheatley, Don Shepherd, Peter Walker, Alan Jones and I turned out in black tie to find ourselves grilled on a possible change in the lbw Law, which the other guest, Mr 'Gubby' Allen, MCC's Treasurer, was about to propagate across the committee tables at Lord's. We were not any old cricketers, however, but perfect research for the man from the *Daily Telegraph* – a swing bowler, an off-cutter, a left-arm spinner, a left-handed batsman and a right-hander. We covered a few angles!

It was luck indeed in 1935 that a planned tour of Bermuda was cancelled and Jim and his fellow cricketers went instead to Jersey where was formed his well-known wandering club, the Arabs. It was miraculous luck indeed that Jim survived the prisoner of war camps in the Far East and that the sniper's bullet hit him only in the elbow, and he confesses to the most wonderful slice of luck in his life that at the Grosvenor House Hotel in December 1957 he met Ann Carbutt (neé de Montmorency), recently widowed. They married only two months later and enjoyed over 40 years together.

Jim Swanton at work, however, prepared massively and had an astounding recall of the events he had seen. He was informed and informative and absolutely single-minded, though his was not an all-embracing world of cricket. Swanton's place was on the regular passage to Australia and New Zealand bound for another Ashes series, studying every move Don Bradman made and valuing greatly the shrewdness of The Don's words in a lifelong friendship. He was a big match writer and I am sure that was all time allowed.

To MCC he gave a life's service and was made one of the few Honorary Life Vice-Presidents. He chaired the steering committee which helped create an indoor school at Lord's; he was a member of the Arts and Library sub-committee from 1975 until his death, being chairman from 1982–85. He made a superb speech at last summer's Special General Meeting, full of cautions and, as he might write it in his famous double negatives, not a little censure of some iconoclastic members. He was Kent's President too.

He was certainly not afraid to give an England captain a ticking off. I remember a Test in Calcutta. You would have to say that India, Pakistan and Sri Lanka were not on his beat, but he did put in a rare appearance in 1973 when over 100,000 turned out for the first day's play. I was the sick captain who had been smuggled into the Grand Hotel by the back door in order to avoid hundreds of yelling cricket fans out front. The security officer who had shepherded me asked, before leaving my bedroom, if I would mind autographing a small white card. I did. 'Please add MCC captain,' he said. I did.

On that first evening Jim came to my room, chauffered from the ground, wearing his usual stylish clothes – a Panama hat, tie with pin, buff coloured jacket, trousers creased for eternity and thoroughly British shoes. He came straight out with a frowned rebuke. 'Really, captain. A most extraordinary fellow took a seat next to me in the press-box, unshaven, not working, and when asked how he gained admission he announced that you had given him a pass and here it is.' Typed on top was: 'Please admit one to press-box.' Signed in my writing – Tony Lewis, MCC captain.

Jim Swanton had such a complete vision of how cricketers should behave and dress, score quick runs or bowl a line and a length – his mind was a manual of perfect performance – that he found it natural to censure flaws in others. I have sat as an Arabs captain on the balcony at Canterbury, delaying my declaration while Jim marched up and down, waving a rolled golf umbrella, insisting that his team, not mine, were told to go out to bowl immediately. 'Well, you were jolly lucky,' he admitted when we won.

It was my great good fortune to have E. W. Swanton as a mentor. 'Try to take part in the whole spectrum of cricket reporting, the writing, broadcasting, the lot,' he once confided with a secretive, sonorous whisper in a London taxi from beneath his Homburg and from behind his white silk scarf. He believed in the promise of youth. Only recently a young writer sponsored by MCC's Arts and Library sub-committee attended the England tour of South Africa to write for MCC on the website. Jim armed the young man with three priceless pages of 'advice to a young cricket-writer'.

For E. W. Swanton, cricket was a serious, sporting pursuit which lost all its charm the moment frivolity barged in and jollity replaced the determined pursuit of victory. And we know he was right.

CHRISTOPHER MARTIN-JENKINS

Former BBC cricket correspondent. Daily Telegraph. The Times
The Cricketer

Readers of *The Cricketer* do not need to be reminded of what a colossus he was who slipped out of the world with a calm acceptance last January 22. Asking me to evaluate Jim the journalist was a little like requesting William McGonagall to assess the poetic works of Alfred Tennyson, but duty and affection demand an attempt from one who, like the page in King Wenceslas, merely stumbled along in the master's giant foot strides.

He was masterful in his prime, too; a mite demanding and overbearing to a diffident student struggling to make headway in his first job, but never unfair and always sympathetic. I worked as his assistant editor on *The Cricketer* for three years, always treating him with immense respect but gradually relaxing in his company to the point where he became a friend.

He taught high standards in everything and he was always eager to help young people wanting to get into cricket writing. Not many of them could meet his expectations, but he was always willing to look for the best in other people. It was his interest in them, especially the young, which kept him so utterly in touch with changes in cricket and society until the end. He maintained a tremendous work-rate into old age and he did not believe in wasting time, once, for example, dictating letters to a secretary from his Jaguar whilst it was being hauled to the top of a ramp for repairs to the exhaust system. To the last, anyone who wrote to him about cricket could be sure of a reply.

His sheer personality dominated in whatever company he was keeping, but Jim took pride-pricking from friends, and criticism from lesser men, completely in his stride. He knew his own worth and proved it daily. It is hard to imagine any job being too much for him, such was his energy and ability, and he did things his way, certainly once he had established himself on the *Daily Telegraph*, with a secretary or assistant close at hand on match days, under firm instruction.

He had begun work as a journalist for the Amalgamated Press after leaving school at Cranleigh in 1924, subsequently wrote on cricket and rugby for the *Evening Standard* before the war and, in the role for which he was best known, for the *Telegraph* until he died but it was as a broadcaster for BBC Radio that he was first widely famous. He started with scripted reports of matches during the 1930s, the very early days of radio, and he was the first broadcaster from England to join an MCC winter tour, working as a freelance commentator for the BBC and the SABA in South Africa in 1938/39. For the rest of my life whenever I think of Jim I shall think first of that rich, plummy voice. It was the very essence of the easy authority which he brought to all his affairs.

As a journalist, the shortage of newsprint for much of his career no doubt helped him to be a meaty rather than a waffly writer. There were few flights of fancy, but plenty of apt fact and strongly worded opinion on matters of technique, propriety or politics. Swanton was never ill-informed and his judgement was as sound as a bell.

In his brilliant address at the funeral in Sandwich, ten days before what would have been Jim's 93rd birthday, Lord Runcie got to the nub of E.W.S. the writer, by stressing the depth of his knowledge and interest in cricket and the strength of his opinion about how it should be played. Knowledge and deep conviction made him a formidable writer, always worth reading, not least in *The Cricketer*, with which he became closely associated, from the moment in the early 1960s that 'Plum' Warner handed his interest in the magazine to his son John. The shrewdest thing young Warner did was to get Jim involved.

He saw it as a challenge, a duty almost, to keep 'the paper' (as he called it) going and he was a driving force for the good for the last thirty-eight years of his life. What he got out of it financially, as sometime editorial director and president, was never the equal of the energy he applied to keeping the magazine interesting and competitive, or to the prestige he lent it by his increasingly legendary status.

CHARLES FRY

Grandson of C.B. Fry, member
of MCC Committee, Arab

On the Arabs' Kent tour in the early 1960s the Arabs were playing the Band of Brothers at the spacious King's School Canterbury ground. With the Arabs fielding and Jim in command, a slow bowler bowled a ball down the leg side and the batsman in his eagerness to hit it swung round and hit the wicketkeeper, standing up, a fierce blow above the eye with his bat. The keeper, not unnaturally, slumped to the ground in a pool of blood. Quick as a flash Jim waved to his wife Ann, who was sitting in the family Jaguar on the boundary, motioning that she should 'come forward'.

Ann drove the Jag directly onto the square and got out to help. Jim, conscious that the prostrate, dazed and bleeding wicketkeeper didn't know Ann, proceeded to introduce them: 'David, I don't think you've met my wife Ann.' Only Jim would have seen such an introduction as a necessity in the circumstances!

NEIL DURDEN-SMITH, OBE

Author, broadcaster, public relations savant

In the late 1950s, when I was appointed as a young Royal Naval Lieutenant to be ADC to the Governor-General of New Zealand, Lord Cobham, he told me about this friend of his, Jim Swanton. Among other things he told me was that if the said Swanton was ever shipwrecked on a desert island his first question would be 'Who is the Governor?' The following year, 1958, I went to Melbourne to see the Australia v. England Test and stayed at Government House when Sir Dallas Brooks, a distinguished former Royal Marine General, was Governor of Victoria. Imagine my astonishment when coming down to breakfast on the first morning of my stay, there tucking into bacon and eggs with His Excellency was an impressive looking, rather portly gentleman who was introduced to me as – you've guessed it – none other than Jim Swanton. I reflected later there was some truth, after all, in Charles Cobham's apocryphal tale!

I saw a lot of Jim following that early encounter, particularly, when on leaving the Navy in 1963, I became a BBC Outside Broadcasts producer. In due course radio cricket production became one of my responsibilities and I found myself working with Messrs Johnston, Arlott, F. R. Brown, Yardley, Arthur Wrigley and Swanton, whose job it was to deliver a live 4-minute close of play summary on each evening of a Test match. (Subsequently I was to join this mighty league of gentlemen as one of the commentators on *Test Match Special*.) It was the era of schoolboyish pranks in the box and on one occasion, during a Lord's Test, Johnners persuaded me to place a colour photograph of a nubile, extremely well equipped blonde, naked to the waist, on top of Jim's notes while he was in full flow. After a cacophony of coughing and spluttering he managed to regain his composure and finish his summary, but he always looked at me decidedly sideways after that!

His great partnership, of course, was with Ann, of whom he was inordinately proud. Not only was she a superb artist and a very good golfer in her time but she was also a wonderful pianist and composer (one of the anthems, 'God is Hope', at Jim's Memorial Service in Canterbury Cathedral, was composed by Ann Swanton). I heard her play – Bacharach, Berlin, Coward, Gershwin, Kern, Porter et al – in such disparate places as the terrace of the Sandy Lane Hotel in Barbados and Pizza on the Park in Knightsbridge, where I joined Ann and her musical friends from time-to-time to have lunch and listen to them play piano – magical. When I next saw Jim after one of these lunchtimes he always asked me about it and Ann told me how pleased he was that one of his cricketing friends enjoyed that part of her life.

As everyone knows, Jim Swanton was the doyen of cricket writers and a very competent broadcaster to boot, but I always thought he was an outstanding speaker as well. His command of the language, attention to detail and, above all, timing, could not be faulted. I heard him make many memorable speeches, particularly those at The Hilton at The Lord's Taverners Dinner for Brian Johnston's 80th birthday where Jim remarked that although he hadn't read Brian's latest book, he expected to be libelled in it as he had been in the previous fourteen. Later there was that splendid occasion in the Long Room at Lord's at the 50th Anniversary Dinner of the Cricket Writers' Club, of which he was the first Chairman. He would even take the trouble to prepare a little gem of a speech when he came to dinner in the clubhouse of his beloved Royal St George's every year on the occasion of the annual match with The County Cricketers' Golf Society at Sandwich.

Ever the perfectionist, I am sure he actively enjoyed crafting and delivering his speeches to suit particular occasions and audiences.

He certainly provided real enjoyment to many throughout the world through this facet of such an outstanding life.

MARK WILLIAMS

Chief Executive, Lord's Taverners

My first encounter with Jim had been as a new member of MCC when I chanced to sit alongside him in one of those high chairs in The Long Room at Lord's on a sweltering hot day in July 1967. I was on leave from the Royal Navy at the time. We might never have spoken. I was a young man of no consequence, E.W.S. even then was the doyen of cricket writing – magisterial, imposing, not to say intimidating. When I offered an opinion on the cricket, I swiftly discovered his legendary kindness to young people with a love for the game.

Ray Illingworth was batting in the Test match against Pakistan and Jim remarked that Ray was all at sea against most forms of spin. Our conversation touched on Oxford, where I had been at school and where Jim had played frequently in the years after the war when he was recuperating at Pusey House after three years as a prisoner of the Japs. Chancing my arm, I said that I was considering a change of career from the Navy and was thinking of writing on cricket. In that case said Jim you had better take some lunch with me next week and help me with my piece.

And so it came about. We met before play. Jim asked me to take notes about the cricket as he was off to do an interview and might miss something. We would meet for lunch in the Tavern Restaurant. I must have passed that first test because an invitation to play for his own side, the Arabs, followed.

The game was at Tonbridge School. Colin Ingleby-Mackenzie was our captain and the redoubtable Blowers kept wicket. I batted passably well, but thought I must have blotted my copybook when, fielding sub for the opposition, I took a blinding catch to dismiss Simon Parker-Bowles who was on the point of winning the match for the Arabs. But Jim's magnanimity did not desert him and an invitation to become a member duly followed.

The Arabs, MCC and Lord's, Sandwich and Royal St George's Golf Club, Barbados and Sandy Lane, the church both at home and overseas – these were all Jim's natural habitat. If he possessed the discretion of a courtier when it mattered, his journalist's ear for a story and his range of contacts made for an unrivalled retailer of the best gossip. 'Did you know that . . .' he would lean forward and say, delivered in a stentorian whisper, which suggested that the fate of nations depended on what he was about to impart.

Finally, Jim's judgement of men and situations was rarely wide of the mark. He stood out against apartheid when the establishment, of which he was a part, would have preferred to turn a blind eye. When Emperor Akihito visited Britain a few years back he went into print against those who would demonstrate their everlasting antipathy to the Japanese in public.

And of all the peoples he had encountered, he perhaps admired the Bajans the most, not least their favourite son, Sir Garfield Sobers. 'Give them the first smile' was his wise comment when I sought his advice before going to live in Barbados.

Of him it may be truly said that we will not see his like again.

RICHARD HUTTON

(Yorkshire & England)
Former editor of The Cricketer.
Before all that Richard Hutton was at Cambridge University and here he gives a student's impression dusted down

At Cambridge we had in the side a lad called Chris Saunders. He was a wicket-keeper and a great wit, and he gave a more than passable impersonation of E.W. Swanton. Saunders eventually achieved as much if not greater success as a schoolmaster, in the process acquiring the headships of Eastbourne and Lancing Colleges, at the latter of which he had himself been a pupil.

In the 1960s, Jim took a keen interest in developments at Oxford and Cambridge and reported the Varsity match in almost as much detail as any Test match. For his part Saunders kept the student body at Cambridge permanently entertained with his Swantonian commentaries, delivered with a typical ecclesiastical gravitas, until one day he went just a bit too far.

In those days, we were lucky to have some expert coaching at Fenner's before the start of the season from Bert (Dusty) Rhodes, the former Derbyshire cricketer who at the time was a Test umpire. He stayed overnight in Cambridge for the best part of two weeks at a local hostelry, the Prince Regent, which was the venue for his farewell party on the last evening of his time with us, prior to his making a quick getaway first thing in the morning.

Without his knowledge Saunders surreptitiously left the bar and soon after Dusty was called to the telephone with the announcement that Jim Swanton wanted to speak to him.

The voice of God came down the line: 'Is that you Rhodes? Jim Swanton here.'

'Oh! Good evening Mr Swanton. What a surprise! How very nice to hear from you.'

'Now look here. I am coming over to Cambridge tomorrow to see how the chaps are getting on under your tutelage. Can I expect to see you there?'

This request caused Dusty great consternation as well as inconvenience because his bags were packed ready for the off. After a hurried mental rearrangement of his schedule, he stammered, 'I er . . . I er . . . I er shall be here . . . all day and I very much look forward to seeing you.'

For the rest of the evening we listened with incredulity to Dusty's excitement about the following day's visitation – how he was cancelling his departure and what he expected from us to give the right impression.

On the next day we practised very hard in preparation for the phantom visit of the cricket correspondent of the *Daily Telegraph*. Resplendent in whites and his MCC touring blazer, Dusty spent most of the day looking at his watch. As the hours passed with no sign of Swanton, Saunders and others behind the deception had to decide whether or not to get Jim off the hook, and how to tell Dusty that he had been duped.

After much agonising they came clean and it didn't take Dusty long to see the funny side of it.

F.G. 'GEORGE' MANN, CBE, DSO, MC

(Middlesex and former England Captain)

Jim and I opened the innings for Middlesex against Cambridge University at Fenners in May 1937. [*A stand of 73 in the second innings during which Mann went on to make 59 and Swanton 26.*] Having mischievously made him gallop extra fast for a third run, taking on a throw from the deep field, he came walking back up the wicket towards me before the next ball could be bowled and panted, 'Now, look here young fella, we've got to play the game properly'.

ROGER KNIGHT

(Gloucestershire, Sussex & Surrey)
Secretary MCC

I have a number of memories of Jim, who was someone whom I admired enormously. Perhaps the most interesting recollection is an event which took place at the opening of the W. G. Grace exhibition in the Lord's Museum. Jim, at the age of 92, was one of the guests and when Primrose Worthington, one of W. G.'s grand-daughters, opened the exhibition, she talked about her memories of sitting on W.G.'s knee and plaiting his beard. The one thing that she could not remember is how she travelled from Croydon to Beckenham to visit him. At that stage, Jim asked whether it was possibly on the No. 16 bus and then added, horse-drawn. Whereupon Miss Worthington thought that it might well have been. The ensuing conversation between the two of them, both in their nineties, with excellent memories, was fascinating to everyone present.

STEPHEN GREEN

Curator of MCC

I knew Jim Swanton for over 30 years. For twenty-five of these he served on the MCC Arts & Library sub-committee. He was its chairman for three years which kept me on my toes.

Almost the last time I saw him was in Canterbury Cathedral last autumn. We were both attending Godfrey Evans' Thanksgiving Service.

Jim was seated opposite me and cut a very fine figure for a nonagenarian. His pew was immediately adjacent to the Archbishop's throne and I thought he frequently cast wistful glances in that direction.

I later mentioned this to Archbishop Runcie and I was pleased when he alluded to this observation in his tribute at Jim's funeral.

I was glad to have seen Jim at Canterbury because the occasion drew together three vital ingredients in his life – a great love of cricket, a deep devotion to Kent and a firm adherence to the Church of England.

We are all the poorer for his passing, even though I no longer wake up each morning in a cold sweat wondering what E.W.S. would make of one of my sins of omission or commission.

DR GERALD HOWAT

Historian and journalist, Member of MCC Arts and Library Sub-Committee

To have known Jim Swanton for the last third of his lifetime was a great privilege. At our first meeting I 'interviewed' him on his recollections of Learie Constantine for my forthcoming biography. He answered my questions with measured judgement, simultaneously making careful notes on the match he was reporting. That professionalism matched by an acute memory must be one of the hallmarks of his success. In later years, and to the very end, one marvelled at the way he could contribute to the debate in committee on cricket publishing ideas which he was unlikely to see brought to fruition. He was more liberal than many suspected in his enthusiasm for the young and his readiness to adapt to the changing time of the last decade or two.

One memory stands out. A group of us were charged with repositioning the pictures in the pavilion at Lord's. We took the best part of two days because Jim would linger over the subjects – Lord Harris, for example – and give us pen-portraits of men he had known from sixty, even seventy, years ago.

No man is perfect. One would be conscious of playing for one's place in E.W.S.' metaphorical 'team'. Perhaps when one was invited to call him Jim one had moved up the order.

His writing output was enormous – *si requiris monumentum, respice libros*.

PAUL SHEAHAN

(Victoria & Australia)
Headmaster, Melbourne Grammar School

I have no recollection of first meeting Jim Swanton, but I do recall quite vividly my devouring his cricket writing when I was quite a young boy.

There was a succinctness but an understanding (as I subsequently discovered) of the intricacies of our great game that few others seemed to possess. His reports of Test matches, unlike the modern genre, had no need to seek for the sensational; they were simple narratives of the day's play that allowed the reader to create a mind's eye picture of the proceedings, punctuated by astute observations of the state of cricket, in general, and English cricket in particular. One would have to say, too, that his comments and opinions were not only voraciously consumed by the readers of his newspaper columns but were eagerly – and I might say sensibly – sought by the administrators of the day.

If I have no recollection of our first meeting, I do remember his generosity as a host, both of his beloved Arabs and of Australians, even if they had not been accorded the honour of joining the wandering band of cricket lovers and sometime players. I count myself as exceedingly privileged and honoured to have been admitted as an Arab, even though my one and only match for them (v Kent Second XI at Yellowhammers) was singularly lacking in success, which earned me the disdain of 'The Founder' for some time!

He gathered a group one day in 1972 at Royal St George's, near Delf House, for a splendid round of golf, followed by lunch. The group was large and included women, two of whom caused much mirth. One let out such an unexpected expletive when she duffed her approach to the eighteenth that E.W.S., basking in the glory of all he surveyed, almost fell backwards off the lip of the greenside bunker into the vast expanse of sand. The other departed considerably from protocol when she suggested to G. O. B 'Gubby' Allen, then chairman of selectors for England, that he had no idea of what he was talking about when he said that Boycott was a certainty for the subsequent England tour of India!

Some thought Jim pompous. At times this was not entirely 'off beam', as he fixed those hooded eyes and looked down at you from an immense height. But, if you were able to stand your ground and argue a point lucidly and with supporting evidence, he became an avid listener and a keen debater. If you managed to strike a resonant chord with humour he would either chuckle and look admiringly or let forth with an enormous belly laugh.

Even an Antipodean could appreciate that Jim was brought up in a different era, an era in which niceties were important (until they got in the way!). However, Antipodeans did not necessarily understand that his was a society in which there were strata and the boundaries between the levels were rarely, if ever, blurred! His style, therefore, would not appeal to everyone but, as I said a moment ago, if you could cut to the chase, there was a heart of gold and a genuine interest in people.

The cricket world will be infinitely the poorer for his passing.

SIR (JOHN) PAUL GETTY, KBE

Philanthropist

Jim always hated to lose. Although he was a fine sportsman, one Sunday at Wormsley, when my team was playing the Arabs, Keith Miller and I heard him saying to an ingoing batsman, 'play for a draw'. Nugget never let him forget!

A PHONE CALL TO SIR GARFIELD SOBERS, OCC

I knew Jim very well. He was a tremendous person and an excellent sports writer. He always said a good word about me and put it in glowing terms, which I appreciated. He was one of those reporters you could talk to, knowing he would keep a confidence.

He loved coming to Barbados and enjoyed meeting the people there and they liked having him there.

He ran the seniors golf tournament – I think you have to be over 55 or over 60 to qualify – for Lord Forte and, in fact, the last time I saw him was on the Westmorland golf course when he arrived in a cart with John Woodcock and came to have a chat. This would be around February, 1999 and he was in fine form.

The whole sporting world will miss him and so will I. He had a wonderful life and career and did all he wanted to do.

SIR TIM RICE

Lyricist, writer and broadcaster. President, Lord's Taverners

I 956 was a watershed in my young life in that it was the year I discovered both E. W. Swanton and Elvis Presley. I cannot be certain that either of these two giants in their respective fields ever fully appreciated the talents of the other, but for me they remain heroes to this day. I did once briefly shake Elvis Presley's hand; that was the extent of our relationship – thirty seconds in which the King of rock 'n' roll might have briefly wondered who I was. But for thirty years I was a good friend of my other 1956 icon, and I value that privilege very highly.

Jim remained a hero to me; I always felt a bit of a young shaver in his presence. His authority tempered with wit and generosity was a formidable combination. In 1971 I wrote him a fan letter after reading the first volume of his autobiography and he responded warmly. Soon the magisterial presence and sonorous vocal tones that had impressed me from a distance, through the pages of the *Daily Telegraph* and over the airwaves of the BBC, were characteristics that I came to know personally.

I worked with Jim on many occasions – if such enjoyable encounters can be described as work. For many years we were both members of the Arts and Library sub-committee of MCC. We made a video together in 1991, 'Lord's – The Home of Cricket'. I made modest contributions to the *Daily Telegraph* cricket pages which Jim bestrode like a colossus for half a century. I spoke at more than a few lunches and dinners with him – and went on a cruise to the West Indies with Jim, J. J. Warr, Hubert Doggart and 200 English cricket lovers.

This latter venture was a fortnight's meander around several West Indian islands, taking in the 1994 England–West Indies Test match in Barbados. Brian Johnston was originally scheduled to be one of the expert commentators and entertainers on this trip, but when he was taken ill, I was signed up as a last-minute replacement. The entire voyage was made memorable by England's great win at the Kensington Oval, led by Alec Stewart's two centuries.

There were plenty of happy cruisers after that triumph. But they were not simply lucky to witness a rare England Caribbean victory; they were doubly fortunate in that every evening after dinner Jim gave them a masterly summary of the day's play. I shall never forget Jim holding us all spellbound below decks with his fluent, incisive analysis, tempered with humour and good manners. Good manners were instinctive to Jim and from that flowed so much of his affable confidence. And I have another warm memory of Jim on that trip; his daily relaxations in the jacuzzi and/or pool on which occasions he had more than a twinkle in his eye for my friend the beautiful South African cricket-lover. She was charmed as were many before her and not a few since; those who knew Jim decades before 1956, those who only knew him in his ninth decade and many in between.

JOHN WOODCOCK

It is appropriate to give the last word to the distinguished former cricket correspondent of The Times *and one of Jim's closest friends*

It may be rather facile to say that there will never be another Swanton – but it is true. He spoke with unrivalled authority, set his own agenda, encouraged and promoted countless young cricketers and journalists, and amassed, over the course of 70 years, a store of friends, memories and cricketing intelligence that would not be possible today, if only because of the pace of life. No sports writer can ever have been paid a much higher compliment than when the incomparable Sir Jack Hobbs, seen leaving a Test match at Lord's one day, half an hour before the close of play, said, 'If I miss anything, I shall be reading Swanton in the morning and he'll fill me in.'

On a more personal note, I'd like to single out Jim's loyalty, both to the game and his friends. It came as a surprise to many, as he grew in years, to find that he was not the dinosaur they had imagined him to be, but a valuator. He knew that cricket never has been what it was, and he never went off it. And as a friend, you couldn't wish for a better.

Index